MW01198995

Lay People in the Asian Church

Peter Nguyen Van Hai

Lay People in the Asian Church
A Critical Study of the Theology of the Laity
in the Documents of the Federation of
Asian Bishops' Conferences with Special Reference to
John Paul II's Apostolic Exhortation *Ecclesia in Asia*
and the Pastoral Letters of the
Vietnamese Episcopal Conference

PETER LANG
EDITION

Bibliographic Information published by the Deutsche Nationalbibliothek
The Deutsche Nationalbibliothek lists this publication in the Deutsche Nationalbibliografie; detailed bibliographic data is available in the internet at http://dnb.d-nb.de.

Cover Image:
Phat Diem Cathedral in Vietnam, built from 1875 to 1898, an architectural inculturation of Christianity in the Asian context. Photograph courtesy of the Diocese of Phat Diem.

Library of Congress Cataloging-in-Publication Data
Hai, Peter Nguyen Van, 1952- author.
  Lay people in the Asian church : a critical study of the theology of the laity in the documents of the Federation of Asian Bishops' Conferences with special reference to John Paul II's Apostolic Exhortation Ecclesia in Asia and the pastoral letters of the Vietnamese Episcopal Conference / Peter Nguyen Van Hai.
    pages cm
  Includes bibliographical references and index.
  1. Laity–Asia. 2. Christianity–Asia. 3. Federation of Asian Bishops' Conferences. I. Title.
  BV687.I126 2015
  262'.1525–dc23
                    2015023482

ISBN 978-3-631-66612-8 (Print)
E-ISBN 978-3-653-05941-0 (E-Book)
DOI 10.3726/ 978-3-653-05941-0

© Peter Lang GmbH
Internationaler Verlag der Wissenschaften
Frankfurt am Main 2015
All rights reserved.
Peter Lang Edition is an Imprint of Peter Lang GmbH.

Peter Lang – Frankfurt am Main · Bern · Bruxelles · New York · Oxford · Warszawa · Wien

This publication has been peer reviewed.
www.peterlang.com

Table of contents

Acknowledgements VII

Abbreviations IX

Chapter 1 Rediscovering the Importance of Lay People
in the Asian Church...1

Chapter 2 The Laity in Historical Context...21

Chapter 3 *Fides Quaerens Dialogum*: Theological
Methodologies of the Federation of Asian Bishops'
Conferences 43

Chapter 4 Features of the FABC's Theology of the Laity 79

Chapter 5 Evaluation of the FABC's Theology of the Laity............ 109

Chapter 6 Models of the Asian Church.. 137

Chapter 7 Church as Context for Lay Mission in Asia..................... 155

Chapter 8 John Paul II's Theology of the Laity and the
Teachings of the Asian Bishops.. 165

Chapter 9 The Mission of Lay People in the Pastoral Letters
of the Vietnamese Bishops with Reference to the
Teachings of John Paul II and the Bishops of Asia........ 195

Chapter 10 The Future of the FABC's Theology of the Laity............ 233

Selected Bibliography.. 259

Index.. 287

Acknowledgements

Special thanks are due to the editorial committees of the following journals for giving me permission to edit and update several of my articles: Chapters 2, 4, 5, and 10 previously published in the *East Asian Pastoral Review* 46:4 (2009) 334–356, 47:1 (2010) 7–37, 47:3 (2010) 234–262, and 49:2 (2012) 107–132 respectively; Chapters 3, 6, and 8 in the *Australian E-Journal of Theology* 8 (October 2006) 1–26, 18 (April 2011) 61–73, and 10 (May 2007) 1–22; Chapter 7 in *Compass: A Review to Topical Theology* 46:2 (2012) 13–20; Chapter 9, a combination of two papers appeared in the *East Asian Pastoral Review* 48:4 (2011) 313–344 and *The Australasian Catholic Record* 89:3 (2012) 333–348. I also thank Ms Ute Winkelkötter, Mrs Andrea Kolb, Ms Lotte Kosthorst, and Mr Richard Breitenbach of Peter Lang International Academic Publishers for their interest and assistance in publishing this work.

Finally, I wish to express my gratitude to my former Jesuit professors at my *alma mater*, St Pius X Pontifical College, Da Lat, Vietnam, for initiating me into the sacred science of theology and scholastic philosophy. To them and all *alumni* I dedicate this book.

Abbreviations

ABM	Asian Bishops' Meeting
ACMC	Asian Colloquium on Ministries in the Church
AMCU	Asian Movement for Christian Unity
AsIPA	Asian Integral Pastoral Approach
BECs	Basic Ecclesial Communities
BIBA	Bishops' Institute for Biblical Apostolate
BILA	Bishops' Institute for Lay Apostolate
BIMA	Bishops' Institute for Missionary Apostolate
BIRA	Bishops' Institute for Interreligious Affairs
BISCOM	Bishops' Institute for Social Communication
BISA	Bishops' Institute for Social Action
FABC	Federation of Asian Bishops' Conferences
FABC I	Statement of the First Plenary Assembly of the FABC
FABC II	Statement of the Second Plenary Assembly of the FABC
FABC III	Statement of the Third Plenary Assembly of the FABC
FABC IV	Statement of the Fourth Plenary Assembly of the FABC
FABC V	Statement of the Fifth Plenary Assembly of the FABC
FABC VI	Statement of the Sixth Plenary Assembly of the FABC
FABC VII	Statement of the Seventh Plenary Assembly of the FABC
FABC VIII	Statement of the Eighth Plenary Assembly of the FABC
FABC IX	Statement of the Ninth Plenary Assembly of the FABC
FABC X	Statement of the Tenth Plenary Assembly of the FABC
FAPA Vol. 1	*For All the Peoples of Asia*, vol. 1
FAPA Vol. 2	*For All the Peoples of Asia*, vol. 2
FAPA Vol. 3	*For All the Peoples of Asia*, vol. 3
FAPA Vol. 4	*For All the Peoples of Asia*, vol. 4
FAPA Vol. 5	*For All the Peoples of Asia*, vol. 5
FIRA	Formation Institute for Interreligious Affairs
OC	Office of Clergy
OCL	Office of Consecrated Life
OE	Office of Evangelization
OEIA	Office of Ecumenical & Interreligious Affairs
OEFF	Office of Education and Faith Formation
OESC	Office of Education & Student Chaplaincy
OHD	Office of Human Development

OL	Office of Laity
OLF	Office of Laity and Family
OSC	Office of Social Communication
OTC	Office of Theological Concerns
SCCs	Small Christian Communities
TAC	Theological Advisory Commission
VEC	Vietnamese Episcopal Conference

Chapter 1 Rediscovering the Importance of Lay People in the Asian Church

As one of the main preoccupations of the Second Vatican Council (1962–1965) the vocation and mission of the laity was the subject of an entire conciliar Decree and several sections of two Constitutions on the Church.[1] In the first Constitution, *Lumen Gentium*,[2] the Council emphasised the basic equality of all the baptised,[3] and the common priesthood of all the faithful in the Church as the people of God.[4]

---

1 See Vatican Council II, "*Apostolicam Actuositatem*: Degree on the Apostolate of the Laity," in *Vatican Council II: Vol. 1: The Conciliar and Post Conciliar Documents*, edited by Austin Flannery, new revised edition (Northport, N.Y.: Costello Publishing Co., 1996) 766–98; "*Lumen Gentium*: Dogmatic Constitution on the Church," ibid. 350–426; "*Gaudium et Spes*: Pastoral Constitution on the Church in the Modern World," ibid., 903–1001. Henceforth, in footnotes the full titles of these conciliar documents will be abbreviated to "*Lumen Gentium*," "*Apostolicam Actuositatem*," and "*Gaudium et Spes*," followed by numbers. The main conciliar teachings on the laity appear in "*Lumen Gentium*," especially chapter 2 on the people of God and chapter 4 on the laity, "*Apostolicam Actuositatem*," and *Gaudium et Spes*," in particular section 43.

2 Contending that one of the lasting contributions of the Council was its "Christological definition of the concept of the Church," Joseph Ratzinger argues that "to understand Vatican II correctly one must always and repeatedly begin with" the first sentence of *Lumen Gentium*, which declares that "*Lumen gentium cum sit Christus*." See *Church, Ecumenism and Politics: New Essays in Ecclesiology* (Middlegreen, Slough, England: St Paul Publications, 1988) 4–5. For Gerard Philips, "from the beginning, the Constitution on the Church explicitly adopts a Christocentric perspective, one which runs like a golden thread throughout the whole treatment" ("The Church: mystery and Sacrament," in *Vatican II: An Interfaith Appraisal*, edited by John H. Miller [New York: Association Press, 1966] 187). Kenan B. Osborne also observes that "for a Christian the Jesus-event is central," and "Jesus alone is *lumen gentium*" (*Ministry: Lay Ministry in the Roman Catholic Church: Its History and Theology* [New York: Paulist Press, 1993] 602). Osborne goes on to assert that "Christology in an ever increasing way will be seen as the basis and substance of ecclesiology." Ibid., 603.

3 *Lumen Gentium*, no. 32.

4 For Yves Congar, one of the most important decisions made by Vatican II was to place chapter 2 of *Lumen Gentium* on the People of God between chapter 1 on the mystery of the Church and chapter 3 on the hierarchy, and that chapter 2 "has the greatest promise for the theological, pastoral and ecumenical future of ecclesiology" ("The People of God," in *Vatican II: An Interfaith Appraisal*, edited by John H. Miller [New York: Association Press, 1966] 197). Thomas P. Rausch notes that "the council took a number

1

Thereby, it provided the dogmatic foundation for the development of a practical theology of the laity in *Apostolicam Actuositatem*, the Decree on the Apostolate of the Laity.[5] At the heart of this Decree is a revolutionary claim that Christ himself calls every faithful to serve the mission of the Church.[6] In the second Constitution, *Gaudium et Spes*, the Council highlighted the special responsibility of lay people in the modern world.[7]

With these teachings, Vatican II, following the twin strategy of *ressourcement* (returning to Christian sources in Scripture, the Fathers of the Church, the liturgy, and philosophy) and *aggiornamento* (renewal or updating the Church), effectively

---

of steps to develop a theology of the laity: First, it used the biblical image of the people of God to describe the Church…and emphasized that the whole Church…are called to holiness…. Pneumatologically, it reclaimed the *charismata* or spiritual gifts 'both hierarchic and charismatic'…. Most important, it stressed that both ordained ministers and all the faithful share in the priesthood of Christ, though in different ways" ("Ministry and Ministries," in *Ordering the Baptismal Priesthood: Theologies of Lay and Ordained Ministry*, edited by Susan K. Wood [Collegeville, Minn.: Liturgical Press, 2003] 57). For a detailed commentary on the notion of the people God in *Lumen Gentium* see Aloys Grillmeier, "The People of God," in *Commentary on the Documents of Vatican II*, edited by Herbert Vorgrimler, vol. 1 (New York: Herder and Herder, 1967) 153–85. Avery Dulles reminds us that "in New Testament times there was, technically speaking, no such thing as the laity, or clergy either. There were diverse ministries, of course, but they were not put into these two categories" ("Can the Word 'Laity' Be Defined?" *Origins* 18:29 [29 December 1988] 470). Dulles' view echoes Congar's observation that "there is no distinction between 'lay people' and 'clerics' in the vocabulary of the New Testament." See Yves M.J. Congar, *Lay People in the Church: A Study for a Theology of Laity*, translated by Donald Attwater, revised ed. (London: Geoffrey Chapman, 1965) 4.

5   A.A. Hagstrom notes that Vatican II was "the first council to treat the laity from a theological, rather than an exclusively canonical, point of view." See "Theology of Laity," in *New Catholic Encyclopedia*, 2nd ed., vol. 8 (Detroit: Gale Group in Association with the Catholic University of America, 2003) 291.

6   *Apostolicam Actuositatem*, no. 3, *Lumen Gentium*, no. 33. For Avery Dulles, "At the council the Catholic Church for the first time in history took up in its full scope the question of the status and role of the laity. If Vatican II had done nothing else, that fact alone would make the council historic" ("Can the Word 'Laity' Be Defined?" *Origins* 18:29 [29 December 1988] 471).

7   Thomas P. Rausch argues that "perhaps the most significant shift represented by the council was the turn toward the world and especially toward the poor" (*Catholicism in the Third Millennium*, 2nd ed. [Collegeville, Minn.: The Liturgical Press, 2003] 16).

renewed the hierarchical and institutionalised ecclesiology,[8] and signalled a shift in the Church's understanding of the identity and role of lay people.[9] First, it abandoned an attitude that was prevalent for centuries, which took for granted a passive role for the laity. Second, it advocated the active participation of lay people in the priestly, prophetic, and kingly mission of Christ,[10] considering it as a duty incumbent on all recipients of the sacraments of Baptism and Confirmation.[11] Consequently, Vatican II has often been hailed as "the Council of the Laity."[12] This Copernican revolution in the conciliar theology of the laity generated in turn a rediscovery of the importance of lay people in the Asian Churches,[13] which, like

---

8   This ecclesiology, "which had lasted almost four centuries," was aptly described as "hiérarchologie," a term coined by Yves Congar in 1947 to characterise the Church presented as "an organized society constituted by the exercise of powers with which pope, bishops and priests were invested." See Yves Congar, *Ministère et Communion Ecclésiale* (Paris: Les Editions du Cerf, 1971) 10; "My Path-Findings in the Theology of Laity and Ministries," *The Jurist* 32 (1972) 170; Thomas F. O'Meara, "Beyond 'Hierarchology'," in *The Legacy of the Tübingen School: The Relevance of Nineteenth-Century Theology for the Twenty-First Century*, edited by D.J. Dietrich and M.J. Himes (New York: Crossroad, 1997) 183, 190.

9   For Giovanni Magnani, the importance of the laity question at Vatican II can be seen in the fact that the term "layman" occurs 206 times in the conciliar documents, not counting the "three instances of 'laity' and seven of the adjective 'lay'." See "Does the So-Called Theology of the Laity Possess a Theological Status?" in *Vatican II Assessment and Perspectives: Twenty-Five Years After (1962–1987)*, vol. 1, edited by René Latourelle (New York: Paulist Press, 1988) 595.

10 *Lumen Gentium*, no. 31.

11 *Lumen Gentium*, no. 33. It is instructive to recall Kenan B. Osborne's insightful remark that the "integration of the sacrament of initiation (baptism-confirmation-eucharist) into the fundamental structure of church ministry is key to the understanding both of the church itself and of the various church ministries, which one finds throughout the Vatican II documents (*Ministry: Lay Ministry in the Roman Catholic Church: Its History and Theology* [New York: Paulist Press, 1993] 1).

12 Yves Congar, "The Laity," in *Vatican II: An Interfaith Appraisal*, edited by John H. Miller (New York: Association Press, 1966) 239; John Nilson, "The Laity," in *The Gift of the Church: A Textbook on Ecclesiology in Honour of Patrick Granfield*, edited by Peter C. Phan (Collegeville, Minn.: The Liturgical Press, 2000) 400.

13 In this book, we use interchangeably the following terms, in singular or plural form: "the Church in Asia," or "the Asian Church." Elsewhere in the text, we also employ the phrase "the Church of Asia." By these terms we mean first and foremost, but not always in an exclusive sense, the Catholic Church in Asia. Theologically speaking, it would be more correct to speak of the "Church in Asia" rather than the "Asian Church" or "the Church of Asia." Indeed, one only needs to recall the custom of Saint Paul, who believes strongly

other Catholic ecclesial communities throughout the world, experienced Vatican II as a theological event and a catalyst for change.[14] One of the notable changes was the establishment of the Federation of Asian Bishops' Conferences (FABC),[15] an

that the local Church is the incarnation of the Church of God, e.g., "to the Church of God in Corinth" (1 Cor 1:2; 2 Cor 1:1), or "… the Church in Cenchrea" (Rom 16:1). Henri de Lubac notes that "Ignatius of Antioch likewise addressed himself to 'the Church of God which is at Philadelphia of Asia', at Magnesia, Tralles, Smyrna, etc. Origen used these formulas again. The *Martyrdom of Polycarp* contains a similar, more explicit greeting: 'The Church of God which resides at Smyrna, to the Church of God which resides at Philomelium and to all the residences everywhere of the holy and Catholic Church." See *The Motherhood of the Church* (San Francisco: Ignatius Press, 1982) 202–3.

14 Continuing the debate of the so-called "*Annales*" school on the meaning of the term "event," and the relationship between *longue durée* and *événement*, Joseph Komonchak explores the theme of "Vatican II as 'Event'," *Theology Digest* 46:4 (Winter 1999) 337–352, making a distinction between "event, experience, and final documents." In his view, "'Experience' refers to contemporary intentions, motives, encounters, decisions, and actions during the Council; the 'final documents' are the product of that experience." "Event" represents a different category, in the sense of a "noteworthy" occurrence, one that has consequences. He concurs with most of the literature on the subject that an "event" represents novelty, discontinuity, a "rupture," a break from routine, causing surprise, disturbance, even trauma, and perhaps initiating a new routine, a new realm of the taken-for-granted.

15 The FABC consists of the Catholic Bishops' Conferences in South, Southeast, East and Central Asia, and comprises member conferences from Bangladesh, India, Indonesia, Japan, Kazakhstan, Korea, Laos-Cambodia, Malaysia-Singapore-Brunei, Myanmar, Pakistan, Philippines, Sri Lanka, Taiwan, Thailand, and Vietnam. The ecclesiastical jurisdictions of Hong Kong (SAR), Macao, Mongolia, Nepal, Kirgyzstan, Siberia (Russia), Tadjikistan, Turkmenistan, Uzbekistan, and East Timor enjoy associate membership. This book covers the first Asian Bishops' Meeting in 1970 and the ten Plenary Assemblies that were held, normally once every four years, between 1974 and 2012, namely: "Evangelization in Modern Day Asia" (1974), "Prayer – The Life of the Church in Asia" (1978), "The Church as a Community of Faith in Asia" (1982), "The Vocation and Mission of the Laity in the Church and in the World of Asia" (1986), "The Emerging Challenges for the Church in Asia in the 1990's: A Call to Respond" (1990), "Christian Discipleship in Asia Today: Service to Life" (1995), "A Renewed Church in Asia: A Mission of Love and Service" (2000), "The Asian Family Towards a Culture of Integral Life" (2004), "Living the Eucharist in Asia"(2009), and "FABC at Forty Years: Responding to the Challenges of Asia: A New Evangelization"(2012). All of the important documents of the FABC issued between 1970 and 2012 were published in the five volumes of *For All the Peoples of Asia*. These volumes will be cited as *FAPA Vol. 1*, *FAPA Vol. 2*, *FAPA Vol. 3*, *FAPA Vol. 4*, and *FAPA Vol. 5*, with the ten FABC Plenary Assemblies being referred to as FABC I, II, III, IV, V, VI, VII, VIII, IX, and X. FABC offices will be abbreviated as

ecclesial body that received its official status in 1972,[16] two years after 180 "Asian bishops" met for the first time around Paul VI in Manila.[17] Another change lies in

---

follows: Office of Clergy (OC), Office of Consecrated Life (OCL), Office of Evangeliza- tion (OE), Office of Ecumenical & Inter-religious Affairs (OEIA), Office of Education & Student Chaplaincy (OESC), now renamed Office of Education & Faith Formation (OEFF), Office of Human Development (OHD), Office of Laity (OL)–now subsumed into the Office of Laity and Family (OLF), Office of Social Communication (OSC), and Theological Advisory Commission (TAC)–later changed to Office of Theological Concerns (OTC). FABC' study institutes and seminars organised by the FABC offices will be referred to as Asian Movement for Christian Unity (AMCU), Bishops' Institute for Biblical Apostolate (BIBA), Bishops' Institute for Lay Apostolate (BILA), Bishops' Institute for Missionary Apostolate (BIMA), Bishops' Institute for Interreligious Affairs (BIRA), Bishops' Institute for Social Communication (BISCOM), Bishops' Institute for Social Action (BISA), Bishops' Institute of Theological Animation (BITA), Faith Encounters in Social Action (FEISA), and Formation Institute for Interreligious Affairs (FIRA). It is important to note that of all the official documents published by the FABC, the final statements of the Plenary Assemblies are the most authoritative. However, the texts produced by the FABC's offices and study institutes, which often refer to the statements of the Plenary Assemblies, also strongly reflect the thinking of the Asian bishops. Domenico Colombo made a similar remark arguing that "queste strutture di settore e i loro testi, ovviamente, non hanno l'autorità delle Assemblee e sono espres- sioni indirette della FABC." See "A Servizio dei Popoli dell'Asia: Camminare sulle orme di Gesù in ascolto dello Spirito," in *Documenti della Chiesa in Asia: Federazione delle Conferenze Episcopali Asiatiche 1970–1995*, edited by Domenico Colombo (Bologna: Editrice Missionaria Italiana, 1997) 14. Colombo went on to suggest that it is important to know these texts to better understand the FABC. Ibid., 18.

16 On 16th November 1972 the Holy See approved the statutes of the FABC *ad experi- mentum* for two years, marking the official establishment of the Federation. See FABC, *Statutes of the Federation of Asian Bishops' Conferences* (Hong Kong: General Secretariat of the FABC, 1995) 1. For a detailed discussion of the history, objectives, functions, structures, and activities of the FABC see Miguel Marcelo Quatra, *At the Side of the Multitudes: The Kingdom of God and the Mission of the Church in the FABC Documents (1970–1995)* (Quezon City: Claretian Publications, 2000) 5–18; Edmund Chia, "Thirty Years of FABC: History, Foundation, Context and Theology" *FABC Papers, No. 106* (Hong Kong: FABC Central Secretariat, 2003) 4–13.

17 FABC, "Asian Bishops' Meeting," arts. 1, 3, *FAPA Vol. 1*, 3; Felix Wilfred, "The Federa- tion of Asian Bishops' Conferences (FABC)," in *For All the Peoples of Asia: Federation of Asian Bishops' Conferences, Documents from 1970 to 1991*, vol. 1., edited by Gaudencio B. Rosales and C.G. Arevalo (Quezon City: Claretian Publications, 1992) xxiii. In this book we employ the terms "the Asian bishops" and "the bishops of Asia" interchangeably to refer to the Catholic bishops of Episcopal Conferences in East Asia that are members of the FABC.

the fact that, in their efforts over forty years–from the historic meeting in 1970–to apply the conciliar teachings in the Asian *Sitz-im-Leben*, the bishops of Asia have developed their own local theologies, including a contextual theology of the laity, which is the topic of this work.

The theme of "the Vocation and Mission of the Laity in the Church and in the World of Asia" was discussed in detail at the Fourth Plenary Assembly of the FABC held in September 1986.[18] While accepting Vatican II teachings,[19] the Asian bishops were acutely aware that "the signs of the times" in their region pointed in directions different from what was assumed at the time of the Council.[20] They also

---

18 FABC IV, *FAPA I, Vol. 1*, 177–98. Besides the Fourth Plenary Assembly, the Asian bishops have further explored the role of the laity in seminars organised by their Office of Laity and the Institute for the Lay Apostolate, and embarked on a programme of integral formation to promote "a New Way of Being Church in Asia." *FAPA Vol II*, 107–11.

19 Vatican II documents such as *Lumen Gentium, Gaudium et Spes, Ad Gentes*, and *Nostra Aetate*, etc. have often been quoted in the statements of the FABC. John Paul II's Encyclicals and Apostolic Exhortations such as *Redemptor Hominis, Tertio Millennio Adveniente, Dominum et Vivificantem*, and *Ecclesia in Asia* are also cited in the FABC documents, e.g., BIRA IV/3, art. 11.2, *FAPA Vol. 1*, 258; FABC VII, Part II.A, Part III.A.5, Part III.C.3, Conclusion.

20 According to *Gaudium et Spes* (no. 4), "At all times the Church carries the responsibility of reading the signs of the times and of interpreting them in the light of the Gospel." T. Howland Sanks notes that "the phrase, 'discerning the signs of the times', had been used by Reinhold Niebuhr as a title for a book of his sermons in 1946, and the phrase was used frequently by Pope John XXIII in his encyclical *Pacem in Terris*. It means, according to Niebuhr, 'to interpret historical events and values' or, according to Vatican II, 'to recognize and understand the world in which we live, its expectations, its longings, and its often dramatic characteristics" ("Reading the Signs of the Times: Purpose and Method," in *Reading the Signs of the Times: Resources for Social and Cultural Analysis*, edited by T. Howland Sanks and John A. Coleman [New York: Paulist Press, 1993] 3). Christopher O'Donnell notes that "the expression 'signs of the times' came into current usage about the time of Vatican II. Though appearing earlier in France, it was used by Pope John XXIII in the apostolic constitution *Humanae salutis* convoking Vatican II: 'Making our own the warnings of Jesus exhorting us to discern 'the signs of the times' (Matt 16:3), we detect in the midst of so much darkness many indications that make us hopeful about the future of the Church and humanity'." See *Ecclesia: A Theological Encyclopedia of the Church* (Collegeville, Minn.: The Liturgical Press, 1996) 424. For José Comblin, this phrase was understood by "John XXIII and the Council in two different senses which are not always clearly distinguished.... In the first place, the signs of the times indicated events and situations in contemporary Western society: that is, the changes taking

realised that, after more than 400 years of active evangelisation, Christians still remain *a pusillus grex* in the vast continent of Asia.[21] This region is home to 60% of the world population,[22] most of which lives in abject poverty. It is also blessed with a plurality of ancient cultures and religious traditions that have shaped the "minds and hearts and lives" of Asian people down through a long history.[23] Therefore, the Asian bishops had to reconsider the mission of the Church to such a world, and the role of the laity within it.

For the Asian bishops, the Church's evangelising mission in Asia experiences the greatest urgency while at the same time needing to find a distinctive form.[24] This mission—"a continuation in the Spirit of the mission of Christ"[25]—will mean a triple dialogue with the cultures, the religions, and the poor.[26] This "dialogue of life,"[27] or "dialogue of salvation,"[28] is "intrinsic to the very life of the

---

place in society.... In the second place, there is a reference to Matthew 16:4, so to eschatological signs, signs of the presence of the kingdom of God in this world. The Council documents and the Pope's speeches tended to conflate the two senses, as though the changes taking place in society had an eschatological meaning" ("The Signs of the Times," *Concilium* 4 [2005] 73).

21 Christians account for approximately 3.9% of the total population of Asia with Catholics representing about 2.8%, concentrated mainly in the Philippines (83% of the population), South Korea, Vietnam, and East Timor. See *The World Almanac and Book of Facts 2003* (New York: World Almanac Books, 2003) 638, 780, 801, 828, 857.

22 ACMC, art. 13, *FAPA Vol. 1*, 69. Daniel G. Groody arrives at a similar figure: "if the 6.5 billion people who live on our planet were proportioned down to a community of 100 people, 60 would be Asian, 14 African, 11 European, 14 American (North, South, Central, and Caribbean), and 1 would be an Australian or New Zealander." See "Globalizing Solidarity: Christian Anthropology and the Challenge of Human Liberation," *Theological Studies* 69 (2008) 253.

23 FABC I, Briefer Statement of the Assembly, art. 11, *FAPA Vol. 1*, 22.

24 FABC V, art. 4.1, *FAPA Vol. 1*, 281.

25 FABC V, art. 3.1.2, *FAPA Vol. 1*, 280.

26 For an in-depth treatment of the theme of triple dialogue, see Peter C. Phan's classic trilogy: *In Our Own Tongues: Perspectives from Asia on Mission and Inculturation* (Maryknoll, New York: Orbis Books, 2003); *Christianity with an Asian Face: Asian American Theology in the Making* (Maryknoll, New York: Orbis Books, 2003); *Being Religious Interreligiously: Asian Perspectives on Interfaith Dialogue* (Maryknoll, New York: Orbis Books, 2004).

27 FABC I, art. 20, *FAPA Vol. 1*, 15; FABC VI, art. 8.1.3, *FAPA Vol. 1*, 288.

28 BIMA I, art. 9, FAPA *Vol, I*, 94.

church, and the essential mode of all evangelisation."[29] At their seventh Plenary Assembly held in January 2000, after years of addressing individual issues confronting the Asian Church, the bishops of Asia finally adopted an inclusive view of the evangelising mission,[30] a term now encompassing inculturation, dialogue, justice, and the option for the poor, not as separate topics but aspects of an integrated understanding of the Church's mission of love and service.[31]

The Significance of this Study

To fulfil the evangelising mission in Asia, the Asian bishops have turned to the lay faithful. They conceded that the lay apostolate still remained basically "parish-oriented, inward-looking and priest-directed."[32] Therefore, they have deepened their theology of the laity and used it as a foundation to develop a lay ministry more oriented to the world. This theology, deeply anchored in a contextual ecclesiology that was developed at the Third Plenary Assembly held in 1982, interprets anew the identity, vocation, and role of lay people, and places emphasis on their co-responsibility in the mission of the Church, in collaboration with bishops, priests, and religious.

For the bishops of Asia, the success of the evangelising mission in Asia will very much depend on how vigorously lay people, agents of evangelisation *par excellence*, have come to understand and implement their dual responsibility in the Church and in the world.[33] Yves Congar, often considered to be the most important Catholic ecclesiologist of the twentieth century,[34] underscores this point by predicting that "if the Church, secure on her foundations, boldly

---

29 BIRA I, art. 9, *FAPA Vol. 1*, 111.
30 The Asian bishops refer to this as a "movement toward active integral evangelization, toward a new sense of mission." FABC VII, Part I.A.5, *FAPA Vol. 3*, 3.
31 FABC VII, Part III, *FAPA Vol. 3*, 8.
32 FABC IV, art. 4.6.2, *FAPA Vol. 1*, 193.
33 FABC V, arts. 3.3.3., 5.1, 8.1.1–8.1.2, *FAPA Vol. 1*, 281, 283, 287.
34 Thomas F. O'Meara, "Beyond 'Hierarchology'," in *The Legacy of the Tübingen School: The Relevance of Nineteenth-Century Theology for the Twenty-First Century*, edited by D.J. Dietrich and M.J. Himes (New York: Crossroad, 1997) 173; Elizabeth T. Groppe, "The Practice of Theology as Passion for Truth: Testimony from the Journals of Yves Congar, O.P.," *Horizons* 31:2 (Fall 2004) 384.

throws herself open to lay activity, she will experience such a spring time as we cannot imagine."[35]

Yet, so far, despite its prominence in the FABC's thought, and its enormous implications for the mission and the future of the Asian Church, the role of the laity in the documents of the FABC has been examined mainly in isolation or only as related to other concerns. By focusing on one aspect of the question of the laity, studies conducted so far have not treated the FABC's theology of the laity in a full and critical fashion. Therefore, to remedy this gap in research, we intend to investigate the FABC's theology of the laity in a more comprehensive fashion by discussing its historical context, its methodologies, its contents and development, and its ecclesiological underpinnings. To bring out the richness and dynamics of the FABC's contextual theology of the laity, we will also compare it with the theologies developed by John Paul II and the Vietnamese Episcopal Conference.

This book, then, will investigate the theology of the laity as proposed by the Federation of Asian Bishops' Conferences. It will situate this theology in the context of post-Vatican II magisterial documents, in particular Pope John Paul II's Apostolic Exhortation *Ecclesia in Asia*,[36] and the pastoral letters of the Vietnamese Episcopal Conference. The book will ascertain whether there has been a development in the FABC's theology of the laity, and to what extent this teaching represents an integration of, and a step beyond, other postconciliar theologies of the laity.

The State of the Question

To date, the documents of the FABC have been the object of over thirty doctoral dissertations and several licentiate or masters theses.[37] They treat a variety of

---

35 Yves M.J. Congar, *Lay People in the Church: A Study for a Theology of Laity*, rev. ed., trans. Donald Attwater (London: Geoffrey Chapman, 1965) xviii.

36 See John Paul II, "*Ecclesia in Asia,*" *Origins* 29:23 (18 November 1999) 357, 359–84. Hereafter, only the title *Ecclesia in Asia* and relevant numbers will be cited in footnotes.

37 For a latest count of these doctoral theses, see http://www.fabc.org/FABCRelated Studies.html (accessed 16 May 2015).

theological and pastoral themes such as the evangelising mission,[38] the kingdom of God,[39] the Catholic social teachings,[40] ecclesiology,[41] Christology,[42] inculturation,[43]

38 Vincent Ezhanikatt, "Evangelization in India in the Light of the Federation of Asian Bishops' Conferences from 1970 to 1991" (D. Miss. Diss., Pontificia Universitas Urbania, 1995); Agustinus Bula, "A Study of the Evangelization Mission of the Church in Contemporary Asia in the Light of the Documents of the Federation of Asian Bishops' Conferences, 1970–1995" (Th.D. diss., Pontificia Universitas Urbania, 1997); Jonathan Yun-Ka Tan, "*Missio ad Gentes* in Asia: a Comparative Study of the Missiology of John Paul II and the Federation of Asian Bishops' Conferences" (Ph.D. diss., The Catholic University of America, 2002).

39 Miguel Marcelo Quatra, *At the Side of the Multitudes: The Kingdom of God and the Mission of the Church in the FABC Documents (1970–1995)* (Quezon City: Claretian Publications, 2000).

40 Lucas Thumma, "An Inquiry into the Ethico-Legal Methodology of the Social Teachings of the Federation of Asian Bishops' Conferences Documents from 1970–1991" (S.T.D. diss., Vidyajyoti College of Theology, 1996).

41 C.B. Putranta, "The Idea of the Church in the Documents of the Federation of Asian Bishops' Conferences (FABC) 1970–1982" (Th.D. diss., Pontificia Universitas Gregoriana, 1985); James Thoppil, "Towards an Asian Ecclesiology: Understanding of the Church in the Documents of the Federation of Asian Bishops' Conferences (FABC) 1970–1995 and the Asian Ecclesiological Trends" (Th.D. diss., Pontificia Universitas Urbaniana, 1998); Lawrence Abraham Kadaliyil, "Toward a Relational Spirit Ecclesiology in Asia: A Study on the Documents of the Federation of Asian Bishops' Conferences" (Th.D. diss., Graduate Theological Union, Berkeley, 2006); Thao Nguyen, "A New Way of Being Church for Mission, Asian Catholic Bishops and Asian Catholic Women in Dialogue: A Study of the Documents of the Federation of Asian Bishops' Conferences (FABC)" (Th.D. diss., Graduate Theological Union, Berkeley, 2013).

42 A. Alangaram, *Christ of the Asian Peoples: Towards an Asian Contextual Christology Based on the Documents of the Federation of the Asian Bishops' Conferences*, rev. ed. (Bangalore: Asian Trading Corporation, 2001).

43 Ladislav Nemet, "Inculturation in the Philippines: A Theological Study of the Question of Inculturation in the Documents of CBCP and Selected Filipino Theologians in the Light of Vatican II and the Documents of FABC" (Th.D. diss., Pontificia Universitas Gregoriana, 1994); Bernadus Agus Rukiayanto, "A New Way of Being Church: A Study of Inculturation in the Church of Asia and of Indonesia, A Roman Catholic Perspective" (S.T.D. diss., Weston Jesuit School of Theology, 2007); Dominic Tran Ngoc Dang, "Inculturation in Missionary Formation According to the Federation of Asian Bishops'Conferences Documents (1970–2006) with Special Reference to the Mission in Vietnam" (Th.D. diss., Pontificia Universitas Urbaniana, 2009).

liberation,[44] inter-religious dialogue,[45] prayer,[46] priestly formation,[47] ordained ministry,[48] and the Asian family.[49] Besides a doctoral thesis discussing the spirituality of lay people in a particular diocese,[50] and one that explores "the Participatory Communion" of the laity in a local church,[51] both with reference to the FABC statements, three other doctoral studies deal with the mission and ministry of the laity in a wider context of Asia.[52]

44 D. Bosco M. Mariampillai, "The Emerging Asian Theology of Liberation in the Documents of the Federation of Asian Bishops' Conferences 1974–1986" (Ph.D. diss., University of Ottawa, 1993); Matthew Paikada, "Characteristics of an Indian Liberation Theology as an Authentic Christian Theology: A Study Based on the Analysis of the Indian Situation and the Documents of the CBCI and the FABC" (Dr. Theol., Westphalia Wilhelms University, 1988).

45 Edmund Chia, "Towards a Theology of Dialogue: Schillebeeckx's Method as Bridge Between Vatican's *Dominus Iesus* and Asia's FABC Theology" (Ph.D. diss., University of Niimegen, 2003); Ruben C. Mendoza, "A Church in Dialogue with Peoples of Other Faiths: A Journey to the Kingdom in the Spirit. The Federation of Asian Bishops'Conferences 1970–2007" (Ph.D./S.T.D. diss., Katholieke Universiteit Leuven, 2009); Herman Punda Panda, "Towards Living Together in Harmony: A Study of Interreligious Dialogue as an Effort to Promote Harmony among Believers of Various Religions, Based on the Federation of Asian Bishops' Conferences (FABC) Documents from 1970 to 1996" (S.T.D. diss., Pontificia Universitas Urbaniana, 2001).

46 Joseph Dinh Duc Dao, "Preghiera Rinnovata per una Era Missionaria in Asia" (D. Miss., Pontifical Gregorian University, 1993).

47 Charles Boromeo, "Priestly Formation in the Light of the Federation of Asian Bishops' Conferences (FABC): Towards a Model in the Burmese Context" (S.T.D. diss., International Carmelite College (Teresianum), 2002).

48 Jeffrey G.L. Chang, "Ordained Ministries in the Mission and Ministry of the Church in Asia, in Light of the Documents of the Federation of Asian Bishops' Conferences, 1970–2005" (S.T.D diss., Fu Jen Catholic University, 2007).

49 Maria Eliza A. Borja. "An Analysis of the FABC Documents on the Asian Family (1979–2013)" (Ph.D. diss., Ateneo de Manila University, 2014).

50 Anatriello Sinani, "Spirituality for the Laity in the Toungngu Diocese in the Light of the Documents of the Federation of Asian Bishops' Conferences (FABC)" (S.T.D. diss., International Carmelite College (Teresianum), 1999).

51 Alphonse Thainese, "Laity in the Participatory Communion in the Local Church of Andhra: An Ecclesiological Inquiry Based on the Documents of the Federation of Asian Bishops' Conferences 1970–2005" (Th.D. diss., Dharmaram Vidya Kshetram and Pontifical Athenaeum of Philosophy, Theology and Canon Law, 2006).

52 Petrus Maria Handoko, "Lay Ministries in the Mission and Ministry of the Church in Asia: A Critical Study of the Documents of the Federation of Asian Bishops' Conferences, 1970–1991" (Th.D. diss., Pontificia Universitas Gregoriana, 1993); Marta Nam

Marta Nam Ki Ok and Petrus Maria Handoko discuss the evangelising role of the lay faithful and lay ministries respectively, using the FABC documents published up to 1991 including the statements of the first five Plenary Assemblies of the FABC (1974, 1978, 1982, 1986, and 1990). Nam Ki Ok's study focuses on the mission of the laity in the social and religious context of Korea, devoting only one of the work's eight chapters to examine the statements of the FABC that deal with the role of lay people. The author's approach to the subject in this chapter is predominantly pastoral, emphasising the importance of the formation for the laity,[53] and containing numerous references to the social and ecclesial situations in Korea.[54] Her analysis of the texts consists of a number of direct quotations taken mainly from the statements of the FABC's Fourth Plenary Assembly on the laity and the Bishops' Institutes for the Lay Apostolate, often sandwiched between general introductory and summary remarks, and arranged under the headings of the role of the laity in the family, in the field of education, in the world of work, and in the local Church of East Asia.[55]

Handoko's thesis provides a more extensive investigation of the FABC's theology of lay ministries in the light of the "paradigm of Kingdom."[56] He situates his treatment of lay ministries "within what is termed a total ecclesiology,"[57] and considers "communion as a mode of mission."[58] However, the author does not discuss the contextual approach of the FABC's theology of the laity, and

---

Ki Ok, "Il ruolo evangelizzatore dei fedeli laici nel contesto socio-religioso in Corea alla luce dei documenti della FABC dal 1980 al 1991" (Th.D. diss., Pontificia Universitas Urbaniana, 1996); Nguyen Van Am, "The Laity in Asia: Mission as Inculturation in the Documents of the Federation of Asian Bishops' Conferences" (S.T.D. diss., Jesuit School of Theology at Berkeley, 2001).

53 Marta Nam Ki Ok, ibid., 120–32.
54 See for instance, Marta Nam Ki Ok, ibid., 132–3, 138–9, 141, 144–5, 148, 150–1.
55 Marta Nam Ki Ok, ibid., 132–68.
56 Handoko, "Lay Ministries in the Mission and Ministry of the Church in Asia," 4. Quatra's thesis provides a much more exhaustive investigation of the theme "Kingdom of God."
57 Handoko, "Lay Ministries in the Mission and Ministry of the Church in Asia," 4. This approach was likely inspired by Yves Congar's observation that "there can only be one sound and sufficient theology of the laity, and that is a 'total ecclesiology'." See Congar's *Lay People in the Church: A Study for a Theology of Laity*, revised edition, with additions by the author, trans. Donald Attwater (London: Geoffrey Chapman, 1965) xvi–xvii.
58 Handoko, "Lay Ministries in the Mission and Ministry of the Church in Asia," 287.

its emphasis on the triple dialogue as the mode of the evangelising mission in Asia.[59] His study could be complemented by a discussion of the theological methodologies employed by the bishops of Asia including the "Asian Integral Pastoral Approach."[60] It could also be strengthened by an examination of the common priesthood of the faithful as "a real priesthood of life" and the basis for lay identity and secularity,[61] an investigation of the ecclesial construct of basic ecclesial communities,[62] and an exploration of the linkage between the mission of the laity and the orientation of the FABC's triple dialogue, namely, inculturation, interreligious dialogue, and liberation or human development. In this way, the richness of the FABC's theology of the laity could better be revealed, and shown to be more encompassing, relevant, and useful to Asian Christians.

Nguyen Van Am's dissertation is the third study on the mission of lay people in Asia, based on the documents of the Asian bishops issued up to 2001. The author investigates the subject under three aspects, in three successive chapters.[63] Chapter 2 "deals with inculturation in a close relationship to the laity."[64] In Chapter 3, which purportedly "points out an Asian lay spirituality implied in the mission of inculturation,"[65] Nguyen Van Am argues that "this is the way in which lay people in Asia develop their lay identity by listening to the Spirit and by working for the Kingdom with the heart detached from wealth and power."[66] Finally, in

---

59 OTC, "Methodology: Asian Christian Theology," *FABC Vol. 3*, 329–419; FABC I, arts. 14–20, *FAPA Vol. 1*, 14–15; BIMA I, art. 10, *FAPA Vol. 1*, 94; BIRA I, art. 9, *FAPA Vol. 1*, 111.

60 Ibid.; Office of Laity, "Asian Integral Pastoral Approach: Towards a New Way of being Church in Asia," *FAPA Vol. 2*, 107–11; "Asian Integral Pastoral Approach (AsIPA): Message to the Churches of Asia," *FAPA, Vol. 2*, 137–9; "Second Asian Integral Pastoral Approach (AsIPA) General Assembly II: Final Statement," *FAPA Vol. 3*, 107–12.

61 FABC IV, art. 4.4.2, *FAPA Vol. 1*, 192.

62 FABC VII, Part III, C.7; *FAPA Vol. 1.*, 76–7; *FAPA Vol. 3*, 15.

63 The first chapter of Nguyen Van Am's dissertation "gives a brief overview of the history of the Federation of the Asian Bishops' Conferences," and the last chapter, Chapter 5, is an attempt "to construct a theological synthesis based on the documents analyzed in preceding chapters." See "The Laity in Asia: Mission as Inculturation in the Documents of the Federation of Asian Bishops' Conferences," vii-viii.

64 Ibid., vii.

65 Ibid.

66 Ibid.

Chapter 4, which "singles out some emphases in the Asian Synod,"[67] he suggests that "through these emphases, the Synod encourages lay people to involve in the mission of inculturation."[68] Throughout his study, the author pays little attention to the dynamic integration between inculturation and the other two pillars of the FABC's threefold dialogical approach, namely the dialogue with other religions and the engagement with the poor.[69] His treatment of the spirituality of the Asian laity could be enriched by an exploration of the FABC's teaching on the spirituality of discipleship and the spirituality of harmony. His discussion on the emphases of the Asian Synod and their impact on the mission of lay people in Asia, could also be broadened by an elaboration on the concept of witness of life, a leitmotif of the Apostolic Exhortation *Ecclesia in Asia*, a discussion of the identity, vocation, and mission of lay people in the context of the Church as a witnessing community of faith built on the two pillars of communion and mission, and some remarks on the continuing debate on the primacy between proclamation and triple dialogue. In general, Nguyen Van Am's examination of the thesis topic tends to be cursory, and some of the sweeping statements that his study contains will not likely go unchallenged. For instance, in the introduction to his dissertation, the author avers that "it is true that Asian lay people are very devout and zealous. The FABC knows this. Consequently, the Asian bishops charge the laity with a challenging mission, the mission of inculturation."[70] In the final conclusion, he summarises his study in four assertions, the last of which reads: "more than ever before, the laity in Asia acknowledges that there is no

---

67 For a comprehensive discussion of the Synod for Asia and its themes, see *The Asian Synod: Texts and Commentaries*, compiled and edited by Peter C. Phan (Maryknoll, New York: Orbis Books, 2002).

68 Ibid.

69 Recalling the FABC's emphasis on "the necessity of doing these three dialogues together," Peter C. Phan states that "inculturation, interreligious dialogue, and liberation form the three-pronged approach to Christian mission in Asia" ("Cultures, Religions, and Power: Proclaiming Christ in the United States Today," *Theological Studies* 65 [2004] 735); see also *Christianity with an Asian Face: Asian American Theology in the Making* (Maryknoll, New York: Orbis Books, 2003) 188–9; FABC I, Briefer Statement of the Assembly, art. 20, *FAPA Vol. 1*, 23. Elsewhere, Phan notes that, for the FABC, these three essential tasks "are not three distinct and separate activities of the church; rather, they are three intertwined dimensions of the church's one mission of evangelization" (*In Our Own Tongues: Perspectives from Asia on Mission and Inculturation* [Maryknoll, New York: Orbis Books, 2003] 19; see also FABC VII, Part III, *FAPA Vol. 3*, 8.

70 Nguyen Van Am, "The Laity in Asia: Mission as Inculturation in the Documents of the Federation of Asian Bishops' Conferences," v.

opposition between being Christian and being Asian. More strongly speaking, Asian Christians are called to bring to light this truth that to be Christian is the best way of being Asian."[71] These assertions do not seem to have clear warrants from the texts of the Asian bishops.

In sum, given the focus, depth, and limited coverage of the aforementioned studies, the role of the laity in the documents of the FABC still remains a topic that merits further systematic investigation. We also note the paucity of the secondary literature on the role of lay people in the documents of the FABC, which comprise a few articles, two of which produced as position papers in preparation for the Fourth Plenary Assembly of the FABC,[72] and several workshop guides.[73] These authors could not deal with the theme in an exhaustive fashion because of the limitations of the genre.

With respect to the vocation and mission of the laity in John Paul II's Apostolic Exhortation *Ecclesia in Asia*, to date, there has not been any scholarly research devoted in a substantial way to the subject. There has also been no systematic study on the mission of the laity as proposed in the pastoral letters of

---

71 Ibid., 185. Also cited here are the main points of the remaining assertions in the conclusion of Nguyen Van Am's thesis: "The century of the laity in Asia has come. The FABC aims at consolidating this *kairos* by entrusting without hesitation the great and challenging mission of inculturation to Asian lay people. More precisely, it is not the church, but Jesus Christ with the Holy Spirit who commissions them through Baptism for the sake of Asians. For this reason, first, for lay people to live must mean to live in Jesus Christ (cf. Phil. 1:21), God-made-man, who should illumine and inspire the incarnational lifestyle of lay Christians in Asia.... **Second**, Spirit-filled lay people should give praise to God for his love endures forever.... The laity in Asia emerges as a sign of the totally new order of history, which is not only above, but also within this history, which is already present, but not fully manifested. Thus, to fulfil the mission of inculturation the laity should walk the earth under the Spirit's lead, the Spirit of Joy, *laetitia*. Therefore, **third**, Asian lay people gradually learn to contemplate *sacrament*-church to better understand their lay identity. Of course, they live in the *sacramental* economy, celebrating the sacraments, not as a mere ritualism, but as the source of life.... This sacramental dynamism defines the lay identity as a longing for God's love amidst its specific secularity in Asian realities..." (bold typeface in the original). Ibid., 184–5.
72 S.J. Emmanuel, "Contemporary Catholic Thought on the Vocation and Mission of the Laity in the Church and in the World," *FABC Papers, No. 44* (Hong Kong: FABC, 1986); Felix Wilfred, "Sunset in the East: The Asian Realities Challenging the Church and Its Laity Today," *FABC Papers, No. 45* (Hong Kong: FABC, 1986.
73 Twelve FABC Papers from no. 46a to no. 46l (Hong Kong: FABC, 1986).

the Vietnamese Episcopal Conference (VEC),[74] except perhaps Ha Van Minh's doctoral thesis, which aims to examine the role of lay people in the context of Vietnam.[75] This work begins with a detailed account of the place and mission of lay people in the history of the Church in Vietnam from 1533 to 1975,[76] drawing mainly from Vietnamese sources. It then provides an exposition rather than a critique of the mission of the laity in the pastoral letters of the VEC,[77] the documents of Vatican II, the 1983 Code of Canon Law, the Apostolic Exhortations *Evangelii Nuntiandi* and *Christifideles Laici*, and finally, the statements of the FABC, covering only the first five plenary assemblies, and the reports of the Asian Bishops' Institute for the Lay Apostolate.[78] Consistent with his predominantly pastoral approach, the author devotes the last part of his work to discuss the cooperation of lay people in the Church in Vietnam and their active participation in the parish.[79] While his thesis contains quotations from several pastoral letters of the Vietnamese Episcopal Conference, issued between 1976 and 1999, it includes, unfortunately, only one reference to the 1980 Pastoral Letter, a watershed document in the history of the Catholic Church in Vietnam. Despite

---

74 Pastoral letters and communiqués in Vietnamese language of the Catholic bishops of Indochina and the Vietnamese Episcopal Conference (henceforth abbreviated to VEC), issued between 1951 and 2001, were published in two collections edited by Trần Anh Dũng, *Hàng Giáo Phẩm Công Giáo Việt Nam* [The Hierarchy of the Catholic Church of Viet Nam] *(1960-1995)* (Paris: Đắc Lộ Tùng Thư, 1996), and *Hội Đồng Giám Mục Việt Nam* [The Vietnamese Episcopal Conference] *(1980-2000)* (Paris: Đắc Lộ Tùng Thư, 2001), and in the 2004 and 2005 Almanacs of the Catholic Church in Vietnam, edited by the VEC's General Secretariat. Documents released after 2001, are available online at http://www.vietcatholic.net, http://www.hdgmvietnam.org, or http://www.eglasie.mepasie.org. The majority of them were translated into English by the Union of Catholic Asia News (UCAN), available online at http://www.ucanews.com, with some published in *Catholic International*, or into French by *Églises d'Asie*, a monthly magazine published by the Société des Missions Étrangères. Unless otherwise stated, translations of other documents written in Vietnamese and French are mine throughout. Footnotes are made to the original texts in Vietnamese or in French in preference to the English translations some of which leave a lot to be desired. Hereafter, a pastoral letter cited will be abbreviated to "VEC's Pastoral Letter" followed by the year of publication and relevant page numbers.

75 Ha Van Minh, *Die Laien in der Kirche Vietnams: Eine pastoraltheologische Studie zu ihrer Rolle in Geschichte und Gegenwart* (Frankfurt am Main: Peter Lang, 2001).

76 Ibid., 22–97.

77 Ibid., 103.

78 Ibid., 98–220.

79 Ibid., 221–320.

the current paucity of scholarly research on the role of the laity in the Church in Vietnam, numerous articles dealing with the Vietnamese laity, mostly of a popular nature and mainly in the Vietnamese language, have appeared in periodicals published by authors inside Vietnam or in the émigré communities.[80]

Scope and Methodology

With a view to complementing the existing studies on the role of lay people in the documents of the FABC, this book aims to offer a systematic exposition and a critical evaluation of the FABC's theology of the laity. The work is divided into three parts.

The first part aims to scope and place the subject of the study in context, and this will be done in the first three chapters. In Chapter 1, we highlight the effort of the FABC to rediscover the dignity and status of the laity in the Asian Church. We will also review the state of the question, and explain the methodology and the importance of this research. In Chapter 2, we offer a chronological survey of the question of the laity, leading up to the particular contributions of postconciliar interpretations. In Chapter 3, we explore the theological methodologies of the FABC, and their influence on the formulation of the documents considered.

In the second part, which comprises four chapters, we provide a systematic exposition (Chapter 4) and a critical evaluation (Chapter 5) of the FABC's theology of the laity. This investigation is conducted against the backdrop of the FABC's contextual ecclesiology, which is presented and analysed in Chapters 6 and 7 respectively.

In the third and concluding part of this study, which consists of three chapters, we employ a critical and comparative methodology to articulate the FABC's theological positions, their relation to the teachings of Vatican II, John Paul II, and the Vietnamese Episcopal Conference. Chapter 8, then, treats the FABC's theology of the laity in the context of post-Vatican II magisterial documents, in particular John Paul II's Apostolic Exhortation *Ecclesia in Asia* (1999). In Chapter 9, we situate the FABC's theology in the context of a local Church in Asia by examining

---

80 Peter C. Phan notes that "Vietnamese Catholics are deeply concerned with preserving their language, culture, and religious traditions. To achieve this goal they publish numerous newspapers, magazines, and journals, among which the most important are *Dan Chua* (People of God), *Duc Me Hang Cuu Giup* (Our Lady of Perpetual Help), *Thoi Diem Cong Giao* (Catholic Periodical), and *Hop Tuyen Than Hoc* (Theological Selections)" ("Vietnamese Catholics in the United States: Christian Identity Between the Old and the New," *U.S. Catholic Historian* 18:1 [2000] 21–2).

in detail the theology of the laity proposed in the pastoral letters of the Vietnamese bishops. Here, we also explicate the interaction between the FABC's theology of the laity and those of John Paul II and the bishops of Vietnam. The course of the development of these three theologies of the laity took place on three ecclesial levels, namely, the regional level of the FABC, the global level of the universal magisterium of John Paul II, and the local level of the Vietnamese Church. In Chapter 10, the final chapter, we provide a general assessment of the FABC's theology of the laity in order to highlight its strengths, and respectfully offer suggestions for further clarification and development. We will also reflect on the future of the FABC's theology of the laity.

Contributions of this Study

Given that the concerns of the FABC, John Paul II, and the VEC are primarily missionary and pastoral,[81] we will probe beneath their official statements to detect the underlying theological foundations. We will also provide a critical and systematic exposition of their theologies of the laity. In embarking on such a journey of research, we hope to make the following contributions:

First, we hope that our critical examination of the content and development of the FABC's theology of the laity from 1970 to 2012, set against a historical survey of the question of the laity and lay ministry, would serve the intention of the Asian bishops, and be a resource for the implementation of their vision.

Second, by offering a comprehensive summary and evaluation of the FABC's thought on the Church, which in turn provides the theological grounding for its theology of the laity, we hope to furnish Asian Christians with a truthful account of the thrust and key ideas contained in the documents of the Asian bishops. It is worth noting that, like Vatican II, which was largely a Council *of* the Church, *for* the Church, and *about* the Church, the statements of the FABC are also, in

---

81 Following Raymond E. Brown, we understand "missionary" as "adding constantly to the number of those who had come to believe in Jesus Christ," and "pastoral" as being "concerned with tending the existing flock." See *The Churches the Apostles Left Behind* (London: Geoffrey Chapman, 1984) 32. We also take note of the explication of the term "pastoral" in an explanatory footnote of *Gaudium et Spes*, which states that this Constitution is called "pastoral" because, "while resting on doctrinal principles, it seeks to set forth the relation of the Church to the world and to the men [*sic*] of today." See Vatican Council II, "*Gaudium et Spes*. Pastoral Constitution on the Church in the Modern World," in *Vatican Council II*: Vol. 1, *The Conciliar and Post Conciliar Documents*, edited by Austin Flannery, new rev. edition (Northport, N.Y.: Costello Publishing Co., 1996) 903.

the main, the documents *of* the Asian Church *for* and *about* the Church in the vast continent of Asia.

Third, we will be filling a research gap by uncovering and explaining the theological methodologies of the Asian bishops. This will in turn underscore the special features of their contextual theology of the laity.

Fourth, by comparing the thoughts of John Paul II and the FABC on the identity and role of the laity we will be making a further contribution, as we analyse the interaction and mutual influence between the universal Church and the regional Churches in Asia, and the theologies that animate them.

Fifth, our study will make an even more specific contribution by examining the emerging theology of the laity in the context of Vietnam, and thus aid further communication between the universal Church and local Catholic communities.

Sixth, our contribution is necessarily a tentative enterprise, as we reflect on the future of the FABC's theology of the laity, and gaze beyond the immediate horizon of the post-Vatican II era, and into the third millennium of Christianity.

Finally, writing this book with Asian Christians, in particular the laity, as the main intended audience, our modest wish is that it would become, not just a theological work to be read from beginning to end, but also as a reference tool to be consulted as pastoral needs arise. We hope to achieve this objective, first, by selecting and organising relevant material from the vast corpus of literature produced by the FABC, John Paul II, the VEC, and Vatican II; second, by offering analyses and summaries of the main tenets of these teachings, often in the format of tables and diagrams for easy reference and teaching purposes; third, by drawing on the insights of numerous theologians of note and providing a wealth of bibliographic references. Our final hope is that our research labours would help the readers to expand their understanding of the FABC's theology of the laity, and hence the dignity, vocation, and mission of lay people in the Church and in the world of Asia.

Chapter 2   The Laity in Historical Context

Since Vatican II, a Council that was concerned primarily with the nature and mission of the Church, ecclesiology has assumed a central position in Catholic theology, and the laity question has also come into focus in a new way in theological reflection.[1] Indeed, in the wake of this Council lay activities have flourished, and efforts have been made in different parts of the world to apply and extend the Council's teachings on the role of lay people in complex and varied situations. This chapter suggests that current theologies of the laity have likewise grown from an interchange between a *ressourcement* in the tradition and a dialogue with the contemporary. They seek to apply conciliar and papal teachings in the current context while drawing on the insights of other interpretations of lay experience. Therefore a critical survey of the historical development of the laity question in the Church, including a review of Vatican II's theology of the laity, would help in the understanding of the role of lay people. This chapter will first provide a historical overview of the status of lay people prior to Vatican II. Secondly, it will summarise the main conciliar teachings on the laity and lay ministry. Finally, it will conclude with a review of the changing meaning of ministry and lay ministry after a brief analysis of Leonard Doohan's theological approaches to the question of lay people.

The Laity Before Vatican Council II (1962–1965)

The terms "lay" or "laity" are derived indirectly from the Greek word *laos*,[2] meaning "people," and early Christian writings often used *laos theou* "people of God" to refer to the community of the Church.[3] Originally it had a positive meaning

---

1   Avery Dulles remarks that "the status and role of the laity have been at the forefront of discussion in the Catholic Church since Vatican Council II" ("Can the Word 'Laity' Be Defined?" *Origins* 18:29 [29 December 1988] 470).

2   Peter Neuner argues that the concept of laity does not come directly from the term *laos* but from the adjective *laikós* which means belonging to the people ("zum Volk gehörig"). See "Aspekte einer Theologie des Laien," *Una Sancta* 43 (1988) 317.

3   Ernst Niermann, "Laity," in *Encyclopedia of Theology: The Concise Sacramentum Mundi*, edited by Karl Rahner (London: Burns and Oates, 1975) 814–5; Leonard Doohan, "Theology of the Laity," in *The Modern Catholic Encyclopedia*, edited by Michael Glazier and Monika K. Hellwig (Newtown, Australia: E.J. Dwyer, 1994) 493; idem, "Theology of the Laity," in *The New Dictionary of Sacramental Worship*, edited by Peter E. Fink (Collegeville, Minn.: The Liturgical Press, 1990) 636.

with the New Testament nuance of election and consecration, and was often complemented by references such as "the chosen," "the predestined," "disciples," or "the saints."[4] Clement of Rome (c. 95), in his Letter to the Corinthians, was the first to employ the Greek word *laikós*, from which "laity" is more immediately derived, to describe the common, ordinary people in contrast to the officials.[5] This negative usage of the term was subsequently fuelled by three movements in the early Christian community: the "neo-platonism's influence on several Church Fathers, the growth of monasticism and the development of the clerical dimension

---

4   Walter Kasper, "The Mission of the Laity," *Theology Digest* 35:2 (Summer 1998) 133; A.A. Hagstrom, "Theology of Laity," in *New Catholic Encyclopedia*, 2nd ed., vol. 8 (Detroit: Gale Group in Association with the Catholic University of America, 2003) 290; see also Bernard Sesboüé, *N'ayez pas peur: regards sur l'Eglise et les ministères aujourd'hui* (Paris: Desclée de Brouwer, 1996) 119. Tertullian (circa 160–223), apologist and Father of Latin theology, went much further to state that "là où il y a trois fidèles, il y a une Église, même si ce sont de laïcs." Ibid.

5   See "The Letter of the Church of Rome to the Church of Corinth, Commonly Called Clement's First Letter" in *Early Christian Fathers*, trans. and ed. Cyril C. Richardson et al. (New York: Macmillan Publishing, 1970) 62; Thomas Halton, *The Church*, Message of the Fathers of the Church, ed. Thomas Halton, no. 4 (Wilmington, Del.: Michael Glazier, 1985) 137; Alexandre Faivre, *The Emergence of the Laity in the Early Church*, trans. David Smith (New York: Paulist Press, 1990) 21. I. de la Potterie proved that ιαϊκός was not a biblical term and it had a special meaning: "le 'peuple' inférieur, en tant que se distinguant de ses chefs." See "L'origine et le sens primitif du mot 'laïc'," *Nouvelle Revue Théologique* 80 (1958) 840–1. For an excellent summary of this instructive paper see Friedrich Wulf, "Über die Herkunft und ursprünglichen Sinn des Wortes 'Laie'," *Geist und Leben* 32 (1959) 61–3. For an enlightening account of the debate on the origin of the term *laikos*, and the usage of the term *laos*, see Kenan B. Osborne, *Ministry: Lay Ministry in the Roman Catholic Church: Its History and Theology* (New York: Paulist Press, 1993) 18–25. Phan Đình Cho [Peter C. Phan's name in Vietnamese] observes that "clearly, for Clement, the laity (though he does not use the noun) form a distinct group of people in the church" ("The Laity in the Early Church: Building Blocks for a Theology of the Laity," *Triết Đạo: Journal of Vietnamese Philosophy & Religion* 4:2 [2002] 40). According to Paul Lakeland the word *laikos* "is not found anywhere in the Bible," but "*Laos* ... is frequently found in the Bible" (*The Liberation of the Laity: In Search of an Accountable Church* [New York: Continuum, 2002] 11). Yves Congar concludes that "there is no distinction between 'lay people' and 'clerics' in the vocabulary of the New Testament." See *Lay People in the Church: A Study for a Theology of Laity*, revised edition, with additions by the author, trans. Donald Attwater (London: Geoffrey Chapman, 1965) 4.

of the Church."[6] By the second century, when the Church emerged with a more clearly defined and organised hierarchical structure the laity began to be regarded as inferior to the clergy.[7] From the fourth century when Church structures were similar to political ones, "the subordination of laity became a firm part of Church life."[8] With the passing of the period of persecutions, early Christians continued to witness to their faith, no longer as martyrs but as hermits, whose monastic

---

6   These three developments gave the "laity the image of second-class citizens because of their involvement with the material world which was thought to make them profane, the equation of holiness with monasticism thus introducing a minimalist approach to lay spirituality, and the introduction of grading or ranking of Church membership that left the laity subordinated and powerless." See Leonard Doohan, "Theology of the Laity," in *The New Dictionary of Sacramental Worship*, ed. Peter E. Fink (Collegeville, Minn.: The Liturgical Press, 1990) 636; "Lay People and the Church," *The Way* (July 1992)169. For Jon Nilson, "Monasticism greatly fostered the sense of a class structure in the Church. Monks were regarded as 'super Christians', wholly devoted to Christ by their poverty and celibacy.... The role of the ordinary Christian was to support those who served them by contemplation and prayer, that is, to monks and those who presided over them, the ordained." See "The Laity," in *The Gift of the Church: A Textbook on Ecclesiology in Honour of Patrick Granfield*, edited by Peter C. Phan (Collegeville, Minn.: The Liturgical Press, 2000) 397.

7   Leonard Doohan, "Theology of the Laity," in *The Modern Catholic Encyclopedia*, ed. Michael Glazier and Monika K. Hellwig (Newtown, Australia: E.J. Dwyer, 1994) 493. Peter C. Phan notes that "by the middle of the third century, the *difference* between the laity and the clergy gradually becomes the *inferiority* of the former to the latter" ("The Laity in the Early Church: Building Blocks for a Theology of the Laity," *Triết Đạo: Journal of Vietnamese Philosophy & Religion* 4:2 [Fall 2002] 43); see also Alexandre Faivre, "Naissance d'un laïcat chrétien: les enjeux d'un mot," *Freiburger Zeitschrift für Philosophie und Theologie* 33 (1986) 428.

8   Doohan, "Theology of the Laity," in *The New Dictionary of Sacramental Worship*, ed. Peter E. Fink (Collegeville, Minn.: The Liturgical Press, 1990) 636; "Lay People and the Church," *The Way* (July 1992) 169; Alexandre Faivre, on the contrary, argues that, except for Clement's use of the term "lay" for the first time toward the end of the first century, "The laity appeared for the first time in Christian history at the end of the second century or the beginning of the third." For him, at that time they did not represent all Christian people but comprised only the "baptized believers of the male sex, the 'husband of only one woman'," and "it was not until the fourth century that the term 'lay' was also applied explicitly to women. From then on, the lay people represented all Christians who were not members of the clergy" (*The Emergence of the Laity in the Early Church*, translated by David Smith [New York: Paulist Press, 1990] 209).

lifestyle became "the model of holiness."[9] The laity, already considered second-ary to the hierarchy, was now depicted as "having chosen the less perfect way"[10] than the monks, and hence was relegated to the third place, after the clergy and the religious.[11] The inferiority and passivity of the laity continued in subsequent centuries,[12] crystallised by Gratianus de Clusio's influential statement, "*Duo sunt genera Christianorum*,"[13] and eventually the Council of Trent (1545–1563) "legiti-mized the separation between clergy and people."[14] The laity's loss of status and dignity lasted until the Second Vatican Council (1962–1965).[15]

9 Doohan, "Theology of the Laity," in *The Modern Catholic Encyclopedia*, ed. Michael Glazier and Monika K. Hellwig (Newtown, Australia: E.J. Dwyer, 1994) 493.

10 Avery Dulles, "Can the Word 'Laity' be Defined?" *Origins* 18:29 (29 December 1988) 470.

11 Leonard Doohan, "Theology of the Laity," in *The Modern Catholic Encyclopedia*, ed. Michael Glazier and Monika K. Hellwig (Newtown, Australia: E.J. Dwyer, 1994) 493.

12 J. Gilchrist, "Laity in the Middle Ages," in *New Catholic Encyclopedia*, 2nd ed., vol. 8 (Detroit: Gale Group in Association with the Catholic University of America, 2003) 293.

13 See "Decretum Gratiani, Concordia Discordantium Canonum, Decreti Pars Secunda, Causa XII, Quaestio I, C. VII," extracted from *Patrologia Latina Database* published by Chadwyck-Healey Inc., Disk 5 [2003].

14 Leonard Doohan, "Lay People and the Church," *The Way* (July 1992) 169. In his 1906 Encyclical Letter "*Vehementer*" Pope Pius X taught that "the Church is essentially an *unequal* society, that is, a society comprising two categories of persons, the Pastors and the flock, those who occupy a rank in the different degrees of the hierarchy and the multitude of the faithful ...; the one duty of the multitude is to allow themselves to be led, and, like a docile flock, to follow the Pastors " (*The Papal Encyclicals 1903–1939*, ed. Claudia Carlen [Raleigh, [N.C.]: McGrath Publishing, 1981] 47–8). The 1917 Code of Canon Law held that "by divine institution clergy are distinct from laity in the Church." Cited by Kenan Osborne in *Ministry: Lay Ministry in the Roman Catholic Church: Its History and Theology* (New York: Paulist Press, 1993) 41–2.

15 In the years immediately prior to Vatican II, several theologians such as Yves M.J. Congar endeavoured to redefine the role of the laity. He associated the Christian usage of *laikos* with the Old Testament concept of *laos*, contending that the word 'lay' "properly meant the sacred people in opposition to the peoples who were not consecrated ...." See *Lay People in the Church*, rev. ed., trans. Donald Attwater (London: Geoffrey Chapman, 1965) 3. Congar also used the distinction between the structure and the life of the church to enhance the status of the laity, arguing that the clergy belongs to the structure of the Church, while the laity pertains to the life of the Church, which is more central. See *Lay People in the Church: A Study for a Theology of Laity*, revised edition, with additions by the author, trans. Donald Attwater (London: Geoffrey Chapman, 1965) 262.

The Laity and Lay Ministries in the Documents of Vatican II

At Vatican II, by placing the second chapter of *Lumen Gentium* on the People of God after the first chapter on the mystery of the Church, but before the chapters on the hierarchy, the laity, and the religious, the Council Fathers formally initiated a change in the Church's understanding of the vocation and the mission of lay people. At the beginning of chapter 4 of *Lumen Gentium* on the laity (no. 30), the Council categorically emphasised the equality of all members of the Church by declaring that "everything that has been said of the people of God is addressed equally to laity, religious and clergy."[16] This fundamental equality,[17] which precedes any differentiation on the basis of diversity of ministries, is based on the sacraments of baptism and confirmation,[18] and a common participation in the priestly, prophetic, and kingly mission of Jesus Christ and the Church.[19] The Council provided further clarification. First, the mission of Christ is given to the whole people of God,[20] and "In the Church there is diversity of ministry but unity of mission."[21] *Apostolicam Actuositatem* states clearly that lay people have a "special and indispensable" role in the Church and their mission is exclusive to them.[22] Second, *Lumen Gentium* emphasises the laity's dignity *qua* baptised,[23] affirming that every lay person "is at once the witness and the living instrument of the mission of the Church itself," because "inserted as they are in the Mystical Body of Christ by baptism and strengthened by the power of the Holy Spirit in confirmation,

---

16 Giovanni Magnani argues that "all the general indications given by the conciliar text as it stands when it makes statements concerning the laity, seem more or less to prepare the way for a status of identity between the 'Christian' and the 'layperson' rather than affirming any substantial differentiation." See "Does the So-Called Theology of the Laity Possess a Theological Status?" in *Vatican II Assessment and Perspectives: Twenty-Five Years After (1962–1987)*, vol. 1, edited by René Latourelle (New York: Paulist Press, 1988) 598.

17 *Lumen Gentium*, no. 32.

18 *Lumen Gentium*, no. 11; *Apostolicam Actuositatem*, no. 3.

19 *Apostolicam Actuositatem*, nos. 2, 10.

20 *Lumen Gentium*, no. 33.

21 *Lumen Gentium*, nos. 32–33.

22 *Lumen Gentium*, nos. 10, 2–3.

23 Hervi Rikhof notes that the dignity of every baptised Christian has two aspects. The first is the Christian's "new being in Christ—in other words, his re-creation or *deification*. The second is that certain functions, tasks, rights and duties are connected with that new existence" ("The Competence of Priests, Prophets and Kings: Ecclesiological Reflections about the Power and Authority of Christian Believers," *Concilium* 197 [1988] 59).

it is by the Lord himself that they are assigned to the apostolate."[24] The laity's mission has two focuses: involvement in the world and its transformation,[25] and involvement in the Church and its growth.[26] The Council moved on to teach that temporal realities are good in themselves, and underscored the importance of family,[27] work, civic, and social life.[28] It related the participation of lay people in the threefold mission of Christ primarily to their place in the world, by affirming that the "secular character is proper and peculiar to the laity," and lay people's unique way of sharing in the mission of the Church is to "seek the kingdom of God by engaging in temporal affairs and directing them according to God's will."[29]

---

24 *Lumen Gentium*, no. 33; *Apostolicam Actuositatem*, no. 3. The Council employed the Latin verb "inserti" (inserted or incorporated) to refer to the laity's incorporation to the Mystical Body of Christ, and "configurantur" (configured) to describe the priest's configuration to Christ the priest. The Latin text of *Apostolicam Actuositatem*, no. 3 reads: "Per Baptismum enim corpori Christi mystico inserti, per Confirmationem virtute Spiritus Sancti roborati, ad apostolatum ab ipso Domino deputantur," and *Presbyterorum Ordinis*, no. 2: "Quare sacerdotium Presbyterorum initiationis christianae Sacramenta quidem supponit, peculiari tamen illo Sacramento confertur, quo Presbyteri, unctione Spiritus Sancti, speciali charactere signantur et sic Christo Sacerdoti configurantur, ita ut in persona Christi Capitis agere valeant." *Sacrosanctum Oecumenicum Concilium Vaticanum II, Constitutiones Decreta Declarationes*, Cura et Studio Secretariae Generalis Concilii Oecumenici Vaticani II, ([Roma]: Typis Polyglottis Vaticanis, 1966) 463, 622–3.

25 *Lumen Gentium*, nos. 3, 31, 33, 35; *Apostolicam Actuositatem*, nos. 6, 7; *Gaudium et Spes*: Pastoral Constitution on the Church in the Modern World, in *Vatican Council II: Constitutions, Decrees, Declarations*, vol. 1, edited by Austin Flannery, new rev. ed. (Northport, N.Y.: Costello Publishing, 1996) no. 21.

26 *Lumen Gentium*, nos. 31, 33; *Apostolicam Actuositatem*, no. 10; *Gaudium et Spes*, 92; *Sacrosanctum Concilium*: The Constitution on the Sacred Liturgy, in *Vatican Council II: Constitutions, Decrees, Declarations*, vol. 1, edited by Austin Flannery, new rev. ed. (Northport, N.Y.: Costello Publishing, 1996) no. 11. Hereafter, the full title will be abbreviated to *Sacrosanctum Concilium*.

27 *Apostolicam Actuositatem*, no. 11; *Lumen Gentium*, no. 35; *Gaudium et Spes*, no. 52.

28 *Apostolicam Actuositatem*, nos. 13–14; *Gaudium et Spes*, nos. 26, 53, 60, 75; *Ad Gentes*: Decree on the Church's Missionary Activity, in *Vatican Council II: Constitutions, Decrees, Declarations*, vol 1, edited by Austin Flannery, new rev. ed. (Northport, N.Y.: Costello Publishing, 1996) no. 12. Henceforth the full title will be abbreviated to *Ad Gentes*.

29 *Lumen Gentium*, no. 31.

The relationship between the laity and the hierarchy and religious was also clarified by Vatican II.[30] According to *Lumen Gentium*, the common priesthood of the faithful and the ministerial or hierarchical priesthood "differ essentially and not only in degree", but "each in its proper way shares in the one priesthood of Christ."[31] However, the Council did not provide "a positive theological definition of the laity, but rather a description of and an outline of their functions."[32] The 1983 *Code of Canon Law*,[33] which was developed based on the theological

---

30 *Apostolicam Actuositatem*, nos. 24–25. Angel Anton contends that Vatican II, while emphasising the baptismal equality of all Christians, did not reconcile "this principle of fundamental equality ... between pastors and ordinary believers, to make any inferences about the participation of the laity with full rights, that is to say, with a deliberative and not merely a consultative note, in decision making of various directive organs instituted since the Council at the local and universal levels of the Church." See "Postconciliar Ecclesiology: Expectations, Results and Prospects for the Future," in *Vatican II Assessment and Perspectives: Twenty-Five Years After (1962-1987)*, vol. 1, ed. René Latourelle (New York: Paulist Press, 1988) 428-9.

31 *Lumen Gentium*, no. 10.

32 Frederick J. Parrella, "The Laity in the Church," *Catholic Theological Society of America Proceedings* 35 (1980) 273. For Parrella, the description of *Lumen Gentium* no. 31 has three essential elements: "(1) in a negative sense, the laity is 'understood to mean all the faithful except those in Holy Orders and those in a religious state sanctioned by the Church'.... (2) In a positive sense, the laity are the 'faithful' who are 'by baptism made one body with Christ and are established among the People of God. They are in their own way made sharers in the priestly, prophetic and kingly functions of Christ'. (3) In a positive light again, what distinguishes the laity from others is 'a secular quality'." Ibid. In his view, "each of these essential elements presents a problem. The first element...defines the laity by what they are not, not what they are. The second element...positively defines the laity but only in a generic sense; what defines the laity also defines the clergy and religious since *all* are baptised, one with Christ and established as the people of God. The third element, the secular quality of the laity which distinguishes them from the clergy and religious, fails to offer a positive definition but merely specifies a function." Ibid. For G. Chantraine, this typological definition has two aspects: the dignity of lay people is determined by the sacrament of baptism, and their place in the Church is made with reference to the ordained and the religious. See "Le laïc à l'intérieur des missions divines," *Nouvelle Revue Théologique* 109 (1987) 362.

33 *The Code of Canon Law: New Revised English Translation*, prepared by the Canon Law Society of Great Britain and Ireland in association with the Canon Law Society of Australia and New Zealand and the Canadian Canon Law Society (London: HarperCollins, 1997). Hereafter, this work will be cited as "The 1983 *Code of Canon Law*" followed by relevant canons, abbreviated to c. and cc.

insights of Vatican II,[34] gives a broader concept of lay people, defining them as the Christian faithful (*Christifideles*) who are not in holy orders.[35] Therefore, canonically speaking, the term laity also includes the unordained religious. In the *Codex*, the term "Christ's faithful" includes not only the laity but also the clerics,[36] who never cease to be the Christ's faithful. The *Codex* divides the Church into two groups: lay and cleric. *Lumen Gentium*, on the other hand, divides the church into three groups: lay, cleric, and religious.[37]

Figure 1 provides a graphic summary of Vatican II's theology of the laity. Of the three ecclesiological frameworks proposed by the Second Vatican Council the first two are by *Lumen Gentium*: (i) The Common Priesthood of the Faithful and (ii) The Priestly, Prophetic and Pastoral Functions, and the third is by *Apostolicam Actuositatem*, which highlights the role of lay people in the Church (*ad intra*), and their double mission in the world (*ad extra*), namely the proclamation of the gospel (*Ad Gentes*) and the contribution to the good of all people (*Gaudium et Spes*).

---

34 In the Bull of Promulgation, Pope John Paul II states that the new Code "can be viewed as a great effort to translate the conciliar ecclesiological teaching into canonical terms." See "Apostolic Constitution," In *The Code of Canon Law: New Revised English Translation*, prepared by the Canon Law Society of Great Britain and Ireland in association with the Canon Law Society of Australia and New Zealand and the Canadian Canon Law Society (London: HarperCollins, 1997) xiv. Thomas J. Green notes that "John Paul II emphasized the following key ecclesiological themes as underlying the code: the Church as the people of God; hierarchical authority as service; the Church as communion with its wide-ranging implications for universal Church-particular Church relationships and primacy-episcopacy relationship; the participation of all the faithful in the threefold functions (*munera*) of Christ with its profound implications for their fundamental rights and duties; and, finally, the importance of the Church's ecumenical commitment" ("The Church and the Law," in *The Gift of the Church: A Textbook on Ecclesiology in Honour of Patrick Granfield*, edited by Peter C. Phan [Collegeville, Minn.: The Liturgical Press, 2000] 374–5).

35 Canon 207 says: "By divine institution, among Christ's faithful there are in the Church sacred ministers, who in law are also called clerics; the others are called lay people." Ibid., 44.

36 The 1983 *Code of Canon Law*, c. 207.

37 *Lumen Gentium*, no. 31.

Figure 1: Vatican II's Theology of the Laity: Three Frameworks

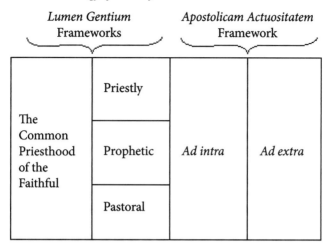

In the documents of Vatican II the terms "minister" and "ministry" occur over two hundred times but only nineteen of them apply to the activity of lay people.[38] A detailed study of these usages shows a clear progression in the Council's understanding of lay ministry, initially with an *ad intra* focus and subsequently as *ad extra* activities of everyday Christian life.[39] The first usage occurs in the Constitution on the Sacred Liturgy *Sacrosanctum Concilium* (nos. 29, 112, 122) where lay people were accepted as liturgical ministers and their ministry relates to the *munus sanctificandi*.[40] In the Degree on the Pastoral Office of Bishops

---

38 Elissa Rinere, "Conciliar and Canonical Applications of 'Ministry' to the Laity," *The Jurist* 47 (1987) 205. This paper provides a summary of her doctoral research on the subject, *The Term "Ministry" as Applied to the Laity in the Documents of Vatican II, Post Conciliar Documents of the Apostolic See, and the 1983 Code of Canon Law*, Canon Law Studies 519 (Washington: The Catholic University of America, 1986).

39 Elissa Rinere, "Conciliar and Canonical Applications of 'Ministry' to the Laity," *The Jurist* 47 (1987) 205–16. Jon Nilson observes that "Vatican II did not foresee all the lay roles and ministries that would emerge since the council" ("The Laity," in *The Gift of the Church: A Textbook on Ecclesiology in Honour of Patrick Granfield*, edited by Peter C. Phan [Collegeville, Minn.: The Liturgical Press, 2000] 407).

40 Analysing nos. 33 and 35 of *Lumen Gentium*, Louis Ligier argues that lay people "can in certain circumstances 'stand in' for ministers of the Church in order to perform cultal and sacramental functions in their place." See "'Lay Ministries' and their Foundations in the Documents of Vatican II," in *Vatican II Assessment and Perspectives: Twenty-Five*

Christus Dominus (no. 33), ministry is used to refer to the laity's participation in the diocesan curia sharing the *munus regendi* of the bishop. According to the Declaration on Christian Education *Gravissimum Educationis* (e.g., no. 7), lay people who teach Catholic children attending non-Catholic schools are said to exercise a true ministry by continuing the *munus docendi* of the hierarchy. In contrast to the preceding documents, *Apostolicam actuositatem* and *Ad gentes* apply the term lay ministry to both activity within the Church—in fulfilment of the hierarchical munera, and work carried out in the world—in fulfilment of the *munera* of the people of God. *Gaudium et Spes*, the last conciliar document, considers the everyday activity of human life as ministry (e.g., no. 38).

The positive understanding of the identity and role of lay people developed in the documents of Vatican II was the continuation of previous papal teachings such as the epochal statement made by Pope Pius XII in 1946: "The laity are the Church,"[41] and the culmination of preconciliar works on the subject by pioneers such as Yves Congar whose postconciliar writings continued to exercise a great influence on other theological interpreters of lay experience.[42] This theological

---

Years After (1962-1987), vol. 1, edited by René Latourelle (New York: Paulist Press, 1988) 164.

41 Giving an address to the new cardinals on 20 February 1946, Pius XII declared that "… i fedeli, e più precisamente i laici, si trovano nella linea più avanzata della vita della Chiesa; per loro la Chiesa è il principio vitale della società umana. Perciò essi, specialmente essi, debbono avere una sempre più chiara consapevolezza, non soltanto di appartenere alla Chiesa, ma di essere la Chiesa, vale a dire la comunità dei fedeli…. *Essi sono la Chiesa*" (emphasis added). See "Acta PII PP. XII: Allocutiones I," *Acta Apostolicae Sedis* 38:5 (1 April 1946) 149.

42 Vatican II adopted the traditional *tria munera* schema that Yves M.J. Congar had used as a framework for his classic work *Jalons pour une theologie du laïcat* [Signposts of a Theology of the Laity] (Paris: Les Editions du Cerf, 1953). An English version of the book appeared as *Lay People in the Church: A Study for a Theology of Laity*, revised edition, with additions by the author, trans. Donald Attwater (London: Geoffrey Chapman, 1965). Earlier, Congar translated a paper by J. Fuchs who wrote a dissertation in 1941 arguing that the triple office schema has a Protestant origin. See "Origines d'une triologie ecclésiologique à l'époque rationaliste de la théologie," *Revue des sciences philosophiques et théologiques* 53 (1969) 185-211. Congar would continue to employ the *tria munera* schema to describe the functions of the laity. See "Sur la Trilogie: Prophète-Roi-Prêtre," *Revue des sciences philosophiques et théologique* 67 (1983) 97-115. In another article, "Prêtre, Roi, Prophète," he observed that the Second Vatican Council applied the trilogy to Christ, the laity and ordained ministers: for the ordained the Council followed the order "docteur, prêtre, pasteur/roi," and used "prêtre, prophète, roi" when referring to lay people. See *Seminarium* 23 (1983) 71. Of the several postconciliar papers which illustrate

reflection was developed in dynamic interaction with many different schools of thought. Hence, an overview of other postconciliar interpretations of the laity, as one surveyed by Leonard Doohan, will assist in situating contemporary theologies of the laity in a proper context.

Leonard Doohan's Theologies of the Laity

According to Leonard Doohan, the motifs of Vatican II's teachings are community, incarnation, and service.[43] In light of these themes, increased emphasis has been given to the values of lay life and lay mission. Doohan contends that three specific developments of Vatican II have arrested the downward trend in the life and role of the laity that began approximately from the end of the third century. The first is Vatican II's stress on the notion of Church as communion, hence encouraging co-responsibility and collaboration of all members of the Church. The other two developments are linked to the Council's universal call to holiness, and its declaration on the autonomy of the temporal order coupled with the teaching that building a better world is part of God's plan.[44] For Doohan, five different theologies of the laity exist, which are "often due to separating one of the three conciliar developments from the other two," and each of these theologies of laity is implied in and depends on a particular model of the Church.[45]

The first theological approach sees the role of the laity being dependent on the hierarchy and their ministry as instrumental to that of the hierarchy. This

---

the development of Congar's thought, the most important text dealing with the role of the laity is a 1971 paper, which appeared a year later in English. See Yves Congar, "Mon cheminement dans la théologie de laïcat et des ministères," in *Ministères et communion ecclésiale* (Paris: Les Editions du Cerf, 1971) 9–30; idem, "My Path-Findings in the Theology of Laity and Ministries," *The Jurist* 32 (1972) 184. This 1971 paper is vintage Congar, who, at the age of 67, engaged in a *retractatio* revisiting several theses of his earlier book. See "Quelques problèmes touchant les ministères," *Nouvelle Revue Théologique* 93 (1971) 792, note 13.

43 Leonard Doohan, "Theology of the Laity," in *The Modern Catholic Encyclopedia*, ed. Michael Glazier and Monika K. Hellwig (Newtown, Australia: E.J. Dwyer, 1994) 494.

44 Leonard Doohan, "Theology of the Laity," in *The New Dictionary of Sacramental Worship*, ed. Peter E. Fink (Collegeville, Minn.: The Liturgical Press) 639.

45 Leonard Doohan, ibid., 639–40; idem, *Laity's Mission in the Local Church: Setting a New Direction* (San Francisco: Harper & Row, 1986) 4–5; idem, *The Lay-Centered Church: Theology and Spirituality* (Minneapolis, Minn.: Winston Press, 1984) 4–23; idem, "Contemporary Theologies of the Laity: An Overview Since Vatican II," *Communio* 7 (1980) 228–41.

theological interpretation assumes that only the hierarchy have received a mission and authority from Christ, and therefore, the laity would need the clergy's authorisation to participate in the Church's mission.

In Doohan's second approach, lay people appear as an ecclesial presence to the world; being naturally inserted into the temporal order, they have a specific and exclusively proper mission. This school of thought is based on the theological conviction that secular realities are good and valuable in themselves, and an understanding of the Church as the sacrament of the world, in the world, and at the service of the world.

The third approach to lay experience, which Doohan calls a theology of world transformation, is related to, and implicit in, the theology of ecclesial presence. The emphasis here, however, is on the exercise of lay ministries in the world; their role is to change the world and redeem it for the glory of God because the world is at the same time the context of human redemption and in need of redemption. This theology postulates that lay people are not only *in* the world but *for* the world, emphasising their social responsibility and their endeavours to eliminate injustices.

Doohan's fourth theological approach advocates a restructuring of the Church based a new understanding of the role of the laity which derives from an emphasis on the Church as community, on co-responsibility and collegiality, and on mission as a function of the entire Church. Other signs that call for ecclesial restructuring include the development of basic ecclesial communities, an emphasis on the priesthood of the faithful, and the creation of new lay ministries to meet community needs.

His fifth type of theological interpretation is the theology of self-discovery for the laity. This is an exploratory approach undertaken by many lay people who engage in new ministries or participate in new forms of faith sharing. Like many existing religious organisations and spiritual movements, these ministries are situational by nature, being created to respond to a specific need. They are at times *ad hoc* initiatives but in some ways also life-styles. Lay people discover their specific mission through these experiences, which often lead them to form a different view of their identity and role in the Church.

Doohan believes that each of these five theologies has its inherent strengths and weaknesses.[46] He contends that there has been a growing demand for an approach to the Church that can be readily understood by all laity, and thus

---

46 Leonard Doohan, *Laity's Mission in the Local Church: Setting a New Direction* (San Francisco: Harper & Row, 1986) 5.

proposes the model of the "Church as family."[47] Each of the five models that Doohan explicates above seems to be biased toward either the maximalist or the minimalist tendency. The former considers all lay activities as "ministry" while the latter restricts the word to apostolic activities performed by the ordained, or to ecclesial functions sanctioned by the Church. The following section will further investigate the various meanings of the terms "ministry" and "lay ministry" in contemporary theologies.

The Changing Meaning of Ministry and Lay Ministry

Since the Second Vatican Council there has been some confusion as to the meaning of the words "ministry" and "lay ministry."[48] The latter term is "definitely a creation of the post-Vatican II church."[49] Both the Council and the 1983 *Code of Canon Law* never used the term "lay ministry," leaving theologians and local Churches the task of developing their definition. The following section provides a chronological survey of some representative definitions or descriptions of the terms "lay ministry" or "ministry" which have been proposed since the end of Vatican II up to the present time.

According to James Coriden, ministry is "the descriptive term for the whole range of service functions performed within the community of Christian believers, the tasks related to worship and sacrament as well as those which seek to

---

47 Ibid., 5–6.

48 John A. Collins observes that "over the past fifty years the word 'ministry' has ceased to mean what it used to mean in ecclesiology. Always once referring to the ordained leadership and pastoral practice of a church, the term was actually only lightly used within Roman Catholic circles, and there more often than not had a reference to ministry in Protestant practice …. Within a few years of the conclusion of the Second Vatican Council such ingrained usage quickly underwent a full circle of change …. The words 'mission', 'apostolate' and 'ministry' itself applied indiscriminately to hierarchical and lay participation in the pastoral life of the Church" ("Fitting Lay Ministries into a Theology of Ministry: Responding to an American Consensus," *Worship* 79:2 [March 2005] 156). For instance, ministerial words in no. 38 of *Gaudium et Spes* apply only to the laity while in no. 24 of *Lumen Gentium* they refer to the office of bishops. Ibid., 156–7.

49 H. Richard McCord, "Lay Ministry: Living Its Questions," *Origins* 19:46 (19 April 1990) 757. Neil Ormerod observes that *Sacramentum Mundi* (1968–70) "has no entry on ministry at all," and the *New Catholic Encyclopedia* (1967–79) "has a telling heading, 'Ministry, Protestant'" ("Mission and Ministry in the Wake of Vatican II," *Australian EJournal of Theology* 1 [August 2003] 2).

satisfy the gamut of human needs, individual and social."[50] In December 1977 a group of Catholic laity and clergy issued the Declaration *The Chicago Declaration of Christian Concern* arguing that "the involvement of lay people in many Church ministries" was leading to "a devaluation of the unique ministry" of lay people in the world.[51] The group emphasises that lay people are the Church-in-the world, and their primary ministry is "to transform the world of political, economic and social institutions" through their professional and occupational lives.[52] Just over a year later, the Latin American bishops, continuing the thrust of the Medellín Conference,[53] issued the Puebla document (Jan-Feb 1979), which gives a clear approval of the two key elements of the practice of liberation theology—the forming of basic ecclesial communities and the preferential but not exclusive love for the poor. These prelates called on Latin American Christians to perceive "the responsibilities of their faith in their personal life and in their social life" through a process of conscientisation.[54]

In 1982, members of the Faith and Order Commission of the World Council of Churches unanimously approved the historical text *Baptism, Eucharist, and Ministry* recommending that "the Church must discover the ministry which can

---

50 James A. Coriden, "Ministry," *Chicago Studies* (Fall 1976) 305.

51 The Chicago Declaration of Christian Concern, in *Challenge to the Laity*, ed. Ed Marciniak et al., (Huntington, Ind.: Our Sunday Visitor, 1980) 20–3.

52 Ibid.

53 Second General Conference of Latin American Bishops, "The Church in the Present-Day Transformation of Latin America in the Light of the Council" (August 26-September 6, 1968 [Medellín, Columbia]), in *Liberation Theology: A Documentary History*, edited with introductions, commentary and translations by Alfred T. Hennelly (Maryknoll, N.Y.: Orbis Books, 1990) 99. In Peru, nineteen Church organisations jointly offered suggestions to the Peruvian bishops attending the Medellín Conference, emphasising that lay people "cannot evade their commitment to social change," and must "participate in the church's work of evangelization, sanctification, and service." See Peruvian Organisations, "The Role of the Laity, (June 1-2, 1968)," ibid., 84–88.

54 [Latin American Bishops], Third General Conference of the Latin American Bishops "Evangelization in Latin America's Present and Future" (Pueblo de los Angeles, Mexico, January 27-February 13, 1979) in *Liberation Theology: A Documentary History*, edited with introductions, commentary and translations by Alfred T. Hennelly, (Maryknoll, N.Y.: Orbis Books, 1990) 225–58. Paulo Freire defines conscientisation—*conscientização* in Brazilian—as a "probing of the ambience, of reality," or a "commitment in time" because it goes deeper than the French expression *prise de conscience* and "implies a historical commitment." See his 1970 paper "Conscientizing as a Way of Liberating," ibid., 6–7.

be provided by women as well as that which can be provided by men."[55] Joseph Komonchak prefers to stress that "the whole Church is the primary minister of Christ in the world," and "the various ministries are the concrete ways in which the Church ... articulates its responsibility for its own self-realization in the world."[56] George Tavard reduces ministry to four functions: "proclamation, worship, education and service."[57] For Thomas O'Meara, Christian ministry is "the public activity of a baptized follower of Jesus Christ flowing from the Spirit's charism and an individual personality on behalf of a Christian community to witness to, serve and realize the kingdom of God."[58] This definition is based on six characteristics which, he argues, constitute the nature of ministry: "Ministry is: (1) doing something; (2) for the advent of the kingdom; (3) in public; (4) on behalf of a Christian community; (5) which is a gift received in faith, baptism and ordination; and which is (6) an activity with its own limits and identity within a diversity of ministerial actions."[59] The 1983 *Code of Canon Law* applies the term

---

55 World Council of Churches, *Baptism, Eucharist and Ministry*. Faith and Order Paper No. 111 (Geneva: World Council of Churches, 1982) 24.

56 Joseph A. Komonchak, "Church and Ministry," *The Jurist* (43:2 (1983) 283–4.

57 George H. Tavard, *A Theology of Ministry* (Wilmington, Del.: Michael Glazier, 1983) 128.

58 Thomas Franklin O'Meara, *Theology of Ministry* (New York: Paulist Press, 1983) 142.

59 Ibid., 136. O'Meara also surveys the change in the meaning of "ministry" in six historical periods of the Church, and argues that each of these periods still has some bearing on the theory and praxis of ministry today. Ibid., 95–133, esp. 97–8. The first period is a "move from communal diversity and universality to a small number of ministries with prominence given to the service of leadership (*episcopalization*) and a further alteration of fulltime ministry to a sacral statement (*sacerdotalization*)." The second period of "*monasticization*" involves "the reforming and ministerial expansion of the monastery." The "dominance of one structure in the order of offices (*hierarchization*)" represents the third period. The "*pastorization* of ministry" wrought by the Reformation represents the fourth, followed by "the Counter-Reformation's organization of ministry along the lines of Baroque papacy and spirituality" where the Pope emerged as the source of all ministries. Finally, the "*romanticization* of the ministry" in the nineteenth century." Ibid., 97–8. Paul Bernier expands O'Meara's schema into thirteen periods or movements by breaking down O'Meara's periods into shorter time frames and adding two periods to cover the post-Vatican years: "The Foundations of Ministry: The Apostolic Age (27–70)"; "Ministry as Charism: The Post-Apostolic Age (70–110)"; "From Ministry to Bishop: The Period of Establishment (110–313)"; "Priesthood as Ministry: From State Church to Empire Collapse (313–500)"; "The Monastery as Minister: The Feudal Period to the East/West Split (500–1054)"; "Ministry as Hierarchy: The Age of Scholasticism (1055–1414)"; "The Reformation of Ministry: The End of the Medieval

ministry to lay activities within the Church in just seven of its 1,752 canons,[60] as "a fulfilment of the hierarchical *munera* only," and their exercise requires ecclesiastical authorisation.[61] In the *Codex*, lay people can participate in common,[62] public,[63] and under certain conditions, jurisdictional ministry.[64]

Writing two monographs on ministry, Edward Schillebeeckx makes a sharp distinction between the notion of ministry between "the *beginning* of the first millennium and the *end* of the second," and proposes "a fourth ministry, alongside the episcopate, presbyterate and diaconate, bestowed by the community of the

---

Church (1415–1565)"; "Ministry as Cult: The Fortress Church (1565–1962)"; "The Reappraisal of Ministry: The Period of *Aggiornamento* (1962–1965)," and "Reappraising Presbyteral Ministry: The New Theology of Vatican II (1962–1965)"; "Unresolved Problems in Ministry: In the Shadow of Vatican II (1965–2000)"; "Toward an Evangelical Ministry: The Third Millennium (2000-)," and "Reintegrating the Laity: The Age of the Laity (2000-)." See *Ministry in the Church: A Historical and Pastoral Approach* (Mystic, Conn.: Twenty-Third Publications, 1992) 11–278.

60 See the 1983 *Code of Canon Law*, cc. 230, 759, 910, 943, 1481, 1502, and 1634; Elissa Rinere, "Conciliar and Canonical Applications of 'Ministry' to the Laity," *The Jurist* 47:1 (1987) 216-20. The *Codex* makes use of the "priest-prophet-king" schema in its structure and content, separating codification concerning *munus regendi* (not mentioned by name in the title of Book II) from that concerning *munus docendi* (Book III) and *munus sanctificandi* (Book IV)." See the 1983 *Code of Canon Law*, cc. 204–1253.

61 Elissa Rinere, "Conciliar and Canonical Applications of 'Ministry' to the Laity," *The Jurist* 47:1 (1987) 216-9. For John Alesandro, "there is still ambivalence in the code: Are laity true lay ministers or are they only supplementary ministers?" See "The Code of Canon Law: Past, Present and Future," *Origins* 37:23 (15 November 2007) 362. Rik Torfs notes that "*munus* does not refer to a specific office but to major tasks which operate also through offices." See "*Auctoritas – potestas – jurisdictio – facultas – officium – munus*: a conceptual analysis," *Concilium* 197 (April 1988) 69. According to Torfs, the term *munus* occurs less than two hundred times in the 1983 Code, and "in many of these instances it appears in the application (task)." Ibid., 70. On the other hand, the term *officium* is used some 260 times in the 1983 Code, and mainly refers to an "ecclesiastical office." Ibid., 68-9.

62 The 1983 *Code of Canon Law*, cc. 225–226.

63 The 1983 *Code of Canon Law*, cc. 145, 229, 230, 339, 443, 493–4, 451, 483, 494, 451, 536–7, 617, 620-1, 627, 636, 651, 1168, 1424, 1428, 1435.

64 The 1983 *Code of Canon Law*, cc. 129, 228, 274, 764, 766, 785, 812, 1111-2, 1421. According the *Codex*, the people of God is made up of the baptised faithful, who are called, "each according to his or her particular condition, to exercise the mission which God entrusted to the Church to fulfill in the world." Ibid., c. 204.

church and its leaders on pastoral workers."[65] In a pastoral letter as Archbishop of Chicago, Cardinal Joseph Bernardin discusses ministry from a functional and relational perspective, and describes it as "a specific activity supported and designated by the Church, which discloses the presence of God in some way in our human situation and empowers us to live more fully in the mystery of God—in communion with God and one another."[66]

With a focus on caring for society, Robert Kinast believes that "the ultimate significance of the term lay ministry is not to be found in a definition," but in the actual experience of the laity, hence the primary task is not so much to define the term as to interpret it.[67] Sharon Euart expands the usage of the term ministry to include a "*common* ministry" which does not require ordination or designation, and includes such activities as love of neighbour, evangelisation in one's

---

65 Edward Schillebeeckx, *The Church with a Human Face: A New and Expanded Theology of Ministry* (London: SCM Press, 1985) 3–4, 266; idem, *Ministry: Leadership in the Community of Jesus Christ* (New York: Crossroad, 1981); also published as *Ministry: A Case for Change* (London: SCM Press, 1981).

66 Cardinal Joseph Bernardin, "Ministry: In Service of One Another," *Origins* 15:9 (1 August 1985) 136. For Bernadin, ministry is "ultimately directed toward establishing a life in communion with God and with one another, a way of life which manifests the kingdom of God in our midst." Ibid., 135. In his view, ministries and ministers could be differentiated in five ways: by different forms of ecclesial recognition and designation; according to the amount of time they devote to their ministry; through the specification of their activities; depending on the background and skills required to undertake the ministries; and according to the setting in which the service is provided. Ibid., 137. It is noteworthy that, for Greek Orthodox theologian John D. Zizioulas, "it is the ministry that more than anything else renders the Church a *relational* reality, i.e., a mystery of love, reflecting here and now the very life of the Trinitarian God," which is constantly revealed by way of a *double movement*: (i) as a baptismal movement which renders the Church a community existentially "dead to the world" and hence separated from it, and (ii) as a eucharistic movement which relates to the world by "referring" it to God as *anaphora* and by bringing to it the blessings of God's life and the taste of the Kingdom to come. It is this double movement of the Church's relational nature that makes the ministry realise its relational character as a movement of the Church both *ad intra* and *ad extra*. See *Being As Communion: Studies in Personhood and the Church* (New York: St Vladimir's Seminary Press, 2002) 220–1.

67 Robert L. Kinast, *Caring for Society: A Theological Interpretation of Lay Ministry* (Chicago: The Thomas More Press, 1985) 61. For Kinast, the experiential meaning of lay ministry encompasses several overlapping and interconnecting feelings ranging from importance to authenticity, from equality to complementarity, from ownership to stewardship. Ibid., 65.

own way, and building up the Church according to one's gifts.[68] For the Cincinnati Archdiocesan Pastoral Council, ministry is "any action of Christian persons which reveals and furthers God's presence in the world on behalf of the church and at the service of those in need."[69] Richard McBrien proposes a working definition of ministry based on four different levels, two being Christian in nature, and two having nothing intrinsically to do with religion.[70]

In *Christifideles Laici*, the Apostolic Exhortation promulgated after the Synod on the Laity in 1987, John Paul II observed that there was "a too-indiscriminate use of the word *ministry*," and stressed the difference between the ministries derived from the sacrament of orders and those derived from the sacraments of baptism and confirmation, teaching that ministries of the lay faithful find their foundation in the sacraments of baptism and confirmation and they should be exercised in keeping with the laity's secular character.[71] In 1990, John Linnan described ministry as "the public and ecclesially recognized roles of those who in the name of Christ serve the community of believers, assisting them in their efforts to become church, the Body of Christ, so that it can continue the work of Christ in the world."[72] Like John Linnan, Michael Lawler borrowed key elements of O'Meara's definition and viewed ministry as "action done in public, on behalf of the church, as a result of a charism of service, proclaimed, made explicit and

---

68 Sharon A. Euart. "Council, Code and Laity," *The Jurist* 47:2 (1987) 496.

69 Cincinnati Archdiocesan Pastoral Council, "An Expanded View of Ministry," *Origins* 16:31 (15 January 1987) 553, 555.

70 These levels of ministry are: (i) General/universal ministry as any service rendered to others, rooted in our humanity, having nothing intrinsically to do with religion; (ii) General/specific ministry as a special service rendered to others, rooted in competence, performed by people who are certified or validated; (iii) Christian/universal ministry as any service rendered to others in Christ and because of Christ, rooted in baptism and confirmation; in this sense every Christian is called to ministry; (iv) Christian/specific ministry as a service rendered in the name of the Church and for the sake of its mission, based on some action of designation by the Church, performed by a small number of Church members. See Richard P. McBrien, *Ministry: A Theological, Pastoral Handbook* (San Francisco: HarperCollins, 1988) 11–4.

71 John Paul II, "*Christifideles Laici: Apostolic Exhortation on the Vocation and Mission of the Lay Faithful in the Church and in the World*," *Origins* 18:35 (9 February 1989) no. 23.

72 John E. Linnan, "Ministry Since Vatican II: A Time of Change and Growth," *New Theology Review* 3(1990) 44.

celebrated in the church in sacrament, to incarnate in symbol the presence of Christ and of the God whose kingdom he reveals."[73]

In a monumental book published in 1993, Kenan Osborne studies the lay ministry question in the Catholic Church over the two millennia of Christian history, highlighting the importance of a "common matrix for all Christians."[74] He proposes three concepts to express this matrix of gospel discipleship, a foundational and primordial basis that is rooted in baptism, confirmation, and the Eucharist,[75] and precedes any distinction of cleric/lay or cleric/religious/lay: the people of God, *Christifidelis*, and priesthood of all believers.[76] For John Collins, there are two types of ministry: "ministry as lowly *diakonia*" where "by baptism all Christians are called into ministry, which is an ongoing gift of the Spirit," and "ministry as high *diakonia*" which is a "responsibility laid upon certain individuals within the church who feel called and are called by the church to proclaim the gospel in word and sacrament."[77]

In a report issued in 1995, the Bishops' Conference of England and Wales understands ministry "as the service based on baptism and confirmation to which all are called. In this sense it overlaps with, and flows into mission. It is the forms of life and activity through which the baptised express their discipleship, in the various areas of their life; home and family; neighbourhood and wider society; parish and diocese."[78] Across the Atlantic Ocean, the U.S. Catholic bishops issued two documents to explain the vocation, mission, and ministry of the laity as four calls—to holiness, to community, to mission and ministry, and to Christian adulthood/Christian maturity.[79] It is of note that in the 1980 statement the U.S. bishops

---

73 Michael G. Lawler, *A Theology of Ministry* (Kansas City, Mo.: Sheed & Ward, 1990) 28; see also Michael G. Lawler and Thomas J. Shanahan, *Church: A Spirited Communion* (Collegeville, Minn., The Liturgical Press, 1995) 64.

74 Kenan B. Osborne, *Ministry: Lay Ministry in the Roman Catholic Church: Its History and Theology* (New York: Paulist Press, 1993) 530–1.

75 Ibid., 597.

76 Ibid., 540–1.

77 John N. Collins, "A Ministry for Tomorrow's Church," *Journal of Ecumenical Studies* 32:2 (Spring 1995) 169.

78 Bishops' Conference of England and Wales, *The Sign We Give* (Essex, England: Matthew James, 1995) 18.

79 National Conference of Catholic Bishops [U.S. Bishops], "Called and Gifted: The American Catholic Laity, 1980, Reflections of the U.S. Bishops," *Origins* (27 November 1980) 369, 371–3; *Called and Gifted for the Third Millennium* (Washington, D.C.: United States Catholic Conference, 1995), http://www.nccbuscc.org/laity/calleden.htm (accessed 7 July 2003).

used the term "ecclesial ministers" to describe "lay persons who have prepared for professional ministry in the Church." In the 1995 pastoral letter, they changed the term to "ecclesial lay ministers," listing a broad range of their roles such as cantors, music directors, readers, Eucharistic ministers, altar servers, and activities such as teaching young people and adults, serving in peace and justice networks, in soup kitchens and shelters, in marriage preparation, in bereavement programs, and in ministry to the separated and divorced. The bishops affirmed that "all these actions, when performed in the name of Jesus and enacted under the aegis of the Church, are forms of ministry."[80]

In 1997, eight Vatican dicasteries jointly issued an Instruction, approved in *forma specifica* by Pope John Paul II, examining the distinction between the ministry specific to priests and the ministries of lay people, and giving "directives to ensure the effective collaboration of the nonordained faithful…while safeguarding the integrity of the pastoral ministry of priests."[81] Instead of proposing

---

80 Ibid., 10. Avery Dulles notes that the U.S. Bishops' 1995 document makes a clear distinction between "the two areas of lay activity: their witness and service in secular society and their service to the church, calling only the latter ecclesial lay ministry" ("Can Laity Properly Be Called 'Ministers'," *Origins* 35:44 [20 April 2006] 729). In 1999 the U.S. Bishops' Subcommittee on Lay Ministry issued another report under the title of *Lay Ecclesial Ministry: The State of the Questions: A Report of the Subcommittee on Lay Ministry* (Washington, D.C.: Committee on the Laity, United States Conference of Catholic Bishops, 1999), this time focusing on lay ecclesial ministry as the new phenomenon of the Church. In 2005 the U.S. bishops revisited the theme, and emphasised the basis of lay ecclesial ministry on both the individual call to ministry and the collective participation in the mission of the Church. See "Co-workers in the Vineyard of the Lord," *Origins* 35:25 (1 December 2005) 405–27. This document provides further clarification: "The ministry is *lay* because it is service done by laypersons. The sacramental basis is the sacraments of initiation, not the sacrament of ordination. The ministry is *ecclesial* because it has a place within the community of the church, whose communion and mission it serves, and because it is submitted to the discernment, authorisation and supervision of the hierarchy. Finally, it is *ministry* because it is a participation in the threefold ministry of Christ, who is priest, prophet and king." Ibid., 408.

81 Eight Vatican Offices, "Instruction: On Certain Questions Regarding Collaboration of Nonordained Faithful in the Sacred Ministry of Priests," *Origins* 27 (17 November 1997) 397, 399–411. In a commentary on this document, Cardinal Joseph Ratzinger stated its purpose as "to avoid, on the one hand, an undervaluing of the ordained ministry and a falling into a 'Protestantization' of the concepts of ministry and even of the Church herself, and, on the other, the risk of a 'clericalization' of the laity" ("Unity of the Church's Mission Involves Diversity of Ministries," *L'Osservatore Romano* 17

a definition Zeni Fox suggests five "namings" of ministries: "ministry as sacramental/liturgical, as stewardship of the tradition, as community building, as prophesy and as caring for society."[82] Reflecting on the diversity of ministries in a postmodern Church, Meyer-Wilmes argues that ministries "represent the church in society" and defined them as "public functions in and by which the church articulates its specific understanding of itself."[83] Opting for simplicity Paul Avis contends that ministry "may be best understood as any work for the church that is recognized by the church."[84] In a similar vein, John Ford remarks that "the different uses of the term 'ministry' reflect the multiplicity of forms that ministry has taken in the twenty centuries of Christianity," and "underlying the variety in usage of the term, the reality represents a fundamental aspect of Christian belief and life: ministry is service for others in imitation of Christ."[85]

To conclude our survey of the representative descriptions of the terms "ministry" and "lay ministry," which often overlap in significant ways, it is fitting to make a distinction between ministry and mission: "the latter pertains to the essence of the Church, the former is one of the Church's activities, though indispensable for mission."[86] In this sense, ministry could be seen as "a mission within

---

[29 April 1998] 18). Ratzinger warns against "a 'functionalistic' conception of the ministry, which sees the ministry of 'pastor' as a *function* and not as an *ontological sacramental reality*." Ibid. Edward Hahnenberg observes that "while at points the document helpfully distinguishes different ministerial tasks, its vision of the priest's sacred ministry is so encompassing that it is hard to imagine any lay activity within the church as anything but a participation in something that properly belongs to the ordained" ("Bishop: Source or Center of Ministerial Life?" *Origins* 37:7 [28 June 2007] 106).

82 Zeni Fox, *New Ecclesial Ministry: Lay Professionals Serving the Church* (Kansas City, Mo.: Sheed & Ward, 1997) 225–7.

83 Hedwig Meyer-Wilmes, "The Diversity of Ministries in a Postmodern Church," *Concilium* 3 (1999) 70.

84 Paul Avis, "Ministry," in *The Oxford Companion to Christian Thought*, ed. Adrian Hastings et al. (Oxford: University Press, 2000) 437.

85 John Ford, "Ministries in the Church," in *The Gift of the Church: A Textbook on Ecclesiology in Honor of Patrick Granfield*, ed. Peter C. Phan (Collegeville, Minn.: The Liturgical Press, 2000) 294.

86 Christopher O'Donnell, *"Ecclesia:" A Theological Encyclopedia of the Church* (Collegeville, Minn.: The Liturgical Press, 1996) 305. Gerard Hall also makes a helpful distinction: "the mission of evangelizing belongs to the whole Church and is the responsibility of all Christians. Ministries, on the other hand, belong to individuals in particular churches. Yet they also exist for, and are expressions of, the Church's universal mission…. The relationship between the universal Church and the local churches

a mission."[87] Ministry also tends to be *ad intra*, an involvement in the Church and its growth while *mission* is primarily *ad extra*, an involvement in the world and its transformation.[88]

Conclusion

This chapter has reviewed the laity question in history with an emphasis on theological developments after the Second Vatican Council. It examines in particular Leonard Doohan's theological interpretations of lay experience, and the changing meaning of lay ministry. Two conclusions can be drawn from this historical survey. The first is the realisation that there was a definitive change in perspective, initiated by Vatican II, whereby lay people are no longer considered to be passive objects of the ministrations of the clergy, but active agents who participate in their own right in the threefold mission of Christ and the Church. The second is the recognition of the existence of a multiplicity of lay ministries in the Church. This ever expanding phenomenon necessitates ongoing theological investigations, which in turn will help to clarify the meaning and scope of lay life and lay mission in the Church and in the world. The various interpretations of the mission and ministry of lay people discussed in this chapter will serve as the context for a detailed exposition and evaluation of the FABC's theology of laity in Chapters 4 and 5 respectively. But, to gain a full and systematic understanding of this rich and dynamic theology we will proceed first with a study into the theological methodologies espoused by the Asian bishops. And, this is our objective in the next chapter.

---

resembles the relationship between mission and ministry: one cannot exist without the other" ("Christian Mission Today," *Compass* 41:3 [Spring 2007] 5).

87 James H. Provost, "Ministry: Reflections on Some Canonical Issues," *The Heythrop Journal* 29 (1988) 291. Neil Ormerod argues that "far from ministry being the central task of the Church, it is mission which defines its purpose." See "Mission and Ministry in the Wake of Vatican II," *Australian EJournal of Theology* 1 (August 2003), http://dlibrary.acu.edu.au/research/theology/ejournal/aejt_1 (accessed 16 March 2004).

88 John E. Linnan, "Ministry Since Vatican II: A Time of Change and Growth," *New Theology Review* 3 (1990) 34; Christopher O'Donnell, *"Ecclesia:" A Theological Encyclopedia of the Church* (Collegeville, Minn.: The Liturgical Press, 1996) 303.

Chapter 3 *Fides Quaerens Dialogum*: Theological Methodologies of the Federation of Asian Bishops' Conferences

For Karl Rahner the Second Vatican Council (1962–1965) marked the beginning of the Church's "official self-realization as a world Church."[1] In his view there were three great epochs in Church history. The first one was a short period of Jewish Christianity, followed by the second, much longer period of the Church in a particular cultural group, namely of Hellenism and European culture and civilisation. With Vatican II the Church has entered into the third period where the Church's living space is the whole world, and has begun the transition from a Western Church to a universal Church.[2] Rahner contends that this caesura or break in the history of the Church can be compared to the opening up of the primitive Church to the Gentiles, and presents many challenges for the integration of non-Western cultures.[3] His world-Church vision suggests an ecclesiology that places emphasis on the local church. In his words, "a world-church as it exists outside Europe cannot simply import and imitate the life-style, law, liturgy and theology of the European church. In all these respects the churches must be independent and culturally firmly rooted in their own countries."[4]

---

1 Karl Rahner, "Towards a Fundamental Theological Interpretation of Vatican II," *Theological Studies* 40 (1979) 717; "Die bleibende Bedeutung des Zweiten Vatikanischen Konzils," *Stimmen der Zeit* 197 (1979) 796. Following Tissa Balasuriya, Paul J. Roy contests Rahner's thesis, and argues that the Council was a largely Eurocentric body, which did not reflect the concerns of the peoples of the third world ("The Developing Sense of Community," in *Vatican II: The Unfinished Agenda*, edited by Lucien Richard, Daniel T. Harrington and John W. O'Malley, [New York: Paulist Press, 1987] 201).

2 Rahner, "Basic Theological Interpretation of the Second Vatican Council," in *Theological Investigations* 20 (London: Darton, Longman & Todd, 1981) 83.

3 Rahner, "Towards a Fundamental Theological Interpretation of Vatican II," *Theological Studies* 40 (1979) 723–4. Rahner emphasises that "this is the issue: either the Church sees and recognizes these essential differences of other cultures for which she should become a world Church and with Pauline boldness draws the necessary consequences from this recognition, or she remains a Western Church and so in the final analysis betrays the meaning of Vatican II." Ibid., 724.

4 Rahner, "The Future of the Church and the Church of the Future," in *Theological Investigations* 20 (London: Darton, Longman & Todd, 1981) 110–1.

Indeed, with Vatican II the global character of the Church was underscored. It emerges as a worldwide community of faith made up of local Churches,[5] each of which is involved in a different cultural and social context. Such a sense of the Church in turn affects theology and its methods. One of these is the growing need for a contextual theology that takes into account human experience and the specific realities of cultures and social changes as these affect both the life of the Church and theological reflection upon it. The more the Church becomes the world Church, the more varied Christianity will become, and the more contextualised theology will be. Christian theology is and has been contextual by definition,[6] but since the event of Vatican II there has been a much greater emphasis on a plurality of theologies,[7] and a keener realisation of the need for

---

5   In this paper "local Church" is used in preference to "particular Church," to refer to a national Church, grouping of Churches, diocese, parish or small Christian communities. The usage of these terms is not consistent across official Church documents. Statistically Vatican II documents use "diocese" more than "particular Church." Half of the twenty-four occurrences of the term "particular Church" in the conciliar documents refer to the diocese with the rest to organic groupings of churches such as rites. "Local Church" is used eight times to refer to the diocese, the parish or groupings of Churches. The Council's expression of "particular Church" has a wider meaning than that adopted by the 1983 Code of Canon Law, which restricts the usage of the term to the diocese. The Code does not use the terms "local Church" and "universal Church." See Theological Advisory Commission, *Theses on the Local Church: a Theological Reflection in the Asian Context*, FAPC Papers no. 60 (Hong Kong: FABC Secretariat, 1991) 9–11; Sabbas J. Kilian, "The Meaning and Nature of the Local Church," *CTSA Proceedings* 35 (1980) 244–55; Joseph A. Komonchak, "Ministry and the Local Church," *CTSA Proceedings* 36 (1981) 56; Leonard Doohan, *Laity's Mission in the Church: Setting a New Direction* (San Francisco: Harper & Row, 1986) 26–7; *The Jurist* 52:1 (1992) 295–7. Henri de Lubac contends that the criterion for the identity of a particular Church (i.e., a diocese) is theological while the criterion of a local church is socio-cultural (Henri de Lubac, *The Motherhood of the Church: Followed by Particular Churches in the Universal Church and an Interview Conducted by Gwendoline Jarczyk*; translated by Sr. Sergia Englund [San Francisco: Ignatius Press, 1982] 193–5). However, for the English Language Group's discussion on the meaning of "local Church" at the International Colloquium on "Local Church and Catholicity" held in Salamanca, Spain from 2–7 April 1991, the difference between the two terms is encountered in their diverse matrices: "While the principal matrix of the word 'local' expresses the notion of place, the word 'particular' is centered on social, historical, and cultural aspects." See *The Jurist* 52:1 (1992) 296–7.

6   Douglas John Hall, *Thinking the Faith: Christian Theology in a North American Context* (Minneapolis: Fortress Press, 1991) 69.

7   Continuing the debate of the so-called *"Annales"* school on the meaning of the term "event," and the relationship between *longue durée and événement*, Joseph Komonchak

a contextual theology that takes into account, or even as a starting point, human experience and contextual realities as resources for theological reflection. Regional and local Churches, including those in Asia, have been developing their theologies from their own cultural, social, and religious situations.[8] In his classic work on *Method in Theology*, Bernard Lonergan contends that "theology is an ongoing process mediating between a cultural matrix and the significance and role of religion in that matrix."[9] It is concerned with the effective communication of Christ's message while such communication presupposes that preachers and teachers enlarge their horizons to include an "understanding of the culture and the language of the people they address."[10] Therefore, theology can be defined as *fides quaerens intellectum* in terms of a local context.[11]

---

explores the theme of "Vatican II as 'Event,'" *Theology Digest* 46:4 (Winter 1999) 337–352, making a distinction between "event, experience, and final documents." In his view, "'Experience' refers to contemporary intentions, motives, encounters, decisions, and actions during the Council; the 'final documents' are the product of that experience." "Event" represents a different category, in the sense of a "noteworthy" occurrence, one that has consequences. He concurs with most of the literature on the subject that an "event" represents novelty, discontinuity, a "rupture," a break from routine, causing surprise, disturbance, even trauma, and perhaps initiating a new routine, a new realm of the taken-for-granted. Reflecting on the controversy surrounding the interpretation of the Second Vatican Council as continuity or discontinuity with the tradition, John W. O'Malley argues that "recent emphasis on the continuity of Vatican II with the Catholic tradition runs the danger of slighting the aspects of the council that were discontinuous. Among those aspects are the literary genre the council adopted and the vocabulary inherent in the genre, different from that of all previous councils" ("Vatican II: Did Anything Happen?" *Theological Studies* 67 [2006] 3).

8   For Robert Schreiter, contextual theologies arose because universal theologies, largely practised in the academy, did not address the most pressing issues in many local situations, such as "the burden of poverty and oppression, the struggle to create a new identity after a colonial past, or the question of how to meet the challenge of modernity ..." (*The New Catholicity: Theology Between the Global and the Local* [Maryknoll, New York: Orbis Books, 1997] 1).

9   Bernard Lonergan, *Method in Theology* (New York: Herder and Herder, 1972) xi.

10   Ibid., 362.

11   Tony Kelly suggests that "the context is something that has to be at once discovered and created, as a more global theological context already in existence doubles back on itself to integrate, however dialectically, our particular context into its framework. In this way, the hitherto voiceless can become participants in a larger conversation, and unknown or neglected historical experiences become part of the data. We are never starting from scratch; but faith, endowed with its millennial traditions and historical experience of many cultures, seeks understanding, integration and expression, now, in

The FABC's theology, viewed over a forty-two year period from 1970 to 2012, has been a development of great significance for the Churches in Asia, paralleling the more comprehensive event of the Second Vatican Council in its import for the whole Church. This chapter begins with a discussion of the imperative of theological contextualisation using Raimundo Panikkar's distinction between *traditum* and *tradendum*,[12] and a summary of Stephen Bevans' models of contextual theology. After a brief review of the Asian context, it presents the contextual methodologies of the FABC's theology,[13] and highlights its distinctive features. The paper suggests that the FABC's theology is best understood in terms of the synthetic contextual model according to Stephen Bevans, and argues that it has in fact initiated a paradigm shift, based on Hans Küng's hermeneutical framework, in response to the growing crisis inherent in the Asian *Sitz-im-Leben*. The chapter concludes that the FABC's theology is a contextual theology par excellence, a faith seeking both understanding and dialogue with the cultures, the religions, and the poor of Asia.

From *Traditum* to *Tradendum*: the Imperative of Theological Contextualisation

Contextualisation of theology or of the Gospel is not a new reality as theology is always contextually conditioned.[14] Throughout the centuries Christians have

---

this particular context" ("Whither 'Australian Theology'? A Response to Geoffrey Lilburne," *Pacifica* 12 [June 1999] 196). This suggestion flows from his earlier exploration of the theme of theology as "Christian faith making new connections" (*An Expanding Theology: Faith in a world of connections* [Newtown, NSW: E.J. Dwyer, 1993] ix).

12 In this essay "contextualisation" is used in preference to "inculturation." For Robert Schreiter, these two terms are often used interchangeably, but contextualisation is "the most widely used term in Roman Catholic circles to describe the proper relation between faith and cultures," and it has "the advantage of emphasizing the importance of context." See "Faith and Cultures: Challenges to a World Church," *Theological Studies* 50 (1989) 747.

13 The Consensus Paper of a workshop on "Local Churches and the Tasks of Mission: Inculturation," part of the International Congress on Mission held in Manila in 1979 to celebrate the 400th anniversary of the foundation of this diocese, recommends that "theologizing should be contextual, taking into consideration the ways of thinking and the sets of meanings and values that shape the lives of the people." (International Congress on Mission, art. 19.c., *FAPA Vol. 1*, 140).

14 Krikor Haleblian contends that it is more correct or proper to speak of contextualisation of the Gospel than the contextualisation of theology as theology is always contextually conditioned. "The Problem of Contextualization," *Missiology: An International Review* 11:1 (January 1983) 95.

lived and witnessed to the values of the Gospel in different cultural, religious, social, political, and economic contexts. Contextualising theology can occur along four fronts: "as an ongoing process in Christendom; at the frontiers of mission, where the church meets other cultures; specifically in the encounter with other religions; and in the interpretation of the Bible."[15] On the second and third fronts especially, the Church has to face different worldviews and is compelled to reflect on the relationship between the Christian faith and human culture, and between tradition and social change. The Church also has to constantly review the entire tradition both in terms of content and as a historical communication. Tradition as the *traditum* is what is handed on, and it is not context-free. Tradition as the *tradendum* is what should be transmitted, in a way that addresses a particular context.[16]

Thus, in this chapter *traditum* means the deposit of faith that must be received, safeguarded and transmitted in all its integrity. On the other hand, the term *tradendum* implies the duty to communicate the Christian message in a manner that is deliberately sensitive to the cultural, historical, religious and social contexts of the intended audience.[17] *Traditum*, therefore, refers to the *what* of the *depositum fidei*, and *tradendum* suggests the *why* and *how*. There is a hermeneutical endeavour within both the *traditum* and the *tradendum*. Consequently, contextual theology is an ongoing process of interpreting the *traditum* and the *tradendum* in reference to the promises, needs, and possibilities of a particular cultural situation, in creative fidelity to scripture and tradition.

---

15 Charles R. Taber, "Contextualization," *Religious Studies Review* 13:1 (January 1987) 33.

16 I owe this distinction to Raimundo Panikkar who associates *traditum* with the "burden of the past" and *tradendum* with the "challenge of the future." See *The Unknown Christ of Hinduism: Towards an Ecumenical Christophany*, revised and enlarged ed. (London: Darton, Longman & Todd, 1981) 1, 20. However Panikkar, who admits that he has "not always made the necessary clarifications and distinctions," uses *traditum* and *tradendum* in a different sense. See ibid., 15. In this seminal work, he appears to use *traditum* to refer to a religion or doctrinal formulations, which are "necessarily limited by cultural factors," of a more universal truth, and *tradendum* to mean the "living Presence" of the ultimate "Mystery which Christians call Christ." (Ibid., 2, 4, 7). For him, the universally valid truth is "an existential truth, not a mere doctrine," and hence "non-objectifiable." (Ibid., 9, 11, 21). *Traditum* seems to mean a "conception of Christ" that Christians bring to other people and religions while *tradendum* refers to the "'Unknown Christ,'" who "remains unknown and yet continues to be Christ." (Ibid., 30).

17 John W. O'Malley observes that "tradition is faithfully passed on only when it is rendered engaging and life-giving" (Vatican II: Did Anything Happen?" *Theological Studies* 67 [2006] 9).

Addressing an international ecumenical symposium held at the University of Tübingen, David Tracy argues that "theology as hermeneutical can be described as the attempt to develop mutually critical correlations in theory and praxis between an interpretation of the Christian tradition and an interpretation of the contemporary situation."[18] In his view, theologians have the task of "rendering as explicit as possible an interpretation of the central Christian message for a concrete situation ..."[19] Each theologian, he contends, must "interpret both 'constants' (the 'present world of experience in all its ambivalence, contingency and change' and the 'Judaeo-Christian tradition, which is ultimately based on the Christian message, the Gospel of Jesus Christ')."[20] Following Tracy's suggestion, *traditum* refers to the Judaeo-Christian tradition whose core is the Gospel of Jesus Christ, while *tradendum* is concerned with transmitting the Gospel faith in the present world of experience in all its ambivalence, contingency, and change.

Theologising, therefore, requires contextualising the gospel by taking into account the cultural, historical, political, and social contexts in which people live and experience the transcendent. It is not simply the case of *id quod traditum est, id quod traditur*. It is clear then that contextualisation is both an essential condition for theological thinking,[21] and an imperative for theological integrity.[22] This is particularly true in contemporary Asia. This vast continent is a mosaic of cultures and religions, as well as being, at times, a theatre of bloody conflicts in the midst of the massive poverty of its population. In this context, the FABC has endeavoured to draw on the fountain of *traditum*, and search for a *tradendum* to communicate to the Asian people. To understand and promote this process, let us now turn to the works of Stephen Bevans.

Models of Contextual Theology according to Stephen Bevans

Stephen Bevans describes contextual theology as the process of doing theology that takes into account four factors: the spirit and message of the gospel, the

---

18 David Tracy, "Some Concluding Reflections on the Conference: Unity Amidst Diversity and Conflict," in *Paradigm Change in Theology: a Symposium for the Future*, ed. Hans Küng and David Tracy (New York: Crossroad, 1991) 462.
19 Ibid.
20 David Tracy, "Hermeneutical Reflections in the New Paradigm," in *Paradigm Change in Theology: a Symposium for the Future*, ed. Hans Küng and David Tracy (New York: Crossroad, 1991) 35.
21 Hall, *Thinking the Faith*, 21.
22 Stephen B. Bevans, *Models of Contextual Theology* (Maryknoll, New York: Orbis Books, 1992) 1.

tradition of the Christian people, the culture in which one is theologising, and social change in that culture, whether brought about by Western technological progress or the grass-roots struggle for equality, justice, and liberation.[23] He then proposes five models of contextual theologies, depicted in a theological map (Figure 1), and provides a description of each one in relation to the polarities of culture and social change on the one hand, and the Gospel message and Christian tradition on the other.[24] The relative position of each model is determined by its leaning toward either of these two poles. Their use is also determined by the different ways they combine the four factors present in any contextual theology. It should be noted that Bevans does not consider that these models are mutually exclusive; nor do they constitute five different paths to contextual theology.[25] Keeping this in mind, let us take up each in turn.

---

23 Bevans, *Models of Contextual Theology*, 1. In the revised and expanded edition of 2002, he speaks of "context" rather than "culture", and considers that "contextual theology is done when the experience of the past" ("recorded in scripture and preserved and defended in tradition") "engages the present context" (individual and social experience, secular or religious culture, social location, and social change"). See *Models of Contextual Theology*, revised and expanded edition, (Maryknoll, New York: Orbis Books, 2002) xvi-xvii.

24 Bevans, *Models of Contextual Theology*, 27. Bevans includes a sixth model, the semiotic model, in an earlier paper, "Models of Contextual Theology," *Missiology: An International Review* 13:2 (April 1985) 185–202. This semiotic model is subsumed into the synthetic model in the 1992 book. He adds a new model, the countercultural model (not shown in Figure 1) in the revised and expanded edition published in 2002, and places it on the extreme right of the continuum as for him "its concern is to challenge the context with the content of scripture and tradition" (*Models of Contextual Theology*, revised and expanded edition, [Maryknoll, New York: Orbis Books, 2002] 32, 117–37). Robert Schreiter has a similar insight stating that the relation of theology to context, "construed as culture, social structure, or social location," is "one of intimacy and distance at the same time," that is, theology must "be rooted in the context, yet be able also to take stock of the context at the same time" (*The New Catholicity: Theology Between the Global and the Local* [Maryknoll, New York: Orbis Books, 1997] 4–5.) As the primary focus of this essay is to discuss the FABC's theological methodologies, we prefer to use the 1992 map of models of contextual theology as it provides ample data for our discussion. As to the revised and expanded edition, Bevans notes that "besides a few style changes, updating bibliography and biographical information," he has "changed very little in most of the text" of the 1992 edition. (Ibid., xvi).

25 Ibid., 28.

Figure 1: A Map of Models of Contextual Theology

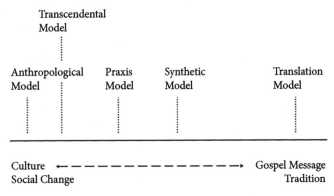

Transcendental
Model

| Anthropological Model | Praxis Model | Synthetic Model | Translation Model |

Culture ← — — — — — — — — — — — —→ Gospel Message
Social Change   Tradition

Source: Stephen B. Bevans, *Models of Contextual Theology*
(Maryknoll, N.Y.: Orbis Books, 1992) 27.

The translation model is the first and most conservative of the five. It places more emphasis on fidelity to the theological sources of scripture and tradition in its insistence that the message of the gospel is unchanging.[26] Its presupposition is that the essential message of Christianity is supracultural. Proponents of this model tend to distinguish between the kernel of the gospel and the husk of culture: an essential, supracultural Christian message can be separated from a nonessential, disposable cultural expression.[27] The contextualising process starts with stripping the Christian message from its cultural wrappings, usually its Western cultural husk. Once the pure gospel is identified, it can be rewrapped, as it were, in a particular cultural husk for communication to the intended recipients. In this approach, culture plays an ancillary role, subordinate to the unchanging Gospel message. Hence any conflicts between the values of the gospel and those of the cultures will be resolved in favour of the Gospel values which must be preserved. The Gospel in this view is the judge of all cultures, which are vehicles of the Gospel message. Thus the model presupposes that revelation is culturally free; that the Christian message brings something that is totally new into a culture; and that all cultures inherently have the same basic structures.

---

26 Bevans, *Models of Contextual Theology*, 30–46.
27 Robert Schreiter highlights the image of kernel and husk: "the basic Christian revelation is the kernel; the previous cultural settings in which it has been incarnated constitute the husk. The kernel has to be hulled time and again, as it were, to allow it to be translated into new cultural contexts." See *Constructing Local Theologies*, (Maryknoll, New York: Orbis Books, 1985) 7.

The anthropological model, on the other hand, takes human culture as the starting point.[28] It focuses on the validity of the human as the place of divine revelation as a theological *locus* on a par with the other sources of scripture and tradition. This model is primarily concerned to preserve and promote an authentic Christian cultural identity. To this end, it emphasises the dignity of the human person, the structure of human community, and the value of culture in its use of anthropological insights. In this regard, God's revelation is viewed not as a separate supracultural message but as a stimulus to meaning and value found in the midst of human life, and in the relationships that constitute social existence. The anthropological model has a creation-centred orientation. It acknowledges God's presence as revealed in the different cultural contexts, which affect both the content, understanding, and presentation of the word of God.[29] Necessarily, this model is also opened to insights gleaned from interreligious dialogues as material from which to develop a culturally sensitive theology.

Thirdly, there is Bevans' praxis model of contextual theology.[30] It highlights the importance of social development, for the interpretation of the Gospel and articulation of faith cannot be politically or economically neutral. It is especially associated with political theology, particularly the theology of liberation,[31] in the recognition that God's saving action is at work not only in the matrix of culture but also in the dynamics of history. Revelation is therefore related to the recognition of God's presence in history, in social, economic and political structures, in the struggle against every form of oppression, as in the events of everyday life. The truth of the Gospel is not primarily on the level of theory, but in the praxis of historical conduct. In contrast to the previously elaborated models, this model is concerned with the promotion of the cultural and social change. In this sense, all believers, not merely theologians, are engaged and called to know the truth

---

28 Bevans, *Models of Contextual Theology*, 47–62.
29 Bevans explains that a creation-centered theology is based on the conviction that "culture and human experience are generally good," and grace can build on nature, in contrast to a redemption-centered theology, according to which grace cannot be understood as perfecting nature as human experience and culture are "either in need of a radical transformation or in need of a total replacement." In his view, in a creation-centred approach, "human experience, current events, and culture would be areas of God's activity and therefore sources of theology." See Bevans, *Models of Contextual Theology*, 16–7.
30 Bevans, *Models of Contextual Theology*, 63–80.
31 Gustavo Gutiérrez defines theology as "critical reflection on historical praxis" (*A Theology of Liberation: History, Politics and Salvation* [Maryknoll, New York: Orbis Books, 1988] 12).

by doing it.[32] We know God best by doing God's saving will, and by uniting ourselves with his saving action.

A fourth model, which Bevans calls synthetic, aims to incorporate the best insights of the three previously described models.[33] As the "both/and" process, it is intent on keeping the integrity of the traditional message, and at the same time, taking seriously culture and social change. In a creative and dynamic dialectic, it promotes an ongoing dialogue between faith and cultures by accepting that every culture or context, though unique in its way, still contains elements common to all. Dialogue, complementarity, and transcultural communication are the key factors.

Bevans' fifth model is described as transcendental.[34] Its focus is not on the content to be articulated but on the articulating subject. Genuine theology is possible only when it emerges from authentically converted subjects, from those who allow God to touch and transform their life. Thus, the starting point of this model is transcendental as it shifts from the world of objects to the world of subjects into the interior world of human persons in their conscious experience of both God and themselves. In this way, theology is a process of self-objectification, rather than a detached objective content. The believing and knowing subject is intimately involved in determining reality. This model presupposes the universal structure of human knowing and responsibility. Consequently, it enables the Christian to come to self-appropriation in the light of God's Word, within the larger world of human experience. In this sense, the best agents of contextual theology are those who have been radically transformed in their deepest subjectivity, as they live and act in their differing religious and cultural contexts.

According to Bevans, each of the above five models is valid. Collectively, they offer a range of methodological options for theologising. Each model will operate more adequately within certain sets of circumstances. Underlying this flexible commitment to contextual theology is the recognition that theological pluralism is desirable in a world of cultural differences, especially in Asia, home to a multitude of cultures and religions. Theology is after all an interpretation of the Gospel for the Church's life in society, and this is what the FABC has endeavoured to do in the particular context of Asia. The following section will provide a *tour d'horizon* of the Christian Church in the Asian context.

---

32 Jon Sobrino, quoted in Alfred T. Hennelly, "Theological Method: The Southern Exposure," *Theological Studies* 38:4 (December 1977) 724.
33 Bevans, *Models of Contextual Theology*, 81–96.
34 Ibid., 97–110.

The Asian Context: Realities, Issues, and Challenges

Most of the statements issued by the FABC begin with a discussion of the contextual realities in Asia.[35] Together these documents depict Asia as a continent of change and crisis, pregnant with difficulties but also showing increasing signs of hope. Right from its first meeting in 1970, prior to the official establishment of the FABC, the Asian bishops observed that Asia, a continent of ancient cultures and religions, home to "almost two-thirds of mankind," is marked by poverty, and scarred by war and suffering.[36] Nearly 60 percent of its people are under twenty-five years of age.[37] With the demise of colonialism, Asian nations have endeavoured to seek and affirm their identity, and the poor masses have expected a better life for themselves.[38] The first plenary meeting of the FABC (1974) recognises that there is a "swift and far-reaching transformation," in Asia, a continent "undergoing modernisation, social change, secularisation and the breakup of traditional societies."[39] In the Second Plenary Assembly (1978) the bishops express a concern that the modern world threatens traditional values and this situation brings to the Church a true crisis.[40] In the following Plenary Assembly (1982) they see signs of hope and signs of the presence and action of the Holy Spirit.[41] The Fourth Plenary Assembly (1986) stresses the need to confront "the dark realities in the heart of Asia" which are associated with "misguided and selfish power politics," and it highlights the plight of the youth and women.[42] It affirms that "the Asian family is the cellular receptacle of all Asia's problems, poverty, repression, exploitation and degradation,

---

35 Except the statement of the Third Plenary Assembly, which commences with a discussion of the ecclesiology of the Asian Church. See FABC III, arts. 6–8.2, *FAPA Vol. 1*, 55–7. For a succinct summary of Asia's realities, not in a chronological progression as presented in this essay, but under its demographic, economic, social, political, and religious aspects, see Peter C. Phan, "Ignacio Ellacuría, S.J. in Dialogue with Asian Theologians: What Can They Learn from Each Other?" *Horizons* 32:1 (Spring 2005) 66–7; see also *The Asian Synod: Texts and Commentaries*, edited by Peter C. Phan (Maryknoll, New York: Orbis, 2002).

36 Asian Bishops' Meeting, art. 5, *FAPA Vol. 1*, 4.

37 Ibid., arts. 6–7. See also FABC IV (1986) art. 3.2.1, *FAPA Vol. 1*, 181; FABC V (1990), art. 2.2.2, *FAPA Vol. 1*, 277.

38 Ibid., arts. 9–10.

39 FABC I, art. 4, *FAPA Vol. 1*, 13.

40 FABC II, arts. 8–9, *FAPA Vol. 1*, 30–31.

41 FABC III, arts. 10–13, *FAPA Vol. 1*, 59.

42 FABC IV, arts 3.0.1–3.3.6, *FAPA Vol. 1*,179–84.

divisions and conflicts."[43] The Fifth Plenary Assembly (1990) raises concerns at the change caused by globalisation, continuing injustice, discrimination against women, and the bleak future of young people.[44] The Sixth Plenary Assembly (1995) begins with a quick scan of Asian realities, retrieving the analyses of previous plenary assemblies, this time emphasising "whatever threatens, weakens, diminishes, and destroys the life of individuals, groups or people."[45] In the Seventh Plenary Assembly (2000) the Asian bishops review in broad strokes problems associated with economic globalisation, authoritarian states coupled with rampant corruption, the rise of fundamentalism, the deterioration of the environment, and the increasing militarisation of societies.[46] The Eighth Plenary Assembly (2004) discerns many "dead-dealing forces" such as "Asia's massive poverty, divisions, conflicts, exploitation, and oppressive structures" which threaten "not only the quality of life but also the very survival of many Asian families."[47] The Ninth Plenary Assembly (2009) reflects on the realities transpiring in various parts of Asia, and see in "the midst of the ruins of life brought about by wars, violence and displacement of peoples...the Asian capacity to celebrate life and to hope for a better life."[48] Finally, in the tenth Plenary Assembly (2012) the bishops of Asia systematically discern the signs of the times and analyse the mega-trends in Asia and ecclesial realities.[49]

For the FABC, despite all the dark realities signs of hope are emerging, and Asia remains "the context of God's creative, incarnational, and redemptive action, the theatre in which the drama of Asia's salvation is enacted."[50] The poor and marginalised of Asia become more recognised, conscious of their human dignity, and do not accept that the situation they are in is an inevitable fate, but "something to be struggled against."[51] There are movements for democracy and human rights, women's movements and ecological movements,[52] and people become more committed to ecumenical and interreligious dialogue.[53]

---

43 Ibid., art. 3.4.1.
44 FABC V, arts. 2.1–2.2.3, *FAPA Vol. 1*, 275–77.
45 FABC VI, arts. 6–7, *FAPA Vol. 2*, 3–4.
46 FABC VII, Part II, *FAPA Vol. 3*, 6–8.
47 FABC VIII, art. 47, *FAPA Vol. 4*, 17.
48 FABC IX, *FAPA Vol. 5*, 11.
49 FABC X, *FAPA Vol. 5*, 58–68.
50 FABC V, art. 1.1, *FAPA Vol. 1*, 275.
51 FABC V, art. 2.3.1, *FAPA Vol. 1*, 277; FABC VI, art. 8, *FAPA Vol. 2*, 4.
52 FABC IX, *FAPA Vol. 5*, 11.
53 FAPA V, arts. 2.0–2.3.9, *FAPA Vol. 1*, 275–279; FABC VI, *FAPA Vol. 2*, 4.

The Christian Church continues to face many problems, which are due to a triple marginalisation: Christianity as a minority religion in Asia,[54] the local Church perceived as a *corpus alienum* planted by Western missionaries on Asian soil,[55] and the universal Church seen to maintain an attitude of superiority towards other religions.[56] Therefore, the FABC is committed to the emergence of the Asianness of the Church in Asia by trying to be an "embodiment of the Asian vision and values of life, especially interiority, harmony, [and] a holistic and inclusive approach to every area of life."[57] Only then can the Church become a "Church of Asia," not simply a "Church in Asia," and will it no longer be considered as an "alien presence."[58]

At the seventh Plenary Assembly (2000), the FABC articulated the vision of the Church in Asia as consisting of eight movements: first, "a movement towards a Church of the Poor and a Church of the Young" [Asian Bishops' Meeting, 1970]; second, "a movement toward a 'truly local Church'" [FABC I, 1974]; third, "a movement toward deep interiority" [FABC II, 1978]; fourth, "a movement toward an authentic community of faith" [FABC III, 1982]; fifth, "a movement toward active integral evangelization, toward a new sense of mission" [FABC V, 1990]; sixth, "a movement toward empowerment of men and women" [FABC IV, 1986]; seventh, "a movement toward active involvement in generating and

---

54 Christians account for approximately 3.9% of the total population of Asia with Catholics representing about 2.8%, concentrated mainly in the Philippines (83% of the population), South Korea, Vietnam, and East Timor. See *The World Almanac and Book of Facts 2003* (New York: World Almanac Books, 2003) 638, 780, 801, 828, 857.

55 OE, "Church Issues in Asia in the context of Evangelization, Dialogue and Proclamation," art. 13, *FAPA Vol. 2*, 195.

56 During a visit to India in 1999, John Paul II inflamed local tensions by openly calling for conversion of Asia to Catholicism saying that the continent is "'thirsting for the living water that Jesus alone can give.'" See Editorials, "Planting the Cross," *Asiaweek* (26 November 1999) 18. Cardinal Joseph Ratzinger, Prefect of the Congregation for the Doctrine of the Faith, once described Buddhism as "un autoérotisme spirituel, en quelque sorte" (Michel Cool, "Le Testament du Panzerkardinal," *L'Express* [20 March 1997] 70). His office's declaration *Dominus Jesus: On the Unicity and Salvific Universality of Jesus Christ and the Church* generated headlines in both Catholic and secular press. See *The Tablet* (November 18, 2000) and *America* (October 28, 2000). *The Washington Post* (September 6, 2000) ran a headline, "Vatican Claims Church Monopoly on Salvation," and the *Los Angeles Times* (September 7, 2000)'s banner read, "Salvation that Reopens the Door to Intolerance."

57 FABC VII, Part III, *FAPA Vol. 3*, 8.

58 BIRA IV/12, art. 50, *FAPA Vol. 1*, 333.

serving life" [FABC VI, 1995]; eighth, "a movement toward the triple dialogue with other faiths, with the poor and with the cultures."[59] Twelve years later, at the tenth Plenary Assembly, they reiterated their vision of "a Church that is: *truly Asian, in triple dialogue* with the religions, cultures and peoples of Asia, especially the poor."[60] This time they also envisaged "a Church in solidarity with the whole creation."[61]

The challenge for the Asian Church is "to proclaim the Good News of the Kingdom of God: to promote justice, peace, love, compassion, equality and brotherhood in these Asian realities,"[62] and to "work for justice and peace along with the Christians of other churches, with people of other faiths, and with all the people of good will, to make the Kingdom of God more visibly present in Asia."[63] The FABC has also endeavoured to motivate the Church of Asia towards a new way of being Church, a Church that is committed to becoming a community of communities, and a credible sign of salvation and liberation.[64] At the seventh Plenary Assembly, the FABC committed itself to direct its mission of love and service to the youth, women, the family, indigenous peoples, sea-based and land-based migrants, and refugees.[65] Facing the 21st century, the Asian bishops acknowledge that they are addressing "needs that are massive and increasingly complex," and they recognise the "need to feel and act 'integrally'," "in solidarity with the poor and the marginalized, in union with all our Christian brothers and sisters, and by joining hands with all men and women of Asia of many different faiths."[66] For the Asian bishops, "inculturation, dialogue, justice and the option for the poor" are aspects of whatever they do.[67] These Asian realities, issues, and challenges are the context in which the Church lives and theology is done in Asia today. In this Asian context, the Church is called to a renewed evangelisation, which requires "a new expression, renewed methods and a renewed fervor."[68]

---

59 FABC VII, art. I.A, *FAPA Vol. 3*, 3–4.
60 FABC X, *FAPA Vol. 5*, 54.
61 Ibid.
62 FABC V, art. 7, *FAPA Vol. 1*, 275.
63 FABC V, art. 2.3.9, *FAPA Vol. 1*, 279.
64 FABC VI, art. 3, *FAPA Vol. 2*, 3.
65 FABC VII, Part III.A.1–5, *FAPA Vol. 3*, 9.
66 FABC VII, Part III, *FAPA Vol. 3*, 8.
67 Ibid.
68 TAC, "Being Church in Asia: Journeying with the Spirit into Fuller Life," art. 51, *FAPA Vol. 2*, 226.

Theological Methodologies of the FABC

Since their first meeting in 1970, the bishops of Asia have consistently followed a contextual approach to theological reflection, "taking into account contextual realities as resources of theology."[69] They draw a distinction between "sources" and "resources" of theology: Christian sources refer to scripture and tradition, and contextual realities are called theological resources.[70] The FABC has employed "the same method in its many conferences and seminars – to start from the analysis of the real situation in its many facets and to base its faith-reflections on the data thus perceived."[71] This consistent pattern has been evident in the plenary assembly statements, the position papers, and the various institutes and workshops organised by the FABC offices. Here we will examine the FABC contextual theological methodologies gleaned from the structure of plenary assembly statements and the passages in the FABC documents that deal explicitly with the subject.

"See, Judge, Act" Process

Of the many documents issued by the FABC, the plenary assembly statements have the highest authority. Each of these statements shows how the Asian bishops confront various contextual issues and propose action plans based on their analysis of the situations, and their interpretation and application of Christian sources and magisterial teachings. Analysing the final statements of the first three plenary assemblies, A.J.V. Chandrakanthan asserts that "a conspicuous lack of methodology is a serious deficiency in almost all the statements of the plenary assembly."[72] One would tend to agree with this contention if by methodology he means a formal, structured theological process, akin to the elaborate method proposed by Bernard Lonergan.[73] However, a detailed analysis of these statements

---

69 OTC, "Methodology: Asian Christian Theology," arts. 3.1, *FAPA Vol. 3*, 355. For a helpful discussion of the Asian context as sources and resources of theology, see Peter C. Phan, "Theology on the Other Side of the Borders: Responding to the Signs of the Times," *CTSA Proceedings* 57 (2002) 98–102.

70 OTC, "Methodology: Asian Christian Theology," arts. 3.1–3.4, *FAPA Vol. 3*, 355–64.

71 TAC, "Asian Christian Perspectives on Harmony," art. 1.1, *FAPA Vol. 3*, 233.

72 A.J.V. Chandrakanthan, "Asian Bishops' Approaches to Evangelisation: A Theological Evaluation and Critique of the Statements of the Plenary Assemblies of the FABC (1970–1983)," *Indian Missiological Review* 9 (April 1987) 105–127.

73 Bernard Lonergan, *Method in Theology* (New York: Herder and Herder, 1972). In his inaugural address at a congress held at the Gregorian University in 2004 on the occasion of the 100th anniversary of the birth of Lonergan, Cardinal Carlo Maria Martini makes an analogy between the *Spiritual Exercises* of Saint Ignatius Loyola and Lonergan's book,

and other documents that were subsequently issued by the FABC shows that the Asian bishops have never intended to develop a systematic method of theology. Their approach is, and has always been, primarily pastoral and missionary. They analyse contextual realities with constant reference to scripture and tradition, aiming to respond to the needs of Asian Christians, and to interpret and devise ways to fulfil the evangelising mission of the Church in Asia.[74] They do not

---

considering the former as "a method for putting order into one's own life," and the latter as "a method for putting order into one's own way of thinking, knowing, reasoning," and concludes that Lonergan's work "constitutes a new 'organon' permitting future generations to situate themselves in the river of human research with strong concepts and persuasions always capable of being perfected." See "Bernard Lonergan at the Service of the Church," *Theological Studies* 66 (2005) 518, 526.

74　The FABC often considers evangelisation as part of the overall mission of the Church, ignoring the distinction of these two terms in various conciliar and papal documents. See "Asian Colloquium on Ministries in the Church," art. 16, *FAPA Vol. 1*, 70; BIMA II, art. 11, *FAPA Vol. 1*, 99; BIMA III, "A Syllabus of 'Mission Concerns'," art. 1, *FAPA Vol. 1*, 106; BIMA IV, "Resolutions," art. A.2, *FAPA Vol. 1*, 293. For the Asian bishops, "the proclamation of Jesus Christ is the center and the primary element of evangelization without which all other elements will lose their cohesion and validity" (BIMA IV, art. 6, [*FAPA Vol. 1*], 292). The Pontifical Council for Interreligious Dialogue and the Congregation for the Evangelisation of Peoples employ the term evangelisation or evangelising mission to mean evangelisation in its broad sense of bringing the good news into all areas of humanity, and use the word proclamation to express the more specific understanding of evangelisation as the clear and unambiguous proclamation of the Lord Jesus. See "Dialogue and Proclamation: Reflections and Orientations on Interreligious Dialogue and the Proclamation of the Gospel of Jesus Christ," *Origins* 21:8 (4 July 1991) 124. The term evangelisation occurs only 31 times in all the documents of Vatican II, which seems to speak of "evangelising" as "the proclamation of the basic Christian message to those who did not yet believe in Christ" (Avery Dulles, "John Paul II and the New Evangelization," *America* (1 February 1992) 53. It becomes a key term in Paul VI's Apostolic Exhortation *Evangelii Nuntiandi* (1975), which uses the term mission very sparsely. See Giancarlo Collet, "Theology of Mission or of Missions? The Treatment of a Controversial Term," *Concilium* 1 (1999) 88. Felipe Gomez notes that mission carries ecclesiological connotations, and evangelisation shifts towards Christology; he recalls that for Paul VI, one single term evangelization defines the whole of Christ's office and mandate (*Evangelii Nuntiandi* 6). See "The Missionary Activity Twenty Years After Vatican II," *East Asian Pastoral Review* 23:1 (1986) 36. In *Redemptoris Missio*, John Paul II defines the term mission in both a theological and geographical sense, emphasising that the Church is "missionary by her very nature" (no. 62). This encyclical distinguishes three situations requiring different activities of the one mission of the Church: the mission *ad gentes* proper, the pastoral activity, and

set out to face this enormous challenge by adopting or developing a systematic theological methodology. Instead, the starting point of their theological reflection and pastoral deliberation is the local, contextual realities, which they use as theological resources, which in turn have significantly shaped their theological method and content.[75]

The Asian bishops' theological approach, expressed in the structure of most of their plenary assembly statements and other documents, seems to follow the simple methodology of "See, Judge, Act," a pastoral process used by the Jeunesse Ouvrière Chrétienne movement, founded by the late Belgian Cardinal Joseph Cardijn (1882–1967).[76] In the first "See" stage of their approach, the Asian bishops use headings or phrases such as "Modern day Asia,"[77] "Some Aspects of the Present Religious Context of Asia and its Challenge,"[78] "The Presence of the Spirit and Signs of Hope in our Communities in Asia,"[79] "Challenges of Asia,"[80] "Challenges and Hopes,"[81] "A Vision of Life Amid Asian Realities,"[82] "Issues and Challenges in

---

the new evangelisation (nos. 33–34). See his *Redemptoris Missio, Origins* 20:34 (31 January 1991) 559, 553, 561.

75 Samuel Rayan asserts that the greatest gain achieved by Third World theology is the articulation of its methodology ("Third World Theology: Where Do We Go From Here?" *Concilium* 199 [August 1988] 129). For Felix Wilfred, "in the thought of the FABC, the pastoral and the theological are intimately linked" ("What the Spirit Says to the Churches (Rev 2:7)," *Vidyajyoti* 62 [1998] 124).

76 Mary Irene Zoti, "Cardijn: A Priest Who Believes in the Priesthood of the Laity," *The Living Light*, 23:4 (June 1987) 312. Australian canon lawyer Stefan Gignacz argues in his Louvain doctoral thesis that "Cardijn's 'see, judge, act' method was actually a continuation of the work of the French lay Catholic democratic movement known as Le Sillon (the furrow), founded by Marc Sagnier, with even earlier roots in often marginalized Catholic lay movements and going back to the inspiration of prophetic figures like Fréderic Ozanam and also to the visionary but excommunicated French diocesan priest of the mid-century Felicité de Lamennais." See Joe Holland, "Roots of the Pastoral Circle in Personal Experiences and Catholic Social Tradition," in *The Pastoral Circle Revisited: A Critical Quest for Truth and Transformation*, edited by Frans Wijsen, Peter Henriot, and Rodrigo Mejía (Maryknoll, New York: Orbis Books, 2005) 9.

77 FABC I, art. 4, *FAPA Vol. 1*, 13.
78 FABC II, *FAPA Vol. 1*, 30.
79 FABC III, *FAPA Vol. 1*, 59.
80 FABC IV, art. 3.0, *FAPA Vol. 1*, 179.
81 FABC V, *FAPA Vol. 1*, 275.
82 FABC VI, *FAPA Vol. 2*, 3.

the Mission of Love and Service,"[83] "Pastoral Challenges to the Family in Asia,"[84] and "Mega-trends in Asia and Ecclesial Realities."[85] For the second "Judge" step of their theological process, they use a variety of phases such as "The Challenge of Discerning the Asian Way,"[86] "The Church's Response and Resolve: To Become More Fully a True Community of Prayer,"[87] "The Evangelization of the Church in Contemporary Asia,"[88] "Theological-Pastoral Reflections,"[89] and "Reflecting in Faith on the Pastoral Situation."[90] In the final "Act" phase of their methodology they use headings and phrases such as "Recommendations of the Assembly,"[91] 'Our Commitment,"[92] "Pastoral Concerns,"[93] "Specific Pastoral Directions, at the Level of Doing,"[94] "A Few Practical Directions,"[95] "Pastoral Recommendations for the Family Ministry,"[96] "Responding to the Pastoral Challenges."[97] Besides this "See, Judge, Act" scheme, the FABC has also developed other more structured methodologies, which will be examined in the next section.

The Pastoral Cycle (1986)

In 1986, at BISA VII, for the first time since its inception, the bishops of Asia discussed a four-stage "pastoral cycle"[98] which revolves around "*prayer* as a

83   FABC VII, *FAPA Vol. 3*, 6.
84   FABC VIII, *FAPA Vol. 4*, 3.
85   FABC XI, *FAPA Vol. 5*, 58.
86   FABC VII, *FAPA Vol. 3*, 9.
87   FABC II, *FAPA Vol. 1*, 31.
88   FABC V, *FAPA Vol. 1*, 279.
89   FABC VIII, *FAPA Vol. 4*, 18.
90   FABC X, *FAPA Vol. 5*, 69.
91   FABC I, *FAPA Vol. 1*, 20.
92   FABC II, *FAPA Vol. 2*, 36.
93   FABC IV, art. 4.7.0, *FAPA Vol. 1*, 194.
94   FABC V, art. 7.3, *FAPA Vol. 1*, 285.
95   FABC VII, *FAPA Vol. 3*, 12.
96   FABC VIII, *FAPA Vol. 4*, 44.
97   FABC X, *FAPA Vol. 5*, 58.
98   Joe Holland identifies three historical roots of the pastoral circle in the tradition of Catholic social thought and action, namely Latin American liberation theology, the "See, Judge, Act" method used by Catholic Action movements, and "the praxis model (*phronesis*) of Aristotelian thought, which entered the Catholic tradition through medieval Scholasticism" ("Roots of the Pastoral Circle in Personal Experiences and Catholic Social Tradition," in *The Pastoral Circle Revisited: A Critical Quest for Truth and Transformation*, edited by Frans Wijsen, Peter Henriot, and Rodrigo Mejía [Maryknoll, New York: Orbis

covenantal relationship in faith": exposure-immersion, social analysis, contemplation or ongoing theological reflection, and pastoral planning.[99] At this institute, the bishops endeavoured "to discover a liberative spirituality for social action among the poor and by the poor," a spirituality that places "the Church at the service of the whole human race."[100] In their view, "only through a deep spirituality grounded in interior prayer" can they experience God in the poor, reflect on that presence in day-to-day situations, and seek to bring to the oppressed what God challenges the Church to do.[101] Exposure brings us closer to the reality of poverty, but immersion enables us to "experience reality from the perspective of the poor themselves."[102] Using social analysis "we evaluate the social, economic, political, cultural and religious systems in society," and try to "discern God's plan in the signs of the times, in the voices of our age, in the events of history as well as in the needs and aspirations" of the people.[103] Social analysis, the bishops affirm, is inadequate as a tool to grasp the whole of reality, and must be integrated with the religio-cultural reality in Asia to discern "its positive, prophetic aspects that can inspire genuine spirituality," and not just its "negative and enslaving aspects."[104] Contemplation, "the stage of ongoing theological reflection," makes us "discover God's presence and activity within social

---

Books, 2005] 5). Contributors to this book note that the terms pastoral cycle, pastoral circle, and pastoral spiral have been used in different settings, with the first term being more popular in Asia, Australia, and the United Kingdom, the second widely used in Africa, Canada, and the United States, and the third "an exclusively Asian term." See "Preface," ibid., xx-xxi. For these authors, the pastoral circle is "a process of answering four basic questions about some experience that we have, either as individuals or in a community setting": What is happening here? Why is it happening? How do we evaluate it? and How do we respond? These questions occur during four moments of the pastoral circle, which mediate the "*experience*" of the situation: Contact, Analysis, Reflection, and Response. See "Steps in the Pastoral Circle," ibid., 229–30.

99 BISA VII, arts. 8–13, *FAPA Vol. 1*, 231–2.
100 BISA VII, art. 4, *FAPA Vol. 1*, 230.
101 BISA VII, art. 13, *FAPA Vol. 1*, 232.
102 BISA VII, art. 8, *FAPA Vol. 1*, 231.
103 BISA VII, art. 9, *FAPA Vol. 1*, 231.
104 BISA VII, arts. 9–10, *FAPA Vol. 1*, 231–2. Peter C. Phan notes that "the FABC does not specify which method of social analysis to be employed," and argues that "implicitly, the FABC considers Marxist social analysis, which was favored by Latin American liberation theology, insufficient for the Asian situation" ("Human Development and Evangelization (The first to the sixth plenary assembly of the federation of Asian bishops' conferences)," *Studia Missionalia* 47 [1998] 213).

reality,"[105] while pastoral planning aims to "translate the previous three stages into actual, realizable plans."[106] In 1995 the FABC declared that the Pastoral Cycle, depicted in Figure 2, must be used in "all expressions of the ministry of the Word, including catechesis."[107] They dropped the term "exposure" from this methodology, and modified slightly the headings of the four stages, which now read as immersion into reality, analysis of this experience, faith-reflection and discernment, and pastoral planning and action. The four-stage pastoral cycle can be mapped to the "See, Judge, Act" process: exposure-immersion and social analysis correlate with "See"; contemplation or ongoing theological reflection corresponds to "Judge"; and there is a parallel between pastoral planning and "Act."

In May 2000, the FABC's Office of Theological Concerns referred to the Pastoral Cycle as a cycle of "social analysis" of the signs of the times, "theological reflection" to discern them in the light of the Gospel, and planning for the future and specifying missionary response.[108] This cycle begins with "our faith in Jesus Christ, the experience of that faith in prayer and in the covenant relationship that we share with our Christian brothers and sisters."[109] It is "a cycle which continually repeats itself and results in a theology different from that of former times, a living theology which constantly strives to discern the working of the Spirit in a rapidly changing world."[110] Five months later, in October 2000, its Office of Ecumenical and Interreligious Affairs discussed this Pastoral Cycle Methodology again in the context of formation for interreligious dialogue and simplified it into three R's: review of experiences, observations and learning, reflection in light of histories and traditions, and responses in the context of present and existential realities.[111] The following year, at the Second Asian Laity Meeting in 2001, the Asian bishops encouraged the use of this process of "exposure, reflection and action" in the formation of the laity.[112] At this meeting, the term "exposure" was used to encompass what is meant by "immersion" as exposure was seen as a means to help Christians

---

105   BISA VII, art. 11, *FAPA Vol. 1*, 231–2.
106   BISA VII, art. 12, *FAPA Vol. 1*, 232.
107   OESC, "A Renewed Catechesis for Asia Towards the Year 2000 and Beyond," *FAPA Vol. 2*, 31.
108   OTC, "Methodology: Asian Christian Theology," *FAPA Vol. 3*, 331.
109   Ibid.
110   Ibid.
111   OEIA, "FIRA III," arts. 5.1, 2.3, *FAPA Vol. 3*, 137, 134.
112   OL, "Second Asian Laity Meeting: Final Statement," art. 4.2, *FAPA Vol. 3*, 115.

"to learn, to see, to feel and share in the suffering of others."[113] By interpreting the Pastoral Cycle Methodology as a three-phase process in the last three interpretations, the Asian bishops have clearly opted for a simplified methodology that fits in with the "See, Judge, Act" process, a framework that they have effectively applied in structuring most of the final statements of their plenary assemblies.[114]

The "Mission Process" (1990)

At the Fifth Plenary Assembly in 1990 the Asian bishops declared that their reflection on Asia's realities in the light of *their mission of evangelisation* [italics mine] has led them to realise "the enduring validity of a process of: (a) *dialoguing* with the realities of Asia from within; (b) *discerning* the movement of God's Spirit in Asia; and (c) *translating into deeds* what the Spirit bids us to accomplish (italics in the original)."[115] For them, this process has to be the general approach for their total response as Church in Asia.[116] We call this process the "mission process" as the bishops would later emphasise the use of this methodology of "dialogue, discernment and deeds" in the context of Christians as the evangelising and liberating force in the struggle for fullness of life,[117] or the explication of this process of "Dialogue-Discernment-Deeds" as "Dialogue with the World of Asia and Discernment as Church in the light of the Gospel" leading us "to be a Prophetic Church."[118]

Figure 2 provides a graphical summary of the main theological methodologies of the Asian bishops. It highlights our argument that it is the "See, Judge, Act" process that underlies their theological and pastoral reflection. Other methods and insights, such as the Asian Integral Pastoral Approach and the discussion on the work of theology in Asia, are also discussed in this section as they provide further clarification and amplification of the FABC's theological methodologies.

---

113 OL, "Second Asian Laity Meeting: Final Statement," art. 2.2, *FAPA Vol. 3*, 114.
114 Jonathan Yun-Ka Tan expands the FABC's theological process into a "five-fold methodology" including (i) a commitment to life, (ii) dialectical social analysis, (iii) critical introspective contemplation, (iv) triple dialogue with Asian cultures, religions and the poor, and (v) quest for harmony in the task of theologizing in the Asian milieu." Tan states that "this division of the FABC's theological methodology into five stages" is his "own division, classification and explication" for the purposes of his essay. See "Theologizing at the Service of Life," *Gregorianum* 81:3 (2000) 544.
115 FABC V, art. 7.1, *FAPA Vol. 1*, 284.
116 Ibid.
117 FABC VI, art. 3, *FAPA Vol. 2*, 2.
118 OHD, "The Prophetic Path to the New Millennium Through Social Advocacy," art. 3.14, *FAPA Vol. 3*, 50.

Figure 2: Theological Methodologies of the FABC

The Pastoral Cycle Methodology					"Mission Process"	
1986	1995	May 2000	Oct 2000	2001	1990	
Exposure Immersion	Immersion into Reality	Social Analysis	Review	Exposure	Dialoguing	"See"
Social Analysis	Analysis					
Contemplation or Theological Reflection	Faith Reflection & Discernment	Theological Reflection	Reflection	Reflection	Discerning	"Judge"
Pastoral Planning	Pastoral Planning & Action	Plan & Response	Response	Action	Translating into Deeds	"Act"

The "Communion Process": Asian Integral Pastoral Approach (1993)

The Asian Integral Pastoral Approach (ASIPA) came into being in 1993 at a Consultation sponsored by the FABC's Office of Human Development and Office of Laity.[119] It is not a theological methodology, but a pastoral process that seeks to promote a new way of being church, a participatory church envisioned and encouraged by the FABC during its Fifth Plenary Assembly meeting held in 1990.[120] The bishops' vision, articulated at this assembly, is that the Church in Asia will have to be "a *communion of communities*, where laity, religious and clergy recognise and accept each other as sisters and brothers," and "a participatory Church where the gifts that the Holy Spirit gives to all the faithful – lay, religious, and cleric alike – are recognised and activated, so that the Church may be built up and its mission realized" (italics in the original).[121]

---

119   Office of Laity and Office of Human Development, "Asian Integral Pastoral Approach: towards a New Way of Being Church in Asia (AsIPA)," *FAPA Vol. 2*, 108.
120   FABC V, art. 8.1.1–8.1.2, *FAPA Vol. 1*, 287.
121   FABC V, arts. 8.1.1–2, *FAPA Vol. 1*, 287.

ASIPA is "Asian" because it seeks to implement the FABC's vision and to face the realities of the Asian peoples.[122] It is "integral" in terms of content, collaboration of different pastoral agents, and coordination of structures at different levels. With regard to content it includes "standing up against injustice," "ecumenical interreligious dialogue," "direct proclamation of the Gospel," "active participation of the laity," "the quest for integrity of creation," "deepening the faith," "aiming at small Christian communities," "forming of communion of communities," [and] "centered on the Presence of the Risen Lord."[123] It is "pastoral" in that it aims to implement "the vision of the new way of being church," involving "the participation of the entire community" and "a new style of leadership which will be an enabling and animating one."[124] ASIPA is both an "approach" and a concrete realisation of the vision of a participatory church. It is also a "community building approach" which awakens the laity at the grassroots level "to discover their common mission and realise their social responsibility."[125] For the FABC, ASIPA is a useful methodology that helps basic ecclesial communities to grow and develop, and as such, it is an indispensable tool in fostering an ecclesial communion marked by authentic participation and coresponsibility.[126] Therefore, we venture to refer to it as a "communion process."

Theology as Service to Life (1994 & 2000)

In 2000, the FABC's Office of Theological Concerns (OTC) issued a lengthy document on theological thinking in the Asian context,[127] stating that "it is rather a continuation of the tradition of the Church, a living tradition which today in Asia experiences an encounter with other Asian religious traditions and Asian cultures."[128] It discusses the question of pluralism, provides an overview of "traditional Christian theological methods in the east and the west," considers the resources used by Asian theologians to develop an Asian theology, investigates the nascent Asian biblical hermeneutics and methods of interpreting the scriptures of other religions in Asia, and finally reviews "the question of the use of

---

122 Office of Laity and Office of Human Development, "Asian Integral Pastoral Approach: towards a New Way of Being Church in Asia (AsIPA)," *FAPA Vol. 2*, 108.
123 Ibid., 109.
124 Ibid.
125 Ibid.
126 FABC VII, art. III.C.7, *FAPA Vol. 3*, 15; OL, "Second Asian Integral Pastoral Approach (AsIPA) General Assembly II," art. 1.4, *FAPA Vol. 3*, 108.
127 OTC, "Methodology: Asian Christian Theology," *FAPA Vol. 3*, 329–419.
128 Ibid., 330.

symbol, narrative, and myth in the Asian religious traditions."[129] The document aims "to shed some light on the emerging theological methods used by Asian theologians," and not "to define 'An Asian Method of Theology'."[130] It mentions briefly "the methods of theological reflection" employed by the FABC.[131] These methods display a consistent pattern in the thinking of the Asian bishops, who consider contextual realities as resources of theology, embodying and manifesting the presence and action of God and His Spirit. Using these resources has become integral to their thought process, and as a result introduced a significant change in their theological methodologies. In 1994, in a statement issued by their Theological Advisory Commission, they assert that theology in Asia is "more than faith seeking understanding but faith fostering life and love, justice and freedom."[132] This theology is first and foremost "a service to life."[133] For them, theology must become "a dynamic process giving meaning to and facilitating the Asian journey to life,"[134] by starting from below, "from the underside of history, from the perspective of those who struggle for life, love, justice, and freedom."[135] Asian theology, they insist, has to "reflect systematically on themes that are important to the common journey of life with other peoples in Asia, to the life of Christians and their churches in Asia, and to the work of the Asian Episcopal conferences."[136] Theology, in this way, becomes "part of the process of becoming and being Church in Asia."[137] It is, according to Vietnamese American theologian Peter C. Phan, "essentially ecclesial" in the sense that it is "at the service of the mission of the church."[138] The salient features of this theology and its Asian way of theologising will be taken up in the next section.

---

129 Ibid., 332.
130 Ibid., 332.
131 Ibid., 356.
132 TAC, "Being Church in Asia: Journeying with the Spirit into Fuller Life," art. 48, *FAPA Vol. 2*, 226. See also Office of Theological Concerns, "Methodology: Asian Christian Theology," art. 3.2.2, *FAPA Vol. 3*, 357.
133 TAC, "Being Church in Asia: Journeying with the Spirit into Fuller Life," art. 48, *FAPA Vol. 2*, 226.
134 TAC, "Being Church in Asia: Journeying with the Spirit into Fuller Life," art. 50, *FAPA Vol. 2*, 226.
135 Ibid., art. 49, *FAPA Vol. 2*, 226.
136 Ibid., art. 48, *FAPA Vol. 2*, 226.
137 Ibid., art. 50, *FAPA Vol. 2*, 226.
138 Peter C. Phan, "Theology on the Other Side of the Borders: Responding to the Signs of the Times," *CTSA Proceedings* 57 (2002) 91.

Characteristics of the FABC's Contextual Theology

There is no doubt that readers of the documents of the FABC issued between 1970 and 2012 will find that its contextual theology, which continues to evolve in a highly creative way in response to the changing context of Asia, is multi-faceted and very rich in content. Therefore, it is simply too daunting a task to attempt to capture all of its features. However, within the limited scope of this chapter, we would like to draw out five of its major characteristics, which complement and enrich each other:

(1) a synthetic contextual character;
(2) a similarity between the FABC's theological methodology and that of Latin American liberation theologies;
(3) a faith seeking dialogue;
(4) an approach that encourages theological pluralism and aims to achieve harmony; and,
(5) a development that constitutes a paradigm shift in theology.

Synthetic Contextual Theology

Discussing inculturation of theology in Asia, Stephen Bevans contends that the FABC's treatment of inculturation implies a "transcendental model" of contextual theology because in this model "what matters is not so much the content of what is written or spoken, but the authenticity of faith and cultural connectedness with which theology is done."[139] For him, the FABC's theology may use concepts and symbols that are not exclusively Asian, but it may still be considered as "authentically Asian" because it is the result of a "community which has striven to express Christian faith as an authentic cultural subject."[140] This view has the advantage of highlighting the sustained efforts of the Asian bishops in their dialogue with the cultures of Asia. However, a close reading of the documents shows that the FABC's theology displays the bolder features of a synthetic model, which incorporates the insights of three models of translation, anthropological, and praxis. First, at the Second Plenary Assembly the bishops state that the handing-on of the traditional values to present and future generations "calls for creative assimilation and 'translation' into contemporary cultural expression."[141] Secondly, this theology reveals an anthropological character in that it takes human culture as a theological resource

---

139   Stephen Bevans, "Inculturation of Theology in Asia," *Studia Missionalia* 45 (1996) 16.
140   Ibid.
141   FABC II, art. 10, *FAPA Vol. 1*, 31.

on a par with other sources of scripture and tradition.[142] Thirdly, it also shows major elements of a praxis model because, according the bishops, "doing the truth comes before the formulation of doctrine," and "Churches in Asia should not wait [for] a satisfactory theological answer before going further in praxis of dialogue and proclamation."[143] The bishops stress that it is "in this systematic reflection on sustained praxis that we discover what God is saying to the Churches."[144] In short, as the synthetic contextual model, the FABC's theology holds in balance four contextual elements of Gospel, tradition, culture, and social change in its ongoing dialogue with the cultures, the religions and the poor of Asia by way of a three-fold strategy of inculturation, interreligious dialogue, and liberation.

Liberation Theology

There is a close resemblance between the FABC's theological approach, which generally follows a "See, Judge, Act" process, and the method employed by Latin American liberation theologies,[145] which is based on "three mediations - socio-analytic, hermeneutical and practical."[146] In contrast to Western theologies which

---

142 OTC, "Methodology: Asian Christian Theology," arts. 3.1, *FAPA Vol. 3*, 356. Felix Wilfred uses "*anthropological*" to mean "cultural forms and expressions, patterns of thought and social relationship, ..." and "*theological*" to refer to "faith, mystery of the church, grace, ..." ("Inculturation as a Hermeneutical Question: Reflections in the Asian Context," *Vidyajyoti* 52 [September 1988] 424).

143 OE, "Church Issues in Asia in the Context of Evangelization, Dialogue and Proclamation," art. 53, *FAPA Vol. 2*, 205.

144 Ibid.

145 Christopher Rowland notes that "liberation theology is above all a new way of *doing* theology rather than being itself a new theology" ("Introduction: The Theology of Liberation," in *The Cambridge Companion to Liberation Theology*, edited by Christopher Rowland [Cambridge: Cambridge University Press, 1999] 3).

146 Peter C. Phan, "Method in Liberation Theologies," *Theological Studies* 61 (2000) 61. Clodovis Boff classifies the theological methodology of Latin American liberation theology into three mediations: social-analytic, hermeneutic, and practical, following more explicitly the "See, Judge, Act" model. See his book *Theology and Praxis: Epistemological Foundations* (Maryknoll, New York: Orbis, 1987). Peter C. Phan notes that Exposure-Immersion "corresponds to *praxis*," a concept understood by Boff as the fundamental *locus* of liberation theology, that is, "its point of departure, its milieu and its finality." See Peter C. Phan, "Human Development and Evangelization (The first to the sixth plenary assembly of the federation of Asian bishops' conferences)," *Studia Missionalia* 47 (1998) 213; Clodovis Boff, ibid., xxi. Phan equates socio-analytic mediation with "social analysis," hermeneutic mediation with "contemplation," and practical mediation with "pastoral planning" (Phan, ibid., 214).

deal with the challenges to faith posed by the non-believer, the locus of liberation theologies is the non-person, understood as the poor, the oppressed, the exploited, and the marginalised. By reflecting and expanding on two motifs of liberation, considered to be the best translation of salvation, and the preferential option for the poor, liberation theology is not just a "theology *about* the poor," but a "theology *for* the poor."[147] Francis Schüssler Fiorenza stresses this point observing that "the interpretation of experience as an experience of oppression is common to all liberation theologies."[148] Therefore, the key questions for liberation theologies are "how to proclaim God as Father in an inhuman world? and "how do we tell the 'non-persons' that they are the sons and daughters of God?"[149] In the context of Asia, Asian bishops seek to address problems and issues associated with, not only the massive poverty of the population, but also the plurality of soteriological religions and the diversity of local cultures.[150] Triple dialogue with these realities is the Asian bishops' theological and pastoral orientation.

Faith Seeking Dialogue

The theological concept of dialogue occupies a special place in the mind of the Asian Catholic Bishops right from their first Plenary Assembly held in 1974 to consider issues and strategies relating to the "Evangelization in Modern Day Asia".[151] This notion has permeated their entire corpus, and culminated in the coinage of the phrase "triple dialogue" or "three-fold dialogue" in the Sixth and

---

147   Peter Hebblethwaite, "Liberation Theology and the Roman Catholic Church," in *The Cambridge Companion to Liberation Theology*, edited by Christopher Rowland (Cambridge: Cambridge University Press, 1999) 179. The late doyen of Vaticanologists also notes that the phrase "option for the poor" was "first used in a letter from Pedro Arrupe to the Jesuits of Latin America in May 1968." See Ibid.

148   Francis Schüssler Fiorenza, "Systematic Theology: Task and Methods," in *Systematic Theology: Roman Catholic Perspectives*, vol. 1, ed. Francis Schüssler Fiorenza and John P. Galvin (Minneapolis: Fortress Press, 1992) 62.

149   G. Gutierrez, "The Task and Content of Liberation Theology," in *The Cambridge Companion to Liberation Theology*, edited by Christopher Rowland (Cambridge: Cambridge University Press, 1999) 28; see also Claude Geffré and Gustavo Gutiérez, "Editorial: A Prophetic Theology," *Concilium* 6:10 (June 1974) 10.

150   For Aloysius Pieris, the Asian Church and its theology must be baptised in the Jordan of Asian religion and on the cross of Asian poverty. See his two classics *An Asian Theology of Liberation* (Edinburgh: T&T Clark, 1998), and *Love Meets Wisdom: A Christian Experience of Buddhism* (Maryknoll, New York: Orbis Books, 1988.

151   FABC I, arts. 14–20, *FAPA Vol. 1*, 14–15.

Seventh Plenary Assembly.[152] The three-dimensional dialogue, social, religious, and cultural, is differentiated into four types: "dialogue of life, dialogue of deeds, dialogue of experts, and dialogue in sharing the experiences of faith."[153] For the bishops, dialogue is, first of all, a "dialogue of life"[154] where people collaborate to promote whatever leads to unity, love, truth, justice, and peace. True dialogue has to respond to the realities in Asia where the majority of people live in poverty, and should lead to "a genuine commitment and effort to bring about social justice" by seeking "the change and transformation of unjust social structures."[155] This dialogue is based "on the firm belief that the Holy Spirit is operative in other religions as well."[156] As "God is present and working through the Spirit in the whole of creation," Christians, together with people of other faiths, must endeavour to discover the transforming love of God and make it "a more living experience."[157] There is also dialogue with the Asian cultures, as the primary focus of evangelisation is to make "the message and life of Jesus truly incarnate in the minds and lives" of the people of Asia.[158] To meet the challenges of evangelisation, the Asian bishops follow the lead of Vatican II,[159] and use the "signs of the times methodology,"[160] to discern particular challenges of the times and formulate pastoral strategies and responses.[161] For them, "identifying and analysing the signs of the times" is the task of the Asian Churches if they want to discover

---

152 FABC VII, Part I, art. A8, *FAPA Vol. 3*, 4; FABC VI, art. 3, *FAPA Vol. 2*, 2.

153 BIRA IV/2, art. 8.5, *FAPA Vol. 1*, 253.

154 FABC I, art. 20, *FAPA Vol. 1*, 15; FABC III, art. 17.4, *FAPA Vol. 1*, 61; FABC IV, art. 3.1.11, *FAPA Vol. 1*, 181.

155 FABC I, art. 21, *FAPA Vol. 1*, 15.

156 BIRA IV/2, art. 5, *FAPA Vol. 1*, 253.

157 FABC, "International Congress on Mission: Workshop III: Dialogue with Other Religious Traditions in Asia," art. 3, *FAPA Vol. 1*, 141.

158 FABC I, art. 9, *FAPA Vol. 1*, 14.

159 *Gaudium et Spes* no. 4 affirms that "at all times the Church carries the responsibility of reading the signs of the time, and of interpreting them in the light of the Gospel." *Vatican Council II: The Conciliar and Post Conciliar Documents, Vol. 1*, ed. Austin Flannery, new rev. ed. (Northport, NY: Costello Publishing, 1996) 905; see also *Gaudium et Spes* no. 11. In a *Relatio* during the Council discussion of *Gaudium et Spes* Philippe Delhaye and F. Houtart define the signs of the times as "phenomena, which due to their generalization and great frequency, characterize an epoch, and through which present humankind expresses its needs and aspirations." Quoted in Felipe Gómez, "Signs of the Times," *East Asian Pastoral Review*, 3–4 (1989) 367.

160 James H. Kroeger, "Signs of the Times: A Thirty-year Panorama," *East Asian Pastoral Review* 2 (1989) 191–6.

161 FABC I, art. 5, *FAPA Vol. 1*, 13.

the path that God want them to follow.[162] The Church, they affirm, becomes truly inculturated when it decentres itself, is catholic in its concerns, appreciates the gifts of others, is ready to "work with others for a world at once more human and more divine," and stands with its "sisters and brothers of other faiths in confronting issues of life and death."[163] At their first Plenary Meeting in 1974, the bishops stressed that the primary focus of the evangelising mission was "the building up of the local church."[164] And building up a local Church means undertaking a threefold dialogue with the cultures (inculturation), the religions (interreligious dialogue) and the poor of Asia (liberation).[165] The local Church thus is called to be a community of dialogue to proclaim "Jesus Christ to their fellow humans in a dialogical manner."[166] This dialogical model, for the FABC, is "a new way of being Church"[167] in a continent marked by a diversity of religions and cultures, which in turn implies and requires an openness to theological pluralism.

Theological Pluralism

Indeed, in Asia, each local Church has to confront a different set of issues when it seeks to dialogue with its local cultures, religions and the poor. Their starting point for reflection on Christian faith is the variety of contextually conditioned experiences, which themselves dictate a theological pluralism. Since their first gathering in 1970 the Asian bishops have encouraged this pluralism in theology.[168] In their view, pluralism is a "positive and creative sign" that "unity is deeper than

---

162 ACMC, art. 20, *FAPA Vol. 1*, 71.

163 BIRA IV/12, arts. 49–50, *FAPA Vol. 1*, 333.

164 FABC I, art. 9, *FAPA Vol. 1*, 14.

165 For a comprehensive treatment of Asian theologies on this triple dialogue, namely inculturation, interreligious dialogue, and liberation, see Peter C. Phan's trilogy: *Christianity with an Asian Face: Asian American Theology in the Making* (Maryknoll, New York: Orbis Books, 2003); *In Our Own Tongues: Perspectives from Asia on Mission and Inculturation* (Maryknoll, New York: Orbis Books, 2003); and *Being Religious Interreligiously: Asian Perspectives on Interfaith Dialogue* (Maryknoll, New York: Orbis Books, 2004).

166 BIRA VI/12, art. 15, *FAPA Vol. 1*, 328; "Church Issues in Asia in the Context of Evangelization, Dialogue and Proclamation: Conclusions of the Theological Consultation, Thailand, 3–10 November 1991," art. 51, *FAPA Vol. 2*, 205.

167 BIRA IV/12, art. 48, *FAPA Vol. 1*, 332; "Church Issues in Asia in the Context of Evangelization, Dialogue and Proclamation: Conclusions of the Theological Consultation, Thailand, 3–10 November 1991," arts. 41–42, *FAPA Vol. 2*, 202–203.

168 OTC, "Methodology: Asian Christian Theology," art. 1.4, *FAPA Vol. 3*, 336.

whatever the concrete technical analysis or viewpoints might show."[169] "Pluralism also gives the advantageous value of complementarity."[170] The bishops affirm "a stance of *receptive pluralism*" recognising "the fact that people encounter the Spirit within their context, which is pluralistic in terms of religions, culture and worldviews" (italics in the original).[171] For them, "it is important to cultivate an all-embracing and complementary way of thinking," as it is "very characteristic of Asian traditions" to "consider the various dimensions of reality not as contradictory, but as complementary (yinyang)."[172] They also recognise the "insufficiency of current human expressions" of the Christian faith, and "such insufficiency allows for pluralism in theology."[173] In their view, diversity "represents richness and strength" and "the test of true harmony lies in the acceptance of diversity as richness."[174] Harmony, they affirm, embodies "the realities of order, well-being, justice and love as seen in human interaction."[175] They believe that "there is an Asian approach to reality, a world-view, wherein the whole is the sum-total of the web of relationships and interaction of the various parts with each other, in a word, *harmony*, a word which resonates with all Asian cultures."[176] According to the FABC, "one of the serious obstacles to harmony is the attitude of exclusivity," and "the failure to view the complementarity which exists between peoples, cultures, faiths, ideologies, world-visions, etc."[177] Therefore, they conclude that some of the common, national and regional problems that the nations of Asia face today are due to a lack of harmony.[178]

The FABC first discussed the theme of harmony in 1984, stating that "harmony seems to constitute in a certain sense the intellectual and affective, religious and artistic, personal and societal soul of both persons and institutions in Asia."[179] Hence, there is an imperative for a study in depth of the theology of harmony in the Asian context, which could lead to interreligious dialogue.[180] For the bishops,

---

169 Ibid. BISA II, art. 10, *FAPA Vol. 1*, 204.
170 Ibid.
171 BIRA IV, art. 16, *FAPA Vol. 1*, 261.
172 BIRA IV/11, art. 20, *FAPA Vol. 1*, 322.
173 OTC, "Methodology: Asian Christian Theology," art. 1.5, *FAPA Vol. 3*, 337.
174 Ibid., art. 15, *FAPA Vol. 1*, 321.
175 BIRA IV/10, art. 4, *FAPA Vol. 1*, 313–4.
176 TAC, "Asian Christian Perspectives on Harmony," art. 6, *FAPA Vol. 2*, 298.
177 BIRA IV/11, art. 20, *FAPA Vol. 1*, 322.
178 Ibid.
179 BIRA IV/1, art. 13, *FAPA Vol. 1*, 249.
180 BIRA IV/1, art. 13, *FAPA Vol. 1*, 249.

"scripture offers a pluriformity of models for harmony: Creation, Covenant, People of God, and Kingdom of God. Although all four models contain the dynamics of God's presence, the Kingdom of God is the core of Christ's proclamation and embodies the first three," and "provides the most action-oriented model for fostering harmony within society."[181] However the FABC stresses that "the promotion of harmony and commitment to action is not the preserve of the small Christian community of Asia."[182] As it is a common task, Christians should "strive for a holistic realization of harmony together with others," including the resources of other faiths to "achieve mutual enrichment."[183] The FABC is "committed to the emergence of the Asianness of the Church in Asia. This means that the Church has to be an embodiment of the Asian vision and values of life, especially interiority, harmony, a holistic and inclusive approach to every area of life."[184] It is clear, then, the transition from a Eurocentric theology to a plurality of theologies in an Asian context has taken place. In the process, it has started a "paradigm shift" in theology. Let us now look at the meaning and implications of this phrase by calling on the work of Hans Küng.

Paradigm Change

An international ecumenical symposium was held at the University of Tübingen in 1989, entitled "Paradigm Change in Theology". There, in the first of his papers, Hans Küng applies Thomas Kuhn's notion of paradigm shift to the whole of Christian theology.[185] Using the latter's definition of paradigm as "an entire constellation of beliefs, values, techniques, and so on shared by the members of a given community,"[186] Küng discusses parallels, differences, and analogies between paradigm changes in natural sciences and those occurring in theology, and endeavours to interpret the present theological situation in terms of paradigm changes.[187] He formulates five theses, the first of which postulates that the

---

181 BIRA IV/1, art. 6, *FAPA Vol. 1*, 314.
182 TAC, "Asian Christian Perspectives on Harmony," art. 6, *FAPA Vol. 2*, 298.
183 BIRA IV/10, art. 5, *FAPA Vol. 1*, 314.
184 FABC VII, Part III, FABC Papers No. 93.
185 Hans Küng, "Paradigm Change in Theology: A Proposal for Discussion," in *Paradigm Change in Theology: a Symposium for the Future*, ed. Hans Küng and David Tracy (New York: Crossroad, 1991) 3–33.
186 Thomas S. Kuhn, *The Structure of Scientific Revolutions*, 2nd ed, enlarged (Chicago: University of Chicago Press, 1970) 175.
187 Küng, "Paradigm Change in Theology: A Proposal for Discussion," 9, 11–29. Küng believes that the term "paradigm" can be ambiguous and prefers to use "interpretive

"theological community has a 'normal science' with its classical authors, text-books and teachers, which is characterised by a cumulative growth of knowl-edge, by a solution of remaining problems … and by resistance to everything that might result in a changing or replacement of the established paradigm."[188] His second thesis states that "in the theological community, awareness of a growing crisis is the starting point for the advent of a drastic change in certain hitherto prevailing basic assumptions and eventually causes the breakthrough of a new paradigm or model of understanding."[189] According to his third thesis, "an older paradigm or model of understanding is replaced when a new one is available."[190] In his fourth thesis, Küng argues that "… in the acceptance or rejection of a new paradigm, not only scientific, but extra-scientific factors are involved, so that the transition to a new model cannot be purely rationally extorted [sic], but may be described as a conversion."[191] His fifth thesis states that "… it can be predicted with difficulty, in the midst of great controversies, whether a new paradigm is absorbed into the old, replaces the old or is shelved for a long period. But if it is accepted, innovation is consolidated as tradition."[192]

Küng firmly believes that a paradigm change does not involve a total break, and "in every paradigm change, despite all discontinuity, there is a fundamental continuity."[193] He contends that "every paradigm change shows at the same time continuity and discontinuity, rationality and irrationality, conceptual stability and conceptual change, evolutionary and revolutionary elements."[194] In his view, the tradition is not recovered but formulated anew in light of a new paradigm.[195]

---

models, explanatory models, models for understanding (*Verstehensmodelle*)," ibid., 7. He employs the terms "paradigm" and "model" interchangeably, ibid., 10.

188 Ibid., 14. According to Küng, the theological community includes "scholars and non-scholars, theologians at a university or in a basic community, professional writers or laity." See "A New Basic Model for Theology: Divergences and Convergences," in *Paradigm Change in Theology: a Symposium for the Future*, ed. Hans Küng and David Tracy (New York: Crossroad, 1991) 443.

189 Küng, "Paradigm Change in Theology: A Proposal for Discussion," 20.

190 Ibid., 23.

191 Ibid., 27. Küng contends that a new paradigm demands something like a conversion, or a new conviction, in the recipients who have to decide for or against. Convincing objective reasons are important for a conversion but in the last resort it is a question of trust. Ibid., 25.

192 Ibid., 28.

193 Ibid., 29.

194 Ibid., 30.

195 Ibid.

In his second contribution Küng attempts to *"periodize* the paradigm change in theology and the church,"[196] and identifies the underlying consensus that exists in each of these periods through and within their differences in theological approaches and methodologies. For him, *"several* theologies are possible within a *single* paradigm."[197]

In the third presentation at the symposium on paradigm change Küng explains that a paradigm develops and matures slowly in a matrix of varying social, political, ecclesial and theological factors, and that it "includes not merely gradual but also drastic changes."[198] For theology, an important criterion for a new paradigm is the capacity to be aware of crises and to cope with them.[199]

According to Küng, "the paradigm theory is no more than a hermeneutical framework."[200] He concludes that it is possible to reach a basic hermeneutical consensus despite all our theological differences and divergences, and that a number of different theologies can co-exist within the one post-Enlightenment, postmodern paradigm of a Christian theology.[201]

---

196 Hans Küng, "What Does a Change of Paradigm Mean?" in *Paradigm Change in Theology: a Symposium for the Future*, ed. Hans Küng and David Tracy (New York: Crossroad, 1991) 212–9. In an earlier work, Küng identifies six *"macro paradigms or epochal global constellations"* in the history of Christianity: "1. the Jewish-apocalytic paradigm of early Christianity; 2. the ecumenical-Hellenistic paradigm of Christian Antiquity; 3. the Roman Catholic paradigm of the Middle Ages; 4. the Protestant-Evangelical paradigm of the Reformation; 5. the modern paradigm of reason and progress; 6. the ecumenical paradigm of post-modernity" ("Islam: Radical Changes in History – Challenges of the Present," *Concilium* 5 [2005] 98). For Claude Geffré, "we are experiencing a *theological turning-point* that is inspired by a new paradigm, that of religious pluralism," even though, in his view, the word paradigm is "undoubtedly too strong to describe the major changes going on within the Christian thought" ("The Crisis of Christian Identity in an Age of Religious Pluralism," *Concilium* 3 [2005] 17).

197 Hans Küng, "What Does a Change of Paradigm Mean?" in *Paradigm Change in Theology: a Symposium for the Future*, ed. Hans Küng and David Tracy (New York: Crossroad, 1991) 215.

198 Hans Küng, "A New Basic Model for Theology: Divergencies and Convergencies," in *Paradigm Change in Theology: a Symposium for the Future*, ed. Hans Küng and David Tracy (New York: Crossroad, 1991) 439–452.

199 Ibid., 444–5.

200 Ibid., 452. See also Hans Küng, "Islam: Radical Changes in History – Challenges of the Present," *Concilium* 5 (2005) 98.

201 Ibid., 451.

In 1970, when 180 Asian bishops met for the first time around Pope Paul VI in Manila, they described the situation in Asia as "grave crises," and sought to discover new ways through which they may be of greater and more effective service to both Catholic communities and other people.[202] They stressed the necessity of the triple dialogue with the religions, the cultures and the poor, and this marked the beginning of a paradigm shift in the Catholic theological refection in Asia.[203] From this momentous meeting the FABC's theological project has gradually matured and become a well-developed theology which originally started with a recognition that Asian Churches were facing a crisis.[204] This fact seems to confirm Hans Küng's contention that an important criterion for a new paradigm is the capacity to be aware of crises and to cope with them.[205] The FABC's theology also does not represent a total break with the tradition as its documents constantly refer to the teachings of Vatican II and papal magisterium. Küng has stressed this point arguing that "in every paradigm change, despite all discontinuity, there is a fundamental continuity."[206] At this stage, it is still too early to assess the full impact of this paradigm shift on the Asian Churches, however, signs of this change have been identified as local Churches and their members continue to be challenged to reinvent themselves.

Concluding Remarks

This chapter has discussed the imperative of contextualisation in theology highlighting the dynamics between *traditum* as the deposit of faith and *tradendum* as the duty to communicate the Christian message in a manner that is sensitive to a particular context. As a contextual theology par excellence, the FABC's theology, while displaying several characteristics of the transcendental model, is best understood in terms of the synthetic model, which incorporates the salient features of all three models of anthropological, praxis, and translation, and hence keeps in balance four key elements of contextual theology, viz. Gospel, tradition, culture and social change. Underlying the FABC's theological methodologies

---

202 "Asian Bishops' Meeting," art. 1, *FAPA Vol. 1*, 3.
203 "Asian Bishops' Meeting," *FAPA Vol. 1*, 3–10.
204 FABC II, art. 9, *FAPA Vol. 1*, 31.
205 Hans Küng, "A New Basic Model for Theology: Divergencies and Convergencies," in *Paradigm Change in Theology: a Symposium for the Future*, ed. Hans Küng and David Tracy (New York: Crossroad, 1991) 444–5; Küng, "Paradigm Change in Theology: A Proposal for Discussion," 20.
206 Ibid. 29.

is a pastoral and contextual process, which consists of an exposure to and an analysis of contextual realities (See), a reflection and discernment in light of the Gospel and tradition (Judge), and a planning of responses and concrete actions (Act). This contextual methodology translates into the Asian Integral Pastoral Approach, or "communion process," to address the needs and aspirations of basic ecclesial communities and lay people in the Church. Theology, the bishops of Asia insist, must be a service to life.

Taken as a whole, the FABC's theology constitutes a theological "event" for the Churches in Asia, and its impact on the Asian Church and Asian Christians continues to be more discernible. While the transition from one paradigm to the next is not always clear-cut, there are increasing signs that the FABC's theology, as faith seeking triple dialogue, has instituted a paradigm change in theological reflection as the bishops reflect and respond to the growing crisis inherent in the Asian *Sitz-im-Leben*. As this theology is still evolving, it is difficult to encapsulate it in an encompassing framework of understanding. However, it is possible to make some preliminary observations as to its major features. As an Asian contextual theology, it has a predominantly pastoral and missionary orientation, aims to build up the local Church, is liberative, prophetic, and committed to all things human, encourages a theological pluralism, and has harmony as a goal. But, first and foremost, it is both a faith seeking understanding through discerning the signs of the times, and a faith intent on engaging in a triple dialogue with the cultures, the religions and the poor of Asia.

Chapter 4 Features of the Fabc's Theology of the Laity

Lay people have always played a vital role in the life and activity of the Church, but never become so much a subject of theological reflection as it is today. In Asia, where Christians are only a tiny minority, their vocation and mission have been one of the primary concerns in the mind of the Asian Bishops who have devoted an entire plenary assembly to the subject and regularly reflected on its themes in the overall context of evangelisation.[1] Indeed, for them, the age of lay people has dawned upon the Churches in Asia.[2] In this chapter we will examine the distinctive concept and role of lay people in the documents of the Asian bishops, and provide a detailed analysis of the elements and developments of their theology of the laity from 1970 to 2012.[3] We will emphasise the centrality of the concept of "priesthood of life,"[4] and argue that there is both fundamental continuity and gradual development in the FABC's theology of the laity. Specifically, in the first section, we examine the identity of lay people, their vocation, mission, ministries, and spirituality. We also summarise the FABC's theology of the laity in an ecosystem to highlight its key tenets and theological approach in the context of the challenges of Asia. In the second section, we discuss the development of the FABC's theology of the laity over a forty-two year period from

---

1 FABC IV, *FAPA Vol. 1*, 177–198. At the "First Asian Laity Meeting" held in 1994, the FABC observed that "there has been a deepened awareness of the vital role of the laity in the life and mission of the Church in the last 30 years." OL, "The Commitment of the Laity in the Church's Mission with Special Reference to Implementing the Social Teachings: Final Report on the First Asian Laity Meeting," *FAPA Vol. 2*, 119; [FABC], "Final Statement of the First Asian Laity Meeting," in *The First Asian Laity Meeting: 4–9 September 1994, Korea*, [edited by] Pontifical Council for the Laity, Federation of Asian Bishops' Conferences Office of Laity, [and] Catholic Lay Apostolate Council of Korea, ([Seoul]: Pontifical Council for the Laity, Federation of Asian Bishops' Conferences Office of Laity, Catholic Lay Apostolate Council of Korea, 1994) 255. The Asian bishops acknowledge that "the contribution by countless numbers of the laity to the life of faith among the People of God in Asia cannot be measured." FABC IV, art. 2.4, *FAPA Vol. 1*, 179.
2 OL, "Fifth East Asian Regional Laity Meeting," art. 1.3, *FAPA Vol. 3*, 93.
3 This analysis is based on the documents of the FABC published in the five volumes of *For All the Peoples of Asia*, covering the period from 1970 to 2012.
4 FABC IV, art. 4.4.2, *FAPA Vol. 1*, 192.

1970 to 2012. Besides a brief explanation of the terminologies and concepts used in the organisation and synthesis of its thought, this chapter is largely based on the FABC's own statements.

Elements of the FABC's Theology of the Laity

Of all the documents of the FABC that deal with the question of laity and ministries, the statements of the Fourth Plenary Assembly on "The Vocation and Mission of the Laity in the Church and the World of Asia," held from 16 to 29 September 1986, and the conclusions of the 1977 "Asian Colloquium on Ministries in the Church" provide the most comprehensive treatment of these topics.[5] Therefore, focusing on these two statements, this section will discuss the identity of the laity, their vocation, mission, ministries, and spirituality.

Identity of the Laity

In their official statements the FABC tends to use the terms "we," "us," or "our" to refer, first, to the participants in the various gatherings,[6] second, to the bishops themselves,[7] and third, to the entire people of God including bishops, priests, religious, and lay people.[8] They often make this fourfold distinction of bishops, priests, religious and laity, though not always following this order, in the introductory paragraphs of their statements.[9] This is not the case with the first "Asian Bishops'

---

5 FABC IV, *FAPA Vol. 1*, 177–98; ACMC, *FAPA Vol. 1*, 67–92.

6 For example, "We, the participants of the Third Assembly of the Federation of Asian Bishops' Conferences ...." FABC III, art. 1, *FAPA Vol. 1*, 55; "We, the participants of the first Bishops' Institute for the Lay Apostolate ...." BILA I, art. 1, *FAPA Vol. 1*, 235; "... we, the delegates to BILA III – bishops, priests, religious and lay people ...." BILA III, art. 13, *FAPA Vol. 1*, 245.

7 For example, in the final statements of the Fourth Plenary Assembly, the FABC writes: "Therefore, we bishops of Asia have come together ... with laity, Religious and priests .... The gathering of ours with the laity ...." See FABC IV, arts. 2.1–2.2, *FAPA Vol. 1*, 178; "We wish now to communicate to you the reflections that the laity, Religious and priests have shared with us ..." FABC IV, art. 4.8.2, *FAPA Vol. 1*, 195; BIBA II, *FAPA Vol. 3*, 231.

8 For example, "the call for us Asian Christians ...." FABC IV, art. 4.1.3, *FAPA Vol. 1*, 191; "In a Church of communion, we, clergy as well as laity, ..." FABC IV, art. 4.7.1.1., *FAPA Vol. 1*, 194.

9 FABC IV, art. 2.1, *FAPA Vol. 1*, 178; FABC V, art. 1.1, *FAPA Vol. 1*, 274; FABC VI, art. 1, *FAPA Vol. 2*, 1; see also the footnote to the Introduction of FABC VII, *FAPA Vol. 3*, 1.

Meeting" in 1970 around Pope Paul VI, and the plenary assemblies held in 1974 and 1978, which identify the participants by the use of phrases such as "we, the bishops of Asia,"[10] "we, Bishops-delegate,"[11] and "we, the Bishops-delegate."[12] The Third Plenary Assembly in 1982 simply uses the words "we, the participants,"[13] to acknowledge the contributions of other attendees besides the bishops.

Indeed, a list of concerns raised by people attending the various workshops held in conjunction with this Plenary Assembly is accepted as an integral part of its final statements.[14] The laity as participants in a plenary assembly are explicitly mentioned in relation to the Fourth Plenary Assembly, immediately after the bishops, and followed by religious and priests in this order, no doubt implying the canonical lay status of the majority of the religious.[15] The Asian bishops employ the words "laity," "lay people," and their cognates to emphasise lay roles and responsibilities.[16] Yet, to date they have not provided an explicit definition of the laity. Rather, they have described lay people in the context of the whole community rooted in Asian realities, and stressed that it is in the Christian communities that people experience that they belong, and that "together they are the Church."[17]

For the Asian bishops, the sacraments of baptism and confirmation are the gateway to Christian discipleship and Church membership.[18] Discussing the messianic

---

10 ABM, art. 1, *FAPA Vol. 1*, 3.

11 FABC I, art. 1, *FAPA Vol. 1*, 12.

12 FABC II, art. 1, *FAPA Vol. 1*, 29.

13 FABC III, art. 1, *FAPA Vol. 1*, 53.

14 FABC III, "The 'Syllabus of Concerns' of the Plenary Assembly," *FAPA Vol. 1*, 63.

15 FABC IV, art. 2.1, *FAPA Vol. 1*, 178. Lay people's participation in various Bishops' Institutes was acknowledged much earlier than FABC IV, e.g., BISA III in 1975, art. 1, *FAPA Vol. 1*, 207; BIMA I in 1978, art. 1, *FAPA Vol. 1*, 93; BIRA III in 1982, art. 1, *FAPA Vol. 1*, 119. Here the FABC seems to adopt the definition of the 1983 Code of Canon Law (Canon 207), which defines the laity as the Christian faithful (*Christifideles*) who are not in holy orders: "By divine institution, among Christ's faithful there are in the Church sacred ministers, who in law are also called clerics; the others are called lay people." See *The Code of Canon Law*, new revised English Translation, prepared by the Canon Law Society of Great Britain and Ireland in association with the Canon Law Society of Australia and New Zealand and the Canadian Canon Law Society (London: HarperCollins, 1997) 44.

16 There are numerous instances in the Statement of the Fourth Plenary Assembly which discusses the vocation and mission of the laity in the Church and in the world. See also "The Role of the Lay Faithful," FABC V, art. 5.0, *FAPA Vol. 1*, 282; "Ministries of Lay People," in ACMC, art. 54, *FAPA Vol. 1*, 78.

17 FABC V, arts. 3.3.3, *FAPA Vol. 1*, 281.

18 FABC IV, art. 4.8.6, *FAPA Vol. 1*, 197.

functions of lay people in the Asian context at the Fourth Plenary Assembly the bishops give an implicit description of the laity by making three interrelated distinctions in three successive paragraphs. First, with reference to the priestly function, the clergy are distinguished from the people of God in general, the faithful, the Christian disciple, and all Christians.[19] Second, in the framework of the prophetic office a distinction is drawn between the hierarchy and the whole community or people of God, and, between the leadership of the Church and the believing community or people of God.[20] Third, within the ambit of the royal function a clear and specific distinction is made between the leadership and the laity, while comparing their respective roles in the building up of the kingdom.[21] These dual references are presented in a tabular form in Figure 1 showing their hermeneutical polarity.[22] Viewed together, they approximate to a descriptive definition of the laity.

Figure 1:

Priestly Function	Clergy	as distinct from	People of God, the Faithful, the Christian Disciple, all Christians
Prophetic Function	Hierarchy, Leadership	as distinct from	Whole Community, People of God, the Believing Community
Royal Function	Leadership	as distinct from	The Laity

19 FABC IV, art. 4.4.2, *FAPA Vol. 1*, 192.
20 FABC IV, art. 4.4.3, *FAPA Vol. 1*, 193.
21 FABC IV, art. 4.4.4, *FAPA Vol. 1*, 193.
22 For Kenan B. Osborne, hermeneutical polarity means that "one term cannot be understood without its correlative term." See "The Meaning of Lay, Laity and Lay Ministry in the Christian Theology of Church," *Antonianum* 63 (1988) 240. We note that in these comparative paragraphs the FABC did not mention the words "priest" or "religious" explicitly, but prefer to use the generic terms of clergy, hierarchy, and leadership. It is also worthwhile to recall Peter C. Phan's insightful remarks on the distinction between the identity and mission of a layperson, a religious, and a member of the hierarchy based on their basic relationship with Christ, the Church, and the world. In his view, "each of these three categories enacts the mystery of Christ in the Church and in the world in a way distinct and appropriate to its state.... In the priestly state the Church and its *transcendent-mediating* mission is symbolized and realized; in the religious state the Church and its *transcendent-eschatological* mission is symbolized and realized; and in the state of the laity the Church and its *incarnating-recapitulating* mission is signified and realized. It is the same mission of being the sacrament of Christ in the world that is represented, manifested and made visible in three different states of life." See "Possibility of a Lay Spirituality: a Re-examination of some Theological Presuppositions," *Communio* 10:4 (1983) 384.

According to the bishops of Asia, lay people are "Asian Christians,"[23] "disciples of Christ,"[24] "full-fledged members"[25] of the Church, "mature subjects and persons with dignity and freedom, with their gifts and powers as well as rights and responsibilities."[26] Sometimes they employ the terms "Christ's faithful"[27] and "Christians" to mean lay people, and also use "Christians" and "Christian laity" interchangeably.[28] At their First Asian Laity Meeting held in 1994 they referred to the laity as "Asian citizens and Christians."[29] The laity's Christian identity, formed by the following of Jesus, is rooted in the realities of Asia,[30] the world's exploited market place, a theatre of conflict and division, a continent of suffering humanity, and at the same time, a cradle of ancient cultures, a birthplace of great religions, and a continent awakening to new challenges and responsibilities.[31] In particular, several challenges of Asia are mentioned, namely, politics, the youth of Asia, Asian women, the family, the world of education, mass media, the world of work, social responsibilities in the world of business, and health services.[32] They are the signs of the times that the Churches in Asia must discern and respond in faith to discover the vocation and mission of the laity.[33]

---

23 FABC IV, art. 4.1.3, *FAPA Vol. 1*, 191.
24 FABC IV, arts. 4.3.1, 4.1.3, *FAPA Vol. 1*, 191.
25 FABC IV, art. 4.5.1, *FAPA Vol. 1*, 193.
26 FABC IV, art. 4.2.2, *FAPA Vol. 1*, 192.
27 OL, "Second Asian Integral Pastoral Approach (AsIPA) General Assembly II, art. 4.3, *FAPA Vol. 3*, 111.
28 South Asia Bishops' Meeting, "Christian Response to the Phenomenon of Violence in South Asia," art. 7, *FAPA Vol. 2*, 16.
29 OL, "The Commitment of the Laity in the Church's Mission with Special Reference to Implementing the Social Teachings: Final Report on the First Asian Laity Meeting," *FAPA Vol. 2*, 119; [FABC], "Final Statement of the First Asian Laity Meeting," in *The First Asian Laity Meeting: 4–9 September 1994, Korea*, edited by Pontifical Council for the Laity, Federation of Asian Bishops' Conferences Office of Laity, [and] Catholic Lay Apostolate Council of Korea ([Seoul]: Pontifical Council for the Laity, Federation of Asian Bishops' Conferences Office of Laity, Catholic Lay Apostolate Council of Korea, 1994) 255.
30 FABC IV, arts. 4.8.2–4.8.3, *FAPA Vol. 1*, 195.
31 FABC IV, art. 3, *FAPA Vol. 1*, 179–191.
32 FABC IV, art. 1.1, *FAPA Vol. 1*, 178.
33 FABC IV, art. 4.0.1, *FAPA Vol. 1*, 191.

Vocation and Mission of the Laity

According to the FABC, Asian Christians, both laity and clergy, are called to a communion with Jesus and a communion of liberation.[34] In the Asian context, their vocation is to form a community of disciples, committed to Jesus the Liberator and united in the service of liberation.[35] As a liberating community they are called to move beyond the confines of their passive *modus vivendi* and become actively involved in the life and activity of the Church in response to the dynamic challenges of the world.[36] Only when the Churches become truly Asian, rooted in the peoples of Asia and in solidarity with their everyday life, is their bond of liberation strengthened.[37] Indeed, in the Church and in the world of Asia, lay people are called to "live their discipleship" of Jesus by living the common priesthood of the faithful, which is the real "priesthood of life," shared by all Christians.[38] They have assumed and continue to play a central role in the evangelising mission, and are called to share in Christ's mission according to their proper lay state in the Church.[39] Their call to holiness and consequently to the mission of the Church, is a demand of their Christian identity, which is based on their baptismal incorporation into Christ and in the Eucharist.[40] Facing an uncertain and challenging future in Asia the Asian bishops have turned to Jesus Christ to renew their vision of the mission of the Church.[41]

For the FABC, there are three priorities of mission.[42] Evangelisation is the highest priority in the mission of the Church followed by the imperative to serve the kingdom of God and the social question.[43] Evangelisation is a complex

---

34 FABC IV, arts. 4.1–4.2, *FAPA Vol. 1*, 191.
35 FABC IV, arts. 4.1.1–4.1.3, *FAPA Vol. 1*, 191.
36 FABC IV, art. 4.2.1, *FAPA Vol. 1*, 192.
37 FABC IV, art. 4.1.3, *FAPA Vol. 1*, 191.
38 FABC IV, arts. 4.8.8, 4.4.2, *FAPA Vol. 1*, 197 and 192 respectively. Following Marie de la Trinité, H.M. Nicholas, and H.U. von Balthasar, G. Chantraine prefers to use the term personal priesthood of the faithful—"sacerdoce *personnel* des fidèles"—rather than the common priesthood, because through the common priesthood the faithful become "fils dans le Fils et ainsi personne" ("Le laïc à l'intérieur des missions divines," *Nouvelle Revue Théologique* 109 [1987] 341).
39 OE, "Evangelization among the Indigenous Peoples of Asia," *FAPA Vol. 2*, 213; FABC IV, art. 4.8.8, *FAPA Vol. 1*, 197.
40 BILA III, art. 6, *FAPA Vol. 1*, 244.
41 ACMC, art. 21, *FAPA Vol. 1*, 71.
42 ACMC, art. 15, *FAPA Vol. 1*, 70.
43 ACMC, arts. 16–8, *FAPA Vol. 1*, 70.

reality, encompassing many aspects such as "witnessing to the Gospel, working for the values of the Kingdom, struggling along with those who strive for justice and peace, dialogue, sharing, inculturation, mutual enrichment with other Christians and the followers of all religions."[44] Its ultimate goal is the ushering in and establishment of God's kingdom, namely God's rule in the hearts and minds of people.[45] In this mission of the Church, lay people have their own assignment.[46] Indeed, they play a vital and irreplaceable role in the evangelising mission by proclaiming Jesus Christ through their life, work, and words.[47] This proclamation, the centre and primary element of "*the grace and task of evangelisation*," is strengthened and supported in Christian families, which make up the people of God.[48] The evangelising mission of the Church has become more urgent and decisive, and it needs to be actualised and contextualised in the Asian realities.[49] Therefore, Asian Churches must discern the signs of the times as signs addressed to them by Jesus, and as signs of the Spirit's active presence in the world.[50] In the context of Asian societies, the mission of the Church, and hence of the laity, is Christ-centred, kingdom-focused, world-oriented, dialogical and liberative.

In this section we will begin with a brief explanation of these concepts, and return to explore them in detail in subsequent paragraphs. First, in the context of the statements of the Fourth Plenary Assembly, Christ-centred means that the disciples follow and reproduce Jesus in their lives, and in particular, in His threefold office of Priest, Prophet and King. As the Asian bishops employ the terms "messianic mission" and "messianic functions" only in the statements of the Fourth Plenary Assembly, and make an explicit reference to the triple mission of Jesus in the context of liberation,[51] it seems likely that they want to employ these terms in a Christological sense to emphasise the meaning of the Hebrew word *messiah*, or the Greek equivalent *christos*, which means "the anointed," a title applied to various figures in the Old Testament, especially, priests, prophets, and

---

44 BIMA IV, art. 5, *FAPA Vol. 1*, 292.

45 BIMA IV, art. 5, *FAPA Vol. 1*, 292.

46 BILA III, art. 2, *FAPA Vol. 1*, 243.

47 BIMA IV, art. 10, *FAPA Vol. 1*, 293.

48 BIMA IV, art. 6, *FAPA Vol. 1*, 292; BIMA III, art. 5, *FAPA Vol. 1*, 104; BIMA III, art. 6, *FAPA Vol. 1*, 104.

49 ACMC, art. 24, *FAPA Vol. 1*, 71–2.

50 ACMC, art. 21, *FAPA Vol. 1*, 71.

51 FABC IV, art. 4.3, 4.4, *FAPA Vol. 1*, 192.

kings.[52] Second, the phrase "Kingdom of God," or the more biblical concept of reign of God, has often been used interchangeably, in an anthropological, ethical, and historical sense to stress the duty of the Christian community to infuse the world with the values of the kingdom, such as "justice, peace, love, compassion, equality and brotherhood."[53] Third, the term "world" encompasses the familial, social, professional, political, economic, religious, and cultural spheres.[54] Fourth, the concept of "dialogue" is a leitmotiv that underlies the entire corpus of the FABC's literature, and it has a threefold orientation: dialogue with cultures (inculturation),[55] dialogue with religions (interreligious dialogue) and dialogue

52 Citing L. Schick's study into the origin and use of the threefold ministry schema, Hervi Rikhof notes that this framework "has been used Christologically in order to explain the name 'Christ'. This use occurred in the patristic period and the Middle Ages and can be found in the *Catechismus Romanus* of the Council of Trent. It was also used in the context of the doctrine of redemption to express the functions of Christ." See "'The Competence of Priests, Prophets and Kings: Ecclesiological Reflections about the Power and Authority of Christian Believers," *Concilium* 197 (1988) 58. For Donald J. Goergen, the threefold ministry approach has "a biblical basis in the naming and proclamation of Jesus as the Messiah. As the 'Anointed One of Israel', Jesus sums up within himself all the anointed ones of Israel. The prophets (1 Kgs 19:16); Sir 48:8), the priests (Exod 29:7; Lev 8:10), and the kings (1 Sam 10:1; 16:12–13) were anointed messiahs in the sense in which that would have been understood early in Israelite history.... There is a theological sense in which Jesus as Messiah came to be understood as having incorporated into his ministry dimensions of priesthood, prophecy, and kingship" ("Priest, Prophet, King: The Ministry of Jesus Christ," in *The Theology of Priesthood*, edited by Donald J. Goergen and Ann Garrido [Collegeville, Minn.: The Liturgical Press, 2000] 190). It is worth noting that, according I. De La Potterie, in the New Testament there was no connection between the theme of anointment and the title of "Christ" (anointed), and "le véritable et, en un sens, l'unique contexte où le Nouveau Testament parle de l'onction du Christ, c'est celui du baptême." See "L'onction du Christ," *Nouvelle Revue Théologique* 80 (1958) 251, 250 respectively. In his view, the explanation of the name of "Christ" by way of the threefold ministry was the result of a later theology (la théologie postérieure). Ibid., 250–1.
53 FABC V, art. 1.7, *FAPA Vol. 2*, 275; FABC IV, arts. 3.1.2, 3.2.3, 4.8.7, *FAPA Vol. 1*, 180, 182, 196.
54 FABC IV, art. 4.8.7–8, *FAPA Vol. 1*, 196–7.
55 Peter Schineller makes a helpful remark that "inculturation takes seriously the *who*, the *where*, the *with whom* and *for whom* one does theology and one builds church. In fact, the local community ideally should become the maker of theology, a theology that is in dialogue with the larger Church, but one that speaks God's word for that particular cultural situation" ("Inculturation as the Pilgrimage to Catholicity," *Concilium* 204 [August 1989] 99).

with the poor (development and liberation). Finally, the liberative feature, which is associated with social justice and social change, implies the idea of transforming the world, and the structures of injustice and economic dependence that oppress the poor people in Asia.[56] This brief overview of the main characteristics of lay mission will serve as a preamble to the following presentation of the FABC's view on the role of the Asian laity.

First, the Asian bishops remind Christian communities that Jesus envisions his mission as priestly, prophetic and pastoral,[57] and he is the messianic leader who leads the Church in the journey to liberation.[58] In this journey of life, it is the duty of all Christian disciples to reproduce Christ in their life by sharing his vision, adopting his behaviour, and sustaining themselves through his word and sacraments.[59] They actualise their baptismal discipleship by exercising the triple function in the concrete realities of Asia.[60] Indeed, in the Asian context, it is an urgent task of the whole people of God, including the clergy, to live the common priesthood of the faithful by reproducing in everyday life the mysteries of Jesus' suffering, death and resurrection.[61] The prophetic function is a witness and a service of the whole community to the saving truth of Christ, and not just limited to the teaching function of the hierarchy.[62] The pastoral function, which is intimately linked to the baptismal priesthood of life, is to be understood as the duty of the entire community to build up the kingdom of God, and not only as the basis for the hierarchy's ministry of governance.[63]

This pastoral focus on the kingdom of God is the second feature of the mission of lay people in the documents of the FABC, who affirm that the laity participate in their own way in the building up of the kingdom through their actions

---

56 The editors of International Catholic Weekly *The Tablet* note that "social justice has a long Catholic pedigree, with the term first coined by the Jesuit Luigi Taparelli in the 1840s, and later being expressed more fully in Leo XIII's encyclical *Rerum Novarum*, in which he emphasised that society should be based on cooperation rather than class conflict." See "Towards Justice and Dignity," *The Tablet* (30 September 2006) 2.
57 FABC IV, art. 4.3.1, *FAPA Vol. 1*, 192.
58 Ibid., art. 4.3.1, 4.4.1, *FAPA Vol. 1*, 192.
59 Ibid., art. 4.3.1, *FAPA Vol. 1*, 192.
60 FABC IV, art. 4.3.1, *FAPA Vol. 1*, 192; Office of Laity and the Catholic Council of Lay Organizations in Thailand, "The Role of the Laity in Church Mission in South East Asia with Special Emphasis on Implementing the Church's Social Teachings," *FAPA Vol. 2*, 130.
61 FABC IV, art. 4.4.2, *FAPA Vol. 1*, 192.
62 Ibid., art. 4.4.3, *FAPA Vol. 1*, 193.
63 Ibid., art. 4.4.4, *FAPA Vol. 1*, 193.

within and outside the Church.[64] In the fast changing societies of Asia, lay people are called to actively participate in the mission of the Church by being both a sign of the reign of God and a leaven in the world.[65] Their mode of mission may vary depending on the social context, but fundamentally, it is a mission of triple dialogue by "witnessing to the values of the Gospel, in order to make the reign of God present in a non-Christian milieu, in secularised society, and especially in places where so much misery and poverty abound."[66] This focus on the kingdom provides new insights into the mission of the laity in the world.[67]

Indeed, the third feature of the mission of lay people is its orientation to the world, a term which encompasses the familial, social, professional, and political dimensions of human life.[68] For the bishops, lay apostolate still remains "parish-oriented, inward-looking and priest-directed."[69] Therefore, it has to change its focus and become "outward – and forward – looking" due to the demand of Asian realities.[70] As an inward-looking community does not fulfil its mission,[71] lay people should initiate and direct newer forms of lay ministries in response to the needs of the local situation.[72]

Fourthly, in the theology of the FABC, the mission and ministries of lay people are linked to the triple dialogue with the cultures (inculturation), the religions (interreligious dialogue) and the poor of Asia (liberation/human development).[73] Dialogue is their mode of mission because their discipleship is rooted in Christ, in the community, and in the Asian context.[74] It is understood as a dialogue of

---

64 Ibid.
65 Ibid., art. 2.4, *FAPA Vol. 1*, 179.
66 BILA III, art. 7, *FAPA Vol. 1*, 244.
67 FABC IV, art. 4.4.4, *FAPA Vol. 1*, 193.
68 FABC IV, art. 4.8.8, *FAPA Vol. 1*, 197.
69 Ibid., art. 4.6.2, *FAPA Vol. 1*, 193.
70 Ibid., arts. 4.3.2, 4.6.2, *FAPA Vol. 1*, 192–4.
71 BILA III, art. 6.9, *FAPA Vol. 1*, 237.
72 FABC IV, art. 4.6.2, *FAPA Vol. 1*, 194.
73 FABC I, arts. 12–24, *FAPA Vol. 1*, 14–6; FABC VII, Part I.A.8, Part III, *FAPA Vol. 3*, 4, 8. Jacques Dupuis reminds us that "interreligious dialogue was hardly spoken of before the Second Vatican Council" ("The Church's Evangelizing Mission in the Context of Religious Pluralism," *The Pastoral Review* 1:1 [2005] 20). For Francis A. Sullivan, "John Paul II is the first pope to recognize interreligious dialogue as a 'part' and 'expression' of the Church's evangelization" ("The Evangelizing Mission of the Church," in *The Gift of the Church: A Textbook on Ecclesiology in Honour of Patrick Granfield*, edited by Peter C. Phan [Collegeville, Minn.: The Liturgical Press, 2000] 241).
74 BILA on Women II, art. 3.2, *FAPA Vol. 3*, 75.

life as they witness to Christ in their cultural environment, their religious traditions, and their socio-economic situation.[75] A commitment to cultural and interreligious dialogue, coupled with a preferential, but not exclusive, option for the poor, is a major thrust of the lay mission.[76] Inculturation, interreligious dialogue, and the preferential option for the poor are part and parcel of any Church's activity.[77] Together with proclamation they are just different aspects of one reality.[78] These ministries should be world-oriented and channelled to address the priorities of human development and promotion of justice in the region, and not just limited to Church-oriented functions.[79]

Finally, the FABC affirms that Asian Christians are called to become the instruments of Jesus in his work of liberation.[80] But to become effective agents of liberation they will need to activate the spiritual character and functions received through baptism.[81] They also must act as an evangelising and liberating force in the struggle for the fullness of life,[82] which involves the task of transforming the Asian realities in order to build up the kingdom of God.[83]

To fulfil this mission, local Churches have to discover their own types and structures of ministry that are suitable for their context.[84] At the Asian Colloquium on Ministries in the Church held in 1977, the FABC discussed ways to make ministries more relevant and better suited to the needs of local people and particular Churches.[85] In its view, most of the needs for service in the Asian context can be met effectively by calling on lay people with special charisms to exercise ministries.[86] Lay people who perform these ministries will exercise in a public manner

---

75 BIMA I, art. 5, *FAPA Vol. 1*, 94; FABC IV, art. 3.1.11, *FAPA Vol. 1*, 181.

76 BILA III, arts. 11, 10, *FAPA Vol. 1*, 245; BIMA II, art. 12, *FAPA Vol. 1*, 100. For Gustavo Gutiérrez, the word "preferential" has "a very important meaning, because we cannot overlook the universality of God's love. The big challenge is to keep together the two aspects of *universality* (meaning that no-one can be excluded from our love), and *preference* for the last ones, the insignificant persons" ("The Church of the Poor," *The Month* [July 1989] 266).

77 FABC VII, Part III, *FAPA Vol. 3*, 8

78 BIRA IV/12, art. 51, *FAPA Vol. 1*, 333.

79 BILA II, art. 9, *FAPA Vol. 1*, 241.

80 FABC IV, art. 1.5, *FAPA Vol. 1*, 179.

81 Ibid., art. 4.3.1, *FAPA Vol. 1*, 192.

82 FABC VI, art. 3, *FAPA Vol. 2*, 2; FABC IV, art. 4.8.7, *FAPA Vol. 1*, 196

83 FABC IV, art. 4.8.7, 4.810, *FAPA Vol. 1*, 196–7.

84 ACMC, art. 25, *FAPA Vol. 1*, 72.

85 Ibid., art. 4, *FAPA Vol. 1*, 68.

86 Ibid., arts. 53–4, *FAPA Vol. 1*, 78.

some aspects of the Christian's triple function of priest, prophet and pastor.[87] Their ministries in the context of the challenges of Asia will be discussed in the next section.

Challenges of Asia and Ministries of the Laity

For the FABC, the Church can only respond adequately and meaningfully to the enormous challenges of the Asian milieu through a diversity of ministries, which will emerge gradually according to the needs of a particular community.[88] By way of example the Asian bishops list a number of lay ministries such as "Evangelist,"[89] "Catechist – Preacher – Religion Teacher,"[90] "Ministry for Liturgy and Liturgical Animation – Prayer Leaders – Acolyte – Lector – Cantor,"[91] "Ministry of Family Apostolate,"[92] "Ministry of Healing – Health Services – Health Education – Counselling,"[93] "Ministry of Inter-religious Dialogue,"[94] "Ministry of Social Concern – Social Leaders – Community Service Peace Officers – Peacemakers,"[95] "Ministry for Youth – University Students – High School Students – Campus Leaders,"[96] "Ministries to Workers – Farmers – Other Occupations,"[97] "Ministry for Education, Formal and Non-formal – Adult Education – Social Education – Literacy,"[98] "Community Builders – Community Leaders – Presidents of Rural Communities – Basic Community Leaders – Organizers – Rural Leaders – Rural Development Workers,"[99] "Ministries of Communication – Mass Media – Group Media,"[100] and "Ministry of Pastoral Community Leadership."[101] At the Fourth Plenary Assembly in 1986, the Asian bishops identified nine challenges that require

---

87   ACMC, art. 54, *FAPA Vol. 1*, 78.
88   Ibid., arts. 53, 57, *FAPA Vol. 1*, 78–99.
89   Ibid., art. 58, *FAPA Vol. 1*, 79.
90   Ibid., art. 59, *FAPA Vol. 1*, 79.
91   Ibid., art. 60, *FAPA Vol. 1*, 79.
92   Ibid., art. 61, *FAPA Vol. 1*, 79.
93   Ibid., art. 62, *FAPA Vol. 1*, 79.
94   Ibid., art. 63, *FAPA Vol. 1*, 80.
95   Ibid., art. 64, *FAPA Vol. 1*, 80.
96   Ibid., art. 65, *FAPA Vol. 1*, 80.
97   Ibid., art. 66, *FAPA Vol. 1*, 80.
98   Ibid., art. 67, *FAPA Vol. 1*, 80.
99   ACMC, art. 68, *FAPA Vol. 1*, 80.
100   Ibid., art. 69, *FAPA Vol. 1*, 81.
101   Ibid., art. 70. *FAPA Vol. 1*, 81.

specific ministries of the laity: politics—their first pastoral priority, youth, women, family, education, mass media, work, business, and health services.

The task of the whole people of God, including lay people, is to engage in politics, understood as a purposeful activity seeking the common good, to infuse the kingdom values of love and justice into the political, economic, cultural, and social world of Asia. Their participation in politics, as a faith witness and a leaven in the world, is a duty that flows from the secular character of their Christian identity and the imperative of the Gospel.[102] It is from inside the political machinery that they can effectively influence the philosophies, programs, and activities of political parties and personalities for the common good in the light of the Gospel.[103] Their ministry is to transform society in politics and the workplace, the pre-eminent places where their involvement has not yet been strong as compared to education and social welfare.[104]

Young people who constitute the majority of Asia's population are the second challenge addressed by the Fourth Plenary Assembly.[105] Their situation which mirrors the manifold problems of Asia, is both negative and positive.[106] On the negative side, many of them are living in extremely poor conditions, worsened by their lack of education and training, and hence become vulnerable to the temptations of materialism, consumerism, ideologies, and destructive substitutes such as drugs, alcoholism, and suicide.[107] On the positive side, they live their lives in witness to the values of the kingdom, and play an important role in social transformation endeavours.[108] Other members of the Church must provide them with full support and trust, and empower them to become evangelisers and instruments of God.[109] The Asian youth are the Asia of today, and if the Church wants to transform this continent of the young, it must become in a certain sense a "Church of the young."[110]

---

102 BILA IV, art. 8.1, *FAPA Vol. 1*, 297; OL, "Participation of the Laity in the Life of the Church: Final Message: Third East Asian Regional Laity Meeting," *FAPA Vol. 2*, 99; FABC IV, arts. 3.1.2–3.1.3, *FAPA Vol. 1*, 180.

103 FABC IV, art. 3.1.6, *FAPA Vol. 1*, 180.

104 OL, "Participation of the Laity in the Life of the Church," *FAPA Vol. 2*, 99; OL, "Second Asian Laity Meeting," *FAPA Vol. 3*, art. 3.5, 115.

105 According to FABC IV, "Of the total population, 60% are between 15 and 24 years of age." See art. 3.2.1, *FAPA Vol. 1*, 181.

106 FABC IV, art. 3.2.1, *FAPA Vol. 1*, 181.

107 Ibid., art. 3.2.2, *FAPA Vol. 1*, 182.

108 Ibid., art. 3.2.3, *FAPA Vol. 1*, 182.

109 Ibid., art. 3.2.4, *FAPA Vol. 1*, 182.

110 Ibid., art. 3.2.5, *FAPA Vol. 1*, 182.

The third challenge faced by the FABC is Asian women, who make up half of the population of Asia.[111] They have suffered enormously from exploitation, degradation, dehumanisation, and many injustices due to discrimination inherent in traditional mores and new economic situations.[112] Their tragic realities now cry out for transformation.[113] However, there is a genuine appreciation of Asian women who are considered to be the heart of the family.[114] They have made numerous contributions in many professions, and in the Church, their contribution is significant in a variety of ministries, especially in person-oriented ministries due to their special capacity to love and give life, and their receptive, sensitive and reflective attitude.[115] Based on "their fundamental equality in the Church's universal ministeriality,"[116] they must be recognised as full partners, and allowed to play their rightful role in the world and in the Church.[117] All members of the Church have a special responsibility to uphold and defend the dignity of women, and to change attitudes, policies, practices, and legislation that lead to the discrimination against, and repression of, women.[118]

The fourth and perhaps the greatest pastoral concern in the minds of the FABC is the Christian family, which is both the cellular receptacle of all social and economic problems plaguing the Asian society,[119] and the domestic Church, where evangelisation initially takes place and a civilisation of love begins.[120] The Asian family is thus both evangelised and called to evangelise others.[121] To ensure that this double gift and task continues to prosper in the family is one of the most urgent ministries of lay people in Asia.[122]

The world of education in Asia, the fifth challenge addressed by the Fourth Plenary Assembly, is characterised by two observations, the illiteracy of the majority of Asians, and the high visibility and reputation of Catholic educational institutions.[123] Catholic schools must reflect the Church's preferential option for

---

111 Ibid., art. 3.3.3, *FAPA Vol. 1*, 183.
112 Ibid., art. 3.3.1, *FAPA Vol. 1*, 182.
113 Ibid., art. 3.3.1, *FAPA Vol. 1*, 182.
114 FABC IV, art. 3.3.2, *FAPA Vol. 1*, 183.
115 Ibid., art. 3.3.2, *FAPA Vol. 1*, 183; ACMC, art. 90, *FAPA Vol. 1*, 83.
116 ACMC, art. 89, *FAPA Vol. 1*, 83.
117 Ibid., art. 93, *FAPA Vol. 1*, 84; FABC IV, art. 3.3.3, *FAPA Vol. 1*, 183.
118 FABC IV, art. 3.3.4, *FAPA Vol. 1*, 183.
119 Ibid., art. 3.4.1, *FAPA Vol. 1*, 184.
120 Ibid., arts. 3.4.8–3.4.9, *FAPA Vol. 1*, 185.
121 Ibid., art. 3.4.9, *FAPA Vol. 1*, 185.
122 Ibid., art. 3.4.10, *FAPA Vol. 1*, 185.
123 Ibid., art. 3.5.1, *FAPA Vol. 1*, 185.

the poor,[124] and act as vehicles of social change.[125] Teachers must consider teaching as a call from God and a formation in values, and not simply as a communication of knowledge.[126]

Mass media rank sixth in the list of challenges confronting the Asian bishops, who observe that the Church lags behind consumer industries in taking advantage of the powerful means of proclaiming the liberating Gospel to Asian people.[127] Lay people in Asia are called to evangelise through the mass media,[128] because the Church "must reach out to millions struggling for social transformation.[129]

In the world of work, the seventh challenge of Asia, workers participate in God's own ongoing process of recreating and transforming the world.[130] Therefore, it is of utmost importance that they retrieve the religious meaning of human work as an expression of human creativity and a participation in the work of the Creator.[131] Asian Christians, especially business people, government officials, managers and policy makers, have to listen with compassion to the problems of the poor and needy workers, and to cooperate with other groups in society to transform exploitative and oppressive work systems.[132]

In this context, lay people in the world of business, the eighth challenge of Asia, are called to live out their faith in accordance with Gospel values and in consideration of the needs of others.[133] This faith witness can range from a simple action based on the values of truth, justice, and love to an active participation in transforming the social structure to achieve "greater worker participation, more discerning consumer guidance, more responsible interventions by governments and a more equitable society."[134]

Health services are the ninth challenge facing the Church but more particularly the laity engaged in the provision of medical services. Here, the issues range from the application of modern medicine to significant bioethical problems.[135]

---

124 FABC IV, art. 3.5.3, *FAPA Vol. 1*, 185.
125 Ibid., art. 3.5.2, *FAPA Vol. 1*, 185.
126 Ibid., art. 3.5.5, *FAPA Vol. 1*, 186.
127 Ibid., art. 3.6.3, *FAPA Vol. 1*, 187.
128 Ibid., art. 3.6.1, *FAPA Vol. 1*, 186.
129 Ibid., art. 3.6.6, *FAPA Vol. 1*, 187.
130 Ibid., art. 3.7.1, *FAPA Vol. 1*, 187.
131 Ibid., art. 3.7.4, *FAPA Vol. 1*, 188.
132 Ibid., arts. 3.7.8, 3.8.1, *FAPA Vol. 1*, 189.
133 Ibid., art. 3.8.5, *FAPA Vol. 1*, 190.
134 FABC IV, art. 3.8.5, *FAPA Vol. 1*, 190.
135 Ibid., art. 3.9.1, *FAPA Vol. 1*, 190.

Hence, lay people have to improve their understanding of the moral dimension of modern medicine and its practice.[136] Their ministry is to bring the saving power of God to transform the world of health care, and in particular, it must reach out to farmers, workers, and the landless and slum dwellers.[137] These nine ministries of the laity are the concrete expressions of an authentic Christian discipleship, which is intimately linked to lay spirituality. In contrast to the traditional neglect of the subject,[138] the FABC has paid special attention to lay spirituality, a topic that will be examined in the next section.

Lay Spirituality

For the FABC, the entire people of God share "one Christian spirituality,"[139] which has six features. First, it is incarnated in Asian realities.[140] Second, it is Christocentric and animated by the Holy Spirit.[141] Third, it is ecclesial and communitarian as Christian discipleship is lived in the community of the Church.[142] Fourth, it is biblical, nourished on the word of God.[143] Fifth, it is sacramental, based on the sacraments of the Church, especially the Eucharist, the summit and the source of Christian liturgy and spirituality.[144] Finally, it seeks to build up the kingdom of God in the concrete experiences of the social, political, economic, and cultural world of Asia.[145] This spirituality is an "involvement-spirituality," bringing Gospel values to the various dimensions of Christian life, and

---

136   Ibid., art. 3.9.3, *FAPA Vol. 1*, 190; see also BILA II, art. 7, *FAPA Vol. 1*, 240.

137   Ibid., art. 3.9.7, *FAPA Vol. 1*, 191.

138   For E. Sellner, "Christian spirituality has taken many forms throughout the centuries. One important form, consistently overlooked and unappreciated, is lay spirituality." Quoted by Kees Waaijman in "Lay Spirituality," *Studies in Spirituality* 10 (2000) 5.

139   FABC IV, art. 4.8.8, *FAPA Vol. 1*, 197.

140   Ibid., art. 4.8.3, *FAPA Vol. 1*, 195.

141   FABC V, art. 9.1, *FAPA Vol. 1*, 288; FABC IV, art. 4.8.3, *FAPA Vol. 1*, 195.

142   FABC IV, art. 4.8.4, *FAPA Vol. 1*, 196.

143   Ibid., art. 4.8.5, *FAPA Vol. 1*, 196.

144   Ibid., art. 4.8.6, *FAPA Vol. 1*, 196.

145   Ibid., art. 4.8.7, *FAPA Vol. 1*, 196. Peter C. Phan shares this view noting that, as a way of living, Christian spirituality has four characteristics: "theocentric (relationship with God), Christic (mediated by and modelled after Christ), pneumatological (empowered by the Spirit) and ecclesial (realized in and through the Church." See "Christian Social Spirituality: A Global Perspective," in *Catholic Social Justice: Theological and Practical Explorations*, edited by Philomena Cullen, Bernard House and Gerard Mannion (London: T&T Clark, 2007) 22.

embracing God's plan for the whole creation.[146] It manifests itself in communion, solidarity, compassion, justice, love, and reconciliation with God the Father.[147] However, within this one Christian spirituality of discipleship and participation in Jesus's mission,[148] a lay spirituality can be identified by its secular character and orientation to the world.[149] It is integrated with a life of authentic prayer, which is also a life of service and love, a self-gift to others, a way of proclaiming the Gospel, and a means of collaborating with the Holy Spirit in furthering the mission of the Church.[150] This spirituality, which entails the duty to transform

---

146 BISA VI, art. 18, *FAPA Vol. 1*, 226; FABC IV, art. 4.8.8, *FAPA Vol. 1*, 197.

147 FABC V, art. 9.3, *FAPA Vol. 1*, 288; FABC IV, art. 4.8.7, *FAPA Vol. 1*, 197. We suggest that, to some extent, the spirituality presented by the FABC can be described as a "Christian social spirituality," a rich concept that was helpfully explicated by Peter C. Phan in "Christian Social Spirituality: A Global Perspective," in *Catholic Social Justice: Theological and Practical Explorations*, edited by Philomena Cullen, Bernard House and Gerard Mannion (London: T&T Clark, 2007) 22. It is also worth recalling Adolfo Nicolás's observation that "the crisis of Christianity in Asia is global," and "at the root and at the core of this global crisis lies *spirituality*" ("Christianity in Crisis: Asia. Which Asia? Which Christianity? Which Crisis?" *Concilium* 3 [2005] 66, 68). For the current Superior General of the Society of Jesus, "this crisis is *a crisis of credibility* that touches the whole evangelization enterprise: words do not match action; the received teachings do not change the life of the believers; rituals do not energize life; Christian professionals, politicians, public servants or even husbands do not seem to perform with greater honesty, fidelity or compassion than their Buddhist or Hindu counterparts.... In Asia we are in crisis because our message is not made visible in our life." Ibid., 66. Father Nicolás, who spent more than forty years in Japan, believes that "'real theology' comes from 'life experience' of the laity." See Robert Mickens, "In the Steps of Ignatius—and Arrupe," *The Tablet* (26 january 2008) 6. He was no doubt influenced by the "non-monastically lay apostolic spirituality" developed by Ignatius when he was still "a layman with absolutely no idea of seeking priestly ordination." Aloysius Pieris, "Vatican II: Glimpses into Six Centuries of Its Prehistory," *East Asian Pastoral Review* 44:4 (2007) 311-2.

148 For Keith J. Egan, "A spirituality of discipleship is the lived experience of following Jesus under the influence of the Holy Spirit" ("The Call of the Laity to a Spirituality of Discipleship," *The Jurist* 47 [1987] 75).

149 FABC IV, art. 4.8.8, *FAPA Vol. 1*, 197.

150 FABC II, art. 27, *FAPA Vol. 1*, 34. For Peter C. Phan, the Asian Chrisan spirituality involves an ecclesial task of realising the Church's mission. See "Asian Christian Spirituality: Context and Contour," *Spiritus* 6 (2006) 225. In this inspiring paper Phan provides an adroit and penetrating exploration of the links between the Asian Christian spirituality and the FABC's triple dialogue, namely, interreligious dialogue, liberation, and inculturation. Ibid, 221-7.

the Asian world in the Spirit of the Gospel,[151] encapsulates the main elements of the FABC's theology of the laity, which will be summarised in a schematic form in the following section.

Ecosystem of the FABC's Theology of the Laity

The oversimplified ecosystem presented here aims to provide some clarity, and is not meant to do justice to the richness of the FABC's theology of the laity. It summarises the salient features of the FABC's theology of the laity by highlighting the challenges of Asia, the theological methodologies employed by the Asian bishops,[152] the centrality of the concept of priesthood of life, and the mission of lay people as both a triple function and a triple dialogue with the cultures, the religions, and the poor of Asia.

Figure 2: FABC's Theology of the Laity - Ecosystem

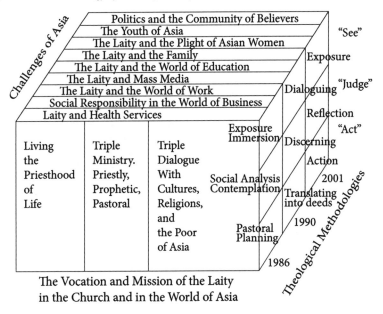

Challenges of Asia
Politics and the Community of Believers
The Youth of Asia
The Laity and the Plight of Asian Women
The Laity and the Family
The Laity and the World of Education
The Laity and Mass Media
The Laity and the World of Work
Social Responsibility in the World of Business
Laity and Health Services

"See"
Exposure
Dialoguing "Judge"
Reflection
"Act"

Living the Priesthood of Life

Triple Ministry. Priestly, Prophetic, Pastoral

Triple Dialogue With Cultures, Religions, and the Poor of Asia

Exposure Immersion
Social Analysis Contemplation
Pastoral Planning
1986

Discerning
Action
2001
Translating into deeds
1990

Theological Methodologies

The Vocation and Mission of the Laity in the Church and in the World of Asia

151 FABC IV, art. 4.8.10, *FAPA Vol. 1*, 197; BILA II, art. 6, *FAPA Vol. 1*, 240.
152 For a detailed treatment of the FABC's theological methodologies see Peter N.V. Hai, "*Fides Quaerens Dialogum*: Theological Methodologies of the Federation of Asian Bishops' Conferences." Australian E-Journal of Theology 8 (2006), http://dlibrary. acu.edu.au/research/theology/ejournal/aejt_8/hai.htm (accessed 1 November 2006).

First, the list of "Challenges of Asia" is taken from the statements of Fourth Plenary Assembly held in 1986 on "The Vocation and Mission of the Laity in the Church and in the World of Asia."[153] The Asian bishops consider "Politics and the Community of Believers" as the first of these challenges confronting the Church followed by the youth of Asia, Asian women, and the family. These challenges continue to be the FABC's pastoral priorities in their subsequent theological deliberations.[154] At the Seventh Plenary Assembly held in 2000 they added "indigenous peoples, sea-based and land-based migrants, and refugees"[155] to the list of concerns that require their pastoral focus. Education, mass media, work, the world of business, and health services are other challenges facing the Asian Churches.

Second, in 1986 the FABC introduced a four-stage "Pastoral Cycle," a theological and pastoral methodology, to be followed in 1990 by another three-phase theological pastoral process of "*dialoguing* with the realities of Asia from within," "*discerning* the movement of God's Spirit in Asia," and "*translating into deeds*" according to the Spirit's biddings.[156] The FABC refers to these methods of theological reflection in other documents, especially in a comprehensive treatment in 2001 of the subject issued by their Office of Theological Concerns.[157] Underlying these theological methodologies is the simple discernment process of "see, judge, act" employed by the Jeunesse Ouvrière Chrétienne movement in the early 20th century.

Third, the mission of lay people is essentially priestly, prophetic, and pastoral, modelled on the ministry of Christ, the leader of the Church.[158] It is linked to the triple dialogue with the religions, the cultures, and the poor of Asia.[159] It is also inseparable from the urgent duty of all Asian Christians to exercise the priestly function by living the priesthood of life, which has "its origins in Christ himself."[160] As the challenges changed so did the Asian bishops' view on lay people and their mission. The following section will endeavour to trace the development

---

153 FABC IV, art. 3.0, *FAPA Vol. 1*, 179–91.
154 FABC VI, art. 15, *FAPA Vol. 2*, 10–2.
155 FABC VII, Part III, A, *FAPA Vol. 3*, 9–11.
156 BISA VII, arts. 8–13, *FAPA Vol. 1*, 231–2; FABC V, art. 7.1, *FAPA Vol. 2*, 284; OHD, "The Prophetic Path to the New Millenium Through Social Advocacy," art. 3.14, *FAPA Vol. 3*, 50; see also FABC VI, art. A.3, *FAPA Vol. 2*, 2.
157 OL, "Second Asian Laity Meeting: Final Statement," art. 4.2, *FAPA Vol. 3*, 115; OTC, "Methodology: Asian Christian Theology," art 3.1, *FAPA Vol. 3*, 356.
158 FABC IV, arts. 4.2.2–4.3.1, *FAPA Vol. 1*, 192.
159 BILA III, art. 7, *FAPA Vol. 1*, 244.
160 FABC IV, art. 4.4.2, *FAPA Vol. 1*, 192.

of their reflection on the role of lay people in the Asian context, from 1970, the date of their first meeting around Pope Paul VI in Manila, to 2012, the last year covered by the fifth of the five-volume collection, which contains all of the important documents issued by the FABC over this period of time.[161]

Development of the FABC's Theology of the Laity

In the statements of the Fourth Plenary Assembly held in September 1986 the FABC admitted that "*in the past*" [emphasis added] they had channelled their efforts to support "an inward-looking" view of the Church, and now realised that they must reassess their priorities and resources to ensure that the Church become "an outward-looking" community.[162] This admission suggests a plausible division of the development of their theology of the laity into two periods marked by the Fourth Plenary Assembly, which was a culmination of the FABC's theological reflection on the subject in the first phase from 1970 to mid-1986, and a change of emphasis in the second period from September 1986 to 2012. This shift of emphasis can be identified in five interrelated areas: its orientation to the world, its contextualisation of the role of the laity based on geographic regions, its emphasis on the empowerment of lay people, in particular the family, women, youth, and the small Christian communities/basic ecclesial communities, its focus on an integral formation *of* and *for* the laity, in particular, the social teachings of the Church, and a deeper exploration of a spirituality of discipleship and a spirituality of harmony.

First, the statements of the FABC, issued in the first period, tend to emphasise the role of lay people in the Church as compared to those produced in the second phase, which show a more pronounced focus on their ministries in the world. Indeed, the 1977 conclusions of the "Asian Colloquium on Ministries in the Church" place more emphasis on the *ad intra* aspects of ministries, discussing their background, context, forms, and formation, and their implications for the life and structure of the Church.[163] However, at the Fourth Plenary Assembly in 1986, the Asian bishops stressed the need to make ministries of lay people more world-oriented and kingdom-oriented because they realised that lay apostolate

---

161 *For All the Peoples of Asia: Federation of Asian Bishops' Conferences, Documents from 1997 to 2001*, vol. 3, edited by Franz-Josef Eilers (Quezon City: Claretian Publications, 2002).

162 FABC IV, art. 4.3.2, *FAPA Vol. 1*, 192.

163 ACMC, *FAPA Vol. 1*, 67–92.

was still "parish-oriented, inward-looking and priest-directed."[164] They reiterated this emphasis in other statements, especially those issued in subsequent plenary assemblies. The Church, they affirmed, has to balance the "efforts on inward looking concerns with concerns for social issues especially regarding workers, women and youth."[165] Lay people should influence the world of business and politics, education and health, mass media and work, by being a servant of the Lord and a companion of all Asians in the journey aiming for full life in the kingdom of God.[166] Their duty is to witness to the values of the kingdom by promoting "justice, peace, love, compassion, equality and brotherhood."[167] This change of emphasis had already been signalled in other documents issued by the FABC in the two years immediately prior to the Fourth Plenary Assembly. The first and second Bishops' Institute for the Lay Apostolate (BILA) in 1984 and May 1986 stress that, to fulfil its mission, the Church has to direct its ministries to the world and society, especially to justice and developmental priorities of the region.[168] The mission of lay people, says BILA III, is to witness to the values of the Gospel by dialoguing with Asians, especially the poor, in a non-Christian milieu and a secularised society.[169]

Secondly, since 1986 the FABC's theology of the laity has become more contextualised with two Asian laity meetings held in 1994 and 2001: the first to discuss the mission of lay people with special reference to the social teachings of the Church, and the second, to reflect on both the Church's social doctrines and the role of the laity as a moving force of love and service in a renewed Church.[170] Regional gatherings of laity were held in East Asia, South Asia, and South East Asia to study the social teachings of the Church in the context of their regional concerns. East Asia consists of Hong Kong, Japan, Korea, Macau, and Taiwan; South Asia comprises Bangladesh, India, Nepal, Pakistan, and Sri Lanka; South East Asia includes Brunei, Cambodia, Indonesia, Laos, Malaysia, Burma, Philippines,

---

164   FABC IV, art. 4.6.2, *FAPA Vol. 1*, 194.
165   BILA V, *FAPA Vol. 2*, 78.
166   FABC VII, art. 6, *FAPA Vol. 3*, 4; see also "The Role of the Laity in Human Development," *FAPA Vol. 2*, 134.
167   FABC V, arts. 1.7, 4.2, *FAPA Vol. 1*, 275, 282.
168   BILA I, art. 6, *FAPA Vol. 1*, 236; BILA II, art. 9, *FAPA Vol. 1*, 241.
169   BILA III, art. 7, *FAPA Vol. 1*, 244.
170   OL, "The Commitment of the Laity in the Church's Mission with Special Reference to Implementing the Social Teachings: Final Report on the First Asian Laity Meeting," *FAPA Vol. 2*, 119–25; OL, "Second Asian Laity Meeting: Final Statement," art. 4.2, *FAPA Vol. 3*, 113–6.

Singapore, Thailand, and Vietnam. The first East Asian regional meeting took place in Taipei in 1986 to discuss "The Role of the Laity in the Local Churches of East Asia," and it was followed by a second meeting in Tokyo in 1989 addressing the theme of "Spiritual Crisis amidst Material Affluence and the Role of the Laity."[171] Five more East Asian regional laity meetings were held in 1992, 1996, 1999, 2005, and 2010 to examine the specific role of lay people in this region, dealing with issues that were more pertinent to East Asia such as the participation of the laity in the life of the Church in East Asia, their role in human development, their formation towards a renewed Church, and the role of women.[172] Two South Asian regional meetings were held in 1995 and 1998 on the theme of the role and mission of lay people in a multi-religious context, and one in 2002 to reflect on the role of women in Church and society.[173] During this period the bishops and laity of South Asia also met to discuss the principles for a Christian response to the growing phenomenon of religious fundamentalism and violence in South Asia, and to emphasise the formation of lay leaders.[174] In South East Asia, two meetings were held in 1996 and 1999 to reflect on the role of the laity in the Church mission with special emphasis on human development and the social teachings of the Church, and one in 2003 on Christian women.[175]

Thirdly, from 1986 on the Asian bishops increasingly emphasised the empowerment of lay people, especially the family, women, youth, and the small Christian communities/basic ecclesial communities, in undertaking their ministries in the Church and in the world. The Fourth Plenary Assembly highlighted the need for developing collaborative Church structures to make full use of lay people's

---

171 OL, "Participation of the Laity in the Life of the Church: Third East Asian Regional Meeting." *FAPA Vol. 2*, 97.

172 OL, "Participation of the Laity in the Life of the Church: Third East Asian Regional Meeting." *FAPA Vol. 2*, 97–100; "The Role of the Laity in Human Development," *FAPA Vol. 2*, 133–5; "Fifth East Asian Regional Meeting: Final Statement," *FAPA Vol. 3*, 93–6; OLF, "Discipleship of Women – Challenges of the 21st Century," *FAPA Vol. 4*, 157–61; OLF, "Mary Truly A Woman of Our Times," *FAPA Vol. 5*, 141–4.

173 OL, "Second South Asian Regional Laity Meeting (SARLM II)," *FAPA Vol. 3*, 83–7; OLF, "Role of Women in Church and Society," *FAPA Vol. 4*, 149–52.

174 "Christian Response to the Phenomenon of Violence in South Asia: South Asia Bishops' Meeting (SABIM)," *FAPA Vol. 2*, 13–8.

175 OL, "The Role of the Laity in Church Mission in South East Asia with Special Emphasis on Implementing the Church' Social Teachings," *FAPA Vol. 2*, 127–31; "Second Southeast Asian Regional Laity Meeting," *FAPA Vol. 3*, 89–92; OFL, "Southeast Asia Meeting on Women: 'Responding to the Challenges of Christian Women in Asia,'" *FAPA Vol. 4*, 153–6.

talents and expertise.[176] The Fourth and Fifth Bishops' Institute for Lay Apostolate in 1988 and 1991 searched for ways to restore to the laity their rightful place and role in the over-clericalised Churches in Asia.[177] The Fifth Plenary Assembly in 1990 emphasised that lay people are the primary evangelisers of cultures and societies.[178] The clergy have to be active in the formation of lay people to enable them to be "*evangelisers of their own* – the young evangelizing the young, workers evangelizing workers, professionals evangelizing professionals, government officials evangelizing government officials, families evangelizing families," and to become a leaven for the transformation of Asian society.[179] Finally, the choice of the Asian family as the topic for the Eighth Plenary Assembly,[180] and the change of name from the "Office of Laity" into the "Office of Laity and Family" together with the creation of the "Women's Desk," the "Youth Desk," and the AsIPA Desk, which regularly organised seminars on the role of women, the Asian youth, and small Christian communities, clearly shows the FABC's commitment of the empowerment of lay people.[181]

Indeed, at the Eighth Plenary Assembly in 2004 the Asian bishops considered "the family as the domestic church," and "the most fundamental community form of the Church."[182] For them, "a family of deep religious faith is a sign of the Church and of the reign of God."[183] Therefore, they challenged church leadership to empower "the family for mission by helping the members to live out their marriage and family life in accord with the values of God's Reign or the teachings of

---

176 FABC VII, art. Part 1,A.6, *FAPA Vol. 3*, 4. Here the FABC might have in mind the collaborative model of ministry of the early Church, a theme that was investigated by Daniel J. Harrington who convincingly argues that "from the earliest times ministry in the Church was collaborative" ("Paul and His Co-Workers," *Priests and People* [August-September 2003] 325). See also "The Collaborative Nature of the Pauline Mission," *The Bible Today* 42:4 (July 2004) 200–6.

177 BILA IV, art. 3, *FAPA Vol. 1*, 295; OESC, "A Renewed Catechesis for Asia Towards Year 2000 and Beyond," *FAPA Vol. 2*, 29; see also OTC, "Being Church in Asia: Journeying in the Spirit into Fuller Life," art. 52, *FAPA Vol. 2*, 227.

178 FABC V, art. 5.1, *FAPA Vol. 1*, 283; OE, "Evangelization among the Indigenous Peoples of Asia," art. 8, *FAPA Vol. 2*, 213.

179 FABC V, arts. 5.1–5.2, *FAPA Vol. 1*, 283.

180 FABC VIII, *FAPA Vol. 4*, 1–61.

181 *FAPA Vol. 4*, 149–85; *FAPA Vol. 5*, 129–72.

182 FABC VIII, art. 99, *FAPA Vol. 4*, 37.

183 FABC VIII, art. 72, *FAPA Vol. 4*, 28.

the Gospel and of the Church."[184] They went on to stress that "how this empowerment takes place has to be a principal concern of family ministry."[185]

The bishops of Asia also acknowledge that discrimination based on gender exists in the family, in economy, politics, culture, religion, and mass media,[186] and women want to be treated more equally in the Church.[187] The first Bishops' Institute on Lay Apostolate on Women in 1995 formally affirms that women are co-evangelists, and active agents in their own transformation.[188] The bishops recognise that Catholic morality and spirituality are biased against women, and traditional Marian spirituality favours the docility of women.[189] To remedy this situation and to empower women, what is required is an inspiring reinterpretation and presentation of Mary as a true disciple, who listens to and acts on the Word of God in the public sphere.[190] At a colloquium held in 1997 to discuss their plans for the Churches in Asia in the 21ˢᵗ century, the Asian bishops considered it a priority to identify the key issues discriminating women in Asia and to promote the empowerment of women in the Church and in society.[191] They proposed that women be invited to become members of theological commissions at national and FABC levels.[192] Between 1995 and 2012, five special Bishops' Institutes on Lay Apostolate on Women and three Women's Desk seminars were held to address issues relating to the role of women in the Church and the world of Asia.[193]

At other forums, the FABC recommended that existing structures within the Church be reviewed and appropriate mechanisms be set up to enable women and youth to participate in the decision-making bodies of the Church.[194] To

---

184 FABC VIII, art. 81, *FAPA Vol. 4*, 31.
185 Ibid.
186 OL and OHD, "Realities and Experiences of Women in Asia," *FAPA Vol. 2*, 114–5.
187 OL, "Participation of the Laity in the Life of the Church," *FAPA Vol. 2*, 98.
188 BILA on Women [I], "Role of Women in Church and Society Toward 2000," art. 1.6, *FAPA Vol. 2*, 92.
189 Ibid., art. 3.7, *FAPA Vol. 2*, 94.
190 BILA on Women II, *FAPA Vol. 3*, 75; BILA on Women [I], "Role of Women in Church and Society Toward 2000," art. 5.4, *FAPA Vol. 2*, 95.
191 OHD, "Colloquium on Church in Asia in the 21ˢᵗ Century," arts. 4.1.2-3, *FAPA Vol. 3*, 37.
192 BILA on Women II, *FAPA Vol. 3*, 76; OL and OHD, "Realities and Experiences of Women in Asia," *FAPA Vol. 2*, 118.
193 BILA on Women [I], *FAPA Vol. 2*, 91–6; BILA on Women II, *FAPA Vol. 3*, 73-7; BILA on Women III, *FAPA Vol. 3*, 79–82; BILA V, *FAPA Vol. 5*, 145–9.
194 OL and OHD, "Realities and Experiences of Women in Asia," *FAPA Vol. 2*, 116; OHD, "Colloquium on Church in Asia in the 21ˢᵗ Century," arts. 4.1.18-19, *FAPA Vol. 3*, 39.

show their deep concern for women and youth they instructed that a women's commission and a youth office be established.[195] In 1997, the first Bishops' Institute on Lay Apostolate on Youth was held to discuss the ministry to Asian youth.[196] The FABC also stressed the need to impart Christian values in children and train them to be agents of change,[197] and held the first consultation on children in 2000.[198] For the FABC, women, youth, the family, as well as other sectors of people such as indigenous peoples, sea-based and land-based migrants, and refugees, are their pastoral priorities, and at the same time, equal partners in the mission of love and service.[199]

Fourthly, after the 1986 Plenary Assembly, there has been an increased emphasis in the FABC's reflection on the "formation *of* and *for* the laity."[200] Three meetings of the Bishops' Institute for Lay Apostolate were held to discuss the topic of lay formation.[201] The FABC identify three levels of formation,[202] the first of which is a general formation of all Christians, in particular lay people, aiming to make them aware of the Second Vatican Council's teachings on their vocation and mission.[203] Special training seminars, weekend courses, and block courses for volunteers and selected leaders belong to the second level of formation,[204] while the third level is the ministerial formation designed for "those who enjoy the charisms for stable ecclesial service."[205] The Asian bishops' vision for the renewal of the Church is based on a holistic formation of the people of God, which

---

195 OL and OHD, "Realities and Experiences of Women in Asia," *FAPA Vol. 2*, 117; OHD, "Colloquium on Church in Asia in the 21ˢᵗ Century," arts. 4.1.15, *FAPA Vol. 3*, 39; OL and OHD, "The Youth of Asia Envisioning the Fullness of Life and Human Dignity in the Church," *FAPA Vol. 2*, 104; OL, "Asian Youth Ministers' Meeting: A Consolidated Report," *FAPA Vol. 3*, 104. Note that this commission and office are commonly referred to as "Women Desk and Youth Desk," see *FAPA Vol. 4*, 149–85; *FAPA Vol. 5*, 129–72.
196 BILA on Youth, *FAPA Vol. 3*, 65–71.
197 OHD, "Colloquium on Church in Asia in the 21ˢᵗ Century," arts. 4.1.15, *FAPA Vol. 3*, 39.
198 OE, "Consultation on 'Missionary Animation of Children'," *FAPA Vol. 3*, 214.
199 FABC VII, art. III.A, *FAPA Vol. 3*, 9.
200 FABC IV, art. 4.7.2, *FAPA Vol. 1*, 194.
201 BILA V, *FAPA Vol. 2*, 77–80; BILA VI, *FAPA Vol. 2*, 81–85; BILA VII, *FAPA Vol. 2*, 87–90.
202 FABC IV, art. 4.7.2.0, *FAPA Vol. 1*, 194.
203 Ibid., art. 4.7.2.1, *FAPA Vol. 1*, 194.
204 Ibid., art. 4.7.2.2, *FAPA Vol. 1*, 194–5.
205 Ibid., art. 4.7.2.3, *FAPA Vol. 1*, 195.

emphasises that lay people's training must be accompanied by the formation of the clergy and religious to enable them to understand and accept the emerging role and responsibility of the laity.[206] They affirm that formation of the lay faithful is an ongoing process and must be placed among the priorities of a diocese.[207] At the Plenary Assembly in 1990, they called for a thorough education of Catholics in the social doctrines of the Church,[208] and repeated the same message at BILA VI in 1992,[209] and the First Asian Laity Meeting in 1994.[210]

In addition to this emphasis on the formation of lay people with special reference to the social teachings of the Church, the Asian bishops recognise the need for lay people to have ongoing formation, and in particular, adequate training "needed for the emerging ministries and for new way of being ministers."[211] They stress that lay formation must be adapted to the cultural contexts of Asia, and involve all members of the Church.[212] As a result of the review of the many programmes and methods that had been implemented, the FABC designed an integral formation process, which they termed "Asian Integral Pastoral Approach" (AsIPA) to promote a new way of being Church in Asia.[213] They devoted two general meetings in 1996 and 2000 to discuss the AsIPA methodology, which they considered to be a very useful means to make the Church a communion of communities and to develop basic ecclesial communities.[214] With an increased emphasis on the contextualised and integral formation of lay people, and a focus on the Church's social teachings in the second period of their theological reflection on the lay experience, the FABC shifted more from a theology *of* the laity to a theology *for* the laity, a theology not focused on dealing with lay people as a

---

206 OL, "The Commitment of the Laity in the Church's Mission with Special Reference to Implementing the Social Teachings," *FAPA Vol. 2*, 121; BILA IV, art. 11, *FAPA Vol. 1*, 297–8.

207 BILA VI, *FAPA Vol. 2*, 77; BILA V, *FAPA Vol. 2*, 77.

208 FABC V, art. 5.2, *FAPA Vol. 1*, 283.

209 BILA VI, *FAPA Vol. 2*, 82.

210 OL, "The Commitment of the Laity in the Church's Mission with Special Reference to Implementing the Social Teachings," *FAPA Vol. 2*, 123; see also "The Role of the Laity in Human Development," *FAPA Vol. 2*, 134.

211 OTC, "The Spirit at Work in Asia Today," art. 4.3.1.2, *FAPA Vol. 1*, 312; BILA IV, art. 9, *FAPA Vol. 1*, 297.

212 FABC VII, art. C.2, *FAPA Vol. 3*, 13.

213 OL, "Asian Integral Pastoral Approach towards a New Way of Being Church in Asia (AsIPA)," *FAPA Vol. 2*, 107–11.

214 OL, "Asian Integral Pastoral Approach (AsIPA) Message to the Churches of Asia," art. 10, *FAPA Vol. 2*, 139; FABC VII, art. III.C.7, *FAPA Vol. 3*, 15.

subject of theological discussion, but aiming to empower them to assume their rightful role in the Church and in the world.

Finally, after 1986, the Asian bishops have further deepened their reflection on the spirituality of all Christians by emphasising that it is a spirituality of discipleship and a spirituality of harmony. First, this spirituality is a journey of authentic discipleship, love, and service in the context of Asia after the pattern of Jesus' death and resurrection.[215] It is a "contextualized Christian spirituality" that discerns the movement of the Spirit who re-enacts in Christians the mysteries of Jesus Christ in the contextual realities of their daily life and struggles.[216] Second, it is a spirituality of harmony which expresses their intimate communion with God, their docility to his Spirit, and their following of Jesus-in-mission.[217] It integrates every aspect of Christian life: liturgy, prayer, community living, solidarity with all and especially the poor, evangelization, catechesis, dialogue, social commitment, etc.[218] It is a spirituality of the new way of being Church, a spirituality of those who trust in the Lord, a spirituality of the powerless and the *anawim*.[219] It is a spirituality that emphasises being over doing, and seeks to challenge the disharmonies of the Asian world by a life of simplicity, humble presence, and service.[220] As such, it is already a living proclamation of Christ, convincing, powerful, and far reaching in its impact.[221] The depth of this spirituality also prepares Christians for ecumenical and interreligious dialogue.[222] At the Sixth Plenary Assembly in 1995, the FABC affirmed that in Asia, where peoples have long traditions of deep religiosity, prayer is absolutely indispensable because the inner life of prayer builds the Church into a credible community of faith, which, in turn, works for a fully human future of Asian peoples.[223] For the FABC, spirituality and social justice go hand in hand, and together they are the keys to the kingdom of God in the world of Asia.[224]

---

215 FABC V, art. 9.1, *FAPA Vol. 1*, 288; OTC, "The Spirit at Work in Asia Today," art. 4.2.2.6, *FAPA Vol. 1*, 308.
216 OTC, "The Spirit at Work in Asia Today," art. 4.2.2.6, *FAPA Vol. 1*, 308.
217 FABC V, arts. 9.1, 9.5, *FAPA Vol. 1*, 288.
218 Ibid., art. 9.3, *FAPA Vol. 1*, 288.
219 Ibid., art. 9.5, *FAPA Vol. 1*, 288.
220 Ibid., arts. 9.5, 10.1, *FAPA Vol. 1*, 288–9.
221 Ibid., art. 9.7, *FAPA Vol. 1*, 289.
222 Ibid., art. 9.6, *FAPA Vol. 1*, 289.
223 FABC VI, arts. 3, 14.1, *FAPA Vol. 2*, 2, 8.
224 OHD, "Colloquium on Church in Asia in the 21st Century," art. 8.1., *FAPA Vol. 3*, 45.

In sum, there was both a fundamental continuity and a gradual progression in the FABC's theology of the laity from 1970 to 2012, which displays a high degree of consistency and integration, coupled with discernible elements of growth.[225] This contextual theology, developed in response to the challenges of Asian societies, was increasingly manifested by an orientation to the world, a more regional contextualisation of the role of lay people, a move towards their empowerment, a focus on their integral formation, and an emphasis on a deeper and more engaging spirituality of discipleship and harmony.

Conclusion

This chapter has reviewed the elements of the FABC's theology of the laity and traced its development over a period of forty-two years from 1970 to 2012. First, in the documents of the FABC, lay people first and foremost are Asian Christians, a contextual reality and constitutive part of the Church, the faithful, the disciples of Christ, the people of God, and the believing community. Their identity is based on the baptismal, common priesthood of life, characterised by the Asian secularity. Their calling is intimately bound to the vocation of local Churches where all Asian Christians are called to a contextualised communion by being committed to Jesus the Liberator and to live the priesthood of life in a communion of integral liberation. Their mission and ministries are essentially Christ-centred, kingdom-focused, world-oriented, dialogical and liberative, as they endeavour to actualise the priestly, prophetic, and pastoral functions in their faith response to the challenges of Asia. Fundamental to their vocation and mission are the two concepts of priesthood of life and contextualised communion, a common matrix for all Asian Christians which, intrinsically linked to their prophetic and pastoral functions, integrates both their *ad intra* role in the Church and their *ad extra* mission in the familial, professional, social, and political world. For the Asian bishops, the entire people of God is priestly, and its common priesthood of life, which has its origins in Christ himself, is more real

---

225 Our observation is inspired by the three selective principles highlighted by Gerard Vincent Hall in his work, *Raimon Panikkar's Hermeneutics of Religious Pluralism* (Ann Arbor, Mich.: UMI, 1994): first, the "*principle of continuity*" implies a "fundamental consistency of the themes, methods and approaches"; secondly, the "*principle of growth*" involves a "transformation and even rupture" of the interpretations and procedures; finally, the "*principle of integration*" is "more than the summation of these first two principles," and "recognises a certain *telos*" in the works produced over a period of time. Ibid., 3.

and inclusive than the ministerial priesthood of the clergy.[226] It encompasses and harmonises two organising frameworks dynamically used by *Lumen Gentium*, namely the common priesthood and the triple mission of the Church. Mission is the purpose of lay ministries, which aim to transform the world by a triple dialogue of life with the cultures, the religions, and the poor of Asia. Evangelisation is the highest priority of mission, and its goal is to build up the kingdom of God.

Secondly, there was both a fundamental continuity and a gradual development in the FABC's theology of the laity from 1970 to 2012. As the challenges of Asia changed so did the teachings of the FABC. Indeed, following the Fourth Plenary Assembly in 1986 its theology of the laity has become more world-oriented with an increased emphasis on the empowerment of lay people, in particular the family, women, youth, and the small Christian communities/basic ecclesial communities, and on the contextualisation of the role of the laity based on geographic regions of Asia, on an integral and contextualised formation *of* and *for* the laity with a focus on the social teachings of the Church, and on a deeper exploration of a spirituality of discipleship and harmony. In this theology, the vocation and mission of lay people is constitutive of the life and activity of the Asian Church, which is called by Jesus to be a community of faith in Asia, a communion of committed disciples working for the liberation of Asia. Their priestly, prophetic, and pastoral ministries are based on the ministry of Jesus Christ who is their model and point of reference. There was no paradigm shift in the FABC's contextual theology of the laity from 1970 to 2012, only a change in emphasis in some areas of pastoral concerns. The following chapter will review the strengths and limitations of this rich and dynamic theology by examining of its context, contents, structure, and resources.

---

226   Gideon Goosen reminds us that "both priesthoods are analogical of the priesthood of Christ. Both mediate; both offer sacrifice; both are go-betweens" ("A New Relationship Between the Ministerial and Baptismal Priesthoods," *Compass* [Winter 1997] 21). For David N. Power, "the use of the word 'priesthood' in the conciliar documents lacks precision. Apart from associating it with the Church's sacramental ministry and eucharistic sacrifice, the council offered no precise definition of Christ's own priesthood, but seemed to take this as a given." See ("Priesthood Revisited: Mission and Ministries in the Royal Priesthood," in *Ordering the Baptismal Priesthood: Theologies of Lay and Ordained Ministry*, edited by Susan K. Wood (Collegeville, Minn.: Liturgical Press, 2003) 91.

Chapter 5   Evaluation of the Fabc's Theology of the Laity

As the first Ecumenical Council where ecclesiology was the central theme, Vatican II has changed the Church,[1] and provided seminal insights into the various aspects of Church life and spirituality. One of its most significant contributions was the development of a new understanding of the vocation and mission of the laity in the Church and in the world. The Council left an important body of texts about the laity (Chapters 2 and 4 of *Lumen Gentium, Apostolicam Actuositatem, Gaudium et Spes*, and *Ad Gentes*), which became the foundation for the FABC's reflection on the identity and role of lay people in the Church in Asia.

In 1974, nine years after the conclusion of the Second Vatican Council, at their first plenary meeting, held to discus the theme "Evangelization in Modern Day Asia," the Asian bishops declared that more and more lay people "must assume

---

1   For a series of discussions on this topic see John Wilkins, "How Vatican II Changed the Church: 1: Earthquake in Rome," *The Tablet* (12 October 2002) 10-1; "How Vatican II Changed the Church: 2: Unfinished Business," *The Tablet* (19 October 2002) 10-2; Alain Woodrow, "How Vatican II Changed the Church: 3: Diary of an Insider," *The Tablet* (26 October 2002) 11-3; Alberto Melloni, "How Vatican II Changed the Church: 4: A Speech That Lit the Flame," *The Tablet* (2 November 2002) 7–8; Robert Blair Kaiser, "How Vatican II Changed the Church: 5: Priest Behind the Scenes," *The Tablet* (9 November 2002) 8–9; John Bowden, "How Vatican II Changed the Church: 6: Priest Behind the Scenes," *The Tablet* (16 November 2002) 10-1; John Marshall, "How Vatican II Changed the Church: 7: My Voyage of Discovery," *The Tablet* (23 November 2002) 8–9; Joseph Komonchak, "How Vatican II Changed the Church: 8: What Road to Joy?" *The Tablet* (30 November 2002) 11-2; John Allen, "How Vatican II Changed the Church: 9: Earthquake in Rome." *The Tablet* (7 December 2002) 8–9; Michael Walsh, "How Vatican II Changed the Church: 10: U-turn on Human Rights," *The Tablet* (14 December 2002) 7–9; Cardinal Franz König, "How Vatican II Changed the Church: 11: 'It Must Be the Holy Spirit,'" *The Tablet* (21–28 December 2002) 4–6; see also *Vatican II: An Interfaith Appraisal.*, edited by John H. Miller (Notre Dame, Ind.: University of Notre Dame, 1966); *The Ecclesiology of Vatican II*, translated by Matthew J. O'Connell, edited by Bonaventure Kloppenburg (Chicago: Franciscan Herald Press, 1974); *Vatican II Assessment and Perspectives: Twenty-Five Years After (1962–1987)*, 2 vols, edited by René Latourelle (New York: Paulist Press, 1988); *Modern Catholicism: Vatican II and After*, edited by Adrian Hastings (London: SPCK, 1991); Dennis M. Doyle, *The Church Emerging from Vatican II: A Popular Approach to Contemporary Catholicism* (Mystic, Conn.: Twenty-Third Publications, 1992).

responsibility in the tasks of evangelisation."[2] In 2001, at the Second Asian Laity Meeting, they observed that "the world of politics and the workplace are the pre-eminent places where the laity are called to transform society."[3] For them, "Basic Ecclesial Communities/Small Christian Communities offer the laity a way to link faith and life,"[4] help them grow in awareness of local situations, and through faith formation "develop a sense of mission and become a moving force to bring about conversation and change in Church and Society."[5] This focus on basic ecclesial communities/small Christian communities together with the emphasis the family, women, and youth was the result of a deepening of FABC's reflection on the role of lay people in the Church and in the world of Asia. Indeed, since Vatican II, in Asia as well as other parts of the Christian world, the theology of the laity has been brought into prominence. This was due to several factors including "a more comprehensive understanding of the mystery of the Church; a more positive sense of the secular world and the mission of the Church within it; [and] new cultural and social conditions which significantly raised the educational level of the lay Christian."[6] Therefore, the FABC's theology of the laity, which is more than simply a canonical or administrative instrument, deserves a comprehensive review.

In this chapter we will evaluate the FABC's theology of the laity (1970–2012) by examining its context, contents, structures, and interaction with other post-Vatican II theologies of the laity. Our main argument is that the concept of priesthood of life, common to all Asian Christians, and intimately connected to the notion of "contextualised communion,"[7] is central to the identity, vocation, mission, and spirituality of lay people in Asia. We also contend that this theology has a contextual and relational dimension, which is implicit in the concept of priesthood of life. Throughout our critical analysis, we will pay particular attention to the underlying assumptions and implications of this rich and dynamic theology.

---

2   FABC I, art. 36, *FAPA Vol. 1*, 17.
3   Second Asian Laity Meeting, art. 3.4, *FAPA Vol. 3*, 115.
4   Second Asian Laity Meeting, art. 3.1, *FAPA Vol. 3*, 115. By promoting Basic Ecclesial Communities/Small Christian Communities as a way to deal with the dichotomy between faith and daily life, the FABC is no doubt concerned with a problem characterised by *Gaudium et Spes* (no. 43) as "one of the gravest errors of our time."
5   Second Asian Laity Meeting, art. 3.1, *FAPA Vol. 3*, 115.
6   Frederick J. Parella, "The Laity in the Church," *Proceedings of the Catholic Theological Society of America* 35 (1980) 269.
7   We coined this term to highlight and condense the FABC's thought on the vocation of lay people.

Vatican II and the FABC's Theology of the Laity

Consistent with the contextual orientation of their theology,[8] the Asian bishops have endeavoured to remain faithful to the Gospel, the tradition, and the universal magisterium, especially the vision of Vatican II, and at the same time, have maintained creativity in adapting these teachings to the concrete realities of Asia. Indeed, many of their statements are based on those of the Second Vatican Council.[9] At the Fourth Plenary Assembly they emphasise the need to make lay apostolate world-oriented or Kingdom-oriented because of the Asian situation and the emphasis of Vatican II.[10]

In other statements on the role of the laity they often use phrases such as "the vision of Vatican II" when they wish to conscientise all the faithful, especially the laity, about "the new vision of Vatican II" with respect to their vocation and mission in the Church and in the world,[11] or to identify the needs and challenges facing the community to realise "the Vatican II vision of Church."[12] They acknowledge the gap between Vatican II's "vision of the Church as the people of God," and the actual situation in the Church, which is due to the passivity of the laity or an unwillingness on the part of the clergy to share responsibility.[13] They encourage the building of a co-responsible Church according to "the vision of Vatican II."[14] They also emphasise the need for the entire community to update their vision of the Church, and learn new methods and skills to enable them to work together in realising "the vision of Vatican II,"[15] or just to highlight efforts made in creating an atmosphere conducive to the realisation of "the vision of Vatican II."[16]

---

8   For a detailed treatment of the FABC's theological methodologies see Peter N.V. Hai, "*Fides Quaerens Dialogum*: Theological Methodologies of the Federation of Asian Bishops' Conferences." Australian E-Journal of Theology 8 (2006), http://dlibrary.acu. edu.au/research/theology/ejournal/aejt_8/hai.htm (accessed 1 November 2006).
9   OEIA and OE, "Consultation on Christian Presence Among Muslims in Asia," art. 12, *FAPA Vol. 1*, 171.
10 FABC IV, art. 4.6.2, *FAPA Vol. 1*, 193–4.
11 FABC IV, art. 4.7.2.1, *FAPA Vol. 1*, 194.
12 BILA V, *FAPA Vol. 2*, 79.
13 BILA I, art. 2–3, *FAPA Vol. 1*, 235.
14 BILA II, art. 14, *FAPA Vol. 1*, 242.
15 BILA I, arts. 2–4, *FAPA Vol. 1*, 235–6.
16 BILA II, art. 2, *FAPA Vol. 1*, 239.

Like Vatican II,[17] the Asian bishops do not provide a rigid definition of the laity, but a typological description by stressing both the generic element and the *differentia specifica*. For the Asian bishops, the generic element is the baptismal priesthood of life of the laity and their participation in the threefold mission of Christ. The specific element is the secular character of lay people who are Christians in the world of Asia.

Following the Second Vatican Council's Degree on the Apostolate of the Laity *Apostolicam Actuositatem*, which states that "the laity, carrying out this mission of the Church, exercise their apostolate…in the world as well as in the Church, in the temporal order as well as in the spiritual,"[18] the statements of the Fourth Plenary Assembly focus on both the *ad intra* and *ad extra* aspects of the vocation and mission of lay people in the Church and in the world. They also emphasise the common priesthood and the *tria munera* of all Christians, the two over-arching frameworks dynamically employed by *Lumen Gentium*, the Dogmatic Constitution on the Church.[19] Moreover, like Vatican II, the FABC's theology of the laity is based on a common matrix which encompasses several tenets such as the common baptismal priesthood of all Christians, their participation in the triple function of Christ, the charisms of lay ministries, and, to a certain extent, the underlying image of the Church as communion.

The indebtedness of the FABC to the teachings of Vatican II is summarised and depicted in Figure 1, which shows the organising framework of the FABC's theology of the laity against the background of the Vatican II documents that deal in a substantial way with lay people, in particular *Lumen Gentium* and

---

17 Richard Gaillardetz notes that Vatican II "was hardly offering an ontological definition of the laity but merely a typological one, that is, a practical definition that captures the 'typical' situation of the vast majority of the laity" ("The Theology Underlying Lay Ecclesial Ministry," *Origins* 36:9 [20 July 2006] 140). See also Bonaventure Kloppenburg, *The Ecclesiology of Vatican II* (Chicago: Franciscan Herald Press, 1974) 312–5.

18 *Apostolicam Actuositatem*, no. 5.

19 Thomas R. Potvin contends that Vatican II uses the *theologoumenon* of *tria munera* to explain the functions of Christ, Christians, the ordained, and the Church, i.e., in Christology, anthropological theology, theology of ordained ministry, and ecclesiology. See "Le baptême comme enracinement dans la participation à la triple fonction du Christ," in *Le laïcat: Les limites d'un système. Actes du Congrès Canadien de Théologie* (Montréal: Fides, 1986) 146–7. For Herwi Rikhof, when the doctrine of Christ's threefold functions was used to explicate the term ministry in ecclesiology, the *tria munera* model "ousted the traditional division of the functions of the Church into two parts, the power of jurisdiction and the power of order" ("The Ecclesiologies of *Lumen Gentium*, the *Lex Ecclesiae Fundamentalis* and the Draft Code," *Concilium* 4 [1995] 61).

Apostolicam Actuositatem. The *ad extra* aspect of *Apostolicam Actuositatem* can be further expanded by juxtaposing two other conciliar documents, viz. *Ad Gentes*, the Degree on the Church's Missionary Activity, which underscores the prophetic ministry of the people of God, and *Gaudium et Spes*, the Pastoral Constitution on the Church in the Modern World, which highlights their pastoral function.

Figure 1: FABC's Theology of the Laity in Vatican II Context

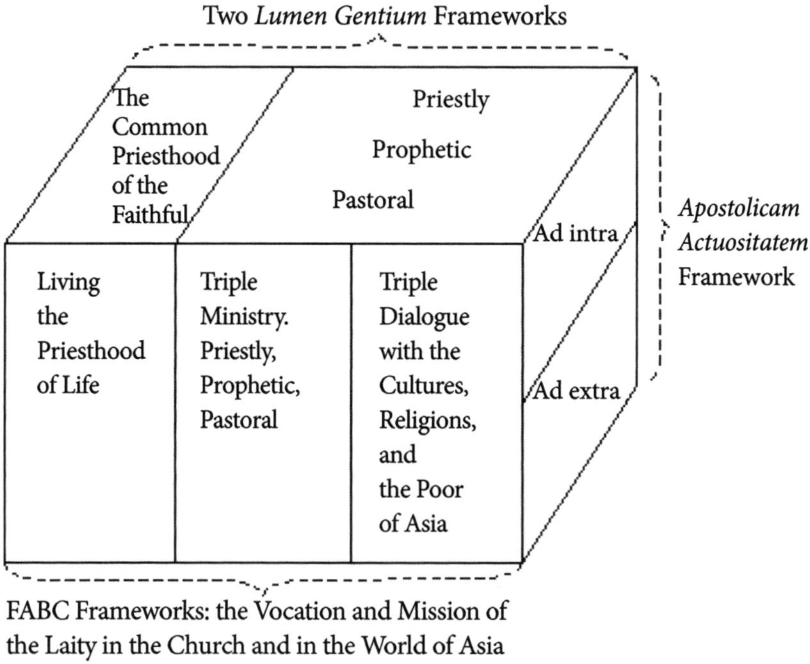

Two *Lumen Gentium* Frameworks

FABC Frameworks: the Vocation and Mission of the Laity in the Church and in the World of Asia

Review of the Contents of the FABC's Theology of the Laity

This section reviews the contents of the FABC's theology of the laity by examining the Asian bishops' view on the identity, vocation, mission, and spirituality of lay people, and concludes with an assessment of its development from 1970 to 2012.

The Identity of Lay People

In the documents of the FABC, the identity of the laity is based on two characteristics: the common baptismal priesthood of life and the secularity of lay people. First, the common priesthood, or to use the FABC's preferred term, the priesthood of life, is the basis for the identity, dignity, equality, vocation, mission, and spirituality of all Christians. It belongs to the whole people God and has its origins in Christ himself.[20] Christians live this priesthood of life by participating in "all the mysteries of redemption, viz., suffering, death and resurrection."[21] This concept implies the interdependency of all vocations in the Church because it is shared by all Christians including the clergy who have the obligation to live this "common priesthood of all before enacting the sacrifice of the Eucharist sacramentally."[22] Through baptism and confirmation believers become Christ's disciples and members of his Church, and are incorporated into Christ and the Eucharist.[23] Here, the FABC seems to expand the common basis of the identity of lay people and all Christians on the three sacraments of Baptism, Confirmation, and the Eucharist.

This description is linked to the concept of *laos*: the lay person is one who is a member of the *laos*, the people of God, in point of fact one who has been baptised and exercises the priesthood of life which belongs to all Christians.[24] For the FABC, "the ministerial priesthood has meaning and fullness only in relation to the common priesthood."[25] Expressed in philosophical terms, one can argue that

---

20 FABC IV, art. 4.4.2, *FAPA Vol. 1*, 192.
21 FABC IV, art. 4.4.2, *FAPA Vol. 1*, 192. Here the FABC seems to draw on Yves Congar's thought on the relation between priesthood and sacrifice. For Congar, who rejects "the popular notion of sacrifice as 'that which costs'," sacrifice is "that which comes from the whole of what we are and have, and totality of our being, our activity and what we possess.... What a Christian does as a Christian is an act of Christ.... For every one of us ... there is an essentially sacrificial life.... It is in this sacrificial sense that the laity partake of Christ's priesthood, by offering the whole of their lives, as Christ offered his." See A.N. Williams, "Congar's Theology of the Laity," in *Yves Congar: Theologian of the Church*, edited by Gabriel Flynn (Louvain: W.B. Eerdmans, 2005) 150-1.
22 FABC IV, art. 4.4.2, *FAPA Vol. 1*, 192. This statement reveals an important strain in the FABC's theology of the laity, which espouses a more nuanced view of the traditionally sharp distinction between the ordained and the laity.
23 FABC IV, art. 4.8.6, *FAPA Vol. 1*, 196; BILA III, art. 6, *FAPA Vol. 1*, 244.
24 In this passage, the FABC seems to take heed of Yves Congar's advice that "today it is the case, rather, that the clergy need to be defined in relation to the laity, who are quite simply members of the people of God animated by the Spirit.... The laity are primarily the baptized. Christians—clergy and lay—are a people of those who have been baptized" (*Fifty Years of Catholic Theology: Conversations with Yves Congar*, edited by Bernard Lauret [Philadelphia, Pa.: Fortress Press, 1988] 65-6).
25 FABC IV, art. 4.4.2, *FAPA Vol. 1*, 192. David Coffey suggests a new term, "the priesthood of the Church," to indicate a category that consists in the integration of the

the priesthood of life is the end and the ministerial priesthood is the means.[26] Also, unlike *Lumen Gentium*, which seems to favour a theology of the laity that seeks to contrast the identity of the lay people with that of the clergy, the concept of priesthood of life has enabled the FABC to adopt a positive vision of the laity, aiming to explore the common matrix for all Christians including the laity and the clergy.[27]

This concept of priesthood of life has three possible theological characteristics. First, it encompasses the incarnational aspect of life realities and the redemptive dimension of life witness.[28] Second, it links the sacramental, *ad intra* participation of lay people in the Church with their daily, *ad extra* engagement in the world.

---

ordained and the common priesthood, both of which have a Christological reference and an ecclesiological nature. For Coffey, "only this insight enables one to reach a clear understanding of the mutual relationship" ("The Common and the Ordained Priesthood," *Theological Studies* 58 [1997] 225).

26 We owe this observation to Phan Đình Cho [Peter C. Phan's name in Vietnamese] who wrote that "in philosophical terms, the baptismal priesthood is the end, and the ministerial priesthood is the means. The latter is an instrument to serve the former" ("The Laity in the Early Church: Building Blocks for a Theology of the Laity," *Triết Đạo:Journal of Vietnamese Philosophy and Religion* 4:2 [2002] 51).See also no. 1547 of the *Catechism of the Catholic Church* (Vatican City: Libreria Editrice Vaticana, 1994), which states that "the ministerial priesthood is at the service of the common priesthood. It is directed at the unfolding of the baptismal grace of all Christians. The ministerial priesthood is the *means* by which Christ unceasingly builds up and leads his Church" (italics in the original). In a similar vein, D. Le Tourneau states that "le service du ministère sacerdotal est un service de quelque chose, donc de quelque chose de préexistant: la *conditio fidelis*. Nou pouvons dire alors que le sacerdoce commun est conceptuellement antérieure au sacerdoce ministériel, en prenant bien garde à ne pas parler de priorité chronologique, ce qui n'aurait pas de sens" ("Le sacerdoce commun et son incidence sur les obligations et les droits des fidèles en general et des laïcs en particulier," *Revue de droit canonique* 39 [1989] 159).

27 For an excellent treatment of a similar theme see the section entitled "A Positive Vision, Not One of Contrast, To Define the Laity" in Giovanni Magnani, "Does the So-called Theology of the Laity Possess a Theological Status?" in *Vatican II: Assessment and Perspectives*, Vol. 1, edited by René Latourelle (New York: Paulist Press, 1988) 597–601, 621, and 624.

28 It is of note that Yves Congar already speaks about the "priesthood of parents," and Donald J. Goergen remarks that "partnering and parenting are a dimension of the priesthood of the laity." See respectively, *Lay People in the Church*, revised edition with additions by the author, translated by Donald Attwater (London: Geoffrey Chapman, 1965) 192–3; "Priest, Prophet, King: The Ministry of Jesus Christ," in *The Theology of Priesthood*, edited by Donald J. Goergen and Ann Garrido (Collegeville, Minn.: The Liturgical Press, 2000) 203.

Third, to a certain extent, it encompasses and harmonises the two schemata of the triple office and the common priesthood of the faithful adopted by *Lumen Gentium*, because, according to the FABC, the royal function, understood as the participation of the laity in the building up of the Kingdom of God, is linked to the priesthood of life,[29] and connected with the prophetic function,[30] which "must be a witness and a service of the whole community to the saving truth of Christ and his Church. This *sensus fidelium*, or faith instinct, of the whole people of God is a gift of the Spirit to all as a body."[31]

Secularity is the second characteristic of the identity of lay people, who are called to live their Christian discipleship and share in Christ's mission according to their lay state in the Church.[32] Their duty is to infuse Gospel values into the various dimensions of their life–familial, social, professional, and political.[33] This secularity is emphasised in the statements of the Fourth Plenary Assembly, which discuss the ministries that must be undertaken by lay people to meet the challenges of Asia such as politics, the youth, Asian women, the family, education, mass media, the world of work, social responsibilities in business, and health services. For the Asian bishops, the primary sphere of service for lay people is the world.[34]

---

29 FABC IV, art. 4.4.4, *FAPA Vol. 1*, 193. Ormond Rush contends that "contemporary ecclesiology needs to address the unresolved tension that remains within *Lumen Gentium* between the rubric of the common priesthood as primary and the threefold *munus* as the overarching framework" ("The Offices of Christ, Lumen Gentium and the People's Sense of the Faith," *Pacifica* 16:2 [2003] 138-9).

30 FABC IV, art. 4.4.3, *FAPA Vol. 1*, 193.

31 FABC IV, art. 4.4.3, *FAPA Vol. 1*, 193. Michael J. Himes notes that for John Henry Newman, "one could think about the sense of the faithful in five ways: a testimony to the fact of apostolic dogma; as a sort of instinct of *phronema*, a Greek term which might best translate as 'fundamental intentionality', deep in the life of the Church; as an action of the Holy Spirit; as an answer to the Church's constant prayer; and as a 'jealousy of error', by which he meant a sensitivity to whether something fits or clashes with the lived experience of the community." See "What Can We Learn from Vatican II?" in *The Catholic Church in the Twenty-First Century: Finding Hope for its Future in the Wisdom of its Past*, edited by Michael J. Himes (Liguori, Miss.: Liguori, 2004) 72. According to Avery Dulles, Newman "adduced five cases in which the sense of the faithful had played a significant role in the preservation or development of Catholic doctrine" such as "the confession of Mary as Mother of God (*theotokos*) in the fifth century;...the definition of the Immaculate Conception of the Blessed Virgin in the 19th century." See "*Sensus Fidelium*," *America* (1 November 1986) 241.

32 FABC IV, art. 4.8.8, *FAPA Vol. 1*, 197.

33 Ibid., art. 4.8.8, *FAPA Vol. 1*, 197.

34 Ibid., art. 4.4.2, *FAPA Vol. 1*, 192.

As Asian Christians their ministry is to live out their double heritage of faith and country as individuals and as a community.[35]

Sometimes the FABC emphasises the cultural identity of lay people before their religious allegiance by referring to them as "Asian citizens and Christians."[36] This picture of the laity, whose identity is rooted in their dynamic relationship with the Church and the societies of Asia, has influenced much of the FABC's thought on lay people's vocation, mission, and ministries. It shows that for the FABC, the dual calling of faith and citizenship is at the heart of what it means to be a lay Catholic in Asia.

In sum, the FABC's understanding of the secular character of the Asian laity is theological, ecclesial, and sociological. First, from the theological perspective, the FABC uses the secularity of lay people as a *locus theologicus*, a necessary element, to describe the identity of the Asian laity and their vocation, mission and ministries. In this sense, the relationship of Asian Christians to the world gives their vocation its uniqueness. Secularity is what qualifies their life and mission in the Church and in the world. Secondly, in an ecclesial sense, the entire Asian Church, not just the laity, is in the world, and has a secular mission with the laity having a particular secularity and mission within this ecclesial secularity. Thirdly, from the sociological or phenomenological point of view, the world is the place where lay people live out their vocation and priesthood of life by participating in secular affairs in the various dimensions of their life.

The Vocation and Mission of Lay People

In the FABC documents, the interrelated concepts of vocation and mission of lay people have a double dimension: contextual and relational. First, vocation and mission are understood as a contextualised communion and a contextualised mission, which express both the contextual and communitarian nature of their calling and activity. Lay people and the entire Christian community are called

---

35 OEIA and OE, "Consultation on Christian Presence Among Muslims in Asia," art. 31, *FAPA Vol. 1*, 170.

36 OL, "The Commitment of the Laity in the Church's Mission with Special Reference to Implementing the Social Teachings: Final Report on the First Asian Laity Meeting," *FAPA Vol. 2*, 119, 125; [FABC], "Final Statement of the First Asian Laity Meeting," in *The First Asian Laity Meeting: 4–9 September 1994, Korea*, edited by Pontifical Council for the Laity, Federation of Asian Bishops' Conferences Office of Laity, Catholic Lay Apostolate Council of Korea ([Seoul]: Pontifical Council for the Laity, Federation of Asian Bishops' Conferences Office of Laity, Catholic Lay Apostolate Council of Korea, 1994) 255, 253.

to a communion with Jesus the Liberator, a communion of committed disciples working for the liberation of Asia, which is rooted in the realities of Asia and in solidarity with the peoples of Asia. They are called to live the Christian priesthood of life, a life committed to Jesus, in the dynamism of communion with the whole people of God, and in a living dialogue and solidarity with the world, especially the poor. It is precisely when they are engaged in temporal affairs that they are engaging in the mission of the Church. For the FABC, their priesthood of life mandates a dialogue of life.

Secondly, for the FABC, underlying the articulation of the vocation and mission of lay people is their relationship with Christ and their role *vis-à-vis* the Church, the clergy and the world.[37] The goal and orientation of lay ministries is to transform the world and build up of the kingdom of God in the footsteps of Christ the Liberator. In the FABC's documents there is a recurrent usage of the terms kingdom of God, "transformation," "transforming," or their cognates.[38] Mission is the purpose of ministries,[39] and evangelisation is the highest priority of mission.[40] Therefore, lay people must assume responsibility for the tasks of evangelisation.[41] While the evangelising mission encompasses many aspects such as witnessing to Christ and the values of the Kingdom, cooperating with people who strive for justice and peace, inculturation, dialogue, and sharing with other Christians and non-Christians,[42] it is essentially the proclamation of Christ by words, works, and especially life.[43] Indeed, proclamation is the centre and primary element of evangelisation,[44] and the ultimate goal of evangelisation is to build up the kingdom of God by a triple dialogue with the religions, cultures and the poor of Asia.[45]

---

37 BILA III, arts. 1-2, 6-7, 13.4, *FAPA Vol. 1*, 243-5; FABC IV, arts. 4.7.1, 4.3.1, 4.4.4, *FAPA Vol. 1*, 194, 192-3.
38 FABC IV, arts. 3.0.2-3.9.3, *FAPA Vol. 1*, 179-190.
39 ACMC, art. 25, *FAPA Vol. 1*, 72.
40 Ibid., arts. 16-8, 25, *FAPA Vol. 1*, 70-2.
41 FABC I, arts. 25, 36, *FAPA Vol. 1*, 16, 7.
42 BIMA IV, art. 5, *FAPA Vol. 1*, 292; BILA III, art. 7, *FAPA Vol. 1*, 244.
43 FABC I, art. 25, *FAPA Vol. 1*, 16; ICM, "Workshop I: Towards a Theology of Mission for Asia Today," *FAPA Vol. 1*, 135.
44 BIMA III, art. 6, *FAPA Vol. 1*, 104; BIMA IV, art. 6, *FAPA Vol. 1*, 292.
45 BIMA IV, art. 5, *FAPA Vol. 1*, 292.

The FABC often uses the terms mission and apostolate interchangeably,[46] especially in relation to the triple mission of Christ.[47] But, unlike the terms evangelisation and mission, which have detailed entries in the indexes of the official collection of the FABC documents, the word apostolate appears as an entry only in the index of the first volume. When they do mention the term lay apostolate, the Asian bishops tend to stress its *ad mundum* dimension, the active mission of the Church in the world, or to emphasise the imperative of triple dialogue, sometimes in conjunction with the term ministries.[48] They also broaden the meaning of ecclesial ministry to include "a pluriformity of ministries" for both the ordained and lay people, a concept which is more biblical and need-oriented.[49] For them, all ministries are modelled on the mission of Jesus the Liberator and based on charisms, but only charisms and services that meet the specific needs of the community will mature into lay ministries, which are recognised and performed with "stability, continuity and responsibility."[50] This charismatic view also underlines the contextual and relational character of the FABC's theology of lay people by stressing that charism is an integral dimension of every ministry, and ministry serves the community.

Hence, lay ministries are essential to the Church, and grounded in the joint missions of Christ and the Holy Spirit. Figure 2 provides a summary and explanation of the terms associated with the FABC's understanding of the concept of mission in a schematic form. It highlights that, in the contextual theology of the FABC, *diakonia* (services and ministries), *koinonia* (communion with Jesus and communion of liberation), and *kerygma* (proclamation) are constitutive of

---

46 Wilhelm Zauner notes that after Vatican II, the substance of the terms "apostolate," "mission," and "sending" have changed: there is little discourse on "apostolate" as a theological idea, and the concept of "mission" has been expanded so much that all countries are now considered to be mission lands, and as a result, the urgency and tension of the latter term is weakened. See "Laien und Priester – eine Kirche," *Theologische Praktische Quartalschrift* 135:3 (1987) 209–10.

47 FABC IV, arts. 4.3.1, 4.4.4, *FAPA Vol. 1*, 192–3; BILA III, arts. 1–2, 6–7, 13.4, *FAPA Vol. 1*, 243–5. It is of note that for Lucien Legrand, the biblical word that corresponds to the term "mission" is the Greek word "'apostolê, tâche ou fonction apostolique," and it is used only four times in the New Testament (Acts 1:25, Rm 1:5, 1 Cor 9:2, and Ga 2:8). See "Vocation à la mission dans le nouveau testament," *Spiritus* 113 (1988) 340.

48 FABC IV, art. 4.6.2, *FAPA Vol. 1*, 194; BILA II, art. 9, *FAPA Vol. 1*, 241; BILA III, arts. 10-1, *FAPA Vol. 1*, 244.

49 BILA II, art. 11, *FAPA Vol. 1*, 241; ACMC, art. 53, *FAPA Vol. 1*, 78.

50 ACMC, arts. 32, 55, *FAPA Vol. 1*, 74, 78; BILA II, art. 12, *FAPA Vol. 1*, 241.

the vocation and mission of lay people, which is in the service of the kingdom of God.

Figure 2: Taxonomy of the FABC's Mission-related Concepts

Kingdom of God	As goal of evangelisation
Evangelisation	As the highest priority of mission
Mission/ Apostolate	As purpose of ministries
	As *ad intra* and *ad extra* ministries
	As living the priesthood of life
	As triple ministry. priestly, prophetic, pastoral
	As triple dialogue with the cultures, the religions, and the poor of Asia
Ministries	As stable, broad-based, recognised, and authenticated services
Services	As spontaneous and occasional ways of sharing in the Church's ministry

Lay Spirituality

In the FABC's theology of the laity, lay spirituality is also contextual and re-lational. First, it is "a spirituality of discipleship"[51] and "a spirituality of daily

---

51 FABC IV, art. 4.8.7, *FAPA Vol. 1*, 196–7. Peter C. Phan provides a helpful remark that "Christian spirituality, whatever its form or orientation, is in essence a following (*se-quela*) or imitation (*imitatio*) or discipleship of Jesus" ("Christian Social Spirituality: A Global Perspective," in *Catholic Social Justice: Theological and Practical Explorations*, edited by Philomena Cullen, Bernard House and Gerard Mannion [London: T&T Clark, 2007] 25). Phan's view echoes what Yves Congar wrote earlier: "Cette vie de service est voulue par le christianisme dans lequel la qualité de disciple et celle de ser-viteur coïncident: car le disciple n'écoute pas seulement son maitre, il l'imite et partage sa vie." See "Laïc et Laïcat," in *Dictionnaire de Spiritualité*, vol. 9 (Paris: Beauchesne, 1976) col. 105.

life,"[52] common to all Christians and based on the priesthood of life, because Christian disciples exercise the priestly function in their everyday life.[53] It is decisively informed by a positive, contextualised engagement by lay people with the world for the purpose of building up the kingdom of God in the existential situation of family life, work, and civic responsibilities. For the Asian bishops, a deep spirituality and prayer-life will have an evangelising and witnessing value. In Asia, they observe, Christians do not impress followers of other religions as people of prayers or contemplative communities.[54] They further note that Asian religions emphasise a deeper awareness of God and self in recollection, silence, and prayer, flowering in openness to others, and in compassion, non-violence and generosity.[55] Therefore, through a sustained and reflective dialogue with believers of other religions, Christians may also hear the voice of the Holy Spirit, expressed in a marvellous variety of ways.[56]

Secondly, the FABC's theology of lay spirituality points to a new way of being Church, giving priority to *being* before *doing*, describing more in terms of what the Church and lay people *are* rather than what they *do*. It is Trinitarian, sacramental, and prayerful with the Eucharist as its font and summit. Most importantly, it links faith and life, ministry and spirituality,[57] stressing that salvation is worked out in and through relationships at home, at work, and in the marketplace.[58] As such, it is also a spirituality of harmony, a spirituality that emphasises "simplicity, humble presence and service."[59]

---

52 BILA II, art. 6, *FAPA Vol. 1*, 240.
53 FABC IV, art. 4.4.2, *FAPA Vol. 1*, 192.
54 FABC II, art. 28, *FAPA Vol. 1*, 34.
55 Ibid., art. 35, *FAPA Vol. 1*, 35.
56 Ibid.
57 For Keith J. Egan "ministry and spirituality are not two distinct areas of the Christian life. One depends on and affects the other. Spirituality shapes ministry and ministry shapes spirituality" ("The Call of the Laity to a Spirituality of Discipleship," *The Jurist* 47 [1987] 83).
58 Without explicitly mentioning the term, the FABC seems to locate the holiness of lay people in their insertion in the world, a point that Peter C. Phan articulated in an article published a quarter of century ago: "Any authentic lay spirituality must reckon with the principle that holiness for the lay person must be achieved *in* and *through* the world and its values, not in the flight of them" ("Possibility of a Lay Spirituality: a Re-examination of some Theological Presuppositions," *Communio* 10:4 [1983] 383).
59 FABC V, art. 9.5, *FAPA Vol. 1*, 289.

The Development of the FABC's Theology of the Laity

While a careful survey of the FABC's theology of the laity from 1970 to 2012 would point out some themes that continue and some notable developments, it is still possible to see in the FABC's thought a coherent and consistent pattern. There is no radical departure in their theological and pastoral journey, but from 1986 the Asian bishops have further developed and clarified their understanding of the role of the laity in response to the challenges of Asian societies. In general, the role of lay people has been more contextualised and differentiated based on the specific needs of different regions of Asia. Their statements show a deeper concern to create of lay people, especially women, youth, and basic ecclesial communities, an active force that would be empowered to work for the kingdom of God in the Church and in the world of Asia. For this task, lay people will need to be educated and trained.

Therefore, the Church has a definite obligation to support the formation of lay people and this education must be suited to the lay life as such. Indeed, the Asian bishops' concern for the formation of the laity and the cooperation between all members of the community to face the changing context of Asia has been one of the most recurrent themes in the FABC documents. Lay people are called to become committed disciples of Christ, to learn the social doctrines of the Church, and to dialogue with peoples of different cultures and religions, especially the poor. Despite the changes in the articulation of the role of lay people, in response to the changing Asian context, the FABC's theology of the laity has remained contextualised and relational, firmly anchored in the teachings of Vatican II and flexibly attuned to the realities of Asia. Its structures will be examined in the following section.

Structures of the FABC's Theology of the Laity

Under the rubric of structures we will review the organising framework of the final statement of the Fourth Plenary Assembly of the Asian bishops, the epistemological perspective, and the hermeneutical approach of their theology of lay people.

The Statement of the Fourth Plenary Assembly of the FABC

The Fourth Plenary Assembly was convened after the FABC had discussed the theme of evangelisation in the world of Asia (FABC I, 1974), the importance of prayer and interiority in the context of Asian realities (FABC II, 1978), and the imperative of responding to the call of Jesus together as a community of faith

(FABC III, 1982). Building on the groundwork laid by these three plenary assemblies the participants of the Fourth Plenary Assembly reflected on the theme of vocation and mission of the laity in the Church and the world of Asia. Consistent with their contextual "see, judge, act" approach, the Asian bishops' treatment of this subject proceeds from an analysis of the signs of the times, through a collective discernment of the will of God, and finally, to a discussion of practical concerns.

After reviewing the challenges facing the Church in Asia, and discussing the theological issues of communion, collegiality, and co-responsibility, the Asian bishops examine the pastoral issues such as lay apostolate, clergy-laity relationship, formation *of* and *for* the laity, and lay spirituality. The organising structure of the Fourth Plenary Assembly statement shows that the FABC's theology of the laity is markedly contextual and relational. It uses the Asian context as theological resources, explores the theological meaning of communion, mission, and ecclesial structure, and finally, addresses pastoral concerns relating to clergy-laity relationship, formation, and spirituality. This theology is influenced by the Asian bishops' epistemological and hermeneutical views on the identity and role of the laity.

Epistemological Perspective

Unlike much of Western theology, which favours a dichotomy between the thinking subject and the object that needs to be analysed and dominated, the Asian bishops have adopted a different epistemology which approaches the reality in its entirety, and in an organic, non-dualistic way, focusing on the inter-relationship of the parts to the whole.[60] For them, Asian religious cultures have a holistic view of reality, seeing human beings, society, and the whole universe as intimately related and interdependent.[61] Adopting this *Weltanschauung*, the FABC stresses the contextualised communion of the entire People of God, and considers both lay people and the clergy as a constitutive part of the whole body of Christ. Unlike *Lumen Gentium*, which makes an ontological distinction between the common

---

60 OTC, "Methodology: Asian Christian Theology," art. 5.1.4, *FAPA Vol. 3*, 408; TAC, "Asian Christian Perspectives on Harmony," art. 3.4, *FAPA Vol. 3*, 276–7.

61 FABC IV, art. 3.1.10, *FAPA Vol. 1*, 181; TAC, "Asian Christian Perspectives on Harmony," art. 4.3, *FAPA Vol. 3*, 278–9. Michael Amaladoss notes that while "Euro-American cultures have a dualistic view of reality," "the Indian *advaita* (non-duality) and the Chinese *tao* (one) deny such a dichotomy. Reality is inter-dependent. It is inter-being. There is a fundamental unity reality. Being is holistic, not dichotomous" ("Contextual Theology and Integration," *East Asian Pastoral Review* 40:3 [2003] 270).

priesthood of the faithful and the ministerial priesthood,[62] the statements of the Fourth Plenary Assembly merely hint at the difference between laity and clergy by referring to the sacramental faculty of the clergy to celebrate the Eucharist, the source and summit of Christian life.[63]

This worldview also underlies much of the Asian bishops' theology of the laity, which seeks to highlight the common matrix of all Christians, laity, religious, and clergy rather than following a contrasting approach.[64] This common matrix is expressed in several main features of their theology. First, it retrieves the pneumatological meaning of charisms as the basis for all Christian services, ministries, and offices. In their view, all Christians are charismatic by vocation and through the sacrament of baptism.[65] Secondly, it uses the model of the Church as a community of faith to emphasise the communitarian vocation of all Christians, not just clergy and religious. Thirdly, it stresses that all Asian Christians are called to be a communion of disciples working for the liberation of Asia, and all share in the common priesthood of life which originates from Christ, though only the clergy can enact the sacrament of the Eucharist.

The two interrelated concepts of priesthood of life and contextualised communion are foundational to their view on the identity and role of the laity. This view is encompassed by their overall vision of a new way of being Church which was articulated at the Third and the Fifth Plenary Assemblies.[66] For the Asian

---

62 *Lumen Gentium* (no. 10) teaches that the common priesthood of the faithful and the ministerial or hierarchical priesthood "differ essentially and not only in degree." Phan Đình Cho [Peter C. Phan's name in Vietnamese] reminds us that "the difference in 'essense' and in 'degree' does not imply that the ministerial priesthood is superior to the common priesthood" ("The Laity in the Early Church: Building Blocks for a Theology of the Laity," *Triết Đạo:Journal of Vietnamese Philosophy and Religion* 4:2 [2002] 51).

63 FABC IV, art. 4.4.2, *FAPA Vol. 1*, 192.

64 The FABC's theology of the laity also seems to move beyond the neat distinctions highlighted by Edward Hahnenberg who observes that "for almost 40 years" theological writing on the topics of ordained and lay ministry "could almost be divided into two separate conversations. One conversation revolves around the theology of priesthood. It is heavily Christological and ontological, emphasizing the priest's ability through ordination to act 'in the person of Christ' and represent Christ to the community.... Another conversation revolves around the theology of lay ministry. It is heavily pneumatological and functional, emphasizing the charisms of the Spirit flowing out of baptism and toward an individual's ministry" ("Ordained and Lay Ministry: Restarting the Conversation," *Origins* 35:6 [23 June 2005] 94).

65 ACMC, arts. 31–37; *FAPA Vol. 1*, 74–5.

66 FABC V, art. 8.0, *FAPA Vol. 1*, 287; FABC III, FAPA Vol. 1, 49–65.

bishops, the Church in Asia will have to be a communion of communities, a participatory Church, a communion of small Christian communities where lay people, religious, and clergy accept each other as brothers and sisters, and a community that witnesses to Jesus Christ in a dialogue of life, and serves as a leaven of transformation and a prophetic sign to the eschatological Kingdom of God.[67] Mission, for the FABC, is more than deeds, and it involves the very being of the Church as a contextualised community of faith in Asia.[68]

Hermeneutical Approach

The FABC's theology of the laity also espouses a hermeneutical approach that seeks to read the "signs of the times" by using simultaneously Vatican II teachings as sources and Asian realities as resources. Applying the "see, judge, act" methodology it describes the laity as Asian Christians and articulates their role as agents of the dialogue of life with the religions, the cultures, and the poor of Asia. In addition to the emphasis on the prophetic-critical dimension to theology and the liberation of the poor and oppressed, favoured by Latin American theologians, and in line with the orientation of African theologies which underline "the inculturation of Christian faith in villages of Africa,"[69] the FABC is cognisant of the existence of a variety of cultures and religions in Asia, and hence, advocates the need for inculturation and interreligious dialogue in addition to the preferential, but not exclusive, option for the poor.

Like *Lumen Gentium*, which discusses the question of the laity from both the ontological and functional points of view,[70] the FABC's treatment of the role of lay people also proceeds from these perspectives, with a more pronounced emphasis on the functional dimension. This functional bias has two advantages. First, it enables them to focus more on the mission and ministries of lay people rather than concentrating on the thorny issue of defining the ontological identity of the laity,

---

67 FABC V, art. 8.0, *FAPA Vol. 1*, 287–8.
68 Ibid., art. 6.1, *FAPA Vol. 1*, 283.
69 Peter Schineller, "Inculturation as the Pilgrimage to Catholicity," *Concilium* 204 (August 1989) 98.
70 Yves Congar observes that "in the dogmatic *Constitution on the Church* the Council avoided treating laymen [*sic*] only from the viewpoint of their apostolate. It fully satisfied the general desire of having a broad exposition of the ontology and dignity of the Christian existence." See "The Laity," in *Vatican II: An Interfaith Appraisal*, ed. John H. Miller (Notre Dame: University of Notre Dame Press, 1966) 243.

a subject considered difficult by Yves Congar,[71] and to place more emphasis on the imperative of communion, co-responsibility, and collaboration of all Asian Christians in giving their faith-response to the massive challenges facing the Churches in Asia. An ontological view of the subject would tend to focus more on the distinction and difference between the ordained and the non-ordained to safeguard the ontological character of ordination, and hence could be seen as perpetuating the laity and clergy divide, and potentially alienating lay people.[72]

The functional emphasis also allows the FABC to concentrate on the realities of Asia, and articulate a specific role of the laity that is more suitable in the Asian *Sitz-im-Leben*. This approach is consistent with the contextual orientation of the theology of the bishops of Asia, who did not set out to develop a systematic theology, but have reflected on the lay experience in the Asian milieu, and issued pastoral statements to guide Asian Catholics in their Christian life and evangelising journey. The interaction between this pastoral and missionary theology and other postconciliar theological interpretations of the laity question will be discussed in the next section.

---

71 According to Yves Congar "it is very difficult to define the laity positively, perhaps even impossible," and "the Council did not wish to commit itself to a definition of the layman [sic]." See "The Laity," in *Vatican II: An Interfaith Appraisal*, ed. John H. Miller (Notre Dame: University of Notre Dame Press, 1966) 241. In an article first published in 1948, Congar understands the "*faithful*" as "those who live normal lives in our own time and culture, and not just people living in a fixed, closed agricultural economy as did our ancestors at the time that our liturgical forms were being created." See "'Real' Liturgy, 'Real' Preaching," *Worship* 82:4 (July 2008) 315. For Peter Neuner, the question of "what is a lay person?" has no correct answer because the question itself is wrong, and he goes on to assert that if we have a correct theology of the people of God we do not need a separate theology of the laity ("Wenn wir eine rechte Theologie des Volkes Gottes haben, so also die These, brauchen wir keine eigene Theologie des Laien"). See "Aspekte einer Theologie des Laien," *Una Sancta* 43 (1988) 322–3. Adopting a different perspective, Susan K. Wood observes that "with the appropriation and exercise of a variety of ministries formerly associated with ordination by the non-ordained, it is becoming increasingly clear that ordained ministry needs to be defined in terms of identity rather than function" ("Priestly Identity: Sacrament of the Ecclesial Community," *Worship* 69:2 [March 1995] 111).

72 It is instructive to recall a quotation that Peter Neuner took from P.M. Zulehner's *Das Gottesgerücht* (Düsseldorf, 1987, p. 74): "Aus der 'Ordination' der einen darf nicht eine 'Subordination' der anderen werden" ("Was ist ein Laie?" *Stimmen der Zeit* 210 [1992] 518); see also "Aspekte einer Theologie des Laien," *Una Sancta* 43 (1988) 324.

The FABC's Theology of the Laity and Other Postconciliar Theologies of the Laity

Studying the FABC's theology of laity, one is to be struck by the close parallels between its themes and other postconciliar interpretations of lay experience, in particular those of Yves Congar and Latin American liberation theologies. This section briefly discusses the notable points of convergence between these theologies, and situates the FABC's theology of the laity in the framework of theological approaches to the question of lay people proposed by Leonard Doohan.

The FABC and Yves Congar's Theology of the Laity

While Yves Congar's theological corpus encompasses three broad categories, namely, ecumenism, questions of fundamental theology, and ecclesiology,[73] four points of convergence between his theology of the laity and the teachings of the FABC are notable. First, like Congar, the FABC provides a definition of ministry based on three characteristics: essentiality, stability, and formal recognition in the context of charisms and services.[74] Secondly, following Congar who employs

---

73 Christopher O'Donnell, *"Ecclesia:"* A *Theological Encyclopedia of the Church* (Collegeville, Minn.: The Liturgical Press, 1996) 102.

74 The Asian bishops distinguish between charisma, services, and ministries as follows: "*Charisms* are enduring gifts given to Church members to be put to use in services and ministries. Endowed with them, different members render different services, thereby contributing, each in his or her own manner, to the Christian mission. All Christians are charismatic by vocation and in virtue of their baptismal consecration; but not all are engaged in the ministry of the Church in the same manner and with the same intensity. We term *services* those ways of sharing in the Church's ministeriality which are undertaken spontaneously and on occasions. These are already in their own manner an expression of the Church's service (diakonia) and indeed indispensable for the Christian presence in the world. *Ministries* apply more properly to those services which Church members undertake with a certain stability and exercise on a sufficiently broad basis, thus sharing formally in the Church's responsibility to signify the presence to men of Christ's saving action. All such ministries must be recognized by the community and authenticated by it in the person of its leader. Thus, every service and ministry of the Church supposes a charism but not every charism blossoms into a ministry." See FABC, "Asian Colloquium on Ministries in the Church," art. 32, *FAPA Vol. 1*, 74. They further clarify that "not every charism or service needs to be recognized as ministry but only those which the life and growth of the community require to be exercised with stability, continuity and responsibility." Ibid., 78. The US Bishops' National Advisory Council quoted approvingly this comprehensive and interesting definition considering it "useful for the Catholic Church in the United States to employ the distinctions made

127

the *triplex munus* schema to examine the role of lay people, the Asian bishops affirm that "lay people with special charisms to exercise ministries" are called to "exercise in a public manner some aspects of the Christian's function of priest, prophet and pastor."[75] They also use the *tria munera* framework to explain in detail the priestly, prophetic, and royal functions of lay people.[76]

Another point of convergence between Congar and the FABC is their emphasis on the common priesthood of the faithful as the background and starting point for their theology of laity. However, whereas Congar employs the term "spiritual priesthood" and considers it to be the background of his theology of lay people, the FABC prefers to call it "priesthood of life" stressing that "the priestly function belongs to the whole people of God."[77]

Finally, as with Congar, the Asian bishops utilise the concepts of communion, collegiality, and co-responsibility as the basis for their explication of the mission of lay people. In their view, the renewal of inner ecclesial structures "consists in creating the right atmosphere of communion, collegiality and co-responsibility for an active and fuller lay initiation, participation and action."[78] As a pastoral movement, Latin American liberation theologies have also called for a greater participation and involvement by the entire people of God. Their influence on the FABC's theology of the laity will be briefly discussed in the next section.

The FABC and Latin American Liberation Theologies

Besides the theology of Yves Congar, the FABC's theology of the laity has drawn on the main insights of Latin America liberation theologies. In its official documents, the FABC has often evoked three distinctive principles of Latin American liberation theologies, namely, an emphasis on historical liberation and human development, a preferential but not exclusive option for the poor, and a bottom-up ecclesiology privileging the experience of basic ecclesial communities and the

---

by the FABC between charisms, ministry and service." U.S. Bishops' National Advisory Council, "The Trust of Lay Ministry," *Origins* 9:39 (13 March 1980) 624.

75 FABC, "Asian Colloquium on Ministries in the Church," art. 54, *FAPA Vol. 1*, 78.

76 FABC IV, art. 4.4.2-4, *FAPA Vol. 1*, 192–3.

77 FABC IV, art. 4.2.2, *FAPA Vol. 1*, 192. For the Asian bishops, the common priesthood of the faithful "is the real priesthood of life" having its origins in Christ himself," and "the clergy have the obligation to live the common priesthood of all before enacting the sacrifice of the Eucharist sacramentally. Ibid.

78 FABC IV, art. 4.5.1-2, *FAPA Vol. 1*, 193; see also FABC III, *FAPA Vol. 1*, 49–65.

process of conscientisation.[79] First, the FABC emphasises the call for Asian Christians "to become a Church deeply committed to Jesus the Liberator," because "such a commitment by all Christians will make the Church a communion of committed disciples – be they clergy or laity – working for the liberation of Asia."[80] Secondly, the FABC highlights the preferential, but not exclusive, option for the poor,[81] and encourages Catholic schools to "reflect the Church's preferential option for the poor."[82] Thirdly, the FABC promotes basic Christian communities, considering them as "the most fundamental ecclesial realities" which embody "the mystery of the Church in their own right."[83]

The Asian bishops also feel that conscientisation is "particularly important today in educating all to justice, especially the young."[84] For them, conscientisation means "to become aware of social conditions surrounding us by reflection and analysis to concrete action,"[85] a process that seeks "the change and transformation of unjust social structures."[86] This commitment to bring about social justice and to transform the world has been identified by Leonard Doohan as one of the main theological approaches to lay experience. It is therefore instructive to provide a brief excursus into the extent to which the FABC's theology of laity fits into Doohan's taxonomy of theological interpretations of the laity question.

---

79 [Latin American Bishops], Second General Conference of Latin American Bishops: "The Church in the Present-Day Transformation of Latin America in the Light of the Council" (August 26-September 6, 1968 [Medellín, Columbia]), in *Liberation Theology: A Documentary History*, edited with introductions, commentary and translations by Alfred T. Hennelly (Maryknoll, N.Y.: Orbis Books, 1990) 89–119; Third General Conference of the Latin American Bishops: "Evangelization in Latin America's Present and Future" (Pueblo de los Angeles, Mexico, January 27-February 13, 1979), ibid., 225–58.

80 FABC IV, art. 4.1.3, *FAPA Vol. 1*, 191.

81 BILA III, art. 11, *FAPA Vol. 1*, 244.

82 FABC IV, art. 3.5.3, *FAPA Vol. 1*, 185.

83 FABC, "Asian Colloquium on Ministries in the Church," art. 40, *FAPA Vol. 1*, 76.

84 BISA II, art. 7, *FAPA Vol. 1*, 204.

85 BISA II, art. 7, note 1, *FAPA Vol. 1*, 205; see also BISA III, art. 8, *FAPA Vol. 1*, 208. Paulo Freire defines conscientisation—*conscientização* in Brazilian—as a "probing of the ambience, of reality," or a "commitment in time" because it goes deeper than the French expression *prise de conscience* and "implies a historical commitment." See his 1970 paper "Conscientizing as a Way of Liberating," in *Liberation Theology: A Documentary History*, edited with introductions, commentary and translations by Alfred T. Hennelly (Maryknoll, N.Y.: Orbis Books, 1990) 6–7.

86 FABC I, art. 21, *FAPA Vol. 1*, 15.

The FABC and Leonard Doohan's Theology of the Laity

Of the five theological interpretations of the laity question identified by Doohan,[87] the third approach, the theology of world transformation, and elements of the fourth approach, the theology of laity and ecclesial restructuring, are most readily discernible in the FABC's theology of laity. First, like the theology of world transformation, the Asian bishops emphasise the duty of all Christians to transform the world, declaring that "through work of every kind we are participating in God's own ongoing process of recreating and transforming our world."[88] In a categorical statement they declare that "to shut oneself totally away from the demands of the political transformation of Asia is, surely, in a sense, a denial of Christian identity."[89]

Secondly, like the variegated features identified in Doohan's fourth theological approach, the bishops recognise the need for ecclesial restructuring based on the "principles of communion, co-responsibility and collegiality,"[90] emphasise the common mission of all Christians,[91] base their theology of laity on an emphasis on the common priesthood of life,[92] propose a model of the Church as a community of faith,[93] and promote the development of basic Christian communities.[94] These theological features together with the focus, context, and intended audience of the FABC's theology of the laity have to be taken into account in order to achieve a balanced assessment of its strengths and areas that may require further amplification and improvement.

Strengths and Limitations of the FABC's Theology of the Laity

The context, contents, and structures of the FABC's theology of the laity, together with its interaction with other postconciliar interpretations of the laity, discussed

---

87 Leonard Doohan, "Theology of the Laity," in *The New Dictionary of Sacramental Worship*, ed. Peter E. Fink (Collegeville, Minn.: The Liturgical Press) 639–40; idem, *Laity's Mission in the Local Church: Setting a New Direction* (San Francisco: Harper & Row, 1986) 4–5; idem, *The Lay-Centered Church: Theology and Spirituality* (Minneapolis, Minn.: Winston Press, 1984) 4–23; idem, "Contemporary Theologies of the Laity: An Overview Since Vatican II," *Communio* 7 (1980) 228–41.

88 FABC IV, art. 3.7.1, *FAPA Vol. 1*, 187, and 188–9.

89 Ibid., art. 3.1.3, *FAPA Vol. 1*, 180.

90 Ibid., art. 4.5.2, *FAPA Vol. 1*, 193.

91 Ibid., art. 4.1.3, *FAPA Vol. 1*, 191.

92 Ibid., art. 4.4.2, *FAPA Vol. 1*, 192.

93 FABC III, *FAPA Vol. 1*, 49–65.

94 FABC, "Asian Colloquium on Ministries in the Church," art. 46, *FAPA Vol. 1*, 77.

in the previous sections show that it is contextual and relational in its approach and orientation. It also reveals that the Asian bishops are not interested in developing a systematic theology of the laity as their theology has always been attuned to the pastoral and missionary questions of the day. It is a contextualised, pastoral theology par excellence, seeking to apply the teachings of the Second Vatican Council to the context of Asia, and marrying theological reflection and social analysis. Its goal is to empower lay people to reclaim their right as full and equal members of the Church, and to be co-responsible with the clergy for the evangelising mission in the world of Asia.

It advocates a common matrix, which is based on a contextualised identity of lay people flowing from a baptismal, common priesthood of life. It includes a call to a contextualised communion, a contextualised mission whose mode is dialogue, a contextualised renewal of ecclesial structure which is adaptable to the Asian realities on the basis of communion, collegiality, and co-responsibility, and a contextualised spirituality of discipleship and harmony which manifests itself in a spirituality of triple dialogue. This common matrix is supported by a contextualised formation *of* and *for* the laity, aiming to help them to assume the task of building up the kingdom of God by engaging in the dialogue of life with the cultures, the religions, and the poor of Asia. Their identity and role is ultimately defined by their triple relationship with Christ, the Asian Church, and the Asian realities.

Indeed, the greatest strength of the FABC's theology of the laity is that it is contextual and relational. It seeks to adapt the "constants" of the Gospel, tradition, and Vatican II to the "context" of cultures and social changes in the Church and in the world of Asia.[95] It draws on lay people's existential relationship with Christ, the Church and the world as theological resources. It is Christocentric and *ad mundum*, stressing lay people's participation in the very mission of Christ and his Church, and decidedly orientated to the world. The Asian bishops consider the vocation of lay people as a communion with Jesus, and link it with a communion of liberation. They show that the laity's vocation is directly connected, not only to Jesus Christ the Liberator, but also to the concrete realities of the world of Asia. Their theology of the laity focuses on exploring the common matrix of Christian vocation, which is based on the sacraments of Christian initiation, expressed primarily by the concept of baptismal, common priesthood of life, a matrix that has a permanent value, and from which different Christian vocations are born,

---

95 For an expanded discussion of these motifs in relation to Christian mission see Stephen B. Bevans and Roger P. Schroeder, *Constants in Context: A Theology of Mission for Today*, American Society of Missionary Series, no. 30 (Maryknoll, New York: Orbis Books, 2004).

rather than insisting on nailing down those elements that distinguish ordained ministries from lay ministries. For them, lay people are Asian Christians pure and simple.[96]

However, the FABC's theology of the laity has certain limitations. The first is that the individual dimension of holiness is somewhat understated. While the Asian bishops were no doubt aware of the universal call of Christians to holiness, a theme that holds a prominent place in *Lumen Gentium*,[97] it did not rate a mention in the statements of the Fourth Plenary Assembly, their *magna carta* for the laity, or in the indexes of the three-volume collection of the official documents of the FABC. Only rarely did the Asian bishops refer explicitly to the universal call of Christians to holiness, and when they did, they discussed it in relation to the clergy and religious.[98] They probably decided that given the audience they were trying to address, the most appropriate point of departure for their theology of the laity was the communal response to the challenges of Asia in light of Vatican II's vision. This approach means that the essential connection of mission with the call for holiness has received less emphasis than it could in another approach to the subject. The bishops also did not discuss explicitly the doxological character of ministry and spirituality, a theological feature that emphasises that the purpose of our daily life and service must be to glorify and to worship the Triune God.

Another limitation of the FABC's theology of the laity is that its emphasis on the common matrix and the autonomy of lay people could blur the clergy-lay distinction, especially with regard to their respective roles in the world.[99] Even though

---

96 Pascal Thomas also emphasises the common identity of all Christians by choosing an eye-catching title for his book on the laity: *Ces chrétiens que l'on appelle laïcs* (Paris: Les Éditions Ouvrières) 1988. It is likely that this title is based on *Lumen Gentium* (no. 30), the Latin version of which reads: "Sancta Synodus, muneribus Hierarchiae declaratis, libenter animum advertit statui illorum christifidelium qui laici nuncupantur." See Sacrosanctum Oecumenicum Concilium Vaticanum II, *Constitutiones, Decreta, Declarationes*, cura et studio Secretariae Generalis Concilii Oecumenicii Vaticani II (Roma: Typis Polyglottis Vaticanis, 1966) 135.

97 *Lumen Gentium*, nos. 39–32.

98 BILA II, art. 6, *FAPA Vol. 1*, 240; BILA III, art. 6, *FAPA Vol. 1*, 244.

99 It is worth noting Kenan B. Osborne's remark that, after Vatican II, "the church is primarily the earthly *communio sanctorum*, an undivided people of God, an undivided community of *christifideles*, a casteless priesthood of all believers. At this fundamental level, terms such as lay and cleric have absolutely no meaning" (*Ministry: Lay Ministry in the Roman Catholic Church: Its History and Theology* [New York: Paulist Press, 1993] 598). For Osborne, in the third millennium, "the very term *sacerdotium* will be replaced by the term *ecclesia*, 'people of God', and the very term *regnum* will be replaced by the

the FABC clearly thinks that laity and clergy have a different role in society, the impression left by this approach can be just the opposite. Once again, this has to do with the starting point. The FABC chooses to proceed with a common matrix to show that sacramental initiation is the basis for the vocation and mission of all Asian Christians, and their mission in the world is synonymous with the mission of the whole Church. Lay people might come to a new appreciation of the empowerment and autonomy in their ministry in the world, but that could lead them to suppose that the clergy have little more to offer. Therefore, the FABC's theology of the laity could be strengthened by an investigation into "an ordering of the baptismal priesthood of all the faithful,"[100] expressed by an ordering of the ministries, both lay and ordained, in service of the mission of Christ.[101]

In this framework of ordered ministries, which is already implicit in the FABC's theology of lay people, all Christians share a common baptismal identity and a common mission before they are further specified by their state in life and their particular ministry.[102] Entrance into ministries or orders then constitutes a new

---

term 'a pluralistic world'. It is no longer a question of *sacerdotium* standing over and against a *regnum*, but rather a community called church within a larger community called a pluralistic world" ("A Profile of the Baptized Catholic Christian at the Beginning of the Third Millennium," *The Catholic World* [January-February 1996] 38). Brian Staudt contends that, unlike Osborne, who sees "the authentic revelation of God in Scripture alone and development beyond Scripture as outside God's plan," J.-M.R Tillard's "examination of the patristic sources and his presupposition that the Holy Spirit played a guiding role in the early church's process of becoming the church that Christ founded leads him to conclude that a division of ministries is necessary and appropriate even within the communion of believers co-equal in dignity." See "The Lay-Cleric Distinction: Tragedy or Comedy?" *Church* 12:3 (Fall 1996) 47; see also J.-M.R Tillard, *Church of Churches: The Ecclesiology of Communion*, translated by R.C. De Peaux (Collegeville, Minn.: The Liturgical Press, 1992).

100 Susan K. Wood, "Introduction: The Collegeville Ministry Seminar," in *Ordering the Baptismal Priesthood: Theologies of Lay and Ordained Ministry*, edited by Susan K. Wood (Collegeville, Minn.: Liturgical Press, 2003) x.

101 The move from the narrow categories of laity and clergy to a broader concept of "ordered ministries" was one of the main conclusions reached by ten noted theologians who gathered at a research seminar in 2002. See *Ordering the Baptismal Priesthood: Theologies of Lay and Ordained Ministry*, edited by Susan K. Wood (Collegeville, Minn.: Liturgical Press, 2003).

102 Edward P. Hahnenberg, *Ministries: A Relational Approach* (New York: Herder & Herder, 2003) 122–50; Susan K. Wood, "Conclusion: Convergence Points toward a Theology of Ordered Ministries," in *Ordering the Baptismal Priesthood: Theologies of*

ecclesial relationship.[103] A deeper reflection on the theme of ordered ministries and the concept of communion as "rightly ordered relationships"[104] with Christ, the Church, and others, would better articulate the FABC's theology of the laity and its emphasis on the vocation of lay people as a communion with Jesus and a communion of liberation, and their priestly, prophetic, and royal mission.[105] It would also reflect more closely the nature of the Church as both communion and mission, and preserve the unity of mission in a diversity of ministries that are grounded in a baptismal, hence Trinitarian, communion. In the Church of Jesus the Liberator, all Christians, lay and ordained, are baptised *for* and *into* communion and mission.

Conclusion

This chapter has evaluated the context, contents, and structures of the FABC's theology of the laity. It also examines the interaction between this theology and other postconciliar theologies of the laity, and provides an assessment of its strengths and limitations. It argues that this theology is eminently contextual and relational, displaying the twin characteristics of fidelity and creativity, adhering to the traditions and teachings of Vatican II, and adapting to the Asian context within the overall vision of a triple dialogue with the religions, the cultures, and the poor of Asia. It is a contextual theology *par excellence*, reforming rather than revolutionary, using the conciliar teachings and the challenges of Asia as theological sources and resources, and aiming to awaken the Asian laity and challenge them to take up their specific mission and ministries in the Church and in the world.[106] It stresses

---

Lay and Ordained Ministry, edited by Susan K. Wood (Collegeville, Minn.: Liturgical Press, 2003) 260.

103 Richard R. Gaillardetz, "The Ecclesiological Foundations of Ministry within an Ordered Communion," in *Ordering the Baptismal Priesthood: Theologies of Lay and Ordained Ministry*, edited by Susan K. Wood (Collegeville, Minn.: Liturgical Press, 2003) 48.

104 Cardinal Roger Mahony, "Church of the Eucharist, a Communion for Mission," *Origins* 33:42 (1 April 2004) 726.

105 FABC IV, arts. 4.1-4.3, *FAPA Vol. 1*, 191–2.

106 In *The Christian Commitment*, Karl Rahner states that "'everything depends on the layperson's understanding that he is, as an individual, irreplaceable, with a specifically Christian and moral task to be performed within groups not directly subject to the church's official control, a task of which he will have to give an account before the judgment seat of God." Quoted by William O'Malley, "The Church of the Faithful," *America* (19 June 1993) 7.

the unity of faith and life, links mission and spirituality, and emphasises the importance of both being and doing. It calls for a contextualised identity of lay people as Asian Christians, a contextualised communion, a contextualised mission, a contextualised renewal of structures, and a contextualised spirituality, supported by a contextualised program of formation *of* and *for* the laity. In this theology, the ministries of lay people are grounded in the inseparable missions of Christ and the Holy Spirit, and their identity and role are ultimately based on their triple relationship with Jesus, the Church, and the world of Asia.

While it has some minor limitations such as an under-emphasis on the universal call for individual holiness, an inadequate treatment of the doxological dimension of lay ministry and spirituality, and a potential blurring of lay-cleric distinction in their respective role in the world, the FABC's theology of the laity offers a view that is well attuned to the Asian context. Its contextual and relational character is summed up by the concept of priesthood of life, a rich matrix that encompasses the ontological aspect of lay people's incorporation into Christ, and the functional dimension of everyday life service and ministry based on the charisms of the Holy Spirit. In this theology of the laity, priesthood of life leads to triple dialogue of life, a theological motif that is also evident in the FABC's theology of the Church. The development and other aspects of this theology of the Church, which provides the ecclesiological underpinnings for the FABC's theology of the laity, will be explored in the next chapter.

Chapter 6   Models of the Asian Church

Like Vatican II, which was largely a Council of the universal church, for the church, and about the church, the statements of the Federation of Asian Bishops' Conferences (FABC) are in the main documents of a local church for and about the Church in Asia. Indeed, since their first meeting in 1970, the Catholic bishops of Asia have issued numerous statements addressing various aspects of the Asian Church. In 1982 they devoted the entire Third Plenary Assembly to reflect on the theme of "The Church – A Community of Faith in Asia."[1] However, consistent with their predominantly missionary and pastoral orientation, they did not develop a systematic ecclesiology. Their ecclesiological interpretations were generally crafted to address the specific challenges facing the churches in Asia. In the first section of this chapter, which begins with an overview of the statement of the Third Plenary Assembly, we will trace the development of the FABC's ecclesiology highlighting its basic continuity and gradual progression. We will then proceed with an investigation into the theological basis and features of this theology of the church, and conclude with a preliminary assessment of its strengths and limitations.

Development of the FABC's Ecclesiology

The statement of the Third Plenary Assembly comprises the main text, which consists of five parts, the "Resolutions of the Assembly," and the "Syllabus of Concerns." It focuses on the church "as a community realizing its communion and mission in its own being and life, and in relation to other communities."[2] Its purpose is to develop a deeper understanding of the mystery of the church from a trinitarian perspective, and its application on the local and community level. Its pastoral aim is "to make local communities more and more authentic communities of faith."[3] Part 1 of the main text is a rapid survey of the FABC's activities and achievements from 1972 to 1982. In Part 2 the Asian bishops explicate the identity, vocation, and mission of the church under the rubric of "a community of faith in Asia." In Part 3 they discuss some of the "inadequacies and failures" of

---

1   FABC III, *FAPA Vol. 1*, 49–65.
2   FABC III, art. 5, *FAPA Vol. 1*, 55.
3   FABC III, art. 14, *FAPA Vol. 1*, 60.

the churches in Asia. This is followed by a more optimistic turn in Part 4 where the bishops identify signs of hope and indications of the presence of the Spirit at work in ecclesial communities in Asia. Finally, in Part 5, they articulate their pastoral vision and priorities.

The title of this statement is significant. It speaks of "a community" "of faith" "in Asia." The emphasis, then, is placed on a particular local church in communion with the universal church and other local churches, and rooted in the concrete, existential, and historical realities of the Asian *Sitz im Leben*. This community is united by faith, "the first single and shared reality by which the Church exists."[4] By this interpretation the FABC appears to adopt the older New Testament understanding of *ekklesia* as a local assembly—the Pauline view—rather than referring to the church as the universal church.[5] It also adheres to the patristic notion of the church as communion,[6] a fertile concept that the 1985 Synod of Bishops proposed as the underlying framework of the church at Vatican II.[7]

After the Third Plenary Assembly, the FABC increasingly turned its attention toward promoting a new way of being church in Asia, which is expressed by four ecclesiological foci: church as communion-in-mission,[8] as community

---

4   Yves Congar, "The Conciliar Structure or Regime of the Church," *Concilium* 167 (September 1983) 3–9, at 4.

5   Analysing the occurrences of the term *ekklēsia* in seventeen of the twenty-seven books of the New Testament, Raymond F. Collins concludes that *ekklēsia* was used in two senses: the first reflects an older usage to connote a local assembly, and the second, a more recent usage, refers to the universal Church. See "Did Jesus Found The Church? Which Church?" *Louvain Studies* 21:4 (1996) 356–64, at 357, 359, 363.

6   J.-M.R. Tillard maintains that "the nature of the Church, as early Tradition understands it" is "summed up in the communion, *koinonia.*" See *Church of Churches: The Ecclesiology of Communion*, translated by R.C. De Peaux (Collegeville, Minn.: The Liturgical Press, 1992) 29.

7   Synod of Bishops, "The Final Report of the 1985 Extraordinary Synod of Bishops." *Origins* 15:27 (19 December 1985) 444–50.

8   OE, "Consultation on Evangelization and Communication," art. 4, *FAPA Vol. 3*, 210; OE, "Consultation on Asian Local Churches and Mission *Ad Gentes*: A New Way of Being Church-in-Mission in Asia," arts. 8–9, *FAPA Vol. 3*, 222; OE, "Consultation on 'Evangelization and Inculturation,'" *FAPA Vol. 3*, 216–7. See also OHD, "Understanding Christian – Muslim Dialogue in South East Asia," *FAPA Vol. 4*, 84.

of dialogue and solidarity,[9] as community of disciples,[10] and as basic ecclesial communities.[11] These ecclesiological understandings do not destroy or reduce, but clarify and complement its primary definition of the church as a community of faith in Asia by relating and re-ordering the reality of the church to the faith experience and the pastoral and missionary needs of Asian Christians. All these understandings of the church in Asia will now be summarised in an architectural model (Figure 1) to highlight their interaction and interdependence. It consists of three concentric circles highlighting the FABC's models of the Asian church.

The first, innermost circle emphasises the centrality of the FABC's view of the vocation of the church as a community of faith in Asia. In all the documents of the FABC, no other definition of the church is as fundamental as this one; it is to this community of faith in Asia that all other images of the church refer, and it is this communion in faith that distinguishes the church from all other communities in the Asian continent. The third, outermost concentric band summarises the Asian bishops' vision for the mission of the church. For them, evangelisation is the

---

9 BIRA IV/12, art. 48, *FAPA Vol. 1*, 332; OEIA, "Consultation on Christian Presence among Muslims in Asia," art. 4, *FAPA Vol. 1*, 166; OESC, "Dialogue between Faith and Cultures in Asia: Towards Integral Human and Social Development," art. 25, FAPA Vol. 2, 25; BIMA 1, art. 11, FAPA Vol. 1, 94; BISA I, art. 2, *FAPA Vol. 1*, 199; BISA V, arts. 6, 12–14, *FAPA Vol. 1*, 218–9; BISA VI, arts. 3, 8–9, *FAPA Vol. 1*, 223, 225; BISA VII, arts. 20–21, *FAPA Vol. 1*, 233; FABC V, arts. 2.3.3–2.3.4, *FAPA Vol. 1*, 278; FABC VI, arts. 3, 14.2, 15, *FAPA Vol. 2*, 2, 8, 10; FABC VII, arts. I.A.8, III, *FAPA Vol. 3*, 4, 8. In 2004, the FABC considered the "Church engaged in the triple dialogue: dialogue with the poor, the religions and the cultures of Asia" as a "contextual model of being Church in Asia." See OEIA, "Fifth Formation Institute for Interreligious Affairs FIRA V: Interreligious Dialogue in Religious Education," *FAPA Vol. 4*, 199; see also OE, "Asian Mission Congress 2006: Telling the Story of Jesus in Asia," *FAPA Vol. 4*, 276.
10 FABC VI, arts. 14, 52, *FAPA Vol. 2*, 1–12, 226.
11 OHD, "Walking Humbly, Acting Justly, Loving Tenderly in Asia," art. 7, *FAPA Vol. 2*, 44; OL, "Second Southeast Asian Regional Laity Meeting," art. 8, *FAPA Vol. 3*, 90; OTC, "The Spirit at Work in Asia Today," art. 2.3.10, *FAPA Vol. 3*, 277; OLF, "SCCs/ BECc Towards a Church of Communion," AsIPA 4th General Assembly," art. 2.3, *FAPA Vol. 4*, 181; "BILA-I on Small Christian Communities (SCCs)," *FAPA Vol. 5*, 163; "Go, You are sent forth! Following Jesus in Mission: Small Christian Communities Serving and Ministering," art. 3.3, *FAPA Vol. 5*, 169. For the FABC the family is "the basic cell of society and the fundamental ecclesial community, the Church that is the home." See FAPA VIII, art. 46, *FAPA Vol. 4*, 16.

primary task and the highest priority for the church,[12] whose purpose is to build up the kingdom of God.[13] Its mission is directed to the world,[14] and its mode "a triple dialogue of life" with the cultures, the religions, and the poor.[15] The second, middle band highlights four main models of the church that the FABC gradually formulated from 1982. These ecclesiological models, which germinated from the basic ideas already existing at or prior to the Third Plenary Assembly, are not distinct from each other but represent different aspects of the vocation and mission of the church that the FABC emphasised in response to the needs and situations of Asian churches. They were developed from the primary, fundamental view of the nature of the church as presented in the innermost circle, and the vision of the church's mission as shown in the outermost band. The arrows used in the outermost band are not meant to indicate any cause-effect relationship between each of these four aspects, but highlight the dynamics and interplay between the various ecclesiological models (in the middle band) and the major aspects of the mission of Asian churches (in the outermost band).

---

12 FABC I, arts. 8, 25, *FAPA Vol. 1*, 13, 16; FABC III, art. 17.3, *FAPA Vol. 1*, 60; FABC V, art. 3, *FAPA Vol. 1*, 279–81; FABC VII, art. III, *FAPA Vol. 3*, 8; BIMA IV, art. 7, *FAPA Vol. 1*, 292.

13 FABC IV, art. 4.4.4, *FAPA Vol. 1*, 193; FABC V, arts. 1.7, 2.3.9, 4.1, *FAPA Vol. 1*, 275, 279, 282; BIRA IV/2, arts. 8.1–8.2, *FAPA Vol. 1*, 252; BILA III, art. 12.2, *FAPA Vol. 1*, 245.

14 FABC III, art. 17.1, *FAPA Vol. 1*, 60; FABC V, art. 3, *FAPA Vol. 1*, 279–81; FABC VII, art. III, *FAPA Vol. 3*, 8; BILA III, art. 13.4, *FAPA Vol. 1*, 245.

15 FABC I, arts. 12–24, *FAPA Vol. 1*, 14-6; FABC III, art. 17.1, 17.4, *FAPA Vol. 1*, 60-1; FABC V, arts. 4.1–4.2, *FAPA Vol. 1*, 282; FABC VI, arts. 3, 15, *FAPA Vol. 2*, 2, 10; FABC VII, art. I.A.8, III, *FAPA Vol. 3*, 4, 8.

Figure 1: Vocation and Mission of the Church: an Ecclesiological Architecture

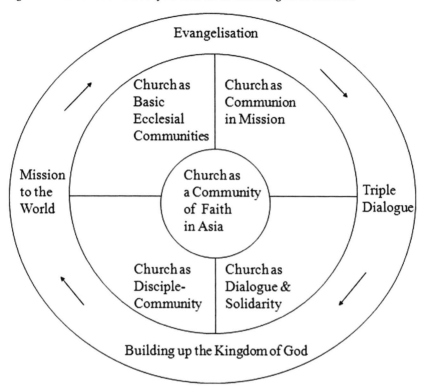

By defining the church as a community of faith in Asia, the Asian bishops have adroitly combined a theological construct and a sociological category to express the vertical and horizontal, divine and human aspects of the church. However, they have decisively moved forward, and developed other ecclesiological images and metaphors in response to the pastoral needs of particular times and places. Our observation is that by proposing these forms of ecclesiality, or new ways being church, the FABC has implicitly adopted an analogical rather than dichotomous (either/or) approach. We also argue that this approach, which is primarily contextual, theologically consistent, and pastorally faithful to the vision of Vatican II,[16] seems to proceed in the opposite direction from that followed by Avery

---

16 For Joseph A. Komonchak, "the reason for a variety of images [of the Church] is to be found in the council's choice of a more biblical, patristic, and liturgical language"

Dulles who started with an exploration of the richness of the reality of the church under five ecclesiological models, and subsequently, developed an encompassing model of the church as a community of disciples.[17] A clear advantage of the Asian bishops' ecclesiological approach is that, like the New Testament ecclesiology,[18] it provides a tensile coexistence of the divergent views of the church, and can avoid the tension caused by the problematic invocation of their teaching to defend conflicting models of the Church in Asia.[19] It also reminds Asian Christians that no one image can exhaust the rich reality of the church, and all frameworks are but weak metaphors trying to reflect the mystery of the church. For the FABC, the Church in Asia has a strongly christological, pneumatological, and trinitarian basis.

Theological Foundations of the FABC's Ecclesiology

Modern Catholic theologians tend to develop their ecclesiology from one of three perspectives: christological, pneumatological, or trinitarian. In a groundbreaking work on ministry, Kenan Osborne champions a vigorous christological orientation, predicting that "Christology in an ever increasing way will be seen as the basis and substance of ecclesiology."[20] J.-M.R. Tillard, on the contrary, develops his ecclesiology based on the concept of communion, and gives great

("The Significance of Vatican II for Ecclesiology," in *The Gift of the Church: A Textbook on Ecclesiology in Honour of Patrick Granfield*, ed. Peter C. Phan [Collegeville, Minn.: The Liturgical Press, 2000] 69–92, at 76).

17 Avery Dulles initially identifies five models of the church, as institution, mystical communion, sacrament, herald, and servant. See *Models of the Church* (Dublin: Gill and Macmillan, 1976). Later, following the lead of John Paul II's *Redemptor hominis* no. 21, he refines and integrates these ecclesiological images into a new model of the church as a community of disciples. See Avery Dulles, *A Church to Believe In: Discipleship and the Dynamics of Freedom* (New York: Crossroad: 1982) 7–14, 18.

18 For T. Howland Sanks, "within the New Testament itself we find a plurality of images and a plurality of self-understandings, which at the same time, maintains communion, koinōnia, among the churches. We find both unity and pluralism in ecclesiology even then" (See *Salt, Leaven, and Light: The Community Called Church* [New York: Crossroad, 1992] 51). He also notes that, according to Paul Minear, there are more than eighty "images and symbols that refer to the community in the New Testament." Ibid., 44.

19 The FABC recognises that "within the Church, there are conflicts between different concepts and models of the Church." See BILA V, *FAPA Vol. 2*, 78.

20 Kenan B. Osborne, *Ministry: Lay Ministry in the Roman Catholic Church: Its History and Theology* (New York: Paulist Press, 1993) 603, 607.

attention to the guiding role of the Holy Spirit in the church. In his view, "the structure of the Church is justified only by its relationship and service to the action of the Spirit, whether it is a question of sacraments, of ministry or of canonical regulation."[21] Focusing on the two poles of Christian faith, "belief in the oneness of the Three Divine Persons and belief in the incarnation of the Second Person," George Tavard accentuates the importance of the Trinity in understanding the church.[22] Here Tavard echoes the view of Hans Küng who emphasises three metaphors of the church as "the people of God, the body of Christ, and the creation of the Spirit."[23] In this article we will argue that the FABC's ecclesiology embraces all three christological, pneumatological, and trinitarian dimensions.

Indeed, in the statements of the FABC, one can distinguish those which are christological from those which are pneumatological and trinitarian. The document issued by the FABC's Theological Advisory Commission on "Being Church in Asia" for instance, has a clearly christological focus and tone. It stresses that the context of Asia requires a deeper awareness of the meaning of the Church as a communion of communions, and a new way of being church that can present a new face of Christ to Asian society.[24] The bishops further underline the christological basis of their ecclesiology by encouraging Asian theologians to develop a cosmic Christology of harmony. Such a Christology will engender a cosmic ecclesiology that moves beyond its institutional attention "to understand the Church essentially as a centrifugal Church, open to the whole universe and present in and for the universe."[25]

However, in spite of this strong christological anchoring, the FABC's ecclesiology retains its pneumatological dimension as it espouses Vatican II's teaching on the church as a community of believers filled with the living Spirit.[26] In accord with the Council, this ecclesiology articulates several principles. First, the Spirit is the church's life principle.[27] Second, the Spirit helps the church interpret

---

21 J.-M.R Tillard, *Church of Churches: The Ecclesiology of Communion* (Collegeville, Minn.: The Liturgical Press, 1992) 29, 32, 52–53.

22 George H. Tavard, *The Church, Community of Salvation: An Ecumenical Ecclesiology* (Collegeville, Minn.: The Liturgical Press, 1992) 244, 29–76.

23 Hans Küng, *The Church* (London: Burns & Oates, 1967) vii-viii, 107–260.

24 TAC, "Being Church in Asia: Journeying with the Spirit into Fuller Life," art. 24, *FAPA Vol. 2*, 221.

25 TAC, "Asian Christian Perspectives on Harmony," art. 5.2.4, *FAPA Vol. 3*, 294.

26 *Lumen gentium* no. 4 summarises the work of the Holy Spirit in the Church.

27 FABC III, art. 15, *FAPA Vol. 1*, 60.

and assess the signs of the times in Asia in light of the Gospel.[28] Third, this ecclesiology considers as very important and relevant to the Asian context Vatican II's teaching on the ecclesial elements outside the visible boundaries of the Catholic Church.[29] Fourth, the church does not live by its hierarchical structure alone but by the variety of its charisms and ministries, which are bestowed by the Spirit for the general good and edification of the church.[30] Fifth, the anointing of all members of the church by the Spirit means that they are called to bear a prophetic witness to the kingdom of God, with the Spirit as the principal agent of mission.[31] Sixth, full communion in the church requires communion in the Spirit.[32] Finally, according to the FABC, the Spirit "seems to be moving the Church strongly in the direction of small Christian communities."[33] And, wherever people come together to build human communities based on love and justice, there is the presence of the Spirit.[34]

This rapid survey of the FABC's documents reveals that the pneumatological dimension is an essential and vital element of the FABC's ecclesiology. But amidst this pneumatological discourse, it continues to insist that the mission of the Spirit is inseparable from that of the Father and the Son: the Spirit makes Christians one by incorporating them into the one body of Christ and leads them to the kingdom of God.[35] The church, according to the FABC, is a people made one with the unity of the Father, the Son and the Holy Spirit.[36] It is essentially "a communication

---

28 OTC, "The Spirit at Work in Asia Today," arts. 4.2.2.7, 4.3.1.2, *FAPA Vol. 3*, 309, 311.

29 FABC III, art. 8.2, *FAPA Vol. 1*, 57; BIRA II, art. 12, *FAPA Vol. 1*, 115; BIRA IV/2, art. 8.5, *FAPA Vol. 1*, 253; BIRA IV/3, arts. 2, 6, 12, *FAPA Vol. 1*, 258–60; BIRA IV/4, art. 2, *FAPA Vol. 1*, 300; BIRA IV/7, arts. 12–13, *FAPA Vol. 1*, 310; BIRA IV/12, art. 7, *FAPA Vol. 1*, 326; OTC, "The Spirit at Work in Asia Today," art. 3.10.2.4, *FAPA Vol. 3*, 299.

30 FABC, Asian Colloquium on Ministries in the Church (hereafter ACMC), art. 31, *FAPA Vol. 1*, 73; BIRA IV/3, art. 9, *FAPA Vol. 1*, 260; OTC, "The Spirit at Work in Asia Today," arts. 4.2.1.1, 4.3.1.2, 4.3.2.1, 5.6, 5.7, *FAPA Vol. 3*, 306, 311, 314, and 323–4 respectively.

31 OE, "Asian-Born Missionary Societies of Apostolic Life (AMSAL)," art. 2.d, *FAPA Vol. 3*, 206.

32 ACMC, art. 23, *FAPA Vol. 1*, 72; FABC III, art. 7.2, *FAPA Vol. 1*, 56.

33 OTC, "The Spirit at Work in Asia Today," art. 4.3.2, *FAPA Vol. 3*, 313.

34 BIRA IV/3, art. 13, *FAPA Vol. 1*, 260.

35 FABC III, arts. 7.2, 15, *FAPA Vol. 1*, 56, 60; BIRA IV/3, arts. 10-1, 13, *FAPA Vol. 1*, 260.

36 FABC III, art. 6, *FAPA Vol. 1*, 55.

which flows out of the communication of the Trinity."[37] Its mission, affirms the FABC, is the *missio Dei*,[38] the very mission of the Trinity.

The christological and pneumatological basis of the FABC's ecclesiology discussed above, we argue, underlines its contextual character, by a constant reference to the Gospel and an emphasis on the social context,[39] coupled with a reading of the signs of the times discerned as promptings and movements of the Holy Spirit. The trinitarian dimension, on the other hand, highlights its relational aspect by stressing the theme of the church as a community of faith rooted in the perfect communion of the three persons, Father, Son, and Holy Spirit. This contextual and relational character in turn provides a framework for understanding the main characteristics of the FABC's ecclesiology, which will be discussed in the next section.

Features of the FABC's Ecclesiology

The first feature of the FABC's ecclesiology is its predominantly "from below" and "from within" methodology, which comprises an inside analysis of the realities of Asia, a reflection of faith, and a plan for action. This methodology reflects a turn to human experience and a reliance on sociological analysis while acknowledging the intrinsic presence and working of God in the very development of human history and society. It has three intertwined elements, namely sociological, christological, and pneumatological. It begins in the faith experiences of local communities, and springs from the Asian bishops' acute awareness of the challenges of Asian societies. It is based on a Christology which is not separated from soteriology, a theme reinforced in the statement of the Fourth Plenary Assembly which highlights the role of the church as the servant and instrument of the liberation of Asia.[40] Therefore, it can also be called a liberation ecclesiology, which is fundamentally contextual and historical.[41] It is anchored in a pneumatology that is also developed from below, a theological endeavour that the FABC hopes will

---

37 OSC, "Communication Challenges in Asia," *FAPA Vol. 2*, 185–6; OSC, "Church and Public Relations," *FAPA Vol. 3*, 185.

38 OE, "Consultation on Asian Local Churches and Mission *Ad Gentes*: A New Way of Being Church-in-Mission in Asia," art. 5, *FAPA Vol. 3*, 222.

39 For the FABC, the statement that "the context determines the Church's mission," is an important principle of the new way of being Church. See OESC, "A Renewed Catechesis for Asia: Towards the Year 2000 and Beyond," *FAPA Vol. 2*, 31.

40 FABC IV, art. 4.1.1, 4.1.3, *FAPA Vol. 1*, 191.

41 Camil Menard asserts that Latin American ecclesiology is "contextuelle et historique." See "L'ecclésiologie des théologiens de la libération: Contexte général and analyse de

"not be a separate, isolated area of the theology, but a leaven which will permeate all of the presently emerging Asian theologies."[42] Theology, it affirms, must be at the service of life,[43] and becomes "part of the process of becoming and being Church in Asia."[44] It is not merely a faith seeking understanding, but a "faith seeking life, love, justice and freedom."[45] It proceeds "from the underside of history, from the perspective of those who struggle for life, love, justice, and freedom."[46] This predominantly from below and from within ecclesiology in turn accentuates the communion of local churches realised in basic ecclesial communities.

Indeed, the recurrent emphasis on basic ecclesial communities or basic Christian communities is the second notable feature of the FABC's ecclesiology.[47] In these communities, members are motivated by love and see things from the perspective of the poor. The study of the word of God and its application to daily life play a central role in these communities, which are often involved in social and political activities. The pastoral process of basic ecclesial communities is explained by Archbishop Orlando Quevedo of the Philippines, who observe that these basic communities generally adopt a "spiral" method of discernment, an analysis of the situation followed by a reflection in light of faith, decision-making, and planning for implementation.[48] This process concludes with action and evaluation, and starts again when another situation emerges. In these communities lay people are empowered to play a leading role and the clergy remain in the supporting function. These communities, especially basic human communities which spring from them, grow by building relationships through intercultural and interreligious dialogue, and by reaching out to others in committed service. Through basic ecclesial communities, a contemporary image of the early Christian community depicted in the Acts of the Apostles,[49]

quelques questions ecclésiologiques discutées par Leonardo Boff," *Eglise et Théologie* 19 (1988) 349.

42 BIRA IV/3, art. 7, *FAPA Vol. 1*, 259; OTC, "The Spirit at Work in Asia Today," art. 4.2.2.1, *FAPA Vol. 3*, 307.

43 TAC, "Asian Christian Perspectives on Harmony," art. 1.1, *FAPA Vol. 3*, 232.

44 TAC, "Being Church in Asia: Journeying with the Spirit into Fuller Life," art. 49, *FAPA Vol. 2*, 226.

45 Ibid., art. 48, *FAPA Vol. 2*, 226.

46 Ibid.

47 FAPA Vol. 1, 249, *FAPA Vol. 3*, 433.

48 Orlando B. Quevedo, "Seeds of the Kingdom," *The Tablet* (30 May 1998) 696.

49 German Martinez, "An Ecclesiology of Peace," *Theology Digest* 38:3 (Fall 1991) 238.

the FABC sees a new way of being church,[50] which is "a communion of ecclesial communities participating in the mission and ministry of Jesus."[51] This symbiosis of communion and mission, explicated as the double finality of the church, is the third feature of the FABC's ecclesiology.

To date, theologians have often explored communion and mission as two distinct but interrelated ecclesiological frameworks through which the church can be understood.[52] Like Yves Congar, Jerome Harmer was one of the first Catholic theologians to propose communion as a theological model for understanding the church.[53] He describes communion as the "permanent form of the unity of the Church."[54] A great many of other Catholic ecclesiologists would follow in his footsteps to investigate this theme. Notably among this cohort are Dennis Doyle and Jean-Marie Tillard.[55] However, the greatest impetus for the emphasis on the church as communion comes perhaps from several official documents, including the concluding report of the 1985 Synod of Bishops, which affirms that "the ecclesiology of communion is the central and fundamental idea of the council's documents,"[56] the letter of the Congregation for the Doctrine of the Faith,[57] the statement of the Second Anglican-Roman Catholic International Commission,[58] and the joint statement issued by the International Consultation Between the

---

50 OHD, "Colloquium on Church in the 21st Century," art. III, 13, *FAPA Vol. 3*, 36; OHD, "Walking Humbly, Acting Justly, Loving Tenderly in Asia," art. 7, *FAPA Vol. 2*, 44.

51 OE, "Consultation on Evangelization and Communication: Orientations and Recommendations," art. 1, *FAPA Vol. 3*, 209.

52 See *The Jurist* 36 (Winter and Spring 1976), and *The Jurist* 39 (Winter and Spring 1979).

53 Yves Congar, *Ministères et communion ecclésiale* (Paris: Les Editions du Cerf, 1970); *Diversity and Communion* (London: SCM Press, 1984).

54 Jerome Hamer, *The Church is a Communion* (London: G. Chapman, 1964) 209.

55 Dennis M. Doyle, *Communion Ecclesiology: Vision and Versions* (Maryknoll, N.Y.: Orbis Books, 2000; J.-M.R Tillard, *Churches of Churches: The Ecclesiology of Communion*, translated by R.C. De Peaux (Collegeville, Minn.: The Liturgical Press, 1992).

56 Synod of Bishops, "The Final Report of the 1985 Extraordinary Synod of Bishops," art. II.C.1, *Origins* 15:27 (19 December 1985) 448.

57 The Congregation for the Doctrine of the Faith declares that the concept of communion is "very suitable for expressing the core of the mystery of the church and can certainly be a key for the renewal of Catholic ecclesiology." See "Letter to the Bishops of the Catholic Church Understood as Communion," *Origins* 15:27 (19 December 1985) 108.

58 Anglican-Roman Catholic International Commission, "The Church as Communion: Agreed Statement of by the Second Anglican-Roman Catholic International Commission," *Origins* 20:44 (11 April 1991) 719–27.

Catholic Church and the World Evangelical Alliance.[59] Literature also abounds on the mission aspect of the church. One of the most articulate interpreters was John Paul II, who declares that "the Church is missionary by her very nature."[60] We note that in all theological discourses on the church, and perhaps more so in the documents of the FABC, the concept of communion tends to accentuate the "nature" aspect while mission highlights the "purpose" of the church.

By coining the term "communion-in-mission" the Asian bishops have adopted an approach that is "both/and" rather than "either/or," stressing both communion and mission as the fundamental dimensions of the church. In so doing, they not only reflect the teachings of Vatican II but also integrate papal and synodal teachings such as those of Paul VI and the 1985 Synod of Bishops.[61] This Synod makes an implicit link between the two concepts of communion and mission by stating that "the Church as communion is a sacrament for the salvation in the world."[62] The Asian bishops do not envisage mission as the sole purpose of the church. Nor do they present communion as relative to mission or vice versa. In fact, they consider both communion and mission are the one *raison d'être* of the church. The advantage of this ecclesiological view is that it avoids the weaknesses identified by Louis J. Luzbetak as associated with the "Church as community" model, such as it "may lead people to become too introspective and not concerned enough about the world outside the Church-community," or "to forget the Kingdom for which the Church exits," or "to forget that the Church is mission."[63] The twin concept of communion-in-mission is also tied to the sacramental and regnocentric dimension of the church, the fourth notable feature of the FABC's ecclesiology.

For the Asian bishops, "the Church is at its deepest level a communion rooted in the life of the Trinity," and a sacrament of "the loving self-communication of

---

59 International Consultation between the Catholic Church and the World Evangelical Alliance, "Church, Evangelization and the Bonds of '*Koinonia*'," *Origins* 33:19 (16 October 2003) 310–20.

60 John Paul II, "*Redemptoris Missio*," art. 62, *Origins* 20:34 (31 January 1991) 559.

61 Vatican II, "*Ad Gentes*. Degree on the Church's Missionary Activity," in *Vatican Council II: Vol. 1: The Conciliar and Post Conciliar Documents*, edited by Austin Flannery, new. rev. ed., (Northport, N.Y.: Costello Publishing Co., 1996) 813–56; Paul VI, "*Evangelii Nuntiandi*," ibid., 427–32.

62 Synod of Bishops, "The Final Report of the 1985 Extraordinary Synod of Bishops," art. II.D.1, *Origins* 15:27 (19 December 1985) 449.

63 Louis J. Luzbetak, *The Church and Cultures: New Perspectives in Missiological Anthropology*, American Society of Missiology Series, no. 12 (Maryknoll, New York: Orbis Books, 1988) 377.

God and the graced response of redeemed mankind in faith, hope and love."[64] They also stress that the local church must endeavour to be a sacrament of unity and harmony of all peoples, because it is the sign and instrument of reconciliation in Christ through the presence and working of the Holy Spirit.[65] As "the sacrament of God's message in the world,"[66] it "constantly moves forward in mission, as it accompanies all humankind in its pilgrimage to the Kingdom of the Father."[67]

In the ecclesiology of the FABC, the notion of kingdom of God is a complex reality which has four preponderant ideas. First, there is an eschatological view in which the kingdom of God is seen to be beyond history.[68] Second, we find an understanding of the kingdom of God which involves an *already* and a *not yet*.[69] Third, there is a prophetic view that sees God's kingdom as norms for individual and political morality.[70] Finally, the Asian bishops speak of the church as the humble servant of the kingdom, and highlight the need for it to be truly missionary, because Jesus expended his whole life for the kingdom of God.[71] By emphasising repeatedly that the church exists for the kingdom of God, they have promoted, according to Peter C. Phan, "a different ecclesiology, one that decenters the Church in the sense that it makes the center of the Christian life and worship not the Church but the reign of God."[72] Indeed, for the FABC, the Church in Asia is called to live in faithfulness to the Gospel and to engage in the works of the triple dialogue, which are a contribution to the civilisation of love, a first sketch of the vision of the kingdom of God on earth. In this sense the FABC's ecclesiology touches Christian life in its deepest spiritual recesses as well as its day-to-day secular realities, because its approach is predominantly from below and from within, characterised by an accentuation on local church and basic ecclesial communities, a symbiosis of communion and mission as the twin finality

---

64 FABC III, arts. 7.1, 15, *FAPA Vol. 1*, 56, 60.

65 See FABC III, arts. 3.6, 7.2, 7.4, 7.9, 13, *FAPA Vol. 1*, 55–6, 59.

66 BIRA II, art. 11, *FAPA Vol. 1*, 115.

67 FABC III, art. 15, *FAPA Vol. 1*, 60.

68 OE, "Consultation on Evangelization and Communication: Orientations and Recommendations," art. 4, *FAPA Vol. 3*, 210; OTC, "The Spirit at Work in Asia Today," arts. 4.2.2.7, 5.1, *FAPA Vol. 3*, 309, 318 respectively.

69 BIRA IV/2, arts. 8.1-8.2, *FAPA Vol. 1*, 252.

70 TAC, "Being Church in Asia: Journeying with the Spirit into Fuller Life," art. 45, *FAPA Vol. 2*, 225.

71 Ibid., art. 44, *FAPA Vol. 2*, 225.

72 Peter C. Phan, *Being Religious Interreligiously: Asian Perspectives on Interfaith Dialogue* (Maryknoll, New York: Orbis Books, 2004) 237.

of the church, and a focus on the sacramental and regnocentric dimension. We will now turn to assess the strengths and limitations of this rich ecclesiology.

Strengths and Limitations of the FABC's Ecclesiology

Like their overall theology, the FABC's ecclesiology is developed from the concrete, existential, and historical situations of Asia, a continent marked by poverty and scarred by war and suffering, and home to a multitude of ancient cultures and religions. That their ecclesiology is contextual can be seen from their faithfulness to the teaching of Vatican II and their primary description of the church as a community of faith in Asia. This contextual character is also discernible in their model of the church as a communion-in-mission, their creative linkage between dialogue and solidarity, and their deeper reflection on discipleship as a new paradigm for understanding the church, realised in basic ecclesial communities. All these ecclesiological appellations are contextual in the sense that they do not merely express the immanent nature of the church but more importantly its economic mission, not only what the church is, but also who and what it is for in the Asian context.

Another strength of the FABC's ecclesiology is its emphasis on the relational character of the church, which is, at its deepest level, a communion grounded in the life of the Trinity. This trinitarian foundation offers a broad framework for integrating the vertical communion with the Triune God and the horizontal communion that has two aspects: *ad intra* between Christians and *ad extra* with humanity. This relational, trinitarian basis of the church seals the intimate connection of communion and mission. The church fulfils its mission to the extent that it is truly a communion, because the mission of the church is first and foremost the mission of the Triune God. In this contextual and relational ecclesiology, the church is not only a community of faith, but also a community of faith, hope, and love in Asia,[73] because it is fundamentally rooted in the mystery of Christ, the Holy Spirit, and the Trinity.

While its contextual and relational character proves to be relevant and fruitful for the needs of the Church in Asia, our argument is that the FABC's ecclesiology is still beset by several theological difficulties. The first difficulty relates to "the relationship between the way we understand God's nature and the way we understand the nature of the Church."[74] Following Peter Fisher, we note that the FABC seems

---

73 FABC III, arts. 7.1, 15, *FAPA Vol. 1*, 56, 60.
74 Peter Fisher, "*Koinonia* and Conflict," *Theology* 104:822 (November-December 2001) 420–8, at 422.

to give an impression that communion "sums up the God-given character of the church, whereas it may, in reality, only represent some aspects of that character," by implying "that we have knowledge *of God*, the three-in-one, of a kind or quality that we do not really possess" and by drawing "conclusions about *the Church* that may not confidently be drawn from assertions or beliefs about the Trinity."[75]

Secondly, like Vatican II, the Asian bishops emphasise the importance of the church as both a local and a universal reality. For *Lumen gentium*, four elements constitute a local church: the presence of the Holy Spirit (nos. 4, 12), the proclamation of the Gospel (no. 5), the celebration of the sacraments (no. 7), and the apostolic ministry of a bishop (nos. 8, 20).[76] Citing the same elements, the Asian bishops declare that diocese and parish are genuine communities of faith, and basic ecclesial communities a new way of being church in Asia.[77] However, there is a certain ambiguity in their statements about the relationship between the local church and the universal church. To date, church leaders and theologians have often co-opted the phrase "in and from which" in *Lumen gentium* no. 23 to argue for the ontological priority of either the local or the universal church. For example, in its letter on "Some Aspects of the Church Understood as Communion," the Congregation for the Doctrine of the Faith states that the universal church is "a reality ontologically and temporarily prior to every individual particular Church."[78] Walter Kasper, on the contrary, argues for the priority of the local church.[79] For the FABC, the church is a communion of communions, and the key question is not which, the universal or the local, has priority, but how the universality of the church is experienced and expressed at the local level of the country, the diocese, the parish, basic ecclesial communities, and the family understood as a miniature church, the church in the home.[80]

---

75 Ibid. 422–3.

76 These four elements are mentioned in the Conciliar Degree *Christus Dominus*, no. 11. French theologians often abbreviate these elements into four E's: "*Esprit,*" "*évangile,*" "*eucharistie,*" and "*évêque.*"

77 FABC V, art. 3.3.2, *FAPA Vol. 1*, 281; ACMC, arts. 38–40, *FAPA Vol. 1*, 75–6; OTC, "The Spirit at Work in Asia Today," art. 4.3.2, *FAPA Vol. 3*, 312–3.

78 Congregation for the Doctrine of the Faith. "Letter to the Bishops of the Catholic Church on Some Aspects of the Church Understood as Communion," no. 9, *Origins* 22:7 (25 June 1992) 108–12, at 109.

79 Walter Kasper, "On the Church: A Friendly Reply to Cardinal Ratzinger," *America* (23–30 April 2001) 8–14; Joseph Ratzinger, "The Local Church and Universal Church: A Response to Walter Kasper," *America* (19 November 2001) 7–11.

80 BIMA III, art. 6, *FAPA Vol. 1*, 104.

Thirdly, the FABC's ecclesiology could also be enriched by a deeper exploration of the immanent aspect of its Trinitarian theology. To date, the bishops' approach to the Trinitarian question seems to be more economic, presenting the "vitality" of communion as an analogical reality that has a vertical and horizontal dimension with the Trinity and among the Christians. For them, the Church is "the community of those who are restored into communion and fellowship (*koinonia*) among themselves, which is a communion and fellowship with God the Father and his Son Jesus in the Holy Spirit."[81] They favour the use of symbolic descriptions of the Trinity because symbols can help in the understanding of theological doctrines and facilitate interreligious relationships.[82] However, they pay scant attention to the immanent Trinity. Peter C. Phan observes that "there has been little interest on the FABC's part in a purely philosophical or even theological discourse on God," and the bishops concentrate instead on the economic Trinity, on "God's activities in the world and God's relationship to us in history, that is, in what God the Father has done for us and the world in his Son Jesus by the power of the Holy Spirit."[83]

Finally, unlike John Paul II who declares that "unless one looks to the Mother of God, it is impossible to understand the mystery of the church, her reality, her essential vitality,"[84] the Asian bishops almost ignore the Marian dimension, except for the recurrent invocation of Mary for her intercession,[85] or some brief statements on Mariology and the Marian devotion.[86] Their ecclesiology is also in contradistinction to Joseph Ratzinger who considers the Marian understanding of the church as "the most decisive contrast to a purely organizational or

---

81 TAC, "Asian Christian Perspectives on Harmony," arts. 3.3.3.1, 4.11, *FAPA Vol. 3*, 274–5, 285.

82 OEIA, "Fourth Formation Institute for Inter-Religious Affairs (FIRA IV)," art. 14, *FAPA Vol. 3*, 2 285.

83 Peter C. Phan, *Being Religious Interreligiously: Asian Perspectives on Interfaith Dialogue* (Maryknoll, New York: Orbis Books, 2004) 121.

84 See "Apostolic Letter *Mulieris Dignitatem* of the Supreme Pontiff John Paul II on the Dignity and Vocation of Women on the Occasion of the Marian Year [15 August 1988]," no. 22, http://www.vatican.va/holy_father/john_paul_ii/apost_letters/documents/hf_jp-ii_apl_15081988_mulieris-dignitatem_en.html (accessed 17 December 2008).

85 For instance, FABC III, art. 24, *FAPA Vol. 1*, 61; FABC IV, art. 5.4, *FAPA Vol. 1*, 198; FABC I, art. 33, *FAPA Vol. 1*, 25; FABC VII, Conclusion, *FAPA Vol. 3*, 16.

86 OL, "BILA on Women II," art. 4.2.8, *FAPA Vol. 3*, 76; OTC, "The Spirit at Work in Asia Today," art. 4.3.3.1, *FAPA Vol. 3*, 315–6.

bureaucratic concept of the Church."[87] For Ratzinger, "it is only in being Marian that we become the Church."[88]

Conclusion

This chapter has examined the FABC's ecclesiological interpretations, which were crafted to make the identity and vocation of the church more intelligible, the preaching more credible, and the social relevance of the evangelising mission clearer. For the Asian bishops, faith is constitutive of the church, and the church defined primarily as a community of faith in Asia. At its deepest level, the church is a communion-in-mission, rooted in the life of the Trinity, comprising the entire local community, incarnated in a people, a defined culture, a specific place, and at a particular time. This mystery of the local church is realised in the diocese, the parish, basic ecclesial communities, and Christian families. The highest priority of the church's mission is evangelisation, which aims to build up the kingdom of God. This mission is oriented to the world, and contextually expressed by a triple dialogue with the religions, the cultures, and the poor of Asia.

From the primary definition of the church as a community of faith in Asia, the bishops have further explored the vocation and mission of the church in the Asian context. For them, the church is also a disciple-community, a communion-in-mission, a community of dialogue and solidarity, and basic ecclesial communities. These ecclesiological expressions are their vision of a new way of being church in Asia. Together they show both a fundamental continuity and a gradual development in the FABC's ecclesiology, one that is essentially christological, pneumatological, and Trinitarian. This theology of the church is distinguished by notable features such as its from below and from within methodology, an emphasis on basic ecclesial communities, a linkage of communion and mission as the integral finality of the church, and finally, a focus on the sacramental and regnocentric dimensions. Despite these ecclesiological elements, which are both faithful to the tradition and fruitful in the Asian context, the ecclesiology of the Asian bishops could be deepened by a clarification of the connection between God's *communio* and the communion of the church. It could also be enriched by a more extensive discussion on the relationship between the local church and the

---

87 Joseph Ratzinger, *Church, Ecumenism and Politics: New Essays in Ecclesiology* (Middlegreen, Slough, England: St Paul Publications, 1988) 20.

88 Ibid.

universal church, a fuller treatment of the theology of imminent Trinity, and an in-depth exploration of the Marian dimension of the church. The following chapter will provide a comparative analysis of the FABC's theologies of the Church and of the laity, highlighting their convergence of thought in terms of contents, development, and methods.

Chapter 7   Church as Context for Lay Mission in Asia

In the years since the Second Vatican Council, especially after the promulgation in 1972 of Paul VI's Apostolic Letter *Ministeria Quaedam*,[1] inviting episcopal conferences to request the establishment of new ministries from the Holy See, lay apostolic activity has flourished in the Church.[2] National conferences of bishops have also issued numerous statements in support of lay ministries.[3] In Asia, at the "Asian Colloquium on Ministries in the Church" in 1977 the Federation of Asian Bishops' Conferences listed more than forty types of lay ministries and predicted that more ministries would emerge in response to the needs of particular communities. Nine years later, in 1986, the Catholic bishops of Asia devoted an entire Fourth Plenary Assembly to examine the question of the vocation and mission of lay people in the Church and in the world of Asia.[4] For the Asian bishops, lay people *qua* Asian Christians are as integral to the Church as the clergy. Hence, the source of their vision for lay responsibility can be found in their understanding of the life, nature, and purpose of the Church.[5] Indeed, their theology of the laity

---

1   Paul VI, "*Ministeria Quaedam*, 15 August 1972: Apostolic Letter on First Tonsure, Minor Orders and the Subdiaconate," in *Vatican II: Vol. 1, The Conciliar and Post Conciliar Documents*, edited by Austin Flannery (Northport, N.Y.: Costello Publishing, 1976) 427–32.

2   According to Peter Hebblethwaite, by granting episcopal conferences the "freedom to experiment" this Apostolic Letter had led to a "ministry explosion" in the 1980s. See *Paul VI: The First Modern Pope* (London: Fount Paperbacks, 1994) 599.

3   See, for examples, U.S. Bishops, "Called and Gifted: The American Catholic Laity, 1980, Reflections of the U.S. Bishops," *Origins* 10:24 (27 November 1980) 369, 371–3; "Called and Gifted for the Third Millennium," *Origins* 25:24 (30 November 1995) 409–15; "Co-workers in the Vineyard of the Lord," *Origins* 35:25 (1 December 2005) 405–27; *Lay Ecclesial Ministry: The State of the Questions: A Report of the Subcommittee on Lay Ministry* (Washington, D.C.: Committee on the Laity, United States Conference of Catholic Bishops, 1999); Bishops' Conference of England and Wales, *The Sign We Give: Report from the Working Party on Collaborative Ministry* (Chelmsford, Essex: Matthew James Publishing, 1995).

4   FABC IV, "The Vocation and Mission of the Laity in the Church and in the World of Asia," *FAPA Vol. 1*, 177–98.

5   Louis Bouyer remarks that "to rediscover the true significance, the true role of the laity, it must be studied in the concrete life of the Church, where the laity are articulated

reflected a particular ecclesiology that had been discussed in detail at the Third Plenary Assembly in 1982, under the theme of "The Church – A Community of Faith in Asia."[6] This chapter will first review the development of the FABC's ecclesiology and its theology of the laity. It will then conclude with a comparative summary of these two theologies under the themes of vocation, mission, theological development, and methodology.

The FABC's Theology of the Church

Back in the mid-1970s the Catholic bishops of Asia foresaw that, by the turn of the 20th century, an estimated 60% of the world population would live in Asia. It was also evident that Asia would remain the least Christian continent in numerical terms. Therefore, in their view, it was imperative that Asian Churches discover their own vocation and become "genuine Christian communities in Asia–Asian in their way of thinking, praying, living, communicating their own Christ-experience to others."[7] Later, the FABC revisited this theme at the Third Plenary Assembly, this time providing a fuller treatment of the subject by reflecting on the nature and structures of the Church, in particular the local Church and basic ecclesial communities. For the Asian bishops, the Church is a community of faith in Asia, "a community realizing its communion and mission in its own being and life, and in relation to other communities."[8] At its deepest level, the Church is "a communion rooted in the life of the Trinity," and essentially "a sacrament of the loving self-communication of God" and the graced response of redeemed people in faith, hope and charity.[9]

Throughout their discourse on the imperatives of the Church in Asia, the Asian bishops emphasise the Christological, pneumatological, and Trinitarian basis of their ecclesiology. First, they encourage Asian theologians to develop a cosmic Christology of harmony, because such a Christology will engender a cosmic ecclesiology that moves beyond its institutional attention "to understand the Church essentially as a centrifugal Church, open to the whole universe and present in and for the universe."[10] Second, their ecclesiology espouses Vatican II's teaching on the

---

with the apostolic ministry." See *The Church of God: Body of Christ and Temple of the Spirit* (Chicago: Franciscan Herald Press, 1982) 408.

6   FABC III, *FAPA Vol. 1*, 49–65.
7   ACMC, arts. 13, 14ii, *FAPA Vol. 1*, 69–70.
8   FABC III, art. 5, *FAPA Vol. 1*, 55.
9   Ibid., art. 7.1, *FAPA Vol. 1*, 56.
10 TAC, "Asian Christian Perspectives on Harmony," art. 5.2.4, *FAPA Vol. 3*, 294.

Church as community of believers filled with the living Spirit,[11] and stresses that the Spirit is the church's life principle.[12] For the FABC, the mission of the Spirit is inseparable from that of the Father and the Son:[13] the Spirit makes Christians one by incorporating them into the one body of Christ and leads them to the kingdom of God.[14] The church, according to the FABC, is a people made one with the unity of the Father, the Son and the Holy Spirit.[15] It is essentially "a communication which flows out of the communication of the Trinity."[16] Its mission, affirms the FABC, is the *missio Dei*,[17] the very mission of the Trinity. We note that the christological and pneumatological basis of the FABC's ecclesiology discussed above underlines its contextual character,[18] by a constant reference to the Gospel and an emphasis on the social context,[19] coupled with a reading of the signs of the times discerned as promptings and movements of the Holy Spirit. The trinitarian dimension, on the other hand, highlights its relational aspect by stressing the theme of the church as a community of faith rooted in the perfect communion of the three persons, Father, Son, and Holy Spirit.

After the Third Plenary Assembly in 1982, the FABC increasingly turned its attention toward promoting a new way of being Church in Asia,[20] which

---

11 OTC, "The Spirit at Work in Asia Today," art. 4.2, *FAPA Vol. 3*, 305.

12 FABC III, art. 15, *FAPA Vol. 1*, 60.

13 BIRA IV/3, arts. 10–11, *FAPA Vol. 1*, 260.

14 FABC III, arts. 7.2, 15, *FAPA Vol. 1*, 56, 60; BIRA IV/3, art. 13, *FAPA Vol. 1*, 260.

15 Ibid., art. 6, *FAPA Vol. 1*, 55.

16 OSC, "Communication Challenges in Asia," *FAPA Vol. 2*, 185–6; OSC, "Church and Public Relations," *FAPA Vol. 3*, 185.

17 OE, "Consultation on Asian Local Churches and Mission *Ad Gentes*: A New Way of Being Church-in-Mission in Asia," art. 5, *FAPA Vol. 3*, 222.

18 For a detailed discussion of the contextual orientation of the FABC's theology see Peter N.V. Hai, "*Fides Quaerens Dialogum*: Theological Methodologies of the Federation of Asian Bishops' Conferences," Australian E-Journal of Theology 8 (2006), http://aejt.com.au/__data/assets/pdf_file/0008/378665/AEJT_8.9_Hai_Fides_Quaerens_Dialogum.pdf (accessed 24 January 2012); translated into Vietnamese by Nguyen Hoang Vinh as "*Fides Quaerens Dialogum*: Cac Phuong Phap Than Hoc Cua Lien Hiep Cac Hoi Dong Giam Muc A Chau," in *Thoi Su Than Hoc* [Contemporary Theological Issues] 55 (January 2012) 110–149.

19 For the FABC, the statement that "the context determines the Church's mission," is an important principle of the new way of being Church. See OESC, "A Renewed Catechesis for Asia: Towards the Year 2000 and Beyond," *FAPA Vol. 2*, 31.

20 For further details see Peter N.V. Hai, "Models of the Asian Church," *Australian E-Journal of Theology* 18:1 (April 2011) 61–73, http://aejt.com.au/2011/volume_18/issue_1/?article=325557 (accessed 30 April 2011); translated into Vietnamese by

is expressed by four ecclesiological dimensions: Church as communion-in-mission,[21] as community of dialogue and solidarity,[22] as basic ecclesial communities,[23] and as community of disciples.[24] Discipleship, declared the FABC, "is a new paradigm for understanding the Church."[25] This concept of discipleship is premised on the intertwined ideas of trinitarian communion, fellowship with other believers, solidarity with all peoples, and mission as service to life and as "sacrament of peace and harmony."[26]

While the Asian bishops already called for an in-depth study of the theology of harmony in the Asian context in 1984,[27] only in 1995 did they develop the initial contours of a theology of harmony, and also "an ecclesiology of harmony" by a triple theological process: first, by reading the ongoing conflicts and growing disharmony in Asian societies as signs of the times, and taking stock of the various attempts at promoting harmony; second, by reflecting on the meaning of harmony in Asian cultures, philosophies, and religions as well as in the Bible and Church traditions; third, by rereading the Gospels to discover "a Cosmic Christology of harmony," and crafting a theology and spirituality of harmony as the basis for an active commitment to harmony and rationale

---

Nguyen Hoang Vinh as "Cac Mo Hinh Giao Hoi A Chau," in *Thoi Su Than Hoc* [Contemporary Theological Issues] 54 (November 2011) 159–186.

21 OE, "Consultation on Evangelization and Communication," art. 4, *FAPA Vol. 3*, 210; OE, "Consultation on Asian Local Churches and Mission *Ad Gentes*: A New Way of Being Church-in-Mission in Asia," arts. 8–9, *FAPA Vol. 3*, 222; OE, "Consultation on 'Evangelization and Inculturation,'" *FAPA Vol. 3*, 216–7.

22 BIRA IV/12, art. 48, *FAPA Vol. 1*, 332; OEIA, "Consultation on Christian Presence among Muslims in Asia," art. 4, *FAPA Vol. 1*, 166; OESC, "Dialogue between Faith and Cultures in Asia: Towards Integral Human and Social Development," art. 25, *FAPA Vol. 2*, 25; BIMA 1, art. 11, *FAPA Vol. 1*, 94; BISA I, art. 2, *FAPA Vol. 1*, 199; BISA V, arts. 6, 12–14, *FAPA Vol. 1*, 218–9; BISA VI, arts. 3, 8–9, *FAPA Vol. 1*, 223, 225; BISA VII, arts. 20–21, *FAPA Vol. 1*, 233; FABC V, arts. 2.3.3–2.3.4, *FAPA Vol. 1*, 278; FABC VI, arts. 3, 14.2, 15, *FAPA Vol. 2*, 2, 8, 10; FABC VII, arts. I.A.8, III, *FAPA Vol. 3*, 4, 8.

23 OHD, "Walking Humbly, Acting Justly, Loving Tenderly in Asia," art. 7, *FAPA Vol. 2*, 44; OL, "Second Southeast Asian Regional Laity Meeting," art. 8, *FAPA Vol. 3*, 90; OTC, "The Spirit at Work in Asia Today," art. 2.3.10, *FAPA Vol. 3*, 277.

24 FABC VI, art. 14, *FAPA Vol. 2*, 1–12.

25 TAC, "Being Church in Asia: Journeying with the Spirit into Fuller Life," art. 51, *FAPA Vol. 2*, 226.

26 FABC VI, art. 14.2, *FAPA Vol. 2*, 8; TAC, "Asian Christian Perspectives on Harmony," art. 3.3.3.1, *FAPA Vol. 3*, 274.

27 BIRA IV/1, art. 13, *FAPA Vol. 1*, 249.

for Asian collaboration.[28] From this "vision of Christ as the sacrament of new harmony" the FABC proposed the metaphors of the Church as the "Sacrament of Harmony" and as "the Servant-Sacrament of Harmony."[29] These images originate from two Vatican II's ecclesiological models: the Church as the sacrament of unity and the Church as "servant of the Kingdom."[30] We note that these metaphors are already implied in the bishops' basic understanding of the Church as a community of faith in Asia, as communion-in-mission, and as community of discipleship.

For the Asian bishops, evangelisation is the primary task and the highest priority for the church,[31] whose purpose is to build up the kingdom of God.[32] Its mission is directed to the world,[33] and its mode "a triple dialogue of life" with the cultures, the religions, and the poor,[34] with a focus on the promotion of social justice.[35] Therefore, lay people must continue "to share zealously in the mission of the Church as a leaven in the world and as a sign of the Reign of God."[36]

The FABC's Theology of the Laity

Indeed, this theme was explored in depth at the Fourth Plenary Assembly on the vocation and mission of lay people in the Church and in the world of

---

28 TAC, "Asian Christian Perspectives on Harmony," arts. 1–4, 5.2, 5.2.4, *FAPA Vol. 3*, 233–255, 255–286, 291–5.

29 Ibid., arts. 5.2.5-5.2.6, *FAPA Vol. 3*, 294–5. It is of note that the heading of section 3.3.3.1 is "The Church as Communion: Sacrament of Harmony." Ibid., 273.

30 Ibid., art. 5.2.6, *FAPA Vol. 3*, 295.

31 FABC I, arts. 8, 25, *FAPA Vol. 1*, 13, 16; FABC III, art. 17.3, *FAPA Vol. 1*, 60; FABC V, art. 3, *FAPA Vol. 1*, 279–81; FABC VII, art. III, *FAPA Vol. 3*, 8; BIMA IV, art. 7, *FAPA Vol. 1*, 292.

32 FABC IV, art. 4.4.4, *FAPA Vol. 1*, 193; FABC V, arts. 1.7, 2.3.9, 4.1, *FAPA Vol. 1*, 275, 279, 282; BIRA IV/2, arts. 8.1–8.2, *FAPA Vol. 1*, 252; BILA III, art. 12.2, *FAPA Vol. 1*, 245.

33 FABC III, art. 17.1, *FAPA Vol. 1*, 60; FABC V, art. 3, *FAPA Vol. 1*, 279–81; FABC VII, art. III, *FAPA Vol. 3*, 8; BILA III, art. 13.4, *FAPA Vol. 1*, 245.

34 FABC I, arts. 12–24, *FAPA Vol. 1*, 14-6; FABC III, art. 17.1, 17.4, *FAPA Vol. 1*, 60-1; FABC V, arts. 4.1–4.2, *FAPA Vol. 1*, 282; FABC VI, arts. 3, 15, *FAPA Vol. 2*, 2, 10; FABC VII, art. I.A.8, III, *FAPA Vol. 3*, 4, 8. We coined the term "a triple dialogue of life" to better reflect the FABC's view of the triple dialogue and its emphasis on the dialogue of life. These two concepts were often used in the same train of thought in their statements; see BIMA I, arts. 5, 9–12, *FAPA Vol. 1*, 94–5; BISA VI, art. 10, *FAPA Vol. 1*, 225.

35 FABC I, arts. 21–23, *FAPA Vol. 1*, 15–16; FABC V, art. 2.3.9, *FAPA Vol. 1*, 279; FABC VI, art. 14.2, *FAPA Vol. 2*, 8; FABC VII, art. III, *FAPA Vol. 3*, 8.

36 FABC IV, art. 2.4, *FAPA Vol. 1*, 179.

Asia.[37] First, for the FABC, lay people first and foremost are Asian Christians, a contextual reality and constitutive part of the Church, the faithful, the disciples of Christ, the people of God, and the believing community. Their identity is based on the baptismal, common priesthood of life, characterised by the Asian secularity. Their calling is intimately bound to the vocation of local Churches where all Asian Christians are called to a contextualised communion by being committed to Jesus the Liberator and to live the priesthood of life in a communion of integral liberation. Their mission and ministries are essentially Christ-centred, kingdom-focused, world-oriented, liberative, and dialogical as they endeavour to actualise the priestly, prophetic, and pastoral functions in their faith response to the challenges of Asia. For the FABC, the entire people of God are priestly, and their common priesthood of life, which has its origins in Christ himself, is more real and inclusive than the ministerial priesthood of the clergy. Mission is the purpose of ministries, and evangelisation is the highest priority of mission.[38] Proclamation is the centre and primary element of evangelisation,[39] and the ultimate goal of evangelisation is to build up the kingdom of God by a triple dialogue with the religions, cultures and the poor of Asia.[40]

Consistent with the contextual orientation of their theology, the Asian bishops have endeavoured to remain faithful to the Gospel, the tradition, and the teachings of Vatican II,[41] and at the same time, maintained creativity in adapting these teachings to the situations in Asia. Their theology also has a markedly relational approach. Indeed, for the FABC, underlying the articulation of the vocation and mission of lay people is their relationship with Christ and their role *vis-à-vis* the

---

37 For a detailed treatment of this subject see Peter N.V. Hai, "Features of the FABC's Theology of the Laity," *East Asian Pastoral Review*, 47:1 (2010) 7–37; idem, "Evaluation of the FABC's Theology of the Laity," *East Asian Pastoral Review*, 47:3 (2010) 234–262; see also idem, "Lay People in the Asian Church: A Study of John Paul II's Theology of the Laity in *Ecclesia in Asia* with Reference to the Documents of the Federation of Asian Bishops' Conferences," *Australian E-Journal of Theology* 10 (2007), http://aejt.com.au/__data/assets/pdf_file/0004/378076/AEJT_10.4_Hai_Lay_People.pdf (accessed 24 January 2012); idem, "*Sentire cum ecclesia*: Laity and Holiness in Papal and Local Theologies," *The Australasian Catholic Record* 89:3 (July 2012) 333–48.

38 ACMC, arts. 26-8, 25, *FAPA Vol. 1*, 70-2.

39 BIMA III, art. 6, *FAPA Vol. 1*, 104; BIMA IV, art. 6, *FAPA Vol. 1*, 292.

40 BIMA IV, art. 5, *FAPA Vol. 1*, 292.

41 OEIA and OE, "Consultation on Christian Presence Among Muslims in Asia," art. 12, *FAPA Vol. 1*, 171; FABC IV, art. 4.6.2, *FAPA Vol. 1*, 193–4; BILA V, *FAPA Vol. 2*, 79; BILA I, art. 2–3, *FAPA Vol. 1*, 235–6; BILA II, art. 14, *FAPA Vol. 1*, 239, 242.

Church and the world.[42] Lay people and the entire Christian community are called to a communion with Jesus the Liberator, a communion of committed disciples working for the liberation of Asia, which is rooted in the realities of Asia and in solidarity with the peoples of Asia.

A striking feature of the FABC's theology of the laity is that there has been a fundamental continuity and a gradual progression in this theology since 1970, the inception date of the FABC,[43] which displays a high degree of consistency and integration, coupled with discernible elements of growth.[44] Indeed, this contextual theology, developed in response to the challenges of Asian societies, has increasingly been manifested by an orientation to the world, a more regional contextualisation of the role of lay people, a move towards their empowerment and greater autonomy, a focus on their integral formation, and an emphasis on a deeper and more engaging spirituality of discipleship and harmony.

Ecclesiological Foundations of the FABC's Theology of the Laity

The figure below aims to highlight the correlation between the Asian bishops' ecclesiology and their theology of the laity. This correlation is important in two ways. First, the bishops of Asia do not emphasise the institutional, clerical or juridical aspect of the Church. This point is not merely terminological; it is substantive. For the issues at stake in defining the role of the laity in the Asian Church are neither exhausted nor chiefly determined by their relationship to the Church as institution, as clergy, and as hierarchy. Our argument is that to correctly understand the FABC's view of the role of the laity one has to restate the question in terms of its fuller understanding of the Church, as in "the role of lay people in the Church as a community of faith in Asia," "the role of lay people in the Church as communion

---

42 BILA III, arts. 1–2, 6–7, 13.4, *FAPA Vol. 1*, 243–5; FABC IV, arts. 4.7.1, 4.3.1, 4.4.4, *FAPA Vol. 1*, 194, 192–3.

43 In November 1970, 180 Catholic bishops of Asia met for the first time around Paul VI to discuss the topic of *Populorum Progressio* in Asia, an event that led to the creation of the FABC. See FABC, "Asian Bishops' Meeting," arts. 1, 3, *FAPA Vol. 1*, 3. Two years later, on 16th November 1972, the Holy See approved the statutes of the FABC *ad experimentum* for two years, marking the official establishment of the Federation. See FABC, *Statutes of the Federation of Asian Bishops' Conferences* (Hong Kong: General Secretariat of the FABC, 1995) 1.

44 Our observation is inspired by the three criteria highlighted by Gerard Vincent Hall in his work, *Raimon Panikkar's Hermeneutics of Religious Pluralism* (Ann Arbor, Mich.: UMI, 1994).

in mission," "the role of lay people in the Church as dialogue and solidarity," "the role of lay people in the Church as disciple-community," "the role of lay people in the Church as basic ecclesial communities," and "the role of lay people in the Church as sacrament of peace and harmony." In any of these considerations the role of the laity ceases to be reduced to a mere discussion of their specific role, rights, and responsibilities as compared to those of the clergy and hierarchy. Lay people are no longer pitted against the clergy and their mutual relationship is not one that is driven by opposition and tension. Secondly, as lay people are defined as Asian Christians—a term that includes the clergy—in the Church viewed primarily as a community of faith in Asia, the role of the laity and the role of the Church are closely integrated.

Ecclesiological Foundations of the FABC's Theology of the Laity: A Comparative Summary

	Theology of the Laity	Ecclesiology
Topics	Themes and Concepts	
Vocation	The laity, as Asian Christians, are called to a communion with Jesus and a communion of liberation	The Church, as a community of faith in Asia, is called to a communion with the Triune God and a discipleship in the Gospel
Mission	1. Christ-centred: triple messianic function: priestly, prophetic, pastoral 2. Kingdom-focused 3. World-oriented 4. Dialogical 5. Liberative	1. Evangelisation 2. Building up God's kingdom 3. Mission to the world 4. Mission as triple dialogue 5. Social justice
Development	After FABC IV (1986) more emphasis on: 1. World orientation 2. Contextualisation based on geographical regions 3. Empowerment of lay people 4. Integral formation *of* and *for* lay people 5. Spirituality of authentic discipleship and harmony	After FABC III (1982) more emphasis on: 1. Church as communion-in- mission to the world 2. Church as dialogue and solidarity 3. Church as disciple-community 4. Basic Christian communities as a new way of being Church in Asia 5. Church as sacrament of peace and harmony

	Theology of the Laity	Ecclesiology
Topics	Themes and Concepts	
Methodology	1. Contextual: faithful to Vatican II and adapting to the Asian context	1. Contextual: faithful to the living presence of Christ (Christological), and attentive to the signs of the times discerned as promptings of the Holy Spirit (Pneumatological)
	2. Relational: triple relationship with Christ, the Church, and the world	2. Relational: Trinitarian

As a summary the table here presented contains only generalisations, and at times the pieces do not nicely fit. However, it hopes to offer a theological spectrum that can assist in the appreciation of the Asian bishops' theology of the laity and their ecclesiology. This figure shows that there is a surprising convergence in both content and structure between their theologies of the laity and of the Church. It underlines the mutual influence of these theological endeavours: the bishops' treatment of the vocation and mission of lay people is based on their ecclesiology, which, in turn, reflects a theological insight and a contextual sensibility that is sharpened by their investigation into the role of the laity as Asian Christians.

For the FABC, not only faith, but faith, hope, and love are the Christian experience and the starting point for theology. In this sense, theology is not merely an endeavour to understand the faith, but also a concrete realisation of the Christian hope and love, in short, a *praxis*; that is, it seeks not just to understand, but to transform.[45] The Church, as a communion-in-mission, a community of dialogue and solidarity, a disciple-community, and a sacrament of peace and harmony, is not only a community of faith, but is also a community of faith, hope, and charity in Asia. This community in turn is concretised and historically realised in basic ecclesial communities, the seedbed of a Church totally geared to the evangelising mission. As such, the FABC's theologies of the laity and of the Church together offer one of the best examples of contextualising the theology of Vatican II.

Conclusion

This chapter has provided a comparative analysis of the FABC's theologies of the Church and of the laity under four categories of vocation, mission, development,

---

45 OTC, "Methodology: Asian Christian Theology," art. 4.2.4.5, *FAPA Vol. 3*, 375–6.

and methodology. It demonstrates that there is a convergence of thought between these two theologies and confirms that the Church and the laity share in the same mission. When Pius XII first lent the Church's authority to the exalted dignity of the laity by declaring in 1946 that lay people are the Church,[46] he formally brought to an end to a theological and pastoral tendency to treat them as merely passive members of the Church. Over the next sixty years, inspired by Vatican II's constitutions *Lumen Gentium, Gaudium et Spes*, and in particular the degree *Apostolicam Actuositatem*, the theology of the laity took on a new course. In the hands of the Catholic bishops of Asia it is intimately linked to their contextual ecclesiology and unifies their teaching on the Church's evangelising mission with such deep insights as the triple dialogue of life and basic ecclesial communities. In fact, the Asian bishops have scarcely issued an official statement where the theme of evangelisation did not dominate. It is the basis of their entire theology, which places particular emphasis on the role of the laity as Asian Christians in carrying out the Church's mission in the world. In the FABC's rich ecclesiology, lay people are the principal agents of the Church's redemptive mission in the world. They are not the bridge in the world; they are the Church in the world. Indeed, the analysis of the FABC's theology of the laity and its ecclesiological framework has touched upon several themes discussed in John Paul II's Apostolic Exhortations *Christifideles Laici* and *Ecclesia in Asia*. A comparative assessment of the FABC's theology of the laity with reference to these Apostolic Exhortations will be provided in the next chapter.

---

46   In his address to the new cardinals on 20th February 1946, Pius XII affirmed that "… i fedeli, e più precisamente i laici, si trovano nella linea più avanzata della vita della Chiesa; per loro la Chiesa è il principio vitale della società umana. Perciò essi, specialmente essi, debbono avere una sempre più chiara consapevolezza, non soltanto di appartenere alla Chiesa, ma di essere la Chiesa, vale a dire la comunità dei fedeli … Essi sono la Chiesa." Acta PII PP. XII: Allocutiones I, *Acta Apostolicae Sedis* 38 (1946) 149.

Chapter 8 John Paul II's Theology of the Laity and the Teachings of the Asian Bishops

In his assessment of John Paul II's achievements in the twilight of his long pontificate Jewish human rights activist Elie Wiesel, who was receiver of the Nobel Peace Prize in 1986, states that if Pope John XXIII had opened the windows of the Church by his vision and actions, then John Paul II opened its doors.[1] Indeed, John Paul II's journeys to all parts of the world highlighted the Catholic presence as never before.[2] During those pilgrimages the pontiff never failed to meet with lay people or to discuss the laity question to emphasise their role and responsibility. Addressing the Italian Episcopal Conference in May 1985 he recalled the importance that Vatican II had placed on the laity's contribution to the mission of the Church in the world and gave two reasons for choosing the vocation and the mission of the laity as the topic of the 1987 Ordinary Synod of Bishops, the first being "the increased awareness of the role that the laity play in the work of salvation," and the second the need to respond to the suggestion of many bishops throughout the world.[3] Fifteen months after the conclusion of this Synod, John Paul II promulgated the post-synodal Apostolic Exhortation *Christifideles Laici*.[4] He would often revisit and deepen this topic in his vast corpus of writings and

---

1 Elie Wiesel, "Pope John Paul II: Pointing the Way to Reconciliation," *Time* (26 April 2004) 67.

2 The Pontiff made 104 overseas trips and 146 pastoral visits inside Italy, and in Rome, he visited 317 of the 333 parishes. See Gianni Colzani, "Between Wojtyla and Ratzinger," *Theology Digest* 52:3 (Fall 2005) 217. For F. Houtart, becoming Pope in 1978, in the difficult post-Vatican II period, John Paul II's twin objective was "to restore a church shaken by the aftermath of the Council and to reinforce its presence in society." See ibid., 219. Australian Prime Minister John Howard describes John Paul II as "a man of enormous courage and dignity whose words of faith and hope inspired millions behind the Iron Curtain to dream again of a Europe whole and free" ("A Tribute to *Quadrant*," *Quadrant* [November 2006] 23).

3 John Paul II, "[Address to the Italian Episcopal Conference:] Propose Suitable Pastoral Lines in the Light of Loreto Discourse," *L'Osservatore Romano* (30 September 1985) 9.

4 John Paul II, "*Christifideles Laici*: Apostolic Exhortation on the Vocation and Mission of the Lay Faithful in the Church and in the World," *Origins* 18:35 (9 February 1989) 561, 563–595. Henceforth, in footnotes the full title will be abbreviated to *Christifideles Laici* followed by numbers.

addresses in subsequent years up until his final pilgrimage on 2nd April 2005. One of the significant writings during this period is *Ecclesia in Asia*,[5] the post-synodal document that he promulgated in 1999, one year after the close of the Synod for Asia. In this *magna carta* for the people of God in Asia, he discusses *inter alia* the role of lay people within the context of evangelisation, a mission that he considers as "an absolute priority"[6] for the Asian Church.

The first section of this chapter provides an overview of the contents and the structure of *Ecclesia in Asia*. The second examines John Paul II's theology of the laity as proposed in this document with reference to *Christifideles Laici* and his other writings and addresses.[7] The final section compares the theologies of the laity of John Paul II and the Catholic bishops of Asia. This chapter argues that it is the logic of faith as gift and evangelisation as task that underlines and unifies the entire post-synodal document, which proceeds from a Christological and Pneumatological perspective to interpret the mission of the Asian Church, in which lay people fully participate. It also contends that "witness of life" is a comprehensive concept that the Pope employs to describe and prescribe the identity and role of lay people in Asia. As a concrete expression of the integration of faith, proclamation, and Christian living, it occupies a central place in *Ecclesia in Asia* and is a succinct summary of its theology of the laity. The chapter proposes a new approach to interpreting John Paul II's theology of evangelisation, one that is based on a basic distinction between the theological firmness (*fortiter*) with which he imposes compliance with the doctrine of proclamation and the pastoral flexibility (*suaviter*) that he encourages in the engagement in the triple dialogue with the cultures, the religions, and the poor of Asia. The chapter concludes that, except for some minor difference in the interpretation of the vocation and mission of lay people in the Asian Church, there is a substantial convergence between John Paul II's theology of the laity and the documents of the Federation of Asian Bishops' Conferences.

---

5   John Paul II, "*Ecclesia in Asia*," *Origins* 29:23 (18 November 1999) 357, 359–84. Hereafter, only the title and numbers will be used in footnotes.

6   *Ecclesia in Asia*, no. 2.

7   While *Christifideles Laici* is the primary source of the Pope's theology of the laity, his view on the role of the laity can also be gathered from the catechetical lectures he gave in general audiences between 27 October 1993 and 21 September 1994. See *The Church: Mystery, Sacrament, Community. A Catechesis on the Creed* (Boston: Pauline Books and Media, 1998) 409–527.

Overview of the Contents and the Structure of *Ecclesia in Asia*

Unlike *Christifideles Laici*, which deals with a single topic, the vocation and mission of the laity, and has as audience the entire universal Church, *Ecclesia in Asia* discusses many theological themes but addresses one single constituency, the local Church in Asia. This choice of coverage suggests that the latter document has a broader theological scope and a more localised approach than the former. This particular orientation is underscored by the post-synodal document's Latin title, taken from its opening words, which translates literally as the "Church in Asia." Therefore, to understand its theology of the laity one has to analyse the document with a double reference to its major themes and the particular situations in Asia. Within this contextual framework, this section provides a brief exposition of the themes and the structure of *Ecclesia in Asia*.

Ecclesia in Asia is organised into seven chapters flanked by an introduction and a conclusion. It focuses on the new evangelisation,[8] the main theme of John Paul II's Apostolic Letter *Tertio Millennio Adveniente*, which details a programme for the Church to welcome the Third Millennium of Christianity.[9] Preparing for the year 2000, he declared, was "a hermeneutical key" of his pontificate.[10] It aims to increase "sensitivity to all that the Spirit is saying" to the Churches in Asia, as well as "to individuals through charisms meant to serve the whole community."[11] The Pope determined that the objective of the third millennium jubilee, the overall context for *Ecclesia in Asia*, is "the strengthening of faith and of the witness of Christians."[12] This jubilee includes the convening of five continental Synods to discuss the challenges of evangelisation according to the needs and situation of each

---

8 *Ecclesia in Asia*, no. 29. John Paul II mentioned the term "new evangelization" for the first time on 9 March 1983 in his address to the Latin American Bishops at Port-au-Prince, Haiti, in the context of the 500th anniversary in 1992 of the first evangelisation of the Americas. See "Apostolic Letter to Latin American Religious on the Occasion of the Fifth Centenary of the Evangelization of the New World," *Origins* 20:13 (6 September 1990) 209, and endnote 1 on page 216.

9 John Paul II, "*Tertio Millennio Adveniente*," *Origins* 24:24 (24 November 1994) 401, 403–16.

10 Ibid., no. 23. According to Peter C. Phan, "this hermeneutical key, which is eschatology, is deeply shaped by the Trinitarian mystery" ("God in the World: A Trinitarian Triptych," in *New Catholic Encyclopedia: Jubilee Volume: The Wojtyla Years* [Detroit: Gale Group in Association with the Catholic University of America, 2001] 33).

11 John Paul II, "*Tertio Millennio Adveniente*," no. 23, *Origins* 24:24 (24 November 1994) 408.

12 Ibid., no. 42.

continent.[13] The theme he chose for the Special Assembly of the Synod of Bishops for Asia, commonly referred to as the Asian Synod,[14] was "Jesus Christ the Savior and his Mission of Love and Service in Asia: 'That they may have Life and have it Abundantly' (Jn 10:10)."[15] In the introduction to the post-synodal document he describes the Asian Synod as "a moment of grace," "a celebratory remembering of the Asian roots of Christianity," and "an ardent affirmation of faith in Jesus Christ the Saviour."[16] He repeats what he declared in an address to the bishops of Asia at the 10th World Youth Day in Manila that evangelisation must be their "absolute priority," and evangelisation is "the joyful, patient and progressive preaching of the saving death and resurrection of Jesus Christ."[17] In the conclusion, he returns to this theme of gratitude and encouragement, entrusting the Church in Asia to Mary, the mother of Christ, and encouraging all Asian Christians to fulfil their mission of love and service, and share with the peoples of Asia "the immense gift" that they have received: "the love of Jesus the Savior."[18]

The seven chapters and fifty-one articles of *Ecclesia in Asia* can be grouped into three parts. Part 1 (chapter 1) provides an analysis of the Asian context. In Part 2, consisted of chapters 2 and 3, the Pope reflects on Jesus Christ as "a Gift for Asia" and the Holy Spirit as "Lord and Giver of Life." Part 3, which comprises the last four chapters, discusses the evangelising duty of all members of the Church as witnesses to the Gospel (chapter 7) through proclamation and inculturation (chapter 4), communion and dialogue for mission (chapter 5), and the service of human promotion (chapter 6). This grouping was likely what John Paul II had in mind when he composed the post-synodal document. First, it displays an organising structure based on the "See, Judge, Act" process, a contextual methodology adopted by the Jeunesse Ouvrière Chrétienne movement, and one that was familiar to the

---

13 *Ecclesia in Asia*, no. 2. Avery Dulles notes that the Synod for Asia deals mainly with "the challenges to evangelization offered by the encounter with the local cultures and with world religions such as Buddhism and Hinduism" ("John Paul II and the Advent of the New Millennium," *America* [9 December 1995] 14).

14 Thomas Menamparampil contends that "historically speaking, the Asian Synod was the most important ecclesial event for Asia from the time of the great Councils (Nicea, Ephesus, Chalcedon)" ("Asia Through Asian Eyes," in *The Future of the Asian Churches: The Asian Synod and Ecclesia in Asia*, edited by James H. Kroeger and Peter C. Phan [Quezon City: Claretian Publications, 2002] 30).

15 *Ecclesia in Asia*, no. 2.

16 *Ecclesia in Asia*, nos. 3–4.

17 *Ecclesia in Asia*, no. 2.

18 *Ecclesia in Asia*, nos. 50–1.

Pope,[19] with Part 1 corresponding to the "See" phase, Part 2, its doctrinal component, to the "Judge" phase, and Part 3, its pastoral and practical component, to the "Act" phase. Second, it is consistent with the three-fold emphasis of *Ecclesia in Asia*, which devotes chapter 4 to proclamation, and inculturation or dialogue with the cultures, chapter 5 to dialogue with other Christian Churches and other religions on the basis of the Church as communion and mission, and chapter 6 to human promotion and dialogue with the people of Asia, especially the poor.

Our grouping differs from what was proposed by James Kroeger, who structured the post-synodal document along three "underlying thematics."[20] His first section, consisting of chapter 1, is "an exploration of the concrete situation of contemporary Asia."[21] His second section, comprising chapters 2, 3, and 4, deals with the "Theological-Doctrinal Aspects of Jesus Christ and the Holy Spirit," and his third section, composed of the last three chapters, discusses "The Church's Mission of Love and Service in Asia."[22] In his view, chapters 2, 3 and 4 together "describe a type of 'doctrinal' orientation to the Church's Asian mission."[23] The strength of this assertion is that it highlights the linkage between chapter 2 "Jesus the Saviour: A Gift to Asia" and chapter 4 "Jesus the Saviour: Proclaiming the Gift", an implicit allusion to the Pope's gift/task idea, a logic that we contend is central to *Ecclesia in Asia*. However, a close reading of these chapters suggests that chapters 2 and 3 offer a set of theological principles based on the Pope's articulation of a Christology and a Pneumatology for Asia, and chapter 4 deals less with the doctrinal aspects of Christ and much more with the primacy of proclamation and the necessity of inculturation, an endeavour to make the Gospel more intelligible and acceptable to Asian peoples. Therefore, we argue that it is more fruitful to group chapter 4 with chapters 5, 6, and 7 as together they constitute the pastoral vision of the Pope for Asia, and reflect better his emphasis on the Church's mission of love and service as proclamation and triple dialogue,

---

19 During the summer vacation in 1947, Father Wojtyla visited France and Belgium where he studied movements such as the Jeunesse Ouvrière Chrétienne (Young Christian Workers) and met with its founder, Canon Joseph Cardijn. See Avery Dulles, *The Splendor of Faith: The Theological Vision of Pope John Paul II* (New York: Crossroad, 1999) 4, 103, 130.

20 James H. Kroeger, "Continuing Pentecost in Asia: Introducing *Ecclesia in Asia*," in *The Future of the Asian Churches: The Asian Synod and Ecclesia in Asia*, edited by James H. Kroeger and Peter C. Phan (Quezon City: Claretian Publications, 2002) 71.

21 Ibid.

22 Ibid.

23 Ibid., 72.

with chapter 7 dealing specifically with Christians as witnesses to, and agents of, the Gospel. This grouping is also aligned with the triple dialogue vision of the Federation of Asian Bishops' Conferences, whose members constituted the majority of the Synod participants.[24] Indeed, in their propositions to the Pope "for his use in composing his Post-Synodal Apostolic Exhortation,"[25] the Synod Fathers affirmed that "the threefold dialogue is one integral movement of the Christian's evangelising mission."[26] They stated explicitly in their final message to the people of God that "the Church in Asia is called upon to enter a triple dialogue: a dialogue with the cultures of Asia, a dialogue with the religions of Asia and a dialogue with the peoples of Asia, especially the poor."[27] This message also acknowledges an increasingly important role of the laity in the mission of the Church, and considers the 21st century as "the Age of the Laity."[28] This view is reinforced in the closing speech by Cardinal Julius Riyadi Darmaatmadja of India, which emphasises the role of lay people in the Church's mission *ad extra*, and insists that their "empowerment and ongoing formation" is essential.[29] Revisiting the overall theme of the Synod for Asia, he declares that "'being Church in Asia' today means 'participating in the mission of Christ the Savior, in rendering his redemptive love and service in Asia,'" so that Asian peoples can more fully achieve their integral human development and "'that they may have life and have it abundantly.'"[30] These statements effectively summarise the major themes and the structure of *Ecclesia in Asia*, and at the same time highlight the critical role of lay people in the mission of the Church in Asia, the subject of our investigation in the next section.

---

24 The Synod for Asia was also attended by a small number of representatives from the Middle-East countries.

25 Peter C. Phan notes that these propositions or recommendations "do not have a deliberative but only a consultative force," and *Ecclesia in Asia* has included all but eight of the fifty-nine propositions (["Editor's Notes,"] in *The Asian Synod: Texts and Commentaries*, compiled and edited by Peter C. Phan [Maryknoll, New York: Orbis Books, 2002] 140).

26 [Synod of Bishops]. "The Synod's Propositions," in *The Asian Synod: Texts and Commentaries*, compiled and edited by Peter C. Phan (Maryknoll, New York: Orbis Books, 2002) 140–65.

27 [Synod of Bishops], "Message to the People of God From the Special Assembly of the Synod of Bishops for Asia," *Origins* 28:2 (28 May 1998) 20.

28 Ibid.

29 Julius Riyadi Darmaatmadja, "A Church With a Truly Asian Face," *Origins* 28:2 (28 May 1998) 26.

30 Ibid.

Critical Analysis of the Theology of the Laity in *Ecclesia in Asia*

Of the many topics and ideas presented in *Ecclesia in Asia*, the concept of "gift" stands out as one that occupies a central place in the Apostolic Exhortation. This observation is borne out by an examination of chapters 2 and 3 that provide the document's doctrinal framework, and chapter 4 that discusses the primacy of proclamation of Jesus the Saviour as the gift to Asia and the challenge of inculturation. In these chapters, the concept of "gift" is intimately linked to the notion of faith. As Jesus himself is the "gift of faith,"[31] it is a task for all Christians, including the laity, to proclaim and share this gift. This gift/task motif (neatly expressed in German as *die Gabe und die Aufgabe* in German) runs through the whole post-synodal document.[32] It is stated with crystal clarity in the first paragraph (no. 1), forcefully at the beginning of chapters 2 and 4 (nos. 10 and 19 respectively), and emphatically as a departing thought toward the end of the post-synodal document (no. 50). For John Paul II, "the Good News of Jesus Christ" is the "gift of all gifts," and "the Church's faith in Jesus is a gift received and a gift to be shared."[33] It is, writes the Pope, "the greatest gift which the Church can offer to Asia."[34] Therefore, "sharing the truth of Jesus with others is the solemn duty of all who have received the gift of faith," and the Church in Asia "cannot cease to proclaim" this "unique gift of faith" which she has received for the good of all.[35] In his view, "what distinguishes the Church from other religious communities is her faith in Jesus Christ; and she cannot keep this precious light of faith under a bushel."[36] Her mission, he insists, is "to share that light with everyone."[37] The Pope emphasises this point again at the conclusion of the Apostolic Exhortation, declaring that the Church's only joy is to share with Asian peoples "the immense gift which she has received – the love of Jesus the Savior."[38] These statements and disquisitions, together with the repeated use of the verb "to share" and its grammatical variants, give rise to our first and overall observation that it is the dynamics of faith as gift and evangelisation as task that underlines and unifies the entire Apostolic Exhortation *Ecclesia in Asia*.

---

31 *Ecclesia in Asia*, nos. 4, 10; see also the headings of chapters 2 and 4.
32 See, for instance, *Ecclesia in Asia*, nos. 1, 10, 12, 19, 20, 31, 35, and 50.
33 *Ecclesia in Asia*, nos. 19, 10.
34 *Ecclesia in Asia*, no. 10.
35 *Ecclesia in Asia*, nos. 10, 1.
36 *Ecclesia in Asia*, no. 10.
37 Ibid.
38 *Ecclesia in Asia*, no. 50.

By emphasising that Jesus is the gift of faith, the post-synodal document retrieves and expands the Christological insights of *Lumen Gentium* and *Redemptor Hominis* (1979), the Pope's very first encyclical and also "the programmatic document" of his entire pontificate.[39] By stressing that this gift must be shared, it captures and contextualises the missionary focus of the Encyclical Letter *Redemptoris Missio* (1990), a document that "represents a new synthesis of the Church's teaching about evangelization in the contemporary world,"[40] and at the same time, articulates his pastoral vision for the remaining fifteen years of his public life. These Christological and missionary concerns are the theological foundation of his gift/task logic and an expression of his contextual approach to the Church in Asia. They reveal that, more than being a philosopher,[41] a poet,[42] a playwright,[43] and a theologian,[44] John Paul II is first and foremost a Christian pastor, intent on being faithful to Jesus, the embodiment of the Christian message and tradition, and at the same time, one who is deeply concerned about the imperative of evangelising mission, the duty to share Jesus the gift with all peoples of Asia in their own cultural and social environment. Therefore, to fully appreciate the theological issues raised in *Ecclesia in Asia*, in particular those relating to the vocation and mission of the laity, one has to explore them with a double reference to the gift/task framework, and the Christological and missionary orientation.

In this post-synodal document, the Pope tends to employ interchangeably the terms "the Church in Asia," "Christians," "the faithful," "all the baptised," "Asian Christians," "Disciples of Christ," "Christian community," "Catholic community,"

---

39 Vatican II's Dogmatic Constitution on the Church actually starts with a Christological affirmation that "Christ is the light of humanity." LG no. 1; Avery Dulles, *The Splendor of Faith: The Theological Vision of Pope John Paul II* (New York: Crossroad, 1999) 10.

40 John Paul II, *Crossing the Threshold of Hope* (London: Jonathan Cape, 1994) 114.

41 In their cover story on John Paul II as *Time*'s 1994 Man of the Year, the authors note that "The Pope's reading is eclectic: philosophy, history, sociology – all in the original languages," and that "Ratzinger is a theologian and John Paul is a philosopher" (Greg Burke, Thomas Sancton and Wilton Wynn, "Lives of the Pope," *Time* [26 December 1994–2 January 1995] 34).

42 George Weigel, *Witness to Hope: The Biography of Pope John Paul II* (New York: HarperCollins, 1999) 117–9.

43 Ibid., 140.

44 According to Peter Hebblethwaite, "Cardinal Wojtyla did not consider himself to be a professional theologian. His real academic work was in ethical philosophy." See *The New Inquisition: Schillebeeckx and Küng* (London: Collins, 1980) 110; Avery Dulles, *The Splendor of Faith: The Theological Vision of Pope John Paul II* (New York: Herder and Herder, 1999) 1–17.

and "the Church" to mean the "people of God" in Asia.[45] These terms obviously include lay people who constitute ninety-nine per cent of the Church's membership,[46] and who are the audience that the Pope intended to entrust in a special way the fruits of the Synod for Asia.[47] Therefore, while the identity of lay people and their specific role are discussed in greater detail in only three sections of the document,[48] the mission and ministry that he assigns to all "Asian Christians" will *ipso facto* apply to the laity. In *Ecclesia in Asia*, this mission is twofold: proclamation of Jesus as Lord, and triple dialogue with the cultures, the religions, and the poor, and its agents are the entire "witnessing Church," including the clergy, the religious, and the laity, in particular, the family and young people.[49] By accenting the dual aspect of mission, the Pope has reiterated his previous teachings in chapter 5 of *Redemptoris Missio*. In this encyclical on missionary activity, he explains that "mission is a single but complex reality" which develops in "a variety of ways," encompassing witness as the first form of evangelisation, proclamation, "the permanent priority of mission," which leads to conversion, baptism, and establishment of local Churches, inculturation of the Gospel in different cultures, interreligious dialogue, and promotion of integral development and liberation by forming consciences.[50] The remarkable alignment between these two papal documents demonstrates that John Paul II has been quite consistent in his view on the meaning, purpose, and importance of the evangelising mission as both proclamation and triple dialogue. What is innovative in the latter document is his constant juxtaposition of these elements of mission to the gift/task idea, a logic that enables him to express a profound gratitude for the grace that has been bestowed on the Church in Asia, and one that heightens his sense of urgency for the missionary task at hand. En route, he opens up a window into his understanding of how God's marvellous plan unfolds in Asia where the God of salvation has chosen to initiate his saving plan, and

---

45 See respectively, *Ecclesia in Asia*, nos. 1–4, 9–10, 18–20, 22, 25, 32, 34, 36, 48, 50; 23, 24, 30–32, 34, 40–42; 32, 35, 45; 43; 51; 50; 23; 34; 2, 10, 20, 23, 24, 29, 32, 34–39, 42; 25, 31, 33, 42.

46 Joseph A. Komonchak, "Christians Must Make a Difference," *The Tablet* (28 September 2002) 4.

47 John Paul II, "Finding the Light," in *The Future of the Asian Churches: The Asian Synod and Ecclesia in Asia*, edited by James H. Kroeger and Peter C. Phan (Quezon City, Philippines: Claretian publications, 2002) 59; *Ecclesia in Asia*, no. 22.

48 The titles of nos. 45, 46, and 47 are respectively "The Laity," "The Family," and "Young People."

49 See respectively, *Ecclesia in Asia*, nos. 19, 20, 23; 21–22; 29–31; 34–38; 42.

50 See respectively, *Redemptoris Missio*, nos. 41; 42–3; 44; 44–9; 52–4; 55–7; 58–9.

puts in context his fervent prayer that the third millennium will be a *kairos* for "*a great harvest of faith* to be reaped in the vast and vital continent."[51]

John Paul II often reiterated the gift/task logic in his speeches to and about the laity throughout his pontificate. In 1980, in a homily delivered in Accra, Ghana, he declared that the laity and all Christians have "a unique opportunity and crucial responsibility" to witness to the "the gift of faith, the tremendous privilege of knowing Christ Jesus as Lord," which is also the greatest treasure and the greatest of all resources entrusted to them.[52] Speaking with the Canadian laity in 1984 he reminded them of "the general call to the apostolate which all Christians have received," and their "specific task of renewing the temporal order by permeating it with the spirit of the Gospel."[53] In a 1991 talk with Polish lay people, he encouraged them "to learn to recognize the gifts" they have received "in order to pass them on to others and in order to strive for them."[54] A couple of years later, reflecting on the topic of the possible participation of lay people in certain aspects of the ordained ministries he insisted that "every office, gift and task should be respected and put to good use."[55]

The gift/task principle is also a recurrent idea in his addresses on the laity given in general audiences between 27 October 1993 and 21 September 1994.[56] In an address on Jesus' earthly life as a model for lay people, he explained that "the call of the laity involves their sharing in the Church's life and, consequently, an intimate communion with Christ's very life. It is a divine gift and, at the same time, it has a correspondent duty."[57] Recalling *Lumen Gentium* (no. 36) and *Christifideles Laici* (no. 14) he affirmed that "living in the truth received from Christ and working to spread it in the world is thus a task and duty of all Church's members, including the laity."[58] Following the teachings of *Christifideles Laici* (no. 24) and *Apostolicam Actuositatem* (no. 3) that charisms should be received in gratitude, and that each

---

51 *Ecclesia in Asia*, no. 1.

52 John Paul II, "The Role of the Laity in Africa," *Origins* 10 (1980) 47.

53 John Paul II, "The Laity's Call to Serve," *Origins* 14:16 (4 October 1984) 255.

54 John Paul II, "Laity and Necessary Church Renewal in Poland," *Origins* 21:6 (20 June 1991) 97.

55 John Paul II, "Do Laity Share in the Priest's Pastoral Ministry?" *Origins* 24:3 (2 June 1994) 41.

56 John Paul II, *The Church: Mystery, Sacrament, Community. A Catechesis on the Creed* (Boston: Pauline Books and Media, 1998) 409–527.

57 General audience of 10 November 1993, in John Paul II, *The Church: Mystery, Sacrament, Community. A Catechesis on the Creed* (Boston: Pauline Books and Media, 1998) 418.

58 General audience of 9 February 1994, ibid., 438.

believer has the right and duty to use charisms, he emphasised that "this right is based on the Spirit's gift and the Church's validation. It is a duty stemming from the very fact of the gift received, which creates a responsibility and demands a commitment."[59] His predilection for the idea of gift extends also to his reflection on lay people and human life. For him, "The presence of children in the Church" is a gift,[60] "Old age is a gift,"[61] and "Life is always a gift."[62] Ten years later, pondering on the linkage between holiness and credibility of proclamation, he declared that "holiness is not only a gift. It is also a task intrinsic and essential to discipleship, which shapes the whole of Christian life."[63]

These selected quotations, taken from the speeches delivered over a period of two decades, show that by connecting the idea of faith as gift and evangelisation as task in *Ecclesia in Asia*, John Paul II has consistently applied a logic that had been central to his thinking. Quoting his own writings from a section of *Redemptoris Missio* that deals with the mission *ad gentes* and the gift of faith,[64] he warns that the Church and all its members "may not keep hidden or monopolize this newness and richness which has been received from God's bounty in order to be communicated to all mankind."[65] He goes on to affirm that people "who are incorporated in the Catholic Church ought to sense their privilege and for that very reason their obligation of *bearing witness to the faith and to the Christian life* as a service to their brothers and sisters, as a fitting response to God" (italics in the original).[66] Here, for the first time in the Apostolic Exhortation, the Pope introduces the term "witness" in conjunction with the themes of faith and Christian life in the context of the gift/task framework, and determines that witnessing to the gift of faith is the task of all Christians.

Indeed, like the gift/task idea, "witness" is one of the most striking and recurrent concepts in *Ecclesia in Asia*.[67] In the section devoted to the laity, where the terms "missionaries," "evangelisers," "witnesses to Christ," and "witnesses

---

59 General audience of 9 March 1994, ibid., 449.
60 General audience of 17 August 1994, ibid., 510.
61 General audience of 7 September 1994, ibid., 521.
62 Ibid.
63 John Paul II, "Holiness and the Credibility of the Church's Proclamation: 'Ad Limina' Address to Bishops From California, Nevada and Hawai," *Origins* 34:3 (3 June 2004) 41.
64 John Paul II, "*Redemptoris Missio*," no. 11, *Origins* 20:34 (31 January 1991) 545.
65 *Ecclesia in Asia*, no. 10.
66 *Ecclesia in Asia*, no. 10; see also John Paul II, "*Redemptoris Missio*," no. 11, *Origins* 20:34 (31 January 1991) 546.
67 *Ecclesia in Asia*, nos. 10, 17, 18, 23, 41–46, 49.

to the Gospel" are used interchangeably to describe their identity and vocation, John Paul II asserts that their proper role in the life and the mission of
the Church consists in being "witnesses to Christ wherever they may find
themselves."[68] Indeed, by baptism and confirmation, lay people are called to be
missionaries in the world "to spread the Gospel of Jesus Christ."[69] In addition
to linking these concepts of witness and mission to the sacraments of initiation and the duty of proclamation, the Pope singles out dialogue with the poor
(liberation and human development) as a unique role of lay people in "rooting
out injustice and oppression" by "witnessing to the Gospel in every area of life
in society."[70] Our second observation is that the term "witness" or its various
usages such as "witnessing," "witnessing to the Gospel," "witnesses to Christ,"
and "witness of life" is a comprehensive concept that John Paul II employs to
describe the identity and prescribe the role of the laity in Asia. Explained as a
concrete expression of the integration of faith and daily living, it is closely connected to his conception of lay people as missionaries and witnesses to Christ.[71]
Equated to Christian life and proclamation,[72] it explicates his insistence on the
proclamation of Jesus as the unique and universal saviour. Prescribed as the
primary mode of evangelisation,[73] it is tightly coupled with the notion of faith
and lies at the heart of *Ecclesia in Asia*. As such, it epitomises and summarises
the contextual theology of the laity proposed in the Apostolic Exhortation.

In this post-synodal document, John Paul II endorses the recommendations
of the Synod Fathers on evangelisation, and concurs that it is "a reality that is both
rich and dynamic."[74] He proceeds to enumerate its many aspects and elements,
starting with the concept of witness, including "witness, dialogue, proclamation,
catechesis, conversion, baptism, insertion into the ecclesial community, the implementation of the Church, inculturation and integral human promotion."[75] As
evangelisation is the overall theme of the Asian Synod and also the theological
focus of *Ecclesia in Asia*, we argue that this loaded list demonstrates his genuine
concerns for the priorities and sensibilities of the Asian bishops. It highlights

---

68   *Ecclesia in Asia*, no. 45.
69   Ibid.
70   Ibid.
71   *Ecclesia in Asia*, nos. 45–6, 42.
72   *Ecclesia in Asia*, nos. 23, 20.
73   Here the Pope reiterates his emphasis in *Redemptoris Missio* (no. 42) that "the witness
     of a Christian life is the first and irreplaceable form of mission."
74   *Ecclesia in Asia*, no. 23.
75   Ibid.

all major tasks and challenges facing the Church in Asia, including an explicit proclamation of Jesus Christ together with a detailed explanation of Christian doctrines and practices (catechesis), the necessity of being incorporated into an ecclesial community via conversion and baptism, the need to establish new communities of faith (implementation of the Church), the triple engagement with the religions (interreligious dialogue), the cultures (inculturation), and the poor of Asia (integral human promotion), and finally, the primacy of leading a life worthy of Jesus Christ and his Gospel (witness).

For John Paul II, "there can be no true proclamation of the Gospel unless Christians also offer the witness of lives in harmony with the message they preach."[76] Everyone in the Church, he declares, "can and must bear this kind of *witness*," and "genuine *Christian witness* is needed" today because people place "more trust in *witnesses* than in teachers, in experience than in teaching, and in life and action than in theories,"[77] especially in Asia, "where people are more persuaded by *holiness of life* than by intellectual argument" (emphasis added).[78] Here, John Paul II seems to have used the term Christian witness to describe the concept of Christian holiness in the Asian context, a motif that is central to both *Lumen Gentium* and *Christifideles Laici*, and one that has generally been defined in these magisterial documents as the perfection of charity.[79]

Elsewhere in the post-synodal document, the Pope emphasises that the credibility of proclamation derives from a living faith and that "Christians who speak of Christ must embody in their lives the message that they proclaim."[80] For him, witness and proclamation go hand in hand, and both are animated by faith and inseparable from it. Faith, received as a gift, is the basis of the identity and vocation of Christians, and witnessing to Jesus Christ and proclaiming his Gospel are their task and mission in the Church and in the world of Asia. This faith demands sharing, and this gift entails task. In *Christifideles Laici* the Pope employs the gift/task logic to stress that ecclesial communion is both a gift and a task for lay people.[81] In *Ecclesia in Asia*, he contextually expands this logic as a recognition by

---

76 *Ecclesia in Asia*, no. 42.

77 Ibid.; *Redemptoris Missio*, no. 42.

78 *Ecclesia in Asia*, no. 42.

79 *Lumen Gentium*, no. 40; *Christifideles Laici*, no. 16.

80 *Ecclesia in Asia*, no. 23.

81 *Christifideles Laici*, no. 20. For a fuller treatment of this theme see Peter N.V. Hai, "Reflections on John Paul II's Theology of the Laity: 20th Anniversary of *Christifideles Laici*," *Australian E-Journal of Theology* 15 (2010), http://aejt.com.au/__data/assets/pdf_file/0008/225395/Hai_Christifideles_GH.pdf (accessed 6 July 2012).

the entire Church, especially the laity (who), of Jesus Christ the Saviour (why) as the gift that must be shared (what) with other peoples through "the joyful, patient and progressive preaching"[82] (when) by becoming authentic witnesses of life (how) in the world of Asia (where). The application of the gift/task logic underscores a key idea of *Ecclesia in Asia* that evangelisation is always "an ecclesial task which has to be carried out in communion with the whole community of faith."[83] This emphasis leads to our third observation that for John Paul II the identity, the vocation, and the ministry of lay people are understood only in the context of the Church as a witnessing community of faith, built on the two pillars of communion and mission.

In line with the teachings of Vatican II, John Paul II affirms that "the entire Church is missionary," and "evangelisation is the duty of the whole People of God."[84] Here the Pope repeats what he categorically stated in his 1990 document *Redemptoris Missio*: "I sense that the moment has come to commit all of the church's energies to a new evangelization and to the mission *ad gentes*. No believer in Christ, no institution of the church can avoid this supreme duty: to proclaim Christ to all peoples."[85] In his view, the Church, "instituted by Christ and made present to the world by the Holy Spirit on the day of the Pentecost" in accordance with the Father's eternal plan, is the mystery of God's loving design, made present and active in the community of the baptised Christians.[86] Therefore, it must be seen as "the privileged place of encounter between God and man," a place in which God reveals the mystery of his inner life and carries out his plan of salvation for the world, and not merely as "a social organization or agency of human welfare."[87] For the Pope, at the heart of the mystery of the Church is the bond of communion which unites Christ to all the baptised.[88] Through this mystery of communion, Christians are united with God and with one another in the Holy Spirit.[89] From this theological perspective, the Pope insists that the primary purpose of the Church is to be the sacrament of "*the inner union of the human*

---

82 *Ecclesia in Asia*, no. 2.
83 *Ecclesia in Asia*, no. 42.
84 *Ecclesia in Asia*, no. 42.
85 John Paul II, "*Redemptoris Missio*," no. 3, *Origins* 20:34 (31 January 1991) 543.
86 *Ecclesia in Asia*, no. 24.
87 Ibid.
88 Ibid.
89 Ibid.

person with God," and rooted in the union with God, it is also *"the unity of the human race"* (italics in the original).[90]

Within this ecclesiological framework, John Paul II makes explicit his view that "whoever enters into communion with the Lord, is expected to bear fruit."[91] He goes on to insist that communion with Jesus is "the indispensable condition for bearing fruit," because communion with others is "the gift of Christ and his Spirit."[92] In this sense, he explains, communion is "both the source and the fruit of mission: communion gives rise to mission and mission is accomplished in communion."[93] Therefore, he is resolute in his view that "communion and mission are inseparably connected."[94] Here, once again the Pope returns to the gift/task logic, this time considering communion as gift and mission as task, and hence situates the vocation and mission of all Christians, including the laity, within an ecclesiological framework that is built on two basic theological concepts of communion and mission.

Like *Christifideles Laici*, in this papal document John Paul II unveils his understanding of the Church by using the concepts of mystery, community of faith, communion, and mission to explicate the nature and purpose of the Church. But, unlike *Christifideles Laici*, which focuses on the role of the laity from a predominantly Trinitarian and ecclesiological perspective,[95] *Ecclesia in Asia* provides a Christological and Pneumatological interpretation of the mission of the entire Church in Asia. Expressing this evangelising mission as proclamation (chapter 4, nos. 19–20, 23), and triple dialogue, namely, inculturation (chapter 4, nos. 21–22), communion and dialogue (chapter 5), and human promotion (chapter 6), often within the gift/task framework, it stresses the distinctive role of lay people, in particular women, the family, and young people, as witnesses to the Gospel in the world of Asia (chapter 7, nos. 45, 46, 47).

Three observations summarise our review of the theology of the laity in *Ecclesia in Asia*. First, by repeatedly applying the idea of faith as gift and evangelisation as task to define and describe the mission of the Church in Asia, John Paul II has effectively used the gift/task logic to unify and underline the entire post-synodal

---

90 Ibid.
91 Ibid.
92 Ibid.
93 Ibid.
94 Ibid.
95 See Peter N.V. Hai, "Reflections on John Paul II's Theology of the Laity: 20th Anniversary of *Christifideles Laici*," *Australian E-Journal of Theology* 15 (2010), http://aejt.com. au/__data/assets/pdf_file/0008/225395/Hai_Christifideles_GH.pdf (accessed 6 July 2012).

document. This logic is intimately linked to a theological motif expounded in *Christifideles Laici*, which postulates that baptismal identity and dignity of Christians, flowing from their faith in Jesus Christ, are the basis of their vocation and mission. The progression from *Christifideles Laici* to *Ecclesia in Asia* can also be discerned in the Pope's accent on the concept of witness of life as the primary mode of evangelisation for Asian Christians, especially the laity. Equated to proclamation, this comprehensive concept is his preferred *locus* to condense and expand his theology of the laity in the post-synodal document. Finally, by considering that the evangelising mission of the witnessing Church as communion and mission, which is incumbent on all members of the Church, has as its fundamental elements both an explicit proclamation of Jesus as Lord, and a triple dialogue with the cultures, the religions, and the poor of Asia, he proves to be a contextual theologian who remains faithful to Vatican II and at the same time is sensitive to the demands of the Church in Asia. Here lies one of John Paul II's most powerful theological syntheses, which addresses a critical issue confronting the Asian Church, namely the relationship between evangelisation and interfaith dialogue.[96] However, while his view on interreligious dialogue is widely welcome in Asia, his insistence on the need to explicitly proclaim Jesus as the universal and only saviour in the Asian milieu has created upset in some theological quarters. Indeed, this contentious issue has received considerable attention from Catholic theologians,[97] and generated a vigorous theological debate, which had already begun in earnest with the

---

96 Michael Barnes notes that "'inter-faith' and 'inter-religious' tend to be used interchangeably; the former has inter-personal, the latter more inter-systemic, connotations" (*Theology and the Dialogue of Religions* [Cambridge: University Press, 2002] 3). Peter C. Phan seems to employ these terms interchangeably as well. See the title of his monumental book, *Being religious Interreligiously: Asian Perspectives on Interfaith Dialogue*, (Maryknoll, New York: Orbis Books, 2004). For Michael Amaladoss, "interreligious dialogue is primarily not between religions but between believers" ("Rationales for Dialogue Among World Religions," *Origins* 19: 35 [1 February 1990] 575.

97 See, for instance, Peter C. Phan, "*Ecclesia in Asia*: Challenges for Asian Christianity," in *The Asian Synod: Texts and Commentaries*, compiled and edited by Peter C. Phan (Maryknoll, New York: Orbis Books, 2002) 249–61; John Mansford Prior, "Unfinished Encounter: A Note on the Voice and Tone of *Ecclesia in Asia*," ibid., 236–48; Luis Antonio Tagle, "The Challenges of Mission in Asia: A View from the Asian Synod," ibid., 212–21; Michael Amaladoss, "Mission in Asia: A Reflection on *Ecclesia in Asia*," ibid., 222–35; Edmund Chia, "Of Fork and Spoon or Fingers and Chopsticks: Interreligious Dialogue," ibid., 273–83; Jacques Dupuis, "FABC Focus on the Church's Evangelising Mission in Asia Today," *Vidyajyoti* 56:9 (1992) 449–68. G. Gispert-Sauch, "John Paul II: Christology, Dialogue, Mission," *Jeevadhara* 35:209

publication of *Proclamation and Dialogue*,[98] a document jointly prepared by two Roman dicasteries, and further intensified with the release of *Dominus Jesus*, a document produced by the Congregation for the Doctrine of the Faith.[99] Some of these scholars at times prefer to contrast rather than compare the Pope's views with those of the FABC,[100] and as a result, have focused more on differences rather than common points between the theologies of evangelising mission according to John Paul II and the Asian bishops. As the whole Church is missionary by nature, and evangelisation is the vocation and mission of all Christians, it is fitting to revisit this debate on evangelisation, proclamation, and dialogue in the next section as a prelude to our comparative assessment of their theologies of the laity.

Comparative Analysis of the Theologies of the Laity of John Paul II and the Asian Bishops

For John Paul II it is an inescapable responsibility of the Church in Asia to proclaim Jesus as Lord and be actively engaged in the threefold dialogue with the peoples, the cultures, and the religions of the continent. In this section we argue that by advocating the double mission of evangelisation as proclamation and triple dialogue, in particular, interreligious dialogue, John Paul II has adopted a

---

(2005) 371–80; Jacob Kavunkal, "Church and Mission in Asia in the Light of *Ecclesia in Asia*: A Critical Study," *Jeevadhara* 30 (2000) 290–9; J. Neuner, "*Ecclesia in Asia*: Towards a New Theology of Proclamation," *Third Millennium* 3 (2000) 110–6; Jonathan Y. Tan, "From 'Missio *ad* gentes' to 'Missio *inter* Gentes'. I: Shaping a New Paradigm for Doing Christian Mission in Asia," *Vidyajyoti* 68:9 (September 2004) 670–86; "From 'Missio *ad* gentes' to 'Missio *inter* Gentes'. II: Shaping a New Paradigm for Doing Christian Mission in Asia," *Vidyajyoti* 69:1 (January 2005) 27–41.

98   The Pontifical Council for Interreligious Dialogue and the Congregation for the Evangelisation of Peoples, "Dialogue and Proclamation: Reflections and Orientations on Interreligious Dialogue and the Proclamation of the Gospel of Jesus Christ," *Origins* 21:8 (4 July 1991) 121, 123–135.

99   The Congregation for the Doctrine of the Faith, "Declaration '*Dominus Jesus*': On the Unicity and Salvific Universality of Jesus Christ and the Church," *Origins* 30:14 (14 September 2000) 209, 211–24. For a helpful discussion of this document in reference to Vatican II and the FABC, see respectively, Aloysius Pieris, "The Roman Catholic Perception of other Churches and other Religions after the Vatican's *Dominus Jesus*," *East Asian Pastoral Review* 38:3 (2001) 207–30, and Edmund Chia, "FABC's 'Response' to *Dominus Jesus*," ibid., 231–7.

100 See, for instance, Jonathan Tan Yun-ka, "From *Ecclesia in Asia* to a Mission of Love and Service: A Comparative Analysis of Two Contrasting Approaches to Doing Christian Mission in Asia," *East Asian Pastoral Review* 41:1 (2004) 68–101.

"both/and" rather than an "either/or" approach, and in the process, provides a most balanced synthesis of mission theology for Asia. This theological posture is fundamentally a contextual approach in the sense that it aims to be faithful to the tradition by an emphasis on proclamation, a duty that flows from Christ's own command,[101] hence belonging to the nature and *raison d'être* of the Church, and at the same time, endeavours to be sensitive and adaptive to the situations of Asia by supporting a strategy of triple dialogue in the Asian context. As a methodology that is both theologically firm (*fortiter*) on goals and pastorally flexible (*suaviter*) on means, it provides a plausible explanation to the Pope's theology of evangelisation, one that is built on two pillars of proclamation and triple dialogue. This approach also provides a framework to harmonise the seemingly opposing views of *Ecclesia in Asia* and the statements of the Asian bishops, which have often been brought into relief by scholars who hold strong views on the subject.

To support these arguments our starting point will be two inspiring statements of *Redemptoris Missio*, an encyclical that John Paul II relies heavily to articulate his mission theology in *Ecclesia in Asia*.[102] In the first statement, the Pope emphasises the need to unite two types of proclamation: "the proclamation of the kingdom of God (the content of Jesus' own *kerygma*) and the proclamation of the Christ event (the *kerygma* of the apostles)."[103] For him "after the resurrection, the disciples preach the kingdom by proclaiming Jesus crucified and risen from death," hence, "the two proclamations are complementary; each throws light on the other."[104] In the second, John Paul II teaches that "the Spirit's presence and activity," which are "universal, limited neither by space nor time," "affect not only individuals but also society and history, peoples, cultures and religions."[105] In *Ecclesia in Asia*, the Pope clarifies this doctrine by affirming that "the universal presence of the Holy Spirit is inseparable from universal salvation of Jesus," and "the presence of the Spirit in creation and history points to Jesus Christ in whom creation and history are redeemed and fulfilled."[106] In his view, "the Holy Spirit's universal presence can never be separated from his activity within the body of

---

101 *Ecclesia in Asia*, no. 20; see also Mt 28:18–20, Mk16:15–6, Lk 24:46–8, Jn 14:6, 20:21, and Acts 1:8.

102 There are at least 19 direct and indirect references to *Redemptoris Missio* in *Ecclesia in Asia*.

103 *Redemptoris Missio*, no. 16.

104 Ibid.

105 *Redemptoris Missio*, no. 28.

106 *Ecclesia in Asia*, no. 16.

Christ, the Church,"[107] and "whatever the Spirit brings about in human hearts and in the history of peoples, in cultures and religions serves as a preparation for the Gospel and can only be understood in reference to Christ, the Word who took flesh by the power of the Spirit."[108] We will conclude that there is more convergence and agreement than divergence and disagreement in the theologies of the laity according to John Paul II and the FABC, and, despite the intense debate on the subject of Christian mission, which has at times verged on a polarisation into evangelisation-as-proclamation and evangelisation-as-triple dialogue, the similitude between their perspectives on evangelisation in Asia and the role of lay people, is more pronounced than their perceived differences. The task of this section is twofold. First, it reviews the state of the question and unfolds John Paul II's theology of evangelisation with a focus on proclamation and interreligious dialogue and in reference to the statements of the FABC. Secondly, it provides a comparative assessment of their theologies of the laity.

John Paul II's theology of evangelising mission has often been seen as ambivalent. This ambivalence is due to the fact that, on the one hand, he emphasises the need for respect for what the Spirit does in the histories, cultures, and religions of all peoples. On the other hand, he affirms that Jesus Christ is the only way, truth and life for humankind, and the Church is the ordinary means of salvation.[109] In fact, choosing the theme of the Synod, John Paul II wanted the Synod to "illustrate and explain more fully the truth that Christ is the one mediator between God and man and the sole redeemer of the world, to be clearly distinguished from the founders of other great religions."[110] Critics of his post-synodal document *Ecclesia in Asia* generally concur that the real issue confronting the Church in Asia is not the *who, what* or *why* of mission, but *how*.[111] Like these Asian theologians, the Pope is also acutely aware of the importance of the *how* of mission. Thus, he

---

107 Ibid.; *Redemptoris Missio*, no. 28.

108 Ibid.; See also *Lumen Gentium*, no. 16.

109 *Ecclesia in Asia*, no. 31.

110 *Ecclesia in Asia*, no. 2.

111 Edmund Chia, "Interreligious Dialogue in *Ecclesia in Asia*," *Jeevadhara* 30 (2000) 300-1; J. Neuner, "*Ecclesia in Asia*: Towards a New Theology of Proclamation," *Third Millennium* 3(2000) 113; Jonathan Tan Yun-ka, "From *Ecclesia in Asia* to a Mission of Love and Service: A Comparative Analysis of Two Contrasting Approaches to Doing Christian Mission in Asia," *East Asian Pastoral Review* 41:1 (2004) 81–6; Peter C. Phan, "*Ecclesia in Asia*: Challenges for Asian Christianity," in *The Asian Synod: Texts and Commentaries*, compiled and edited by Peter C. Phan (Maryknoll, New York: Orbis Books, 2002) 255; John Mansford Prior, "Unfinished Encounter: A Note on the Voice and Tone of *Ecclesia in Asia*," ibid., 239–41.

writes, "the great question now facing the Church in Asia is *how* to share with our Asian brothers and sisters what we treasure as the gift containing all gifts, namely the Good News of Jesus Christ" (italics in the original).[112] In his view, "the new evangelization, as a call to conversion, grace and wisdom, is the only genuine hope for a better world and a brighter future. The question is not whether the Church has something essential to say to the men and women of our time, but *how* she can say it clearly and convincingly" (emphasis added).[113] Therefore, what needs to be asked is why the Pope is fully aware of the difficulties facing the Church is Asia, but continues to insist on the need for Asian Christians to explicitly proclaim that Jesus is the universal and only saviour. By focusing mainly on the doctrinal aspects of his theology of evangelisation, Asian theologians have generally assessed the Pope's view on evangelisation in his capacity as a theologian rather than as a theologian *cum* pastor, and in the process accented the differences rather than the similarities between his theology of evangelisation and that of the FABC. This requires remedy because of the importance of proclamation and dialogue in the Asian context, their profound implications for the Churches in Asia, and their prominence in *Ecclesia in Asia* and the documents of the Asian bishops.

In a brilliant chapter on approaches to doing mission in Asia, Jonathan Tan Yun-ka provides a helpful exposition and evaluation of John Paul II's mission theology in contrast to theologies of the FABC by making a series of observations, which are bolstered by many direct and lengthy quotations from several prominent Catholic theologians who have written extensively on the subject.[114] First, the author argues that the focus of *Ecclesia in Asia* is Christocentric with an emphasis on the need "to focus on the verbal, explicit proclamation of the uniqueness and necessity of Christ for the salvation of the world."[115] This focus is different from the approach adopted by the Asian bishops who "are more interested in exploring

---

112 *Ecclesia in Asia*, no. 19.

113 *Ecclesia in Asia*, no. 29.

114 Theologians quoted in this paper include Michael Amaladoss, William Burrows, Edmund Chia, Donal Dorr, Jacob Kavunkal, James Kroeger, Josef Neuner, Peter C. Phan, Aloysius Pieris, John Mansford Prior, Aylward Shorter, and Felix Wilfred. It is noteworthy that Tan did not quote Jacques Dupuis, a *cause célèbre* due to a two-year investigation by the Congregation for the Doctrine of the Faith for his magisterial work *Toward a Christian Theology of Religious Pluralism* (Maryknoll, New York: Orbis Books, 1997).

115 Jonathan Tan Yun-ka, "From *Ecclesia in Asia* to a Mission of Love and Service: A Comparative Analysis of Two Contrasting Approaches to Doing Christian Mission in Asia," *East Asian Pastoral Review* 41:1 (2004) 73.

how Christ's salvific message relates to the deep soteriological dimensions of Asian cultures and religions."[116] Secondly, while John Paul II teaches that "the universal presence of the Holy Spirit is inseparable from universal salvation in Jesus," the FABC concurs with the Pope that "there is only one economy of salvation," but prefers to adopt a different view in which "Christ is subsumed within the Spirit."[117] Thirdly, the Pope takes "a linear and evolutionary view of salvation history," and subscribes to a fulfilment theory, which postulates that "other religions are fulfilled in Christianity."[118] Fourthly, the Pope seems to perceive "dialogue as *preparatio evangelica*, in the sense that dialogue is linked with proclamation, and should lead to a proclamation of the fullness of salvation alone."[119] Fifthly, while recognising "the important role of life-witness" the Pope "does not expand on the life-witness approach," but prefers "to speak of proclamation with its focus on theory, argument, teaching and confrontation."[120] In contrast with the "essentialist approach" of John Paul II, which "presupposes an unchanging deposit of truth," the FABC is more at home with life-witness as "the Asian way of proclaiming the Christian Gospel in Asia."[121] Finally, unlike the Asian bishops who adopt "a combined *inductive-deductive* approach," which starts from "the life experiences of the Asian peoples," and "working its way back to the Church's dogmatic and creedal traditions," John Paul II opts for "a *deductive* method of theology," which begins "from basic, a priori abstract assertions to conclusion, from general, universal principles to particular situations."[122] Therefore, in contrast to the Pope's emphasis on proclamation "as the primary task of mission," which takes precedence over

---

116   Jonathan Tan Yun-ka, ibid., 74.

117   See respectively, *Ecclesia in Asia*, no. 16; Jonathan Tan Yun-ka, ibid., 77.

118   Jonathan Tan Yun-ka, ibid., 78–80. For Michael Amaladoss, *Ecclesia in Asia* "operates with a linear view of history of salvation," which considers Jesus and Christianity "as the fulfillment of the other religions" ("The Image of Jesus in the *Church in Asia*," *East Asian Pastoral Review* 37:3 [2000] 236); John Mansford Prior observes that "the theology of religions in *Ecclesia in Asia* follows the fulfilment theory." See "Unfinished Encounter: A Note on the Voice and Tone of *Ecclesia in Asia*," in *The Asian Synod: Texts and Commentaries*, compiled and edited by Peter C. Phan (Maryknoll, New York: Orbis Books, 2002) 241. The Asian bishops also seem to adopt this theory by affirming that "the Church as the Sacrament of union with God and of the unity of all humankind has the mission to promote in various ways the fulfillment which is God's will and gift for all persons in Christ" (BIRA III, art. 3, *FAPA Vol. 1*, 120).

119   Jonathan Tan Yun-ka, ibid., 81.

120   Ibid., 84–5.

121   Ibid., 84, 87.

122   Ibid., 89–90.

life-witness and dialogue,[123] the bishops of Asia accent "a threefold dialogue with the life-realities of myriad cultures, religions and economic-political realities,"[124] and "see dialogue as the only viable means of mission."[125]

Notwithstanding the merit of, and the profit from, these scholarly labours, John Paul II's contextual approach to evangelisation in Asia is yet to be plumbed for a more plausible explanation. For John Paul II, the theologian *cum* pastor, "in the light of the economy of salvation, the church sees no conflict between proclaiming Christ and engaging in interreligious dialogue."[126] His explicit instruction to Asian Christians is to "recognize the gift that is theirs in Christ" so that they may be able "to communicate that gift to others through *proclamation* and *dialogue*" (italics in the original).[127] We argue that this statement, with a deliberate emphasis on the terms proclamation and dialogue, and their listing order, provides a key for understanding the Pope's mission theology in Asia.

To resolve the vexing issue associated with John Paul II's insistence that the Church in Asia must proclaim Jesus as the only saviour, Peter C. Phan proceeds from the perspective of preaching and catechesis rather than theology, and notes that "the immediate goal of the proclamation of the gospel is to enable a person to accept Jesus as his or her 'personal Savior.'"[128] For him "it is this personal and total commitment of the catechumen to Jesus that is being promoted, not the rejection of the *possible* ways in which God can reach *other* people, a possibility that can no longer be denied after Vatican II. The vital question before all else is not whether and how *other* people can be saved but *how I* can fully enter a personal relationship with God" (emphasis in the original).[129] S.J Emmanuel, on the other hand, emphasises the communitarian aspect of proclamation stating that "the new missionary activity … is a proclamation and invitation to live the gospel as a community becoming church."[130] These statements amplify beautifully the view of the Asian bishops who affirm that "the primary task of the Church is

---

123 Ibid., 97.

124 Ibid., 90.

125 See respectively, ibid., 97, 90, 93.

126 *Redemptoris Missio*, no. 55.

127 *Ecclesia in Asia*, no. 31.

128 Peter C. Phan, "*Ecclesia in Asia*: Challenges for Asian Christianity," in *The Asian Synod: Texts and Commentaries*, compiled and edited by Peter C. Phan (Maryknoll, New York: Orbis Books, 2002) 256.

129 Ibid.

130 S.J. Emmanuel, "Asian Mission for the Next Millennium? Chances and Challenges," *The Way* (April 1999) 108.

the proclamation of the Gospel of Jesus Christ, *calling to a personal faith* in Him, inviting to *membership in the Church* those whom God has chosen, and celebrating salvation through Christ in our belonging to His Church. Every other task of the Church flows from and is related to this proclamation and its acceptance in faith" (emphasis added).[131] This statement leads us to make another observation that there is a fundamental agreement between *Ecclesia in Asia* and the documents of the Asian bishops on the primacy of proclamation.

Indeed, at the "All-Asian Conference on Evangelization" held in South Korea, in 1988, the bishops of Asia affirmed that "the ultimate goal of all evangelization is the ushering in and establishment of God's Kingdom," and while evangelisation has many essential aspects such as "witnessing to the Gospel, working for the values of the Kingdom," and the triple dialogue with the poor, the cultures, and the religions of Asia, "there can never be true evangelization without the proclamation of Jesus Christ," and "the proclamation of Jesus Christ is the center and the primary element of evangelization without which all other elements will lose their cohesion and validity."[132] For them, "to be at the service of the Kingdom means for the Church to announce Jesus Christ."[133] They emphasised this point at the Fifth Plenary Assembly in 1990 and added that "proclamation *through* dialogue and deeds" is the "the first call to the Churches in Asia"

---

131   BIMA IV, art. 7, *FAPA Vol. 1*, 292 [misprinted as BIMA I which was held in 1978 in the Philippines, *FAPA Vol. 1*, 93].

132   BIMA IV, arts. 5–6, *FAPA Vol. 1*, 292; see also BIMA III, art. 6, *FAPA Vol. 1*, 104. Miguel Marcelo Quatra also places the Kingdom of God at the centre of the Church's evangelising mission, but contends that "any attempt to place the various activities in hierarchical order with proclamation at the top, gives an unbalanced picture which does not correspond to reality." See *At the Side of the Multitudes: The Kingdom of God and the Mission of the Church in the FABC Documents (1970–1995)*, (Quezon City: Claretian Publications, 2000) 193. Earlier, Michael Amaladoss cautioned against a narrow understanding of evangelization "as proclamation leading to baptism and, what is worse, look upon other types of activity as merely means or first steps to proclamation" (Making All Things New: Dialogue, Pluralism, and Evangelization in Asia [Maryknoll, New York: Orbis Books, 1990] 57).

133   OE, "Church Issues in Asia in the Context of Evangelization, Dialogue and Proclamation," art. 33, *FAPA Vol. 2*, 201. At a symposium on evangelisation in 2002, using the gift/task logic of *Ecclesia in Asia*, the FABC declared that "the good news of Jesus that we bear is our most precious gift to Asia," and "to share him with others is the ultimate reason for all our pastoral activity. This mission is a faith imperative." [OE], "Evangelization in Asia: Final Statement of FABC Symposium," art. 4, *Origins* 32:16 (26 September 2002) 273.

(emphasis added).[134] Earlier, in 1974, right at their first plenary assembly held to reflect on "Evangelization in Modern Day Asia," the Asian bishops affirmed that "evangelization is the carrying out of the Church's duty by word and witness the Gospel of the Lord," and "through" the tasks associated with the triple dialogue that "local churches can most effectively preach Christ to our peoples."[135] This convergence between the Pope and the FABC on the primacy of proclamation and the importance of dialogue is also expounded by veteran theologians such as Jacques Dupuis, Peter C. Phan, and S.J. Emmanuel.

Contrary to the general thrust of Jonathan Tan's essay, Dupuis argues that there is a "substantial agreement" on the centrality and priority of the proclamation of Jesus Christ, a view that we are in deep agreement with, between the documents of the FABC over its first two decades of existence and the teachings of John Paul II, especially his *Redemptoris Missio*, an encyclical that the Pope often refers to in *Ecclesia in Asia*.[136] Likewise, for Peter C. Phan, "ever since its first plenary assembly in Taipei, Taiwan, 1974, the FABC has repeatedly insisted that the *primary task* of the Asian Churches is the proclamation of the gospel. But it has also maintained no less frequently that *the way* to fulfil this task in Asia is by way of dialogue, indeed a triple dialogue with Asian cultures, Asian religions and the Asians themselves, especially the poor" (emphasis added).[137] In the same article, he expands this idea by stressing that "this new focus of the church's mission must be the light guiding the ordering of its priorities and the choice of its policies, which must not aim at serving the internal interests of the church but the proclamation of the gospel *through* the triple dialogue" (emphasis added).[138] Discussing proclamation in the context of the United States with insights from the FABC, Phan states that "it is *through* this triple dialogue ... that the Church in Asia performs its evangelizing mission and thus becomes the local church. Hence, dialogue is not a substitute for proclamation or evangelization; rather, it is *the way*, indeed the most effective way, in which the proclamation of the good news is done in Asia" (emphasis added).[139] Phan's observations and the statements of the FABC mentioned above, which are

---

134 FABC V, art. 4.1, *FAPA Vol. 1*, 282.

135 FABC I, art. 25, *FAPA Vol. 1*, 16.

136 See Jacques Dupuis, "FABC Focus on the Church's Evangelising Mission in Asia Today," *Vidyajyoti* 55:9 (September 1992) 468.

137 Peter C. Phan, "*Ecclesia in Asia*: Challenges for Asian Christianity," in *Christianity with an Asian Face* (Maryknoll, New York: Orbis Books, 2003) 179.

138 Ibid., 182–3.

139 Peter C. Phan, "Cultures, Religions, and Power: Proclaiming Christ in the United States Today," *Theological Studies* 65 (2004) 729.

peppered with words such as "through" and "the way," point to a clear distinction between the goal and the means of mission, with proclamation as the objective, and dialogue and witness as the ways. S.J. Emmanuel also refers to this distinction by a discussion of "proclamation and/through the three dialogues."[140] In our view, this essential distinction would permit a more fruitful reading of *Ecclesia in Asia*.

Therefore, to fully understand John Paul II's theology of evangelisation and to assess it more thoroughly, we propose a contextual interpretation of *Ecclesia in Asia* based upon a clear distinction between the *firmness* with which he imposes compliance with the *doctrinal* principle of proclamation and the *flexibility* that he allows in the *pastoral* practice of triple dialogue. For the Pope, explicit proclamation is a non-negotiable duty and a mandate that is part and parcel of what constitutes the very identity and mission of the Church. However, in difficult situations such as those facing the Churches in Asia, a gradual and pedagogical approach to evangelisation is also acceptable, one that includes both witness and triple dialogue.

In our view, by insisting that Asian Christians must proclaim Jesus as the universal and only saviour, John Paul II has simply followed Christ's command and the teachings of Vatican II on Jesus as the way, the truth, and the life.[141] By affirming that triple dialogue, especially interreligious dialogue, is integral to evangelisation, he has demonstrated a lot of pastoral flexibility by incorporating the concerns of the Asian bishops. This approach shows that while he is firm on theological principles, regardless of whether the audience is the universal Church as in the case of *Redemptoris Missio*, or a local Church as in *Ecclesia in Asia*, he is quite prepared to be flexible by wholeheartedly accepting the mission strategy of triple dialogue as proposed by the bishops of Asia. Like the two types of proclamation discussed in *Redemptoris Missio*, which are complementary, proclamation and triple dialogue should go hand in hand.[142] Explicit proclamation is obviously the same as the Encyclical's proclamation of the Christ event (the *kerygma* of the apostles), and triple dialogue, with its accent on the building

---

140 S.J. Emmanuel, "Asian Mission for the Next Millennium? Chances and Challenges," *The Way* (April 1999) 108.

141 *Ecclesia in Asia*, nos. 19–20; Vatican Council II, "*Nostra Aetate*. Declaration on the Relation of the Church to Non-Christian Religions," no. 2, in *Vatican Council II: Vol. 1: The Conciliar and Post Conciliar Documents*, edited by Austin Flannery, new rev. edition (Northport, N.Y.: Costello Publishing Co., 1996) 739.

142 The FABC also considers that "dialogue and proclamation are complementary." BIRA III, art. 4, *FAPA Vol. 1*, 120.

up of the Kingdom of God, relates to the proclamation of the kingdom of God (the content of Jesus' own *kerygma*).

John Paul II's policy of theological firmness and pastoral flexibility is probably the outcome of what he learned from the failure to write a *relatio* that could bring two opposite theological positions at the Synod on Evangelisation in 1974 into a meaningful synthesis. This Synod ended in "a kind of ecclesiastical gridlock,"[143] as the final text, prepared by the then Cardinal Wojtyla, the appointed relator, and the two theologian-secretaries, was not accepted by the Synod participants.[144] At the time, one view was espoused by Father Domenico Grasso who represented "the older classical model of the Roman School," and the other adopted by Father Duraisamy Simon Amalorpavadass who proposed "a new voice from the contemporary world of experience."[145] This tension and the subsequent failure to deliver the final report had surely played a part in his subsequent dealings with local Churches as the supreme Pontiff, and his design of a missionary approach based on two pillars of proclamation and triple dialogue in *Ecclesia in Asia*. By insisting on the primacy and centrality of proclamation John Paul II has effectively returned to the Christian sources (*ressourcement*) as the duty of proclamation is based on the very commission of Christ, the *Ur*-tradition. By prescribing the triple dialogue as the fundamental task of Asian Christians, he has adapted (*aggiornamento*) the evangelising mission of the Church to the realities of contemporary Asia. So, in *Ecclesia in Asia*, one can detect a replay of the contest at Vatican II between the so-called conservatives and progressives, only this time it is presented on a grander scale and to the wider world of Asia.

By adopting the *fortiter and suaviter* approach to doing Christian mission in Asia, John Paul II has shown himself to be a contextual theologian and pastor par excellence, one who is faithful to the Gospel and the Church's tradition, and at the same time, sensitive to the religious, cultural, and social situations of Asia. This approach also demonstrates that there is no inherent contradiction in his theology of Christian mission as presented in *Ecclesia in Asia*, but a coherent synthesis and a consistency of thought that have the capacity to harmonise

---

143   George Weigel, *Witness to Hope: The Biography of Pope John Paul II* (New York: HarperCollins, 1999) 221.

144   According to Weigel, the Synod Fathers, "unable to agree on a text of their own, handed the whole business over to a post-synodal commission, which in turn handed all the material generated by the Synod to Paul VI, suggesting that he do something about it." The result was the Apostolic Exhortation *Evangelii Nuntianti*, "one of the finest documents of Paul VI's pontificate." See ibid.

145   Rembert Weakland, "Archbishop's Welcome," *CTSA Proceedings* 56 (2001) viii.

different emphases and different shades of meaning often brought into relief by Asian theologians when they reflect on the mission of the Church in Asia. For the Pope, evangelisation in the Asian context includes proclamation, witness, and triple dialogue, and it is our argument that these tasks are also what the FABC prescribes for all Asian Christians, in particular lay people.[146] The final part of this section will explore further this symbiosis between theologies of the laity of the Pope and the Asian bishops. It also highlights some inevitable divergence in their views given that they see the Church's mission from two different perspectives, one universal and the other local, one rooted in the Western rational thinking and the other steeped in the humus of Asian traditions.

In addition to proclamation and triple dialogue, the tasks that are incumbent on all Asian Christians, both John Paul II and the FABC emphasise witness of life as the fundamental role and mission of the Asian laity. Indeed, for John Paul II, witness of life is the cornerstone of the mission of the Asian laity. In the only section of *Ecclesia in Asia* that carries the heading "The Laity", John Paul II encourages "all lay people to assume their proper role in the life and mission of the People of God as witnesses to Christ wherever they may find themselves."[147] Elsewhere, in a speech to promulgate the post-synodal document in India, he emphasises that lay people are called to "bear witness" to their faith "in a world of contrasts," and to "transform society by infusing the 'mind of Christ' into the mentality, customs, laws and structures of the world" in which they live.[148] In his presentation of this papal document, Cardinal Paul Shan of Taiwan also draws attention to the notion of witness. In his words, "as we get to the end of the Apostolic Exhortation we can sense that the most fervent desire of the Holy Father is to see the Church become in the Third Millennium a community of faithful witnesses, a more genuine and transparent witnessing Church."[149] The Asian bishops, like John Paul II, place an

---

146 Felix Wilfred observes that, for the FABC, "proclamation is interpreted in terms of witness, dialogue and liberation, without exhausting it in these" ("Images of Jesus Christ in the Asian Pastoral Context: An Interpretation of Documents from the Federation of Asian Bishops' Conferences," *Concilium* 2 [April 1993] 55).

147 *Ecclesia in Asia*, no. 45.

148 John Paul II, "Finding the Light," in *The Future of the Asian Churches: The Asian Synod and Ecclesia in Asia*, edited by James H. Kroeger and Peter C. Phan (Quezon City, Philippines: Claretian publications, 2002) 61; *Ecclesia in Asia*, no. 22.

149 Paul Cardinal Shan, "Presentation of the Post-Synodal Apostolic Exhortation *Ecclesia in Asia* of His Holiness John Paul II on Jesus Christ the Savior and His Mission of Love and Service in Asia: 'That They May Have Life and Have It Abundantly' (Jn. 10:10)" *Japan Mission Journal* 53 (1999) 263–76 at 275.

enormous importance on the Christian witness of life. At their Seventh Plenary Assembly in 2000, held only two months after the promulgation of *Ecclesia in Asia*, they affirmed that "the most effective means of evangelization and service in the name of Christ has always been and continues to be the witness of life."[150] They went on to insist that "this witness has to become the way of the Gospel for persons, institutions and the whole Church community."[151] For them, witness of life is central and indispensable to true proclamation.[152] It is also noteworthy that in *Christifideles Laici* Christian holiness is defined as the perfection of charity, but in *Ecclesia in Asia* it seems to be associated with genuine witness of life, a view that is much closer to the thinking of the Asian bishops.

Where John Paul II and the FABC may seem to diverge is in regard to the identity of lay people. In *Christifideles Laici*, the Pope provides a definition of the laity based on three pillars of baptism, secularity, and participation of lay people as sharers of the triple mission of Christ.[153] In *Ecclesia in Asia*, he highlights their secular character by speaking of them as missionaries and witnesses to the Gospel in the world. Unlike John Paul II, the FABC describes the laity as Asian Christians,[154] a generic term that emphasises the dual calling of faith and cultural belonging, and one that lies at the heart of what it means to be a Christian in Asia. It encompasses laity, religious, and the clergy who, while not ceasing to be Asian Christians, have the specific role of serving and leading the laity in the project of establishing the Kingdom of God.[155] It is at their Fourth Plenary Assembly held to reflect on the vocation and mission of the laity that the bishops of Asia discuss the triple mission of the clergy, that is, with reference to the laity.[156] John Paul II, on the contrary, tends to put more emphasis on the different roles and responsibilities of the pastors, the religious, and the laity in the one mission of

---

150   FABC VII, art. Part III.C.1, *FAPA Vol. 3*, 12.

151   Ibid., 12-3.

152   [OE], art. 16, "Evangelization in Asia: Final Statement of FABC Symposium," *Origins* 32:16 (26 September 2002) 274.

153   *Christifideles Laici*, no. 9. For John Paul II, this secularity must be understood not only in its anthropological and social meanings, but also in a theological sense. Ibid., no. 15. It is interesting to recall that during the 1950's the motto of the French Workers Priests movement was "Présence au monde est présence à Dieu" [To be present in the world is to be present to God]. This movement was banned by Rome but a decade later its theme became the starting point for *Gaudium et Spes*, Vatican II's Pastoral Constitution on the Church in the Modern World.

154   FABC IV, arts. 4.1.3, 4.4.2–4.4.4, *FAPA Vol. 1*, 191, 192-3.

155   FABC IV, art. 4.4.4., *FAPA Vol. 1*, 193.

156   FABC IV, art. 4.4, *FAPA Vol. 1*, 192-3.

the Church[157]. His distinction between the clergy and the laity is anchored in the concept of secularity or presence to the world, which, in his view, is a distinctive character of lay people.

Our discussion in this section shows that the theologies of the laity of John Paul II and the FABC are both based on the teachings of the Second Vatican Council. However, what informs the Pope and the Asian bishops in the intervening years differs completely from what informed the Council fifty years ago. Hence, each of these theologies is by no means a fixed set of tightly developed doctrines and pastoral directions. Rather, each explores a number of themes, which have evolved in response to the challenges of the day, one from a universal view and the other with a more localised concern. The trajectory of the parallel development of these contextual theologies displays some variance in response to different needs and challenges, hence spawning different theological interpretations. However, with respect to, and within the ambit of, their theologies of the laity, there is a substantial convergence in the thinking of John Paul II and the Asian bishops.

Conclusion

This chapter has examined John Paul II's theology of the laity in *Ecclesia in Asia* and his other writings with reference to the documents of the Catholic bishops of Asia. It argues that it is the logic of faith as gift and evangelisation as task that underlines and unifies the entire post-synodal document. Central to this theology of the laity is the theme of "witness of life," a comprehensive concept that the Pope employs to describe and prescribe the vocation and mission of lay people in the Asian Church. As a contextual expression of the integration of faith, proclamation, and Christian living, it lies at the heart of the papal document and succinctly summarises its theology of the laity. In this document, the Pope proceeds from a Christological and Pneumatological perspective to explicate the identity and role of lay people as missionaries and witnesses to the Gospel, who share in the mission of the Church as a witnessing community of faith. This evangelising mission has as its key elements and aspects, inculturation, communion, solidarity, and ecumenical and interreligious dialogue.

This chapter also proposes a new approach to interpreting John Paul II's theology of evangelisation, one that is based on a basic distinction between the doctrinal firmness (*fortiter*) with which he imposes compliance with the imperative of proclamation and the pastoral flexibility (*suaviter*) that he encourages

---

157   *Ecclesia in Asia*, nos. 43–45.

in the exercise of the triple dialogue with the cultures, the religions, and the poor of Asia. This approach underscores the logic, coherence, and consistency of thought in John Paul II's theology of mission, and offers a modest way to harmonise the different viewpoints on the relationship between evangelisation, proclamation, and interreligious dialogue.

In the works considered, both John Paul II and the FABC have followed a contextual approach in their probing into the question of the laity. Both draw their inspiration from the same theological sources, especially the teachings of the Second Vatican Council, but each addresses a different audience and confronts a different set of issues, one of a universal character and the other of a localised context. While in *Ecclesia in Asia*, the Pope seems to maintain a distinction, but not separation, between the laity and the clergy by an emphasis on the secularity of lay people, the FABC prefers to opt for an encompassing description of the laity as Asian Christians. However, their main findings on the issue of the laity are remarkably similar, and their thoughts on the role of lay people converge. In this post-synodal document, holiness of life is associated with witness of life, a concept that is fundamental to the true proclamation of Jesus Christ, and one that is also adopted by the Asian bishops. For both John Paul II and the FABC, the mission of Asian Christians, in particular the laity, includes the proclamation of the Gospel, the triple dialogue, and the imperative of witness of life, an integral dimension of these activities, and a special calling of lay people in Asia. The tenets of John Paul II's theology of the laity offer a fruitful line of thought for Asian Christians, and serve as a reminder that the construction of theology should never be divorced from both the Gospel and the local context.

In short, the statements of John Paul II and the Asian bishops on the role of lay people are the outstanding means by which the teachings of Vatican II are assimilated and implemented in the universal Church and in the local Church in Asia. To gain a deeper insight into the contextual interpretation and application of Vatican Council teachings, it would be necessary to advance the investigation of the role of the laity in the context of a local Church in one particular country. And this is the journey that we intend to take in the next chapter by conducting a theological study into the vocation and mission of lay people in the Catholic Church in Vietnam.

Chapter 9 The Mission of Lay People in the Pastoral Letters of the Vietnamese Bishops with Reference to the Teachings of John Paul II and the Bishops of Asia

Remembering Sören Kierkegaard's famous observation that we live our lives looking forward but understand them looking backward, we can hardly find a better way to appreciate the theology of the Vietnamese Episcopal Conference (VEC) than to review its pastoral letters issued over the past six decades.[1] Indeed, on 24 April 1980, nearly five years after a North Vietnamese tank crashed through the iron gates of the Presidential Palace in Saigon, the seat of the former South Vietnamese Government, the Catholic bishops of both North and South Vietnam were permitted to hold their first joint plenary meeting in Hanoi, the capital of a unified Vietnam under the communist control. For Vietnamese Catholics this date marked the end of the division of their church into two ecclesial communities that had begun concomitantly with the political partition of the country into two states, the Communist Democratic Republic of Vietnam in the North and the non-communist State of Vietnam in the South, and signalled the beginning of a new period of reflection and engagement, one that endeavoured to interpret the new signs of the times in light of the Gospel.

At the conclusion of this historic gathering on 1 May 1980 the bishops published the statutes of the VEC,[2] and promulgated their first pastoral letter to the

---

1   Pastoral letters and communiqués in Vietnamese language of the Catholic bishops of Indochina and the Vietnamese Episcopal Conference (henceforth abbreviated to VEC), issued between 1951 and 2001, were published in two collections edited by Trần Anh Dũng, *Hàng Giáo Phẩm Công Giáo Việt Nam* [The Hierarchy of the Catholic Church of Viet Nam] *(1960–1995)* (Paris: Đắc Lộ Tùng Thư, 1996), and *Hội Đồng Giám Mục Việt Nam* [The Vietnamese Episcopal Conference] *(1980–2000)* (Paris: Đắc Lộ Tùng Thư, 2001). Documents released after 2001, are available online at http://www.vietcatholic. net, http://www.hdgmvietnam.org, or http://www.eglasie.mepasie.org.

2   VEC, "Quy Chế Hội Đồng Giám Mục Việt Nam 1980" [Statutes of the Vietnamese Episcopal Conference 1980], in *Hàng Giáo Phẩm Công Giáo Việt Nam (1960–1995)*, edited by Trần Anh Dũng (Paris: Đắc Lộ Tùng Thư, 1996) 266–74.

people of God in the whole country.[3] This letter expresses the common destiny that the church shares with the entire nation. It demands new ways of thinking and acting, and is a watershed in the history of the Catholic Church in Vietnam– on at least two counts. First, from 1954 to 1979, South Vietnamese bishops addressed their pastoral letters only to the faithful in the South, while this ecclesial instrument was not available to their counterparts in the North. Secondly, this letter proposes a pastoral vision of the VEC for a unified church that had to live and operate under the watchful eye of a new government.[4] This new vision was carefully articulated by the VEC who was acutely aware of the enormous implications of its message for the Church in Vietnam.

The outstanding feature of the 1980 pastoral letter was the bishops' decision to define the evangelising mission of the Church in Vietnam as "Sống Phúc Âm giữa lòng dân tộc để phục vụ hạnh phúc cuả đồng bào" ["Living the Gospel in the midst of the people for the service of the happiness of our compatriots"].[5] We would argue that this condensed definition, often substantially reiterated in subsequent letters, came to summarise the vocation and mission of the entire church and all Vietnamese lay people. Consequently, it is a key expression of the contextual theology of the Catholic bishops of Vietnam. It signalled a change in their thinking on the role of the church and lay people in the new society, and is testimony of the search for a contextual expression of the mission of the church, which had to deal with a crisis of being church in a communist-governed country.

Though adopted at the historic gathering in 1980, there were historical antecedents. In fact, a localised quest to find a *modus vivendi* with the communist regime had already begun in 1954 in the dioceses in North Vietnam, where church activities were closely regulated and severely curtailed over the next two decades.[6] This attempt was intensified after April 1975 in concert with the ecclesial community in the South, which had previously been accustomed to a good deal

---

3 Hội Đồng Giám Mục Việt Nam, "Thư chung 1980 của Hội Đồng Giám Mục Việt Nam" [Pastoral Letter of the Vietnamese Episcopal Conference 1980], in *Giáo Hội Công Giáo Việt Nam: Niên Giám 2005* [The Catholic Church in Vietnam: Almanac 2005], 240–7. Henceforth, the 1980 common or pastoral letter will be abbreviated to "VEC's Pastoral Letter 1980" followed by section numbers.

4 Missi, "Une Eglise sous haute surveillance: Les difficiles rapports entre l'Etat communiste et les catholiques," *Missi* 2 (February 1991) 16-9.

5 VEC's Pastoral Letter 1980, no. 14. This English translation is my own.

6 While no bishops from North Vietnam were allowed to attend the Second Vatican Council, sixteen bishops from the South, eleven Vietnamese and five expatriates, participated in conciliar sessions.

of religious freedom, and now manifested a spirit of courageous adaptation after an initial experience of the shock of restriction on religious liberty. Therefore, in addition to a careful study of the pastoral letters issued by the bishops of South Vietnam from 1954 to 1979, we will also review previous pastoral letters such as those published between 1951 and 1953 in the name of the Episcopal Conference of Indochina. At that time, this conference included the three regions of Vietnam, Laos, and Cambodia.

In this chapter we will focus on the contextual theology of the VEC in the 1980 pastoral letter, which we argue is essentially Christocentric and dialogical. It draws on the teachings of the Second Vatican Council, Paul VI, and John Paul II, and emphasises *inter alia* the primacy of the human person, the centrality of the ideas of service and solidarity, the double mission of the church in regard to the world–that is, the proclamation of the Gospel and the contribution to the good of all people, and finally, the imperative of witness and holiness of life. We also provide a comparative assessment of the VEC's theology of the laity and the teachings of John Paul II and the FABC. Our observation is that, with the advent of the Asian Synod, the promulgation of *Ecclesia in Asia*, and especially, the increased participation of the Vietnamese bishops in the meetings of the FABC, the VEC's theology of the laity has become more closely aligned with the thinking of both John Paul II and the Asian bishops.

There is no doubt that the 1980 pastoral letter of the Vietnamese bishops is a profoundly missionary and courageous statement in that it places an enormous responsibility on the shoulders of the church, in particular lay people. Its central theological motif is, as we stated above, "living the Gospel in the midst of the people for the service of the happiness of our compatriots." The rich connotations of such a statement reflect a sense of the role of the church in an unprecedented juncture in the history of the country. It is distilled from a period of sustained theological reflection from 1975 to 1980, and draws on the extensive experience of the ecclesial community in North Vietnam–one that had already lived under the communist regime for two decades. It hints at the ambiguity and tension inherent in the situation: the bishops wanted to be faithful to the church's mission and also endeavoured to accommodate the aims of a new Government in regard to the reconstruction of a new society.

This ambiguity and tension can be detected in two diverging interpretations of the statement in question: one emanated from a former Vietnamese Prime Minister, and the other from the then Archbishop of Saigon. In an interview granted to the editor-in-chief of the Government-sanctioned weekly *Công Giáo và Dân Tộc* (Catholicism and Nation), Vietnamese Prime Minister Võ Văn Kiệt explicated his understanding of the phrase. For him, it simply means that religion must take care of life.[7] In his view, living the Gospel is to serve the happiness of all compatriots and not just people who belong to a religion. This involves adopting a life-long commitment, walking the same rhythm with the people, respecting the rights of all, honouring national independence, upholding state legislation, and being concerned with problems confronting the nation, including issues relating to church-state relations. He went on to praise Archbishop Nguyễn Văn Bình of Hồ Chí Minh City. According to the former prime minister, the Archbishop had sincerely adopted this vision, even if not all the bishops were so convinced, so as to fall short of implementing such a programme in their respective dioceses. This official interpretation of the theological phrase is in marked contrast with the one given by Archbishop Nguyễn Văn Bình himself, who emphasises service as the main element of the message. Indeed, in a 1995 interview published in the Sài Gòn Giải Phóng [Saigon Liberated], the Communist Party's daily for Hồ Chí Minh City, the prelate declared that the orientation of the Catholic Church in Vietnam condensed in the summary statement was the right pastoral direction at that time, and he prayed that the church would take advantage of all new opportunities to present more clearly the face of a servant church.[8] For him, a triumphant or powerful church only creates envy and fear. On the contrary, a servant church will be welcomed by all, especially in a country like Vietnam, one that needs this service and values it highly. With these two interpretations serving as an introductory remark, this paper will briefly review the contents and structure of the 1980 pastoral letter, and proceed with a critical analysis of its theology of the laity and its underlying ecclesiological framework.

Overview of the Contents and Structure of the 1980 Pastoral Letter

In terms of content and structure, the 1980 pastoral letter of the VEC consists of four parts and fifteen sections. In Part One (nos. 1–4), which deals mainly with general church business, the Vietnamese bishops ask all the faithful to join them

---

7   Eglises d'Asie, "Entretien de M. Vo Van Kiet, chef du gouvernement, sur un certain nombre de questions touchant le catholicisme," *Eglises d'Asie* 173 (16 March 1994), http://www.eglasie.mepasie.org (accessed 15 December 2006).

8   Eglises d'Asie, "Après vingt années d'attente: Une interview de Mgr Paul Nguyen Van Binh [Archbishop of Saigon]," *Eglises d'Asie* 199 (16 May 1995), http://www.eglasie. mepasie.org (accessed 15 December 2006); originally published in the daily "Sai Gon Giai Phong" [Saigon liberated], a publication of the Communist Party in Ho Chi Minh City.

in thanking God for the first plenary assembly that they longed to hold ever since the establishment of the Vietnamese Catholic hierarchy by Pope John XXIII in 1960,[9] and more so, since the formal unification of the country in 1976. The bishops also express their thanks to the Government for supporting and facilitating the plenary meeting. The purpose of their week-long gathering, say the bishops, was to pray and to reflect on the mission of the church at a historic turning-point of the country. After a brief mention of the meaning of their forthcoming *ad limina* visit and their attendance at the Synod of Bishops on the Christian family, they highlight the importance of the establishment of the Vietnamese Episcopal Conference as an ecclesial institution that would enable them to fulfil their duties more effectively. Finally, the prelates note that they had gone to pay their respects at the mausoleum of Hồ Chí Minh, and to visit the Prime Minister prior to the conclusion of their plenary assembly.

Part Two, comprising seven sections, explicates the VEC's pastoral direction under two major headings: "A Church for the People" (nos. 5–7), and "A Church in the Midst of the People" (nos. 8–11). In the first section (no. 5) the bishops discuss the pastoral direction of the Church in Vietnam. Here, they recall three major concerns that Pope Paul VI raised in his first encyclical *Ecclesiam Suam*, namely the church's self-knowledge, its renewal, and its dialogue with the world. They suggest that all church members should meditate on these ideas every day. The next section (no. 6) provides a brief exposition of their understanding of Vatican II's conception of the church as the people of God. This is followed by an explication of the mission of the Church in Vietnam, which is to continue the mission of the Lord Jesus Christ who has come to serve and not to be served (no. 7). Following the teaching of John Paul II's first encyclical *Redemptor Hominis*, which offers a lucid vision of a Christological anthropology, the bishops insist that for the church all ways lead to mankind. In section 8, their reflection starts with an affirmation that, in order to fulfil this mission, the Vietnamese Church must be the church of Jesus Christ in the midst of the people. They go on to reflect on the meaning of this pastoral direction for the church *ad intra* and *ad extra*. Commenting on the solidarity of the church with all peoples in Vietnam, the bishops declare that the country itself is the place where all the faithful are called to live their vocation as children of God and to serve as both citizens and

---

9 John XXIII established the Vietnamese Catholic hierarchy by his Apostolic Constitution *Venerabilium Nostrorum* dated 24 November 1960. See [John XXIII], "Sắc Chỉ *Venerabilium Nostrorum* Thiết Lập Hàng Giáo Phẩm Việt Nam [Apostolic Constitution *Venerabilium Nostrorum* on the Establishment of the Vietnamese Hiearchy]," in *Giáo Hội Công Giáo Việt Nam: Niên Giám 2005*, 235–9.

members of the church (no. 9). This solidarity translates into two concrete tasks. First, church members must actively work with all people to defend and develop the country (no. 10). Second, they must build up in the church a lifestyle and an expression of faith that conforms with the tradition of the nation (no. 11).

In Part Three, the Vietnamese bishops send separate messages to the laity (no. 12), the religious (no. 13), and the priests (no. 14), explaining their specific vocation and mission. Finally, they close the pastoral letter with a brief reflection on the past, the present, and the future, and encourage church members to rely on the love of God, the life-giving Word of Jesus, and the power of the Holy Spirit, and hence to have the courage to face reality and to trust in the future (Part Four, no. 15). This seminal document is replete with theological insights and these will be examined in detail in the following section.

Critical Analysis of the VEC's Theology in the 1980 Pastoral Letter

Like all other pastoral documents issued by the VEC to date, the 1980 pastoral letter bears the marks of the times in which it was composed. Therefore, it must be evaluated in light of the circumstances in which it was written and the concrete problems it aimed to address, along with the conciliar and papal documents that it draws from, in particular *Gaudium et Spes*, and the first encyclicals of Paul VI and John Paul II. Any attempt to sketch the VEC's theology in this pastoral letter must, first of all, take into account the fact that it did not purport to offer a systematic presentation, and developed only certain topics of current relevance. It aimed to unite the church, clarify its evangelising mission, and exhort all church members, in particular lay people, to practice a more intense Christian life in a country run by an avowedly atheistic Government. Secondly, given these pastoral and practical concerns, a careful analysis of the theology proposed in this letter must pay attention to its underlying assumptions, themes, and emphases. Thirdly, this orientation suggests the need to adopt a hermeneutical approach that takes into consideration the intended mixed audience of the letter, and also distinguishes between what was meant from what was actually written.

Indeed, besides its primary audience–all members of the Vietnamese Church–this historic letter was meant to convey a positive message of dialogue and cooperation to the Communist Government. This mixed audience explains the peculiarity of some of the statements of the pastoral letter: it mingles elements of the bishops' theology of mission and ecclesiology with issues relating to the Government's policies and directions. Hence, to unravel their double-layered meaning, we will have to reckon with the varied nuances of the bishops' thoughtful expressions by delving into the historical and linguistic tradition of the country in order to explicate the meaning of its key terms. In this sense, our presentation of the VEC's theology, in particular its theology of the laity, will be both descriptive and evaluative. Finally, as the composition of the pastoral letter occurred against the backdrop of a political instability and an economic decline which were due in no small part to Vietnam's overthrow of the Pol Pot regime in Kampuchea in 1979, the year of calamity,[10] and the subsequent war against the Chinese invasion, we also find it necessary to revisit the political and social context of Vietnam in the periods surrounding the momentous year 1980.

Addressing to the entire people of God in an unprecedented period of social and political upheaval in the history of the country the bishops of Vietnam summarise their first pastoral letter and the mission of the church in a single statement: "Living the Gospel in the midst of the people for the service of the happiness of our compatriots." This motif encompasses three concepts of "service," "solidarity," and "witness of life," a threefold theme that expresses their preferred mode of engagement and dialogue with the Vietnamese society. The role of the lay faithful, as both loyal members of the church and good citizens of the country, is further differentiated in that their call to holiness is related to the fulfilment of their temporal duties. These constitutive elements of the mission of the church are derived from this motif with "witness of life" corresponding to "living the Gospel," "solidarity" paralleling "in the midst of the people," and "service" being a shorthand summary of the phrase "for the service of the happiness of our compatriots." While these theological concepts are not new and in fact, were all drawn from various conciliar and papal documents, the Vietnamese bishops have combined them to give a compelling expression to the mission of the church at a critical juncture in the history of the country. Therefore, to make an overall assessment of the 1980 pastoral letter, there are three points to note:

- the etymological explication of the key terms employed in the summary statement;
- the alignment of the 1980 pastoral letter with the conciliar and papal teachings; and,
- the political and social situations of Vietnam at the time.

As the king-pin of the 1980 pastoral letter, the summary statement, which comprises a string of Vietnamese and *Hán-Việt* or Sino-Vietnamese terms, calls for a

---

10 John C. Donnell, "Vietnam 1979: Year of Calamity," *Asian Survey* 20:1 (January 1980) 19–25.

detailed etymological examination. The term "dân tộc" is derived from a combination of two Sino-Vietnamese words: the first means "people in a country or in
a region," and the second denotes "extended family." Depending on the context
of its occurrence in the 1980 pastoral letter, this term can be translated as "people," "nation," or "race." In section 11 for instance, this term refers to each of the
various ethnic groups that live in Vietnam. The term "đồng bào" is also formed
by a juxtaposition of two Sino-Vietnamese words which mean "of the same pla-
centa," and denote, in a narrow sense, children of the same father and mother,
and in a broader sense, people of the same country. It was translated into Latin as
"*germani fratres*" in an influential 18th century dictionary.[11] The Sino-Vietnamese
term "hạnh phúc" denotes "happiness," emanating from two discrete words, which
mean respectively "luck" and "good things" such as wealth, nobility, and longev-
ity. It occupies a third place, after the words "độc lập" (independence) and "tự
do" (liberty), in a trio of terms that are printed on all official documents and
emblems under the official name of the country, namely the Socialist Republic
of Vietnam. There is no doubt that the Vietnamese bishops had this ubiquitous
term "hạnh phúc" in mind when they deliberated on the choice of words to express the theme and the summary statement of the 1980 pastoral letter.

Unlike these last three Sino-Vietnamese terms, the phrase "giữa lòng" (nos. 13
and 14) or "trong lòng" (no. 8) is a pure Vietnamese construct which means, in a
psychological and moral sense, "in the midst of" or "in the heart of" respectively.
In a physiological sense, the words "giữa" and "trong" denote respectively "in the
middle" or "at the centre," and the term "lòng" refers to the heart or the viscera.[12]
Like the term "đồng bào," this prepositional phrase connotes a sense of together-
ness and solidarity.

By employing such evocative terms and linking them with the concepts of
"living the Gospel," "solidarity," and "service," the catch-phrase of the 1980 pastoral letter encapsulates the VEC's seismic shift from a church primarily concerned with securing its own institutional wellbeing, to one willing to move with
the world. This theological posture is moreover anchored in the long tradition

---

11 *Dictionarium Anamitico-Latinum: Primitus Inceptum ab Illustrissimo et Reverendissimo*
    Episcopo Adranensi, Vicariio Apostolico Concincine, edited by J.L. Taberd, Episcopo
    Isauropolitano, *Vicariio Apostolico Concincine, Cambodie, et Ciampe, Asiatice Societatis*
    Parisiensis, nec non Bengalensis, Socio Honorario (Serampore [Bengal, India]: Freder-
    icnagori Vulgo Serampore, 1838), s.v. "Đồng bào," 149.
12 For an interesting discussion of the various meanings of the term "lòng," see Léopold
    Cadière, *Croyances et Pratiques Religieuses des Annamites*, [volume 3], (Paris: Ecole
    Française D'Extrême-Orient, 1957) 147–55.

of Catholic mission and social thought, which culminates in the teaching of Vatican II. This tradition postulates that the human person and human dignity, realised in community and solidarity with others and with the whole of God's creation, are the norms against which every political institution and all aspects of social and economic life must be measured. Therefore, we will examine the pastoral letter with a focus on the primacy of the human person, and explore the fuller implication of this theological approach under five interrelated elements: service, solidarity, mission *ad extra* [to the world], witness of life, and holiness.

Mission as Service

In the 1980 pastoral letter, the concept of service is rendered by the Sino-Vietnamese term "phục vụ" which means either "to serve" or "service." This term appears eleven times in the text, expounding now one, now some other aspect of the mission of the people of God in Vietnam. It is used either as a direct or indirect verb in ten occurrences (nos. 4, 7, 9, 10, 12, 13), and once as a noun (no. 10). As a verb, four times it is preceded by the preposition "để" which means "in order to" (nos. 4, 7, 9, and 13), suggesting a teleological focus; and seven times it commands a direct object (nos. 10, 12, 13, and 14) to highlight the recipients of the church's action. For the Vietnamese bishops, "phục vụ" is a more complex kind of concept than appears at first sight. It is a concrete expression of the mode of engagement and dialogue of the church with the society of Vietnam. As an essentially anthropological and Christocentric theme, it also displays the theological features that are central to the theology of Vatican II, in particular its masterpiece *Gaudium et Spes*.

For the VEC, the duty of the church is to continue the mission of Jesus who came not to be served but to serve every person.[13] Following John Paul II's declaration in his first encyclical–the human person is the way for the church–[14] the bishops of Vietnam emphasise the centrality of the human person as the meeting point between the church and the world. Recalling section 21 of *Gaudium et Spes*, which deals with the attitude of the church towards atheism, they insist that all people, "those believe as well as those do not, should help to establish right order in this world where all live together."[15] For them, the people of Vietnam are the community that God has entrusted to the Christian faithful to serve in their dual capacity as citizens and members of the church. Therefore, the object of the

---

13 VEC's Pastoral Letter 1980, no. 7.
14 John Paul II, *Redemptor Hominis*, no. 14 (Melbourne: A.C.T.S. Publications, 1979) 25.
15 *Gaudium et Spes*, no. 21.

church's service is not only God and the church, but also fellow human beings and the country. This service, illuminated by the Gospel and animated by universal charity, has as its objective the happiness of the people. But in addition to the common materialistic understanding of the term happiness, the VEC expands the meaning of this concept by giving it an encompassing religious sense, and placing it in an eschatological context of new heaven and new earth (Rev 21:1), thereby implicitly referring to the Beatitudes.

By choosing the concept of service as the pivotal idea of the present letter, the VEC's theology proposed in the 1980 pastoral letter coheres with the teaching of Vatican II and the Christological anthropology of *Gaudium et Spes*. Indeed, in his closing speech at the fourth session of Vatican II, Pope Paul VI declares that all the doctrinal wealth of the Council aims at just one thing: to serve people, and this means everybody, whatever their misery and needs.[16] He goes on to affirm that the idea of service has occupied a central place in the Council, and that the Catholic religion is for humanity and in a certain sense it is humanity's life. By stressing that the ultimate beneficiary of the church's service is the whole Vietnamese people, that is, the human community in its concrete, existential, and historical circumstances, the VEC has effectively applied the social doctrines of *Gaudium et Spes*, and followed its approach of dialogue and engagement with the world. This Pastoral Constitution affirms the unity of the orders of creation and redemption in the history of salvation. Its starting point is an anthropology that is essentially grounded in Christology, succinctly summarised in the words of no. 22: "In reality it is only in the mystery of the Word made flesh that the mystery of man truly becomes clear."[17] This Christological anthropology became the basis of the Vietnamese bishops' engagement and dialogue with the communist society of Vietnam.

Indeed, by employing the notion of service of the people as a concrete expression of the engagement with the communist-dominated society of Vietnam, the Catholic church has effectively suggested a new mode of ecclesial and communal living for the church in this country. It gave expression to a formal structure of dialogue, which now included a willingness to engage in a sincere dialogue with the Communist Government despite the large measure of control imposed on the *ad intra* operations of the church—such as the selection of candidates to the priesthood, and the appointment and movement of the clergy—and the restriction of the church's *ad extra* activities, even in the charitable and educational domains.

---

16 See Paul VI, "*Homilia*," Acta Apostolicae Sedis 58 (1966): 57.

17 *Gaudium et Spes*, no. 22.

This openness to dialogue with the Government is inspired by the vision of the Second Vatican Council and stems from the insights of Paul VI's encyclical *Ecclesiam Suam* and John Paul II's encyclical *Redemptor Hominis*.[18] It is somewhat akin to the *Ostpolitik* initiative in the 1960s when the Vatican sought to negotiate agreements with communist Governments in Eastern Europe to protect the survival of the Catholic Church in these countries.[19] It can be termed a "paradigm shift" in the pastoral theology of the VEC, in contrast to the former confrontational approach deriving from the teachings of Popes Pius XI and Pius XII. Indeed, back in 1951, the common letter of the Catholic Bishops of Indochina,[20] that is, besides the nuncio, the nine prelates and three diocesan representatives from the church in Vietnam, and one from the church in Cambodia,[21] was an outright condemnation of Communism and its tactics. This two-page letter opens with a warning to Vietnamese Catholics on the grave danger of the atheistic ideology, and recalls a Vatican degree released on 1 July 1949 under the authority of Pope Pius XII that forbids Catholics to join the communist Party or collaborate with them in setting up a communist state.

Nine years later, on the Ash Wednesday of 1960, at the height of the cold war and amid all that period's ideological *Sturm und Drang*, the bishops of South Vietnam issued another pastoral letter dealing with Communism.[22] It continued the general thrust of the 1951 communication and reiterated the injunction of the 1949 Degree that forbids Catholics to join the Communist Party under the pain of automatic excommunication. It also retrieved the teaching of Pius XI's encyclical

---

18 Peter Hebblethwaite notes that the contribution of Paul VI's *Ecclesiam Suam* was "a shift from a world-denying to a world-affirming attitude" (*Pope Paul VI: The First Modern Pope* [London: HarperCollins, 1993] 380). At the time of its release in August 1964, the Pope recognised that dialogue with communist political regimes was "very difficult, not to say impossible," but asserted that "for the lover of truth discussion is always possible." See *Ecclesiam Suam*, no. 102.

19 Gregory Baum, "The Impact of Marxist Ideas on Christian Theology," in *Twentieth Century: A Theological Overview*, edited by Gregory Baum (Maryknoll, New York: Orbis Books, 1999), 173.

20 "Thư Chung Các Giám Mục Đông Dương" [Pastoral Letter of the Bishops of Indochina], in *Hàng Giáo Phẩm Công Giáo Việt Nam (1960–1995)* 93–5.

21 Five of the ten bishops of the Catholic Church in Vietnam were Vietnamese with the rest being foreign missionaries.

22 See "Thư Chung về vấn để Cộng sản vô thần cuả các Đức Giám Mục Miền Nam, Muà Chay, 02-03-1960" [Pastoral Letter on the Question of Atheistic Communism of the South Vietnamese Bishops, Lent, 2 March 1960], in *Hàng Giáo Phẩm Công Giáo Việt Nam (1960–1995)*, 125–38.

Divini Redemptoris to explain the theory and practice of Communism, and Pius XII's encyclical *Ad Apostolorum Principis Sepulchrum*, in order to condemn *inter alia* the illicit ordination of bishops, the creation of Party-controlled Catholic Patriotic Associations, and the imposition of "three autonomies" on local churches. This "three-autonomies" policy of the communist Government was often referred to as the Three-Self Movements. It stipulates that the church should be self-governing, self-supporting, and self-propagating. However, one should not read into this principle a statement of support for the rightful autonomy of a local church with regard to the universal church. Rather, it is a political scheme designed to sever the links between a local church and the Holy See, so as to end the so-called foreign and papal interference in the internal affairs of a sovereign country. Introduced in China in the 1950s, the policy of three-autonomies was a strategy of the Chinese Communist Party to channel all religions into the mainstream and to put them under governmental control and supervision. This strategy has since become one of the guiding principles governing the officially-sanctioned Chinese Catholic Patriotic Church which operates without the cooperation of the "underground" Catholics who loyally maintain their ties with the Holy See.

Following the Chinese model, the Vietnamese Government established the national Catholic Patriotic Association as a member organisation of the Patriotic Front in November 1983 with the purported objective being to mobilise Catholics to participate with all the people in building and defending the country and the peace. In October 1990 its name was changed to the Committee for Solidarity of Vietnamese Catholics and a new objective was added to the first article: "To look after the interests of the spiritual and material lives of Catholics, and make known the hopes of the faithful to the state so that they may be legitimately satisfied."[23] It is noteworthy that in the early 1980s the VEC did not reach a common agreement on the nature and purpose of the Catholic Patriotic Association. Thus, in the Archdiocese of Ho Chi Minh City, a Liaison Committee of Patriotic Catholics, the precursor to the local Catholic Patriotic Association, was established in January 1980 with the express support from Archbishop Nguyễn Văn Bình. However, in 1983, Archbishop Nguyễn Kim Điền of Huế Archdiocese opposed the establishment of the Catholic Patriotic Association based on a declaration of the Vatican Congregation for the Clergy.[24]

---

23 See Cardinal Angelo Sodano's letter, "Priests and the 'Catholic Patriotic Association'," *Catholic International* 4:2 (February 1993) 7.
24 Jean Maïs, "1975–1985: 10 ans de relations entre l'Église et l'état au Vietnam," *Echange France-Asie* (May 1986) 24–5.

In his view, this association is "an instrument of the state to control and divide the Church."[25] The following year "he was subjected to 50 days of interrogation during which he was told that the application of the Roman declaration in Vietnam was a violation of the law, and that 'to oppose the Catholic Patriotic Association is to oppose the state'."[26] Except this rare case of policy rift between these two prominent members of the hierarchy, the VEC has since always presented a unified public view on ecclesial matters. In fact, according to Bishop Nguyễn Minh Nhật of Xuân Lộc diocese, President of the VEC in 1990, the Vietnamese Episcopal Conference has become an effective instrument in the service of individual dioceses and a body of coordination and unification.[27] He also notes that, in reality, the Committee for Solidarity of Vietnamese Catholics has had very few activities in the provinces except in Ho Chi Minh City where it has been quite active.

Unlike other religious groups, and quasi-governmental organisations in the country such as the Vietnam Women's Union, the Ho Chi Minh Communist Youth Union, the National Peasants' Union, and the Vietnam Confederation of Workers, the Church in Vietnam has never been a member of the Vietnam Fatherland Front, an operational instrument of the party for mobilising public opinion to support party policies and to provide the party with an accurate assessment of moods and attitudes among these key social groups, even though some diocesan priests participated in its activities. So, unlike the divided Church in China, the Church in Vietnam has been spared this intra-ecclesial division. This is due largely to the unity of the bishops and their loyalty to the Pope, a strong *sensus fidelium*, the vigilant support of the Vietnamese Catholic communities in the diaspora, and in particular, the foresight of the architects of the 1980 common letter. The bishops had in fact advocated a *modus vivendi* that was acceptable to both the faithful and the Government.

While the 1951 and 1960 pastoral letters described the official position of the Vietnamese Church towards Communism at that time, anti-communist sentiments, expressed by clergy such as J.M. Thích, a diocesan priest, already existed well before the creation of the Vietnamese Communist Party.[28] These views were

---

25 See Cardinal Angelo Sodano, ibid., 7.

26 Ibid.

27 Eglises d'Asie, "Fidélité et Espérance: Une interview de Mgr Nguyễn Minh Nhật, évêque de Xuân Lộc, président de la Conférence épiscopale du Vietnam," *Eglises d'Asie* 101 (16 December 1990), http://www.eglasie.mepasie.org (accessed 15 December 2006).

28 See for example, J.M. Thích, *Vấn Đề Cộng Sản* [The Question of Communism], (Qui Nhon: Imprimerie de Quinhon, 1927), cited by David G. Marr, *Vietnamese Tradition on Trial, 1920–1945* (Berkeley, Calif.: University of California Press, 1981) 85–6.

to be altered with the advent of Vatican II, the Council that seeks to engage in dialogue rather than condemnation, and makes a crucial distinction between Communism and its followers, while continuing to deplore the blatant violations of religious liberty and human rights. To a certain extent, it softened the earlier anti-communist stance of Pius XI and Pius XII, whose encyclicals were prompted largely by the horrible persecutions of Christians in several communist countries during their pontificates. This later change in ecclesiastical policy gradually fomented a Copernican revolution in the VEC's theology of the church. It culminated in the 1980 pastoral letter and its key expression, "living the Gospel in the midst of the people for the service of the happiness of our compatriots."

The marked break of the Vietnamese Church with the past has also drawn on the teaching of Paul VI's *Ecclesiam Suam*, prominently quoted at the beginning of the main text of the 1980 pastoral letter, and thus effectively setting the tone for the rest of the statement. In this encyclical, the first of his pontificate, Paul VI reflects on the mission of the church in the world, stressing that representatives of both spheres "should meet together and get to know each other and love one another."[29] The 1980 pastoral letter captures the three fundamental ideas of this encyclical, namely, the church's self-awareness, renewal, and dialogue. For Paul VI, the church, first of all, must "look with penetrating eyes within itself, ponder the mystery of its own being, and draws enlightenment and inspiration from a deeper scrutiny of the doctrine of its own origin, nature, mission, and destiny."[30] Second, it must compare "the ideal image of the church as Christ envisaged it, His holy and spotless bride, and the actual image which the church presents to the world today," so that such ecclesial self-awareness should inevitably lead to "the Church's heroic and impatient struggle for renewal."[31] These two attitudes give rise to the third, the relations between the church and "the surrounding world in which it lives and works."[32] Following Paul VI in this regard, the Vietnamese bishops propose that all members of the Vietnamese Church meditate on such attitudes every day. Also like the Pope, who affirms that the task of the church is to serve society, the bishops highlight the concept of service as the mode of engagement with the society. In line with *Gaudium et Spes*, they link the imperative of service with the notion of the church's solidarity with all humanity, the second major theme of the 1980 pastoral letter that we propose to examine in the next section.

---

29 *Ecclesiam Suam*, no. 3.
30 *Ecclesiam Suam*, no. 9.
31 *Ecclesiam Suam*, nos. 10–11.
32 *Ecclesiam Suam*, no. 12.

Mission as Solidarity

Following *Gaudium et Spes* teaching that the church "travels the same journey as all mankind and shares the same earthly lot with the world,"[33] the Vietnamese bishops declare that the Church in Vietnam, living in the midst of the people and drawing on the tradition of the nation, is determined to embrace the destiny of the country and inserts itself into the very life of the land. Therefore, all the faithful must journey with the people because this country is the place and the mother's womb where they are called to live and to act as the children of God. Moreover, the Vietnamese people are the community that the Lord has entrusted to them to serve in their capacity as citizens of the nation and members of the people of God. This journey with the people and immersion in their daily life is expressed by two specific missions. The first is the church's active participation with the people of the whole country, so as to defend and to develop the nation. The second has to do with building up in the church a lifestyle and an expression of faith that is consonant with the traditions of all the peoples in the country. Both of these missions deal with the theme "in the midst of the people," one with its *ad extra* aspect and the other its *ad intra* element. In some significant way they clarify the mission of the Vietnamese Church in the concrete, existential, and historical circumstances of Vietnam.

It is noteworthy that in providing a theological rationale for the church's journey and engagement with the people the VEC has dug deep into the cultural and linguistic traditions of the peoples to retrieve the four different terms already mentioned. Each denotes one aspect or another of Vietnamese life: namely, dân tộc, quê hương, đất nước, and tổ quốc. As discussed before, depending on the context of its occurrences, the term "dân tộc" can mean people, nation, or race. The term "quê hương," a juxtaposition of a Vietnamese word and a Sino-Vietnamese term, is usually translated as country or homeland, and conjures up an image of one's own native village in the countryside just as the Sino-Vietnamese term "hương" denotes village.

In one of the classic books which provides penetrating insights into Vietnamese character and society, John T. McAlister and Paul Mus note that "village life is the most fundamental expression of Vietnamese society."[34] The term "đất nước," which comprises two Vietnamese words that denote land and water respectively, is a

---

33 *Gaudium et Spes*, no. 40.
34 McAlister, John T. and Paul Mus, *The Vietnamese and Their Revolution* (New York: Harper & Row, 1970) 117.

cultural and historical term that underlines the importance of land and water in the life and sustenance of the ancestors of the Vietnamese peoples today. The term "tổ quốc" can be rendered as nation or homeland, and literally means the country of the forefathers because the term "tổ" means the forebears or the ancestors. Used together in one paragraph, these four terms amplify the meaning of the deceptively simple phrase "in the midst of the people," a construct inspired by the documents of Paul VI and the Second Vatican Council. They also refer to the peoples who have for centuries inhabited the land of Vietnam, a country that they have built up to be one of the most resilient and fiercely independent nations in the world.

In the first instance, this solidarity "in the midst of the people" is expressed by the patriotism of all the Vietnamese faithful. Following Vatican II's Degree on the Church's Missionary Activity *Ad Gentes*, the bishops of Vietnam insist that, for the church, the love of the country and the love of other people are not only a necessary natural sentiment but also a requirement of the Gospel. In their view, love of country must be real, and this implies awareness of the current problems of the country, knowledge of the goals, policies, and laws of the Government, and willingness to cooperate with all people to defend and turn Vietnam into a rich, powerful, free, and happy country. For its part, the Gospel will provide the inspiration and strength needed to overcome the difficulties and egoistic tendencies, and to promote a spirit of service and universal charity, in anticipation of a new heaven and earth, the ultimate object of Christian hope.

Mission to the World

The above mission-related statements contain political overtones and require further explanations. First, the formulation of the first mission of the Vietnamese Church has to do with the patriotism of the bishops, and their apprehension of the Government's suspicion of church activities. Second, by placing the mission of the faithful to defend and develop the country before their responsibility for inculturation of the Christian faith in the society of Vietnam, the bishops have given prominence to the *ad extra* aspect of the mission of the church before its *ad intra* dimension, and thereby placing the duty of the faithful as citizens before their responsibility as members of the church. Third, by encouraging the faithful to actively participate with the people of the whole country for the defence and development of the nation, the VEC is obviously referring to the political and social situation of Vietnam around 1980. Indeed, 1980 was a year when the country was still at war with two of his neighbouring countries, namely Kampuchea and

China, and its economy was literally in ruins with the majority of people living in abject poverty.[35]

On Christmas Day 1978, Vietnam launched a huge dry season offensive against the Khmer Rouge regime in Kampuchea with the help of the small army of the Kampuchea National United Front for National Salvation (KNUFNS). Within three weeks, it was claimed that this pro-Vietnamese front was in control of almost all of the country. However, the Pol Pot forces of between 20,000 to 30,000 escaped the swift invasion and continued to harass the Vietnamese and the KNUFNS forces, forcing Vietnam to increase its troops in Kampuchea, by the end of 1979, "to an estimated 150,000 to 200,000 men." So, instead of an expected quick victory, Vietnam found itself "bogged down in a protracted, costly and frustrating pacification campaign in Kampuchea." The international reaction was very sharp, and from 17 to 26 February 1979 Chinese troops invaded Vietnam penetrating some 25 miles inside its border and entering the northern town of Lạng Sơn on 2 March. On 5 March China announced that its troops were withdrawing after achieving its objectives, and after wreaking "havoc on border region communities and the northern economic infrastructure." At the same time "Hanoi proclaimed a general mobilization of all men between 18 and 45 and women between 18 and 35 in the militia, guerrilla and self-defence forces."[36] By 1980, Vietnam had the fourth largest standing army in the world totalling about 1.1 million. The resultant military spending took a heavy toll on the economy. Indeed, partly as the result of these military operations, the economic situation in Vietnam in 1980 was extremely bleak: poverty steadily increased to the point where the population was threatened with malnutrition. Per capita income was estimated at only $US150 to $200 per year.[37]

In addition to the political and economic factors that prompted the Vietnamese bishops to emphasise national defence and development as a specific mission of the faithful, their fear of the victorious Government was another reason. Even in 1995, Archbishop Nguyễn Văn Bình of Hồ Chí Minh City frankly admitted that he still had a great fear of the communists.[38] For him, there was a vast discrepancy between the Government's policies and the assurances of its high-ranking officials

---

35 Douglas Pike, "Vietnam in 1980: The Gathering Storm?" *Asian Survey* 21:1 (January 1981) 84–5.

36 All four quotations are taken from John C. Donnell, "Vietnam 1979: Year of Calamity," *Asian Survey* 20:1 (January 1980) 21, 23, 31.

37 Ibid., 30.

38 *Eglises d'Asie*, "Après vingt années d'attente," *Eglises d'Asie* 199 (16 May 1995), http://www.eglasie.mepasie.org (accessed 15 December 2006).

on the one hand, and, on the other, the confidential reports that he received from the clergy, the religious, and the laity. As a result, the political situation was never far from apprehension and ambiguity.

Mission of Inculturation

We now turn to the second specific mission of inculturation. This issue has occupied the minds of the bishops since 20 October 1964 when the Holy See formally permitted the Vietnamese hierarchy to apply the instruction *Plane compertum est* (8 December 1939),[39] allowing for the observance of the traditional honours to Confucius and the veneration of ancestors and heroes, and thus bringing to an official end the Chinese Rites Controversy in four brief articles. As the church in Vietnam is slowly shedding its Western images, architectures, and practices for others more suited to Vietnamese cultures and mores, the challenge confronting the bishops is to promote a common expression of faith that is consonant with the traditions of the people, a task that was of vital concern to the missionaries in the early years of the establishment of the church. As it has often been raised by the Vietnamese bishops, in particular at the 1998 Synod for Asia,[40] and treated in detail by numerous authors, mainly in the Vietnamese language, we will not rehearse the whole question here, but only offer observations on some of its more important challenges.

First, for Trần Văn Toàn, there was no evidence to support a prevailing view that the early European missionaries had sought to destroy the Vietnamese culture when they romanised the Vietnamese language.[41] He supports his argument by two observations. First, unlike Confucianism, Taoism, and Buddhism, which were introduced into Vietnam through the Chinese language and the Chinese

---

39 For the full text of the instruction *Plane compertum est* (8 December 1939) see *100 Roman Documents Relating to the Chinese Rites Controversy (1645-1941)*, translations by Donald D. St. Sure, [and] edited by Ray R. Noll, (San Francisco: The Ricci Institute for Chinese-Western Cultural History, 1992) 87-8.

40 At the Asian Synod in 1998, the Vietnamese bishops called for a greater inculturation of Christian beliefs and practices in ways more understandable and acceptable to the Vietnames people. See Archbishop Stephen Nguyen Nhu The, "Inculturation in the Context of the Veneration of Ancestors," in *The Asian Synod: Texts and Commentaries*, 124-6; Bishop Paul Nguyen Van Hoa, "Evangelization in Vietnam," ibid., 122-4.

41 Trần Văn Toàn, "La doctrine des 'trois pères': Un effort d'inculturation du christianisme au Vietnam," *Mission* 9:1 (2002) 89-104.

writings, Christianity was preached by the missionaries in *chữ nôm*,[42] the Vietnamese national writing system at that time. Moreover, if the missionaries had romanised the Vietnamese language they did so in order to facilitate their learning of the Vietnamese language. This Latin-based writing system would be used mainly by the missionaries and Vietnamese Catholics together with the *chữ nôm*, until the 20th century when the romanised form became the official writing system of Vietnam. The author concluded that the early European missionaries had seriously endeavoured to inculturate Christianity in the traditions of Vietnam rather than destroy its cultures.

Trần Văn Toàn's second thesis is a cogent argument against a popular view that in Vietnam, Christianity suffered from a lack of inculturation and consequently remained a foreign religion in the early years of evangelisation.[43] In his view, when Christianity was introduced into the country towards the end of the 16th century, Confucianism had already become the doctrine of the state while Buddhism and Taoism were in decline.[44] Therefore, instead of having to engage in dialogue with all three religions, the early missionaries had to deal mainly with Confucianism. This ethical and political traditional worldview has as its basic principles the three social relationships or bonds (tam cương) and the five common virtues or relations (ngũ thường). These bonds are "between king and subject, between husband and wife, and between parents and children."[45] The five virtues or constants include nhân (benevolence, compassion, goodness, humanity) as the central virtue, nghĩa

---

42 According to Brian Eugene Ostrowski, "it was in Nôm, rather than romanized Vietnamese, that most Christian liturgical, scriptural, and doctrinal documents circulated in early modern Vietnam." See "The Nôm Works of Geronimo Maiorica, S.J. (1589–1656) and their Christology," Ph.D. diss., Cornell University, 2006, xii.

43 Trần Văn Toàn, ibid., 91. In a brilliant essay on the role of Catholicism in Vietnam, Jacob Ramsey argues against the contemporary myth of "Catholicism's essential foreignness" or incompatibility with cultural traditions, and stated that this religion has become "just as much as a Vietnamese faith as Buddhism and for that matter, Confucianism." See "Miracles and Myths: Vietnam Seen through Its Catholic History," in *Modernity and Re-enchantment: Religion in Post-revolutionary Vietnam*, ed. by Philip Taylor, Vietnam Update Series (Singapore: Institute of Southeast Asian Studies, 2007) 371–2.

44 Trần Văn Toàn, ibid., 92. Nguyễn Thế Anh notes that "until the fifteenth century, Vietnam was essentially a Buddhist country," and "not until Lê Thánh-tông's reign (1460–97) did Confucian orthodoxy in state ideology reach full bloom" ("From Indra to Maitreya: Buddhist Influence in Vietnamese Political Thought," *Journal of Southeast Asian Studies* 33, no. 2 [June 2002] 225, 235).

45 Peter C. Phan, "The Christ of Asia: An Essay on Jesus as the Eldest Son and Ancestor," *Studia Missionalia* 45 (1996) 33.

(justice, goodness), lễ (civility, ethical behaviour), trí (wisdom, cleverness), and tín (faithfulness, reliability). Realising that Christianity has two tenets that were not acceptable to the followers of Confucianism at that time, namely monogamy and the absence of the formal veneration of ancestors, the early European missionaries emphasised instead the fact that Christianity also accepts the moral principles of three relationships and five cardinal virtues, the fundamental basis of Confucian ethics.

From this dialogical engagement with the Vietnamese traditions these European missionaries articulated the doctrine of the "three fathers" right from the beginning the 17th century. This doctrine combines the Christian idea of God the Father with the ethics of Confucianism; it was first discussed in the 1651 *Cathechismus* of Alexandre de Rhodes.[46] In this bilingual (Latin-Romanised Vietnamese) catechism, the author, considered by many as the founder of Vietnamese Christianity, notes that the concept of the "three fathers" had already existed in Vietnam before the missionaries set foot on Vietnamese soil, and that, what the missionaries did was simply to make it clearer and more precise. For de Rhodes, "there are three grades of superiors or fathers who require commensurate veneration and reverence from us. The lowest grade is composed of the father and mother who give birth to our bodies; the middle grade of the king who governs our country; lastly, the highest grade of the Lord of heaven and earth, the true Lord above all things."[47] Therefore, we have to show filial piety, respect, and obedience towards our parents, to honour the king, who is the father of the entire nation, and to worship God, "the supreme Father and Lord of all things, who creates and preserves heaven and earth and all things."[48] This doctrine, according to Trân Văn Toàn, was the outcome of a successful inculturation of the Christian faith in the cultures of Vietnam, and it actually became a new theological element and a key message that the missionaries communicated to the Vietnamese people at that time. However, despite this early success, and given the continuing perception of the Vietnamese people that the Catholic religion was a foreign cultural implantation, the Vietnamese bishops in 1980 still considered that inculturation of the Christian faith in the context of Vietnam was a major challenge for the church, second only to the *ad extra* mission of the faithful to share in the struggle of all the people of Vietnam to defend and develop the country.

---

46 Trân Văn Toàn, ibid., 95–8, 102–3.

47 See "*The Catechismus* of Alexandre de Rhodes, s.j.," in Peter C. Phan, *Mission and Catechesis: Alexandre de Rhodes and Inculturation in Seventeenth-Century Vietnam* (Maryknoll, N.Y.: Orbis Books, 1998) 220.

48 Trân Văn Toàn, ibid., 97–8.

This *ad extra* [to the world] mission of the church, a third focus of the 1980 pastoral letter, is a theological theme that is linked to the above-mentioned motifs of service and solidarity. It is also a fundamental idea that the Vietnamese bishops draw from the documents of the Second Vatican Council, which teaches that the church carries on a double mission to the world, one a prophetic in character, the other pastoral. The first aspect of this mission, discussed at length in the Degree on the Church's Missionary Activity *Ad Gentes*, is to proclaim the Gospel with the express purpose of converting people. The second element of the church's *ad extra* mission, which purports to aid the world to succeed in its own project, is explicated in *Gaudium et Spes*. According to Walter Kasper, this theme 'ecclesia ad extra' was the determining factor in the final version of this Pastoral Constitution.[49]

By applying the conciliar idea of mission to the world in the context of Vietnam in 1980, the VEC affirmed that the mission of the Vietnamese faithful is to live the Gospel in the midst of the people for the service of the happiness of their compatriots: it was to be concretely implemented in the first place in the defence and development of the nation. Thus, the Vietnamese bishops held together the two dimensions of the *ad extra* mission explained by Vatican II. Firstly, they retained the primacy of evangelisation but understood it, not as a verbal and explicit proclamation, but as a living proclamation by way of "living the Gospel" or giving a witness of life. Secondly, they brought into relief the other aspect of the church's mission to the world, which is to seek the good of the people and to help the world succeed in its own activities. In this manner, they implicitly connected the prophetic and pastoral dimensions of the church's *ad extra* mission with the concept of witness of life, the fourth major theme of 1980 pastoral letter.

Mission as Witness of Life

In this historic document, the Vietnamese bishops discuss the theme of life witness in their exhortations addressed to the laity, the religious, and the priests of Vietnam. First, drawing on *Lumen Gentium* no. 31 and *Gaudium et Spes* no. 43, they encourage lay people to live the Gospel of Christ by engaging in temporal affairs. Secondly, quoting directly from the Apostolic Exhortation *Evangelii Nuntiandi* of Paul VI the VEC highlights the special vocation of the religious as "the living expression of the church's aspiration to respond to the more exigent demands of the beatitudes," and "by their manner of life they

---

49 Walter Kasper, "The Theological Anthropology of *Gaudium et Spes*," *Communio* 23 (Spring 1996) 135.

constitute a symbol of total dedication to the service of God, of the church, and of their follow men."[50] Finally, speaking to both diocesan and religious priests, considered as their closest collaborators, the bishops encourage them to demonstrate to the laity by their manner of life how the Gospel is to be lived in a spirit of love and faithfulness to the church. For the VEC, all members of the church will receive the necessary grace of the risen Christ to become new persons who act with justice and holiness.

The Call to Holiness

Following Vatican II, the VEC affirms that the vocation of the laity is to sanctify themselves in the world by living the Gospel in the midst of earthly responsibilities. Through lay people's presence and activity, the church is present to the society and contributes to the material and spiritual life of the nation. Their lofty mission is to live as the faithful members of the church of Christ and to act as the good citizens of the nation. Therefore, they must develop a sense of truth and justice, and a willingness to serve the good of the nation. The grace of the Holy Spirit will assist them in their life of prayer, both in private and in the family or parish, and through religious instruction and catechesis within the family. The family, writes the VEC, should become a school of faith, a place of prayer, an environment for nurturing a life of charity, and the place for forming an apostolic spirit required by the witnesses of God.

Ecclesiological Framework

The five major themes of the 1980 pastoral letter discussed above, namely service, solidarity, mission *ad extra*, witness of life, and for the laity, sanctification in the midst of the world, clarify and amplify the encompassing mission of the Catholic Church in Vietnam. Taken together, they are the way that the Vietnamese bishops intend to address the two overriding pastoral issues in the context of Vietnam. First, how can the Vietnamese Church evangelise? Second, how can the church engage the communist society and culture? Their answers to these questions arise from grappling with three fundamental questions: What is the church? What is the church for? Where is the church?

For the VEC, the church is the people of God (no. 6), a community of Christians that exists for humanity (no. 7), yet lives in the midst of the people (no. 8). First of all, then, the church is the people of the new covenant, the church of

---

50 VEC's Pastoral Letter 1980, no. 13; *Evangelii Nuntiandi*, no. 69.

Christ that comprises peoples from all the countries, united by the Holy Spirit and having a new commandment which is charity and love. It has a structure right from its inception with various functions established by the Lord for the benefit of the Mystical Body. Its purpose is to continue to build up the Kingdom of God until the end time. Secondly, its mission is to permeate the world with the spirit of the Gospel and to bring the temporal realities to completion. Therefore, no human activity is alien to the mission of the church and every ecclesial activity has to do with human life. The ultimate purpose of all activity of the church is to bring all humanity and all realities of the human world into participation in the life, the charity, and the truth of God. Recalling *Gaudium et Spes* (no. 43), the VEC declares that Christians who seek to escape their earthly responsibilities are shirking their duties towards their neighbours, neglecting God, and hence endangering their eternal salvation. The mission of the church is, in a nutshell, to continue the mission of the Lord who came, not to be served but to serve all humanity. Finally, this church must be the holy church of the Lord Jesus Christ that lives in the midst of the nation.[51] For the Vietnamese bishops, to be the church of the Lord means to live in communion with Christ and in unity with the universal church, to maintain communion with the Pope and with others, and to remain faithful to the spirit of the Second Vatican Council, in an attitude of openness, dialogue, and solidarity with the society in which one lives.

Church and State Relations

There is no doubt that this new attitude of Vatican II towards the world came at an opportune moment for the church in Vietnam, which subsequently adopted a similar *novus habitus mentis* [a new way of thinking]. It provided this church with a pastoral impetus for dialogical engagement, rather than confrontation and condemnation, with the Communist Government.[52] Nonetheless, a careful analysis of the 1980 pastoral letter shows that its relationship with the Government was fundamentally dialectical. On the one hand, the Vietnamese Church wished to engage in a sincere dialogue and a full cooperation with the Government to achieve commonly shared goals.[53] On the other hand, it took a prophetic stand on

---

51 VEC's Pastoral Letter 1980, no. 8.

52 Gaudium et Spes, no. 42.

53 Vu Kim Chinh considers this type of cooperation as a form of mutual liberation. See his paper "Cooperation as Mutual Liberation – Background of Emerging Relationship Between the State and the Catholic Church in Vietnam," in *Church & State Relations*

the centrality of the human person as the ultimate basis for its dialogical engagement with the Government.

By placing the human person at the centre of its contextual theology, the VEC has closely followed the lead of *Gaudium et Spes* and explicated the church's positive relationship with society on the basis of three fundamental realities of human existence, namely human activity, human community, and the centrality of the human person.[54] This observation suggests that the 1980 pastoral letter is, to a large extent, a contextual interpretation of the teaching of the Pastoral Constitution in the Vietnamese *Sitz-im-Leben*.

We also note that in the very sensitive context of Vietnam in 1980, they VEC has deliberately refrained from making any explicit reference to the first chapter of Part One of *Gaudium et Spes*, which deals with the dignity of the human person and atheism, and the Declaration on Religious Liberty *Dignitatis Humanae*, another conciliar masterpiece of the Council. In this Declaration the Council asserts that "the human person has the right to religious freedom," and this right is based on "the very dignity of the human person as known through the revealed word of God and by reason itself."[55] It moves on to acknowledge the legal authority of the state but affirms that the church will choose to follow God if a policy of the Government does not comply with the will of God. We argue that this judicious decision of the bishops of Vietnam, which was based on a careful reading of the signs of the times, did not cloud nor compromise their theological principles but laid a solid foundation for a pastoral development that always centers on the human person. Indeed, by placing the human person at the heart of the theology of the 1980 pastoral letter, the bishops have adopted a theological position that will inevitably lead them to insist on the need for the Communist Government to respect religious freedom,[56] human

---

in *21ˢᵗ Century Asia*, edited by Beatrice Leung (Hong Kong: Centre of Asian Studies, The University of Hong Kong, 1996) 175–202.

54 VEC's Pastoral Letter 1980, no. 7; *Gaudium et Spes*, no. 40.

55 *Dignitatis Humanae*, no. 2.

56 In 1988, Hanoi declared that "'the proposed canonization [of 117 Vietnamese martyrs in Rome in June 1988] is a violation of the national sovereignty and an act harmful to the bloc of national unity." See Nguyen Minh Nhat, "Les relations entre l'Eglise et l'état: vues par le président de la conférence épiscopale," *Missi* 2 (February 1991) 50.

dignity and human rights,[57] and to ensure the basic justice for all people,[58] especially the poor.

Such a person-centred and incarnational theology seeks to bring the church in Vietnam into the heart of Vietnamese society. It speaks in humble and sincere terms to all members of the church and offers a theological framework for dealing with the numerous problems facing the country. By envisaging the church in service of the people in their concrete, existential and historical circumstances, the 1980 pastoral letter sets a new direction for the evangelising mission of the Church in Vietnam. In the process, it fosters a rebirth of Vietnamese Catholic identity, and indicates a decisive transition from the focus on internal consolidation of the church to the promotion of evangelisation by witness of life and engagement with the wider society. Therefore, the 1980 pastoral letter must be evaluated within the larger framework of religious integrity and social responsibility. To a large extent it is successful on three criteria–unity, clarity, and relevance. First, its theology provided a framework for uniting the two ecclesial communities in North and South Vietnam. Second, its ecclesiology clarified the mission of the church and the laity in a new society that was centrally re-engineered by an atheistic Government. Third, its message was highly pertinent to the social and political situation of the church and the country at the time. Therefore, despite its seemingly ambiguous character, the encompassing summary statement of the 1980 pastoral letter must be seen as a vehicle that the Vietnamese bishops utilised to enlighten (*lumen*) the faithful rather than to limit (*limen*) the full scope of the evangelising mission of the church in Vietnam. Indeed, with this historic document, a new chapter in the history of the Catholic Church in Vietnam has begun, and it would unfold in the pastoral statements issued in the following decades. To date, the most significant of these documents is the 2001 pastoral letter.

---

57 In a submission to the Seventh Congress of the Communist Party, the Vietnamese bishops stressed that "everywhere, what people want most is political democracy." See "Toward Genuine Religious Freedom: the Submission by the Bishops of Vietnam to the Seventh Congress of their Country's Communist Party," *Catholic International* 2 (September 1991) 772.

58 It is instructive to recall the affirmation of Benedict XVI that "justice is the both the aim and the intrinsic criterion of all politics" ("*Deus Caritas Est*: Encyclical," no. 28, *Origins* 35:33 [2 February 2006] 551).

Overview of the 2001 Pastoral Letter

In retrospect, with the inaugural meeting of the entire Vietnamese episcopate in 1980 and the promulgation of the first pastoral letter, the Catholic bishops of Vietnam rejected the marginal role that the government prescribed, and affirmed that the church shares the same destiny and travels the same journey with all the peoples of the country. This vision was reiterated and strengthened in subsequent pastoral letters until 2001 when they took a major step forward in response to the onslaught of globalization on a mainly agrarian society, firmly in the grip of a one-party Government, and its attendant marginalization of the majority of the population. Therefore, the development of a pastoral theology in these pastoral letters can be divided into two phases. The first is the period of flexible responses to the government's pressures for an active cooperation, leading up to the pastoral letter in 2000 when the VEC celebrated *inter alia* the twentieth anniversary of the 1980 pastoral letter. A prominent feature of the VEC's pastoral letters in this phase is their constant reference to the key message of the 1980 pastoral letter. The second time frame is marked by the specific topics that each letter addresses, commencing with the 2001 pastoral letter, which articulates a new way of mission in Vietnam.

Indeed, the 2001pastoral letter offered an entirely new pastoral direction focusing on the "mission of love and service." It closed a chapter in the history of the Catholic Church under the communist governance that lasted for twenty-one years, and opened a new one, strategically and pastorally more promising. In many ways it epitomized the process of re-writing the church's relationship with the communist-controlled society which started in 1980 and further deepening the church's identity and mission. From 2001, the church became decidedly more prophetic by regularly raising its concerns on numerous issues confronting the nation, especially the need for the government to respect human dignity and human rights. This period has also been distinguished by a fresh outlook on the church, and the result was the construction and celebration of a more articulated mission for the church, an endeavor that took expression in the pastoral letters issued between 2001 and 2012. Given the focus and limit of this chapter we will not be able to discuss in detail the contents of these statements, except the 2001 letter, which requires a fuller treatment.

The 2001 pastoral letter comprises three parts: "Context," "Pastoral Directions in the New Context," and "Developing the Capacities to Implement the Pastoral Directions." Its purpose is stated right in the opening sentence: to look back at the life of the church during the last decades of the previous century and to reflect on the road ahead in the new millennium. The key questions raised were:

what are the particular contexts of the country and the church at the beginning of the new millennium, and, what should be the appropriate pastoral directions to fulfill God's will that "they may have life and have it to the full." The bishops' answer is that the task of the church is "to continue the Lord Jesus's mission of love and service."[59] To accomplish this duty the faithful have to journey with the people, to dialogue with the poor, the ethnic minorities, the migrant workers, believers and followers of other religions, to inculturate the faith in local cultures, and to work with all peoples to reduce the culture of death, lies, oppression, injustice, violence, and inhumanity by building up a new society of truthfulness, justice, respect for life and human rights, and at the same time, developing a civilization of love and peace as encouraged by John Paul II in his letter on the third millennium. To achieve these objectives the faithful must renew their way of thinking and acting, both individually and as communities, from the family, society, youth, women, dioceses, parishes, and religious congregations to church groups and movements.

Four observations illustrate the fresh approach of the 2001 pastoral letter. First is the recurrent use of the term "mới," which means "new." It appears fourteen times in instances such as new millennium, new phase, new problems, new context, new challenges, "dialogue is a new name of hope," "new class people," "new society," "renew the way of thinking and doing," and "self-renewal and renewal of ecclesial communities."[60] The second feature has to do with the call for respect of the human dignity and human rights, the sensitive topics that were not explicitly addressed in previous pastoral letters. Thirdly, there is a closer alignment between the thinking of the Vietnamese bishops and those of John Paul II and the Federation of Asian Bishops' Conferences (FABC). This theological and pastoral convergence crystallizes around the themes of love and service, which were the focus of the VEC's 2001 pastoral letter, and finds expression in both the title of The Final Statement of the Seventh Plenary Assembly of the FABC, "A Renewed Church in Asia: A Mission of Love and Service,"[61] and the theme of John Paul II's Apostolic Exhortation *Ecclesia in Asia*, which the Pontiff personally stated as: "Jesus Christ the Savior and His Mission of Love and Service in Asia: 'That they may have life and have it

---

59 VEC's Pastoral Letter 2001, nos. 6, 9.
60 Ibid., nos. 10-1, 15-6, 20-2. The actual verb used is "đổi mới," a Vietnamese term that comprises two words: "to change" and "new."
61 FABC, "A Renewed Church in Asia: A Mission of Love and Service," in *For All the Peoples of Asia: Federation of Asian Bishops' Conferences, Documents from 1997 to 2001*, vol. 3, ed. by Franz-Josef Eilers (Quezon City: Claretian Publications, 2002) 1–16.

abundantly' (Jn. 10:10)."[62] Finally, for the first time, with a clear reference to the FABC's vision of triple dialogue, the Vietnamese bishops discuss the dialogue with the poor and oppressed such as the ethnic minorities and the migrant workers, the religions, and the fifty-four distinct cultures in Vietnam. However, this pastoral letter is still very much connected to the 1980 document by its emphasis on the centrality of the human person, and the concepts of service, solidarity, dialogue, inculturation, renewal, and development of the country and society. These themes are also often discussed in the statements of John Paul II and the Asian bishops, and the burden of the following section is to identify the notable differences and the points of convergence in these theologies of the laity.

Differences and Convergences

When the teachings on the laity of John Paul II, the FABC, and the VEC are placed side by side, what naturally comes to mind are the ideas that they hold in common. After all, they share the same Gospel and draw their sources from the same teachings of Vatican II, and deal with the same subject, the vocation and mission of lay people. However, in important ways their theologies are distinct in regard to the imperative of proclamation, the concepts of the common priesthood and the ministerial priesthood, the vocation of lay people and their call to holiness, the identity of the laity, their preferred ecclesiological frameworks, and their theological motifs.

Proclamation

The first noticeable difference between these theologies relate to the treatment of proclamation. Unlike John Paul II who insists on the primacy of explicit proclamation,[63] the Vietnamese bishops, in the 1980 pastoral letter, considered witness of life, or living the Gospel in the midst of the people, as the best way to proclaim the Gospel in the communist-dominated society where public preaching was forbidden outside the physical confines of local churches.[64] Their vision

---

62 John Paul II, *Ecclesia in Asia*, no. 2.
63 See Peter N.V. Hai, "Lay People in the Asian Church: A Study of John Paul II's Theology of the Laity in *Ecclesia in Asia* with Reference to the Documents of the Federation of Asian Bishops' Conferences."
64 VEC's Pastoral Letter 1980, no. 12. In their response to the *Lineamenta* prior to the Asian Synod, the VEC declares that the Church in Vietnam "thinks of evangelization first as a sharing in life, a life as Jesus himself lived it: a life of love for all, a love which goes to the end .... In other words, to evangelise is synonymous with being a witness

of the mission at this particular time did not highlight the imperative of explicit proclamation. In subsequent years, when religious restrictions were increasingly relaxed, they began to explain the mission of the faithful as both living and proclaiming the Gospel.[65] However, for them, living and witnessing to the Gospel still takes precedence over verbal proclamation. Indeed, while the Vietnamese bishops acknowledge that the duty of proclamation derives from the very nature of the Gospel, they declare that, in the context of Vietnam, life witness remains the primary and likely the only way of proclaiming the Good News.[66] In the 2001 and 2011 pastoral letters,[67] they expanded this theme by affirming that the mission of the church is to continue Jesus' mission of love and service. The FABC, on the other hand, while stressing the primacy of proclamation, prefers to explicate this motif by a Christological and pneumatological expression stating that mission is 'a continuation in the Spirit of the mission of Christ,' and it means a triple dialogue with the religions, the cultures and the poor of Asia.[68]

Common Priesthood versus Ministerial Priesthood

The second divergence between John Paul II and the bishops of Asia and Vietnam has to do with the ontological difference between the common and the ministerial priesthood. Whereas this distinction seems to occupy an important place in the Pontiff's theology, it is not a significant issue for the Asian and the Vietnamese bishops. Our observation is that John Paul II tends to focus on a theology *of* the laity, an endeavour to foreground his understanding of the role of lay people against the background of *Lumen Gentium*, which teaches that the common priesthood

---

to Jesus Christ … through a life worthy of being his disciple." See VEC, "Catechesis and Pastoral Ministry," in *The Asian Synod: Texts and Commentaries*, compiled and edited by Peter C. Phan (Maryknoll, New York: Orbis Books, 2002) 50.

65 The VEC devotes the entire 2003 Pastoral Letter to reflect on the theme of proclaiming or preaching the Gospel; see also VEC's Pastoral Letter 2001, no. 6, VEC's Pastoral Letter 2006, no. 4, and VEC's Pastoral Letter 2007, no. 9.

66 VEC Pastoral Letter 2000, no. 4.

67 See for instance VEC, "Thu Chung Hau Đai Hoi Dan Chua 2010 Gui Toan The Cong Đong Dan Chua Viet Nam," [released 1 May 2011] [Post-2010 Assembly of the People of God Pastoral Letter to the People of God in Vietnam], http://hdgmvietnam.org/thu-chung-hau-dai-hoi-dan-chua-2010-gui-toan-the-cong-dong-dan-chua-viet-nam/2881.116.3.aspx (accessed 30 June 2011) nos. 9, 16.

68 FABC V, art. 3.1.2, *FAPA Vol. 1*, 280.

and the ministerial priesthood 'differ essentially and not only in degree.'[69] The FABC and the VEC, on the other hand, prefer to articulate a theology *for* the laity, an invitation for lay people to understand their role in the church and in the world, and to treasure their everyday life as a sacramental opportunity to build up the kingdom of God, to serve others and work out their salvation. So, while the Pope seems to start his theology of the laity from above, with its roots in the conciliar teaching on the ontological differences between the two priesthoods, the bishops start their theologies from below, beginning with the concrete, existential and historical contexts. For John Paul II, the call to the ministerial priesthood must be located within the broader vocation as the church, which is a *mysterium vocationis*.[70]

Vocation of Lay People and the Call to Holiness

To identify the differences between the theologies of vocation, especially the call to holiness, according to John Paul II, the FABC and the VEC,[71] we will press into service the biblical understanding of the concept of vocation proposed by Donald Senior.[72] For him, 'the life of discipleship begins not with a choice but with a call,'[73] and the biblical meaning of vocation has four elements:

---

69 *Lumen Gentium*, no. 10. In a 1994 address John Paul II declared that the fullness of ministry lies with the ordained. See "Do Laity Share in the Priest's Pastoral Ministry?" *Origins* 24:3 (2 June 1994) 40-2.

70 John Paul II, *I Will Give You Shepherds: Pastores Dabo Vobis: Post-Synodal Apostolic Exhortation of John Paul II to the Bishops, Clergy and Faithful on the Formation of Priests in the Circumstances of the Present Day*, no. 34 (Boston, MA: St. Paul Books and Media, [1992]) 66.

71 Edward P. Hahnenberg notes that the term "vocation" had become so problematic that the U.S. bishops 'speak of the 'call' to lay ecclesial ministry' throughout their document ["Co-workers in the Vineyard of the Lord (November 2005)]." See 'When the Church Calls,' *America* 195:10 (9 October 2006), 10-4, http://find.galegroup.com/itx/start.do?prodId=AONE (accessed 11 October 2007), Gale Document Number: A152742193; see also U.S. Bishops, "Co-workers in the Vineyard of the Lord," *Origins* 35:25 (1 December 2005), 405-27. For Hahnenberg, "we are still waiting for a truly post-conciliar theology of vocation," and "it is no surprise that bishops end their document 'Co-Workers' with a call for 'a more thorough study of our theology of vocation.'" See "The Vocation to Lay Ecclesial Ministry," *Origins* 37:12 (30 August 2007) 181; U.S. Bishops, ibid., 67.

72 Donald Senior, "The Biblical Heritage and the Meaning of Vocation: Address to Third Continental Congress on Vocations," *Origins* 31:46 (2 May 2002) 765.

73 Ibid., 762.

first, vocation as a gift of God; second, 'vocation as a fundamental call to life and holiness before God'; third, 'vocation as essentially linked to mission, to a participation in the divine work of transforming the world, a sharing in the mission of Christ to establish the reign of God'; and finally, 'vocation as requiring lifelong conversion of heart and personal transformation.'[74]

First, unlike John Paul II who insists that 'each Christian vocation comes from God and is God's gift,'[75] the FABC and the VEC do not emphasise this important idea.[76] Secondly, whereas John Paul II and the VEC often reflect on the theme of holiness with an emphasis on the need to live out this holiness in the midst of the world,[77] the FABC does not accord the same treatment in their documents including the Statement of the Fourth Plenary Assembly on the vocation and mission of the laity.[78] However, all three often link vocation with the church's mission of transforming the world and building up the kingdom of God.[79] They also stress that conversion and renewal are part and parcel of Christian life and vocation.[80]

---

74 Ibid., 765, also 763–4.

75 John Paul II, *I Will Give You Shepherds: Pastores Dabo Vobis*, no. 35 (Boston, MA: St. Paul Books and Media, [1992]) 66.

76 The FABC did mention that "the *sensus fidelium*, or faith-instinct, of the whole people of God is a gift of the Spirit to all as a body." FABC IV, art. 4.4.3, *FAPA Vol. 1*, 193.

77 John Paul II, "*Novo Millennio Ineunte*," nos. 30-1, *Origins* 30:31 (18 January 2001) 499; *Christifideles Laici*, no. 17. In a public address in Baltimore in 1995, John Paul II declared that "the challenge of the great jubilee of the year 2000 is the new evangelization: a deepening of faith and a vigorous response to the Christian vocation to holiness and service" ("Homily in Oriole Park," *Origins* 25:18 [19 October 1995] 313). To underscore the possibility of holiness in lay life, the Pope beatified two laymen, Lorenzo Ruiz (18 October 1987) and Giuseppe Moscati (25 October 1987), while the Synod on the Laity was in session. See "Annual Address to the Roman Curia," *Origins* 17 (28 January 1988) 575. See also VEC's Pastoral Letter 1980, no. 12; VEC's Pastoral Letter 2006, nos. 3–4.

78 Thomas C. Fox notes that at the FABC's Seventh Plenary Assembly in 2000 there was a total of twenty-three workshops, and "when it was announced that a workshop on 'holiness' failed to attract a single person, the bishops burst into laughter" ("Polite Toward Rome, True to their Mission," *National Catholic Reporter* [28 January 2000] 11).

79 See for example, FABC IV, arts. 2.4, 3.1.2–3.1.3, 3.2.3, 3.5.5, 3.7.1, 3.7.4–3.7.5, 3.8.5, 3.9.3, *FAPA Vol. 1*, 179, 180, 182, 186, 187, 188, and 190 respectively; VEC's Pastoral Letter 1980, nos. 9, 12; VEC's Pastoral Letter 1992, no. 16; VEC's Pastoral Letter 2001, nos. 9, 21–22; John Paul II, *Christifideles Laici*, no. 9; idem, *I Will Give You Shepherds: Pastores Dabo Vobis*, no. 35, 67.

80 For instance, BIRA III, art. 3, *FAPA Vol. 1*, 120; OL, "Second Asian Laity Meeting," art. 3.1, *FAPA Vol. 3*, 115; VEC's Pastoral Letter 1980, no. 8; VEC's Pastoral Letter

It is noteworthy that in *Christifideles Laici* John Paul II defines Christian holiness as the perfection of charity, stating that it is 'the prime and fundamental vocation' of the lay faithful that 'the Father assigns to each of them in Jesus Christ through the Holy Spirit.'[81] The Pope also affirms that holiness is 'the greatest dignity conferred on a disciple of Christ.'[82] In the inspiring Apostolic Letter *Novo Millennio Ineunte*, his message for the church at the beginning of the third millennium, he explains that holiness is 'the dimension which expresses best the mystery of the church.'[83] For him, the rediscovery of the church as mystery and as people of God goes hand in hand with the rediscovery of holiness.[84] Therefore, all pastoral initiatives, he insists, 'must be set in relation to holiness.'[85] However, in his Apostolic Exhortation *Ecclesia in Asia* John Paul II seems to associate it with mission and the witness of life, a view that is closer to the thinking of the bishops of Asia and the VEC.[86]

Unlike John Paul II, in the theology of the FABC, the individual dimension of holiness is somewhat understated. While the Asian bishops were no doubt aware of the universal call to holiness, a theme that holds a prominent place in *Lumen Gentium*,[87] it did not rate a mention in the final statement of the Fourth Plenary Assembly on the laity, and only twice in the five-volume collection of the documents of the FABC (1970–2012).[88] In one of these instances, the FABC states that God is the source of holiness, and 'to become Holy is to carry out his mission – to serve the poor and marginalised beyond the boundaries of any religious beliefs.'[89] On the contrary, for the Vietnamese bishops, all members of the church will receive the necessary grace of the risen Christ to become new persons who act with

---

2001, no. 16; John Paul II, '*Tertio Millennio Adveniente*,' no. 42, *Origins* 24 (24 November 1994) 412.

81 *Christifideles Laici*, no. 16.

82 Ibid.

83 John Paul II, "Apostolic Letter '*Novo Millennio Inenunte*' for the Closing of the Jubilee of the Year 2000," no. 7, *Origins* 30:31 (18 January 2001) 492.

84 Ibid., 499.

85 Ibid.

86 See John Paul II, "*Ecclesia in Asia*," *Origins* 29:23 (18 November 1999) 357, 359–84. See also Peter N.V. Hai, "Lay People in the Asian Church: A Study of John Paul II's Theology of the Laity in *Ecclesia in Asia* with Reference to the Documents of the Federation of Asian Bishops' Conferences."

87 *Lumen Gentium*, nos. 39–32.

88 BILA II, art. 6, *FAPA Vol. 1*, 240; BILA III, art. 6, *FAPA Vol. 1*, 244.

89 OHD, "Understanding Christian – Muslim Dialogue in South East Asia," Part III, art 2, *FAPA Vol. 4*, 84.

justice and holiness.[90] Following Vatican II, the VEC affirms that the vocation of the laity is to sanctify themselves in the world by living the Gospel in the midst of earthly responsibilities.[91]

The Identity of Lay People

Another area where these three theologies may seem to diverge is in regard to the identity of lay people. Whereas the Vietnamese bishops offer no definition of the laity, the Pope presents a description based on three pillars of baptism, secularity, and participation of lay people as sharers of the triple mission of Christ.[92] Unlike John Paul II, the FABC describes the laity as Asian Christians,[93] a generic term that emphasises the dual calling of faith and cultural belonging, and one that lies at the heart of what it means to be a Christian in Asia. It encompasses laity, religious, and the clergy who, while not ceasing to be Asian Christians, have the specific role of serving and leading the laity in the project of establishing the kingdom of God.[94]

Ecclesiological Frameworks

The fifth distinction between these three theologies of the laity relates to the ecclesiological frameworks. Whereas the Vietnamese bishops tend to anchor their theology of the laity in the framework of the church as the people of God, and expanded this theme in the May 2011 Pastoral Letter by a deeper reflection on the communion aspect of the church as the family of God,[95] John Paul II and the FABC, while not ignoring the richness of the Vatican II concept of the church as the people of God, prefer to emphasise an ecclesiology of communion.

Theological Motifs

Finally, in terms of theological motifs, it can be said that 'triple dialogue' is for the FABC what 'baptismal dignity' for John Paul II,[96] and 'service' for the Vietnamese bishops.

However, beneath these theological differences common points can be discernible in their theologies. First, the VEC's pastoral letters have displayed a

---

90 VEC's Pastoral Letter 1980, no. 10.
91 VEC's Pastoral Letter 1980, no. 12; *Lumen Gentium*, no. 31, *Gaudium et Spes*, no. 43.
92 *Christifideles Laici*, no. 9.
93 FABC IV, arts. 4.1.3, 4.4.2–4.4.4, *FAPA Vol. 1*, 191, 192–3.
94 FABC IV, art. 4.4.4., *FAPA Vol. 1*, 193.
95 VEC's Pastoral Letter 2011, nos. 10–1, 20–3, 48.
96 Peter N.V. Hai, "Reflections on John Paul II's Theology of the Laity," 9–12.

gradual alignment with the thinking of John Paul II and the Asian bishops, especially from 1998 when the Vietnamese bishops participated in the entire process of the Synod for Asia and later, in 2000, in the Seventh Plenary Assembly of the Asian bishops.[97] This theological convergence crystallises around the ideas of love and service, which was the focus of the VEC's 2001 pastoral letter,[98] and found expression in both the title of The Final Statement of the Seventh Plenary Assembly of the FABC, 'A Renewed Church in Asia: A Mission of Love and

---

97 According to Bishop Nguyen Minh Nhat of Xuan Loc diocese, the *ad limina* visit of the Vietnamese bishops in 1990 "marks the first time that almost all the Ordinaries of Vietnam have the honour of assembling around the throne of Christ's Vicar on earth." See "The Hardships of the Church in Vietnam," *L'Osservatore Romano* 48 (26 November 1990) 2. It is also noteworthy that in 1995, for the first time since April 1975, four Vietnamese bishops attended the Sixth Plenary Assembly of the FABC held in Manila. See John S. Cummins, "Asia, Continent at a Crossroads," *America* (14 October 1995) 4. Pope John Paul II addressed this assembly during his visit to The Philippines capital to celebrate the World Youth Day and commemorate the 400th year of the Archdiocese of Manila. The Vietnamese Government initially permitted only three bishops to travel to Manila stating that it was the Episcopal Conference of South Vietnam that was a member of the FABC, and that the VEC had not requested nor obtained the government's approval to become a member of the FABC. See "Les évêques du Vietnam et la Féderation des conférénces épiscopale d'Asie," *Eglises d'Asie* 186 (1 November 1994), http://www.eglasie.mepasie.org (accessed 15 December 2006). Fourteen years later, in 2009, again for the first time, a meeting of the FABC was held in Vietnam. See Asia-News, "For the first time a meeting of Asian Bishops takes place in Vietnam," http://www.vietcatholic.net/News/Html/72469.htm. Finally, in 2012, the Tenth Plenary Assembly of the FABC was held Xuan Loc and Ho Chi Minh City. It is of note that when the Asian bishops first met together around Pope Paul VI from 23 to 29 November 1970 to discuss the topic of *Populorum Progressio* in Asia, nine South Vietnamese bishops participated in this inaugural meeting, an event that would lead to the creation of the FABC. See Trần Anh Dũng, *Hội Đồng Giám Mục Việt Nam* [The Vietnamese Episcopal Conference] *(1980-2000)* 3-10.

98 See the first sentence of no. 9 of the VEC's Pastoral Letter 2001, which is quoted here in the French translation provided by the priests of the Missions Etrangères de Paris: 'Face à cette situation sociale et ces nouveaux défis, l'Eglise a conscience que sa mission est de perpétuer la mission d'amour et de service du Seigneur Jesus.' See VEC, "Lettre commune de la Conférence épiscopale du Vietnam envoyée à la communautée du peuple de Dieu pour l'année 2001," *Eglises d'Asie* 338 (1 October 2001) 24. The convergence of thought between the VEC, John Paul II, and the Asian bishops becomes even more apparent when one comes to the heading of the second part of this pastoral letter: "Orientation pastorale à l'interieur du contexte nouveau: amour et service: 'Pour qu'ils aient la vie et qu'ils l'aient en abondance' (Jn 10,10)." Ibid.

Service,' and the theme of John Paul II's Apostolic Exhortation *Ecclesia in Asia*, which the Pontiff stated as: 'Jesus Christ the Savior and His Mission of Love and Service in Asia.'[99] By focusing on the themes of love and service the FABC and the Vietnamese bishops have effectively kept their theologies in synchronisation with the papal magisterium, and in the process, demonstrated their commitment to *sentire cum ecclesia*, to think and feel with the church.

In addition to the motifs of love and service, all three theologies also converge on a number of other themes: the centrality of Jesus, the emphasis on life witness as the fundamental expression of the role of lay people, the triple dialogue, and the respect of human dignity and human rights. First, these theologies make Jesus Christ the centre of the church's witness, and that shapes all their thinking. For John Paul II, it started right from his first encyclical *Redemptor Hominis*[100]; for the FABC, it was the Statement of the Fourth Plenary Assembly on the vocation and mission of the laity that presents Jesus as the Liberator,[101] and for the VEC, it was manifest in the pastoral letters of 1980 and 2001.[102] Secondly, all three theologies stress that witness of life is a fundamental concept to describe and prescribe the role of lay people.[103] Thirdly, by its accent on inculturation, and the dialogue with other religions, the poor, and the people of no religion, in the 2001 pastoral letter and other subsequent pastoral statements,[104] the VEC's theology has become more closely aligned with the thought of John Paul II and the FABC who both high-lighted the need for triple dialogue in the Asian context.[105] Finally, like Vatican II, there is no condemnation of Communism in these theologies.[106] However, all

99   *Ecclesia in Asia*, no. 2.
100 John Paul II, *Redemptor Hominis* (Melbourne: A.C.T.S. Publications, 1979).
101 For example, in this statement the FABC declares that "the call today for us Asian Christians is to become a Church deeply committed to Jesus the Liberator. Such a commitment by all Christians will make the Church s communion of committed disciples–be they clergy or laity–working for the liberation of Asia." See FABC IV, art. 4.1.3, *FAPA Vol. 1*, 191.
102 VEC Pastoral Letter 1980, nos. 7–8; VEC Pastoral Letter 2001, no. 9.
103 See For instance, VEC's Pastoral Letter 1980, no. 12, VEC Pastoral Letter 2000, no. 4.
104 VEC's Pastoral Letter 2001, nos. 10, 13–15; VEC's Pastoral Letter 2003, nos., 9, 11–12; VEC's Pastoral Letter 2004, no. 9; VEC's Pastoral Letter 2011, nos. 15, 39–42.
105 It is of note that for John Paul II and the FABC, proclamation, dialogue, incultura-tion, and the preferential option for the poor, are not separate topics but aspects of an integrated understanding of the church's mission of love and service. See FABC VII, Part III, *FAPA Vol. 3*, 8; *Ecclesia in Asia*, no. 23.
106 According to the FABC [1978], "Communism plays a very important role in Asia by the very fact that some 46% of all Asians live in Communist states. We are aware

three emphasise the need for governments to respect human dignity and human rights,[107] the bedrock of Catholic social teachings.[108] Here, the Vietnamese bishops go a step further than the FABC in that they seek to expand the triple dialogue model with a fourth type of dialogue, namely, the dialogue with the national government.[109] While this pastoral area has been accorded a high priority by both John Paul II and Benedict XVI,[110] it has not received sufficient attention in the

---

that communism presents different faces throughout the world. But its Asian face makes us apprehensive, although we cannot deny that they also present some positive aspects. We have criticized classical capitalism because while professedly promoting economic growth, it has deprived man of the just fruits of his labor. We now criticize communism because, while professedly promoting liberation, it has deprived man of his just human rights. In their historical realization both have hindered true human development, the one creating poverty in the midst of affluence, the other destroying freedom in the pursuit of equality." See BISA IV, art. 13, *FAPA Vol. 1*, 213.

107 VEC's Pastoral Letter 2001, nos. 11, 20; VEC's Pastoral Letter 2006, no. 7; VEC's Pastoral Letter 2007, no. 33.

108 Interviewed on the occasion of the launch of the English version of the "Compendium of the Social Doctrine of the Church," Cardinal Renato Martino states that the Compendium is centred on "the centrality of the human being and of human dignity. Human rights descend from this basis." See Philip Crispin, "Church's Best-Kept Secret," *The Tablet* (11 June 2005) 8.

109 This remark was first made by Peter N.V. Hai in "Lay People in the Asian Church: A Critical Study of the Role of the Laity in the Contextual Theology of the Federation of Asian Bishops' Conferences (1970–2001) with Special Reference to John Paul II's Apostolic Exhortations *Christifideles Laici* (1989) and *Ecclesia in Asia* (1999), and the Pastoral Letters of the Vietnamese Episcopal Conference" (Ph.D. diss., Australian Catholic University, 2009) 432, 441; see also idem, "The Contextual Theology of the Vietnamese Episcopal Conference in the 1980 Pastoral Letter," *East Asian Pastoral Review* 48:4 (Oct-Dec 2011) 338; idem, "Reflections on the Future of the FABC's Theology of the Laity," *East Asian Pastoral Review* 49:2 (April-June 2012) 113–4; and idem, "*Sentire cum ecclesia*: Laity and the Call to Holiness in Papal and Local Theologies," *The Australasian Catholic Record* 89:3 (July 2012) 347. It is noteworthy that one of the recommendations made by the FABC at the Tenth Plenary Assembly was to "encourage a continued dialogue between the Church in Vietnam and the government and indeed between all Churches in the FABC territory and their respective governments." See FABC X, *FAPA Vol. 5*, 83–4.

110 Benedict XVI, "Letter to Chinese Catholics," *Origins* 37:10 (2 August 2007) 145–58; also appeared as "Letter of the Holy Father Pope Benedict XVI to the Bishops, Priests, Consecrated Persons and Lay Faithful of the Catholic Church in the People's Republic of China"; John Paul II, "*Ecclesia in Asia*," nos. 8–9, *Origins* 29:23 (18 November 1999) 362–3.

deliberations of the Asian bishops.[111] Given the high degree of political and social controls exerted by several regimes in Asia, the pioneering work of the VEC in the field of dialogical engagement with the national government could serve as a model for other local churches in Asia.

Conclusion

This chapter has reviewed the theologies of the laity and of the Church in the pastoral letters of the Vietnamese bishops with a special emphasis on the 1980 and 2001 pastoral statements, the two significant milestones in the history of the Catholic Church in Vietnam. In 1980 the bishops of Vietnam articulated the evangelising mission of the entire church, and hence of the laity, as "living the Gospel in the midst of the people for the service of the happiness of our compatriots." This summary statement, which emphasises the centrality of the human person, describes a dialectical relationship between the Vietnamese Church with the Government, one that is based on a sharing of the common goals such as defence and development of the nation, but also one that raises, in a gentle but firm voice, a clear opposition to all violations of the human person and the human dignity. Twenty-one years later, in 2001, the Vietnamese bishops revisited and deepened this mission and reformulated it as "to continue the Lord Jesus's mission of love and service." Underlying these two missionary statements, which were composed to meet the changing pastoral needs and challenges, is a constant reference to Jesus Christ, an emphasis on the motif of service, and a central role accorded to the faithful in the church's mission to the world. These themes are intimately linked to, and strengthened by, the concepts of solidarity, mission to the world, witness, and holiness of life, the ideas that are central to Vatican II documents, especially *Gaudium et Spes*, its longest and closing text. In line with the teaching of this Pastoral Constitution, the VEC's theology is underpinned by an anthropological orientation that is Christocentric, and draws on the insights of both Paul VI and the Second Vatican Council. Therefore, we conclude that the richest legacy of the 1980 pastoral letter is Jesus Christ, who is the foundation and purpose of the vocation and the mission of all the faithful.

A new dimension of the VEC's theology proposed in the 1980 pastoral letter is a theological exploration of a pastoral dialogue with a Communist Government,

---

111   At the Tenth Plenary Assembly, for the first time, the bishops of Myanmar suggested the idea of a "quadruple dialogue," one that would include "a dialogue with atheism, the product of either radical secularism or of political ideology." See FABC X, *FAPA Vol. 5*, 77.

an area that has received little attention from the Federation of the Asian Bishops' Conferences. In view of the authoritarian nature of several national Governments in Asia, this dialogical model may provide other local churches in the region with some useful theological and pastoral pointers, and will benefit further from a collective and deeper reflection of the bishops of Asia. Relying on the doctrinal principles of Vatican II and Paul VI, and using them as a theological starting point, the Vietnamese bishops have articulated not only a theological vision but also a pastoral process for the Church in Vietnam. This vision and process was crafted in 1980, in the midst of a dramatic interaction between the church and the communist society, a complex dialogue that is marked by a latent confrontation between two contrasting visions of the human. One is based on an atheistic and dialectic materialism, and takes human autonomy as the ultimate good, and the other promotes a Christ-centred vision of human wholeness and development,[112] and places human dignity at the centre of its philosophical reflection.[113]

In sum, the 1980 pastoral letter and other pastoral statements of the VEC present a contextual theology that is fundamentally Christological and dialogical. Such a theology is in the first place meant to be an inspirational resource for the Vietnamese faithful. But it also intends to send a clear message to the political authorities of the church's unique contribution to the socio-political order. This message is firmly based on the Catholic Social Teaching on the dignity and value of the human person,[114] one that serves as a constant reminder to the Vietnamese Government to respect religious freedom and human rights.

---

112 For John Paul II, Christian humanism "implies first of all an openness to the transcendent," and "advocates a vision of society centered on the human person and his inalienable rights, on the values of justice and peace, on a correct relationship between individuals, society and the state, on the logic of solidarity and subsidiarity." Quoted by J. Michael Miller, "Three Megatrends Influencing Catholic Higher Education Globally," *Origins* 36:36 (22 February 2007) 570.

113 For Benedict XVI, "respect for the person promotes peace and that, in building peace, the foundations are laid for an authentic integral humanism" ("Respect for Rights of All," *The Tablet* [30 December 2006] 372.

114 John Paul II also articulated this point clearly by affirming that the church's "contribution to the political order is precisely her vision of the dignity of the person revealed in all its fullness in the mystery of the Incarnate Word." See *Encyclical Letter Centesimus Annus of the Supreme Pontiff John Paul II on the Hundreth Anniversary of Rerum Novarum*, no 47 (Sydney: St Pauls Publications, 1991) 89.

Chapter 10 The Future of the Fabc's Theology of the Laity

As this book comes to its conclusion, it would be worthwhile to recall what prompted our journey of research in the first place and where we have come in this exploration. This study set out to examine the role of the laity in the contextual theology of the Federation of Asian Bishops' Conferences (1970–2012) with special reference to John Paul II's Apostolic Exhortations *Christifideles Laici* (1989) and *Ecclesia in Asia* (1999), and the pastoral letters of the Vietnamese Episcopal Conference. Throughout this study a twofold question has constantly been raised—has there been a development in the FABC's theology of the laity, and to what extent does this theology represent an integration of, and a step beyond, other postconciliar theologies of the laity? In the course of responding to this question, we have considered the entire corpus of the FABC, all relevant material produced by John Paul II, the pastoral letters of the VEC, in particular those issued in 1980 and 2001, and other literature that deals with the question of the laity and its underlying ecclesiological framework. Given the scope of this study and the period of the development of these theologies, the methodology employed has been at the same time diachronic and synchronic, critical, analytical, and comparative.

Three general observations emerged from our investigation of this topic. First, there is both a fundamental continuity and a gradual development in the Asian bishops' theology of the laity, which was formulated in tandem with their ecclesiology from 1970 to 2012. This theology of the Church developed according to a similar trajectory to the theology of the laity, marked, as it was, by basic continuity and gradual change in response to the changing situations in Asia.

Secondly, to better explicate the FABC's theology of the laity and to highlight its distinctive features we have compared it with the theologies crafted by John Paul II and the Vietnamese bishops. These three theologies were developed concurrently but at various levels and in different contexts: the Pope's proceeding at the global level of the universal Church, the FABC's at the continental level with the Asian context as its theological locus, and the VEC's at the national level of the local Church in Vietnam. Our comparative analysis shows that the FABC's theology of the laity integrates the major themes and fundamental tenets of the teachings of John Paul II and the Vietnamese bishops, in particular the emphasis on the mission of the Church and the laity as proclamation, witness of life, and triple dialogue, coupled with a spirituality of discipleship expressed in a life of love, service, and solidarity. It also encompasses the motifs of other postconciliar theologies emanating from other parts of the world, e.g., the focus on liberation and the preferential option for the poor in Latin America, the accentuation on the inculturation of faith in African theologies, and the pressing concern of Western theologies with interfaith dialogue.

Thirdly, we have demonstrated that, by maintaining both the contextual character and the universalising dimension, the FABC's theology of the laity represents a step beyond other postconciliar theologies of the laity including those of John Paul II and the Vietnamese bishops. This assertion is based on our observation that the theology of the Asian bishops straddles both the local and the global spheres. As a contextual theology it begins with the local context and arrives at a robust description of the laity as Asian Christians. This articulation of the identity of lay people retrieves the original understanding of the followers of Christ as disciples, a conception that existed at the time of the New Testament and the Church of the first and second centuries when there was as yet no distinction between the laity and the clergy. It also brings into bold relief the historical, concrete and existential dimensions of the life of Asian Christians in Asia, and suggests that their vocation and mission is fundamentally the same as that of the entire Church in Asia.

The universal appeal of the theology of the FABC, on the other hand, is due mainly to the fact that the questions it raises and the theological responses it proposes deal with global, contemporary issues facing the whole Church. Indeed, the FABC's theology of triple dialogue has offered fresh ideas to address at least three current global trends in society. These are: the revolution in communications technologies which blurs the cultures and spurs local communities to search for their own, distinct cultural identity; the increasingly open conflicts between followers of different religions which highlight the urgent need for interreligious dialogue; and finally the inexorable advance of globalisation,[1] which

---

1   T. Howland Sanks reminds us that "as recently as 1979, when Karl Rahner offered his now famous theological analysis of Vatican II as the emergence of the global Church, the term 'globalization' was hardly in use" ("Globalization and the Church's Social Mission," *Theological Studies* 60 [1999] 625). For John Paul II, "one of the Church's concerns about globalization is that it has quickly become a cultural phenomenon. The market as an exchange mechanism has become the medium of a new culture.... The market imposes its way of thinking and acting, and stamps its scale of values upon behaviour. Those who are subjected to it often see globalization as a destructive flood threatening the social norms which had protected them and the cultural points of reference which had given them direction in life." See "Towards a Common Ethical Code for Humankind: *Address to the Pontifical Academy of Social Sciences 2001*,"

leaves in its aftermath the poverty and oppression of the masses, and calls for the commitment to human development, the preferential option for the poor, and the promotion of social harmony. By adopting an integrated approach to proclamation, witness of life, and triple dialogue, the FABC's theology, which places the kingdom of God at the centre of the life and mission of Church, offers innovative insights that can help other local Churches in other parts of the world in their efforts to deal with issues confronting them in the third millennium.

Summary of the Findings

This book consists of three parts besides an introduction (Chapter 1) and a conclusion (Chapter 10). In the first part we examine the question of the laity and lay ministry throughout the history of the Church (Chapter 2) and provide an analysis of the theological methodologies adopted by the FABC (Chapter 3). Building on this historical and methodological framework, the second part investigates (Chapter 4) and reviews (Chapter 5) the theology of the laity in the documents of the FABC issued between 1970 and 2012. This is followed by an exposition (Chapter 6) and a critique (Chapter 7) of this theology's underlying ecclesiological foundations. In the third and concluding part we compare and contrast the FABC's theology of the laity with those of Pope John Paul II (Chapter 8) and the Vietnamese Episcopal Conference (Chapter 9).

In the first chapter we look at the rediscovery of the importance of the laity in the Asian Church, review the state of the question, and highlight the significance and major contributions of the book. We argue that the rediscovery of the status and mission of lay people in the Asian Church emanates from the Copernican revolution in the theology of the laity initiated at Vatican II, a theological event that the Church in Asia experienced as a catalyst for ecclesial change.

Chapter 2 reviews the laity question in history by examining the status, vocation, and mission of lay people in the documents of Vatican II, and also in the periods before and after the Council. We pay particular attention to the postconciliar theologies of the laity according to Yves Congar and Leonard Doohan, and survey the changing meaning of the terms ministry and lay ministry.

Concilium 4 (2001) 12. Kenneth R. Himes suggests that whereas in the past Catholic social teaching "had been primarily directed to issues of economics and secondarily of politics, the new context of globalization will force the tradition to attend more to issues of culture and identity" ("Globalization with a Human Face: Catholic Social Teaching and Globalization," *Theological Studies* 69 [2008] 281).

Chapter 3 discusses the theological methodologies of the FABC and their characteristics. It suggests that these methodological approaches are based on a basic framework of "see, judge, act," and contends that the theology of the Asian bishops, in particular their theology of the laity, is fundamentally a contextual theology, a faith seeking triple dialogue with the cultures, the religions, and the poor of Asia. Chapters 2 and 3 together set the stage and provide a theological springboard for an exploration of the FABC's theology of the laity in the next two chapters.

Chapter 4 examines the features of the FABC's theology of the laity and contends that there is both fundamental continuity and gradual development in this theology from 1970 to 2012. The key elements of this theology include a description of lay people as Asian Christians based on their common, baptismal priesthood of life and their special presence to the world, an explication of their vocation as a call to a contextualised communion with Jesus, an articulation of their mission that is Christ-centred, kingdom-focused, world-oriented, dialogical, and liberative, and finally, a spirituality that is defined primarily as a spirituality of discipleship and a spirituality of daily life. The development of this theology follows a trajectory that is characterised by an increased emphasis on world-orientation, a geographical contextualisation of the role of lay people, an empowerment of the laity, an integral formation *of* and *for* the laity, and lastly an investigation of a spirituality of harmony.

Chapter 5 reviews the FABC's theology of the laity and contends that it has a contextual and relational dimension, which is implicit in the concept of the priesthood of life. This concept together with the notion of contextualised communion is central to the identity, vocation, mission, and spirituality of lay people in Asia, described first and foremost as Asian Christians. This theology also suggests that the vocation and mission of the laity are developed from the concept of the priesthood of life, and while evangelisation occupies the highest priority in the ministries of lay people, it is the kingdom of God that is the ultimate goal of all these activities. The key tenets of this theology are contained in the final statements of the Fourth Plenary Assembly of the FABC held in 1986, the structure of which is based on an epistemological perspective and a hermeneutical approach that are distinctively Asian. While the strength of this theology lies in its contextual and relational character, certain limitations can be identified, namely a lack of emphasis on the universal call to holiness, a concept that is central to *Lumen Gentium* and *Christifideles Laici*, and the blurring of the lay-cleric distinction in the role of the Asian laity in the world.

Chapter 6 analyses the features of the FABC's theology of the Church as the underlying context for the lay vocation and mission, and argues that there is both fundamental continuity and gradual development in the FABC's ecclesiology from

1970 to 2012. This ecclesiology focuses on the kingdom of God and provides an understanding of the Church as communion-in-mission, as dialogue and solidarity, as disciple-community, and finally as basic ecclesial communities. The combination of these ecclesiological models represents a new way of being Church in Asia.

Chapter 7 explores the ecclesiological foundations of the FABC's theology of the laity noting the concurrent development from 1970 to 2012 between the FABC's theology of the laity and its ecclesiology. Both of these theologies are essentially contextual and relational. We also suggest that the Asian bishops have developed their initial conception of the Church as a community of faith in Asia into a matrix of theological models, according to which the Church is called to become a community of faith, hope, and charity in Asia, realised in basic ecclesial communities. This ecclesiology from below, which proceeds from a Christological, pneumatological, and Trinitarian basis, rests on the two ecclesiological pillars of communion and mission. It privileges basic ecclesial communities as a theological locus to integrate the Church's universal, local, and eschatological elements by emphasising their sacramental and regnocentric dimensions.

Chapter 8 examines Pope John Paul II's theology of the laity in his Apostolic Exhortations *Ecclesia in Asia* (1999) and *Christifideles Laici* (1989) with reference to the documents of the FABC, and argues that this theology is based on the baptismal identity and dignity of Christians. As a reflection on the three motifs of vocation, communion, and mission, rooted in the teachings of Vatican II and the 1985 Synod of Bishops, *Christifideles Laici* focuses on the role of lay Christians from a predominantly Trinitarian and ecclesiological perspective, and, aiming at a universal audience, it pays less attention to the social and cultural context of local Churches. Here we offer four observations relating to the question of the laity. First, John Paul II uses the concept of baptismal dignity as the leitmotif to define the vocation and mission of lay people. Secondly, for him, communion ecclesiology is the context for understanding the role of the laity. Thirdly, the universal call to holiness lies at the heart of this papal document. Finally, the Pope's definition of the laity is based on three pillars of baptism, secularity, and participation of lay people as sharers of the triple mission of Christ.

In *Ecclesia in Asia* the Pope provides a Christological and pneumatological interpretation of the mission of the entire Church in Asia, including the laity. Expressing this mission as proclamation, inculturation, communion, dialogue, and human promotion, he underscores the distinctive role of lay people, in particular women, the family, and young people, as missionaries and witnesses in the world of Asia. Here we make three observations. First, it is the logic of faith as gift and evangelisation as task that underlines and unifies the entire Apostolic Exhortation.

Secondly, the term "witness of life" or its variants is a comprehensive concept that John Paul II employs to described and prescribe the identity and role of the laity in Asia. As a concrete expression of the integration of faith, proclamation, and Christian living, this notion lies at the heart of the papal document and succinctly summarises its theology of the laity. Thirdly, the identity, the vocation, and the ministry of lay people are understood only in the context of the Church as a witnessing community of faith, built on the two pillars of communion and mission.

This chapter proposes a new way of interpreting John Paul II's theology of mission, one that is based on a distinction between, on the one hand, the theological firmness (*fortiter*) with which he imposes compliance with the principle of proclamation and, on the other, the pastoral flexibility (*suaviter*) that he encourages in the practice of triple dialogue with the cultures, the religions, and the poor of Asia. This chapter concludes that, except for some minor difference in the interpretation of the identity and role of lay people in the Asian Church, there is a substantial convergence between the theologies of the laity according to the Pope and the Asian bishops.

Chapter 9 investigates the theology of the laity in the pastoral letters of the VEC with a focus on those issued between 1980 and 2012, and with reference to the teachings of John Paul II and the Asian bishops. This contextual and relational theology emphasises the centrality of the human person, and articulates the relationship of the Church and the laity with Vietnamese society as the mission of love and service, and the commitment to solidarity, mission *ad extra*, witness of life, and sanctification. We argue that this theology and its ecclesiological framework are underpinned by an anthropological orientation that is Christocentric, and that the richest legacy of the pastoral letters is the presentation of Jesus Christ as the foundation and purpose of the vocation and mission of the Church and the Vietnamese lay faithful.

The VEC's theology of the Church and of the laity also draws heavily on the insights of Paul VI, John Paul II, and the Asian bishops. We note that "triple dialogue" is for the FABC's theology of the laity what "sacramental dignity" is for John Paul II, and "love and service" for the VEC. However, with the advent of the Synod for Asia, the promulgation of John Paul II's Apostolic Exhortation *Ecclesia in Asia*, and the increased participation of the Vietnamese bishops in the meetings and activities of the FABC, the VEC's theology has become more aligned with the thoughts of both John Paul II and the Asian bishops, who teach that the mission of the Church in Asia has as its key elements proclamation, witness of life, and the triple dialogue with the cultures, the religions, and the people of Asia, especially the poor, those afflicted by a reality that includes the economic, social, political, cultural, and spiritual dimensions of life.

In Chapter 10, this concluding chapter, we provide a summary of the findings and situate the FABC's theology of the laity in the global context of society over the past fifty years, highlighting some of the salient shifts in the contexts of mission facing both the universal Church and the churches in Asia. We will also make some suggestions as to the possible directions of this theology. Finally, we will review the mindsets that govern much of the current thinking on the question of the laity, and suggest that a paradigm shift is required to resolve the simmering tension between the role of the clergy and the rise of the laity in the Asian Churches.

The FABC's Theology of the Laity in the Global Context

In retrospect, there is little doubt that as a result of a sustained interaction with the local settings over this period of time, and partly in response to the universalising theologies of the West, which did not take up issues that were most pressing to the cultural, religious, and social situations of Asia, the Asian bishops have developed their own theologies, including their theology of the laity, to address issues that pertain to the identity and mission of the Church in Asia, a continent marked by a diversity of cultures, a plurality of religions, and the massive poverty of the majority of its population. Like any local theologies, the FABC's theology of the laity bears the marks of the times in which it was developed. In terms of its time span, it seems to overlap with the last two of the three phases of missionary activities suggested by Robert Schreiter.[2] The dominant image of the society in the second phase between 1945 and 1989 was growth and development.[3] It was "the period of the bipolar world of the Cold War, of capitalism versus socialism, with the poor majority of the world's peoples oscillating between the two,"[4] and the Church's theological response was its mission of solidarity, understood as "dialogue, inculturation, and liberation – three forms of solidarity."[5] The third

---

2 Robert J. Schreiter suggests that "there are three discernible periods in those five hundred years of history of the Church's mission": the period of expansion (1492–1945), the period of solidarity (1945–1989), and the period of globalisation (1989-). See *The New Catholicity: Theology Between the Global and the Local* (Maryknoll, New York: Orbis Books, 1997) 122, 123–7; see also "The Theological Meaning of a Truly Catholic Church," *New Theology Review* 7 (November 1994) 10–13.

3 Robert J. Schreiter, *The New Catholicity: Theology Between the Global and the Local* (Maryknoll, New York: Orbis Books, 1997) 125.

4 Ibid., 124–5.

5 Robert J. Schreiter, ibid., 126. For him, these three forms of mission, along with proclamation, emerged "out of the 1981 SEDOS Seminar in Rome." See footnote 12, ibid. For a detailed discussion of these missionary activities see *Mission in Dialogue: the*

period, which commenced with the fall of the Berlin Wall in 1989, is marked by the emblematic concepts of global capitalism and communication, and calls for "a renewed and expanded concept of catholicity,"[6] understood as the extension of the Church throughout the world, fullness of faith, and exchange and communication, as a theological response of the Church to the challenge of globalisation.[7] Schreiter suggests that the mode of mission in this phase would be the elaboration of a praxis around one of the themes of "new humanity, genuine peace [and] reconciliation as a new creation."[8]

On the scale of the Church's history, the fifty years of the development of the FABC's theology of the laity is quite a short time. However, our observation is that the FABC has already laid a solid theological foundation, and this theology is on a new stage of development, one that centres on the search for a stronger sense of Catholic identity in the world of Asia.[9] Some of the global trends that have

---

Sedos Research Seminar on the Future of Mission March 8–19, 1981, Rome, Italy, edited by Joseph Lang and Mary Motte (Maryknoll, New York: Orbis Books, 1982) 634. At the SEDOS seminar held in April 2000 he reiterates this observation and contends that "mission for Roman Catholics after the Second Vatican Council and after the end of colonial empires took on a strong sense of the *accompaniment* of people through dialogue, inculturation, and the liberation of the poor." See "Mission in the Third Millennium," in *Mission in the Third Millennium*, edited by Robert J. Schreiter (Maryknoll, N.Y.: Orbis Books, 2001) 155. We simply note here that proclamation and these three modes of mission had already been discussed in depth at the First Plenary Assembly of the FABC, held in Taipei in 1974. See FABC I, arts. 6–28, *FAPA Vol. 1*, 13–6.

6   Schreiter, ibid., 127.

7   Schreiter, ibid., 128–32.

8   Robert J. Schreiter, ibid., 131. Schreiter argues that, in a globalizing world, "the fullness of faith offers a number of theological *teloi* for a guiding vision of humanity and society": one is a new theological anthropology, based on Genesis 1:26, that articulates "the full dignity of all human beings in a world that drives many of them deeper into misery"; the second involves "the possibility of an ontology of peace to counteract the centrifugal tendencies of globalization"; the third derives from the Pauline vision of reconciliation as the 'new creation' (2 Cor 5:17)." See ibid., 43, 131, and also 113.

9   In his first press conference the day after he was elected to be the sixth general secretary of the World Council of Churches, Rev Dr Samuel Kobia observes that "the twentieth century was dominated by the politics of ideology. It is likely that the twenty-first will be dominated by the politics of identity. Many people define their identity in a religious way. If we are to overcome violence and create peace and justice, we need a multi-faith approach." See G. Gispert-Sauch, "The New Protestant 'Pope,'" *Vidyajyoti* 67:10 (October 2003) 854. Kenneth R. Himes suggests that whereas in the past Catholic social teaching "had been primarily directed to issues of economics and secondarily

affected the Asian Church and will spur further this theological development include the rise of globalisation,[10] the coincidence of religion and violence,[11] the secularisation of society, the rise of Islam, and the erosion of the environment.[12] To these we might add the biotech revolution and the pervasiveness of the wireless world.[13] These global shifts in the contexts of mission, together with the advent of postmodernism,[14] the collapse of the meta-narratives that had bound

of politics, the new context of globalization will force the tradition to attend more to issues of culture and identity" ("Globalization with a Human Face: Catholic Social Teaching and Globalization," *Theological Studies* 69 [2008] 281).

10   Malcolm Waters observes that "just as postmodernism was *the* concept of the 1980s, globalization may be *the* concept, the key idea by which we understand the transition of human society into the third millennium" (*Globalization*, 2nd ed. [London: Routledge, 2001] 1).

11   For Emilio Platti, there is a shift in emphasis from the "Class of Civilizations" to the "Class of Theologies," and "the world is split...along religious fault lines." See Anthony O'Mahony, "Into the Age of Uncertainty," *The Tablet* (19 July 2008) 4; see also Samuel P. Huntington, "The Clash of Civilizations?" *Foreign Affairs* 72:3 (Summer 1993) 22–49.

12   These five shifts in context, which received special attention during the SEDOS Congress held in April 2000 in Rome, were summarised by Robert J. Schreiter in "Mission in the Third Millennium," in *Mission in the Third Millennium*, edited by Robert J. Schreiter (Maryknoll, New York: Orbis Books, 2001) 149–52.

13   In 2008 Gartner researchers identified seven major trends in information technologies (IT) that are "wide-ranging and affect every organization to some extent": "Green IT," "The Consumerization of IT," "Alternative Acquisition and Delivery Models" [i.e., focusing on business outcomes rather than use of IT], "Cloud Computing" [i.e., delivering services across the Internet to multiple customers], "The Modernization of IT," "IT That Matters" [i.e., "IT investments can create, expand and protect an enterprise's strategic competitive advantages], and "The Business Impact of Social Computing" [i.e., IT plays "a critical role in shaping the behavior and activities of people, enterprises and industries"]. See Stephen Prentice et al., "2008 Research Themes Summary," *Gartner Research* (6 March 2008), ID Number G00154624.

14   For Stanley J. Grenz, "The term *postmodern* may first have been coined in the 1930s to refer to a major historical transition already underway and as the designation for certain developments in the arts. But postmodernism did not gain widespread attention until the 1970s. First it denotes a new style of architecture.... Eventually it surfaced as the description for a broader cultural phenomenon. Whatever else it might be, as the name suggests, postmodernism signifies the quest to move beyond modernism" (*A Primer on Postmodernism* [Grand Rapids, Mich.: William B. Eerdmans Publishing, 1996] 2). Grenz further notes that "scholars disagree among themselves as to what postmodernism involves, but they have reached a consensus on one point: this phenomenon marks the end of a single, universal worldview. The postmodern ethos

cultures, religions, and nations, and the sustained deconstruction that charac-
terises the current conversation about religions,[15] will push the FABC's theology,
in particular its theology of the laity, into uncharted waters. While no one can
accurately predict the direction of this vast and continually developing topic, an
ambitious project that is well beyond the scope of this present book, we wish to
offer here some suggestions as to its possible pathways in the future.

Possible Directions for the FABC's Theology of the Laity

One possible direction for the FABC is to undertake a new, comprehensive analysis of these global trends and assess their impact on the local Churches in Asia.[16]

---

resists unified, all-encompassing, and universally valid explanations." Ibid., 11–2. It is
worth noting that the term postmodernism was only widely used in the intellectual
world subsequent to the release of a report commissioned by the Conseil des Uni-
versités of the Government of Quebec in 1979. This report aims to study "the condition of knowledge in the most highly developed societies," and Jean-François Lyotard
"decided to use the word *postmodern* to describe that condition." See *The Postmodern
Condition: A Report on Knowledge*, Translation from the French by Geoff Bennington
and Brian Massumi, Foreword by Fredric Jameson, Theory and History of Literature,
vol. 10 (Manchester: Manchester University Press, 1984) xxiii. Michael Paul Gallagher
notes that "there is a tendency to use 'postmodernism' for the more *intellectual* school
of thinking associated with Lyotard or Derrida, or even tracing its origins as far back
as Nietzsche, and then to reserve 'postmodernity' for a wider *cultural* context that includes ways of life as well as forms of thinking.... The two realities are not completely
separate" (*Clashing Symbols* [London, Longman and Todd, 1997] 87).

15 The authors of a special report in *The Economist* note that "for much of the 20th century religion was banished from politics. For most elites, God had been undone by
Darwin, dismissed by Marx, deconstructed by Freud. Stalin forcibly ejected Him, but
in much of western Europe there was no need for force: religion had been on the slide
for centuries." See "In God's Name: a Special Report on Religion and Public Life," *The
Economist* (3 November 2007) 4.

16 In 2012, at the Tenth Plenary Assembly, on the anniversary of the "FABC at Forty Years"
the Asian Bishops undertook a comprehensive environmental scan and discernment
of the signs of the times analysing the "Megatrends in Asia and Ecclesial Realities." See
FABC X, *FAPA Vol. 5*, 49, 58–77. This suggestion was made by Peter N.V. Hai back in
2009. See "Lay People in the Asian Church: A Critical Study of the Role of the Laity in
the Contextual Theology of the Federation of Asian Bishops' Conferences (1970–2001)
with Special Reference to John Paul II's Apostolic Exhortations *Christifideles Laici*
(1989) and *Ecclesia in Asia* (1999), and the Pastoral Letters of the Vietnamese Episcopal
Conference" (Ph.D. diss., Australian Catholic University, 2009) 424. See also idem,

This analytical exercise corresponds to the "see" phase, the first moment of the contextual methodology of the theology of the Asian bishops.[17] It is a holistic endeavour to take into account the location of its context within the global society, and also a prerequisite for crafting a more relevant theology *of* and *for* the Asian laity. As such it may call for a fresh articulation of the role of the Church and of the laity in the postmodern world of Asia.

Four Theological Foci

Within the ambit of the "judge" phase, the second moment of their theological methodology, we suggest four interrelated topics that the bishops of Asia could further develop to enrich their theology of the laity. These include an emphasis on the theme of *missio Dei*, an exploration of the conception of the Church as a structured or ordered *communio*, a consideration of lay functions and lay repositioning from the perspective of "ordered ministries," and a deepening of a theology of the laity anchored in the sacrament of baptism. These proposed areas of theological reflection warrant further clarification.

Our first suggestion has to do with the theme of *missio Dei*,[18] a rich and profound theological concept that has not received sufficient attention from the

---

"Reflections on the Future of the FABC's Theology of the Laity," *East Asian Pastoral Review* 49:2 (April-June 2012) 109.

17 For a detailed treatment of the subject see Peter N.V. Hai, "*Fides Quaerens Dialogum*: Theological Methodologies of the Federation of Asian Bishops' Conferences." Australian E-Journal of Theology 8 (2006), http://dlibrary.acu.edu.au/research/theology/ejournal/aejt_8/hai.htm (accessed 1 November 2006).

18 The term *missio Dei* "came into currency in the 1930s," and "Karl Barth was one of the first to use the term." Robert J. Schreiter, "Mission in the Third Millennium," *Mission in the Third Millennium*, edited by Robert J. Schreiter (Maryknoll, New York: Orbis Books, 2001) 155. David J. Bosch notes that until the sixteenth century, the term "mission" was used "exclusively with reference to the doctrine of the Trinity, that is, of the sending of the Son by the Father and of the Holy Spirit by the Father and the Son" (*Transforming Mission: Paradigm Shifts in Theology of Mission* [Maryknoll, N.Y.: Orbis Books, 1991] 1). This classical doctrine was "expanded to include yet another 'movement': Father, Son, and Holy Spirit sending the church into the world." See ibid., 390. In Bosch's view, "the recognition that mission is God's mission represents a crucial breakthrough in respect of the preceding centuries," and "it is inconceivable that we could again revert to a narrow, ecclesiocentric view of mission." Ibid. 393.

Asian bishops.[19] While the idea of the mission of God is clearly manifested in their discussion of the Trinitarian dimension of the mission of the Asian Church,[20] the term *missio Dei* or "mission of God" is listed only once (volume 4) in the indices of the five volumes of their documents. This concept emphasises that mission is not primarily an activity of the Church, but is first and foremost the work of the Trinity who initiates it. Mission belongs to the nature of the triune God who loves the world, and the Church is simply called to participate in it. God is missionary because God is love. As the people of God, the Church must also be missionary. In this sense, the mission to further the kingdom of God on earth is the *raison d'être* and the most important duty of the whole Church including the laity. Therefore, it would be fruitful if the Asian bishops could retrieve the original meaning of this theological concept, and further explore its implications and applications for the Church in Asia. Such a rediscovery would avoid the danger of an overemphasis on the horizontal, functional understanding of mission as a series of functions and activities, and encourage all the faithful to embrace an eschatological humility appropriate to a pilgrim Church and to place more reliance on the grace of God in the furtherance of the kingdom of God in Asia. It could also counter a perennial temptation that sees mission purely in terms of visible outcomes, results, and numbers. In Asia, where Christians are likely to remain a very small minority in the foreseeable future, a focus on the *missio Dei* would serve as a constant reminder to the entire Church, especially the laity, that it is the triune God who is the author and the main agent of mission, and they are simply unworthy labourers in God's vineyard. Like Paul and Apollos, the Church can sow the seed and water the plant, but it is God who makes it grow.[21]

---

19 The FABC seems to employ the term *missio Dei* only once. See "Consultation on Asian Local Churches and Mission *Ad Gentes*: A New Way of Being Church-in-Mission in Asia," art. 5, *FAPA Vol. 3*, 222.

20 FABC V, arts. 3.1–3.2.4, *FAPA Vol. 1*, 279–81.

21 See 1 Cor 3:6.

The second focus that we propose relates to the theme of the Church as a *structured communio*,[22] or as an ordered communion.[23] This concept has not been discussed by the FABC. As explicated by Walter Kasper, the expression *communio* encompasses five meanings.[24] In Kasper's view, fellowship with God represents the most fundamental aspect of *communio*, a concept that can also be understood as participation in the life of God through word and sacrament, as an ecclesial unity in communion, as communion of the faithful expressed by the participation and co-responsibility of all, and finally as the communion of the Church as sacrament for the world.[25] The concept of the Church as a *structured communio* incorporates the meaning of the term *communio hierarchia*,[26] an ecclesiological phrase that was coined by the Fathers of the Second Vatican Council to hold in tension both the papal and the episcopal elements, and to highlight

---

22 Ladislas Orsy explains this *structured communio* as follows: "Initially through the sacraments of initiation and the reception of God's word, all the faithful are united in a mysterious way. Then, within this fundamental unity, through the sacrament of orders another *communio* emerges, that of the servant-leaders who are given the privilege to be qualified witnesses of God's revelation and to serve and govern with power the people. Finally, from early times a special type of *communio* emerged in the church, that of 'religious' or 'consecrated' communities. While their origins are not in a sacrament, they are the fruits of the Spirit" ("The Church of the Third Millennium," in *Common Calling: The Laity and Governance of the Catholic Church*, edited by Stephen J. Pope [Washington, D.C.: Georgetown University Press, 2004] 235). For Orsy, *structured communio* is a better expression than "hierarchical communion" as the latter term does not speak of service. Ibid., 239.
23 Richard Gaillardetz prefers to refer to the Church as an "ordered communion." See "The Ecclesiological Foundations of Ministry within an Ordered Communion," in *Ordering the Baptismal Priesthood: Theologies of Lay and Ordained Ministry*, edited by Susan K. Wood (Collegeville, Minn.: Liturgical Press, 2003) 31.
24 For a helpful discussion of this phrase see Walter Kasper, *Theology and Church* (London: SCM Press, 1989), 156–61. Francis George notes that the word *communio* appears 285 times in the documents of Vatican II, but this fact is not immediately evident because it is translated into English by different terms such as fellowship, community, and fraternity. See "The Parish in the Mission of the Church," *Chicago Studies* 46:1 (Spring 2007) 24.
25 Walter Kasper, *Theology and Church* (London: SCM Press, 1989) 148–165.
26 The term "hierarchical communion" occurs five times in the documents of Vatican II: *Lumen Gentium*, nos. 21, 22; *Christus Dominus*, nos. 4, 5; *Presbyterorum Ordinis*, no. 7. As an adjective, "hierarchical" means "by divine order." As a noun, "hierarchy" comes from two Greek words which mean "sacred source," "sacred origin," or "sacred principle."

"the essential organic expression of the essential structure of the church, its unity in catholicity, and its catholicity in unity."[27] However, the term *structured communio* expresses better the reality of ecclesial communion as it maintains the full intent of the phrase *communio hierarchia*, but avoids the explicit reference to the term "hierarchy," a category that has often been associated with the concept of "domination."[28] Francis A. Sullivan reminds us that "hierarchical authority is related to ecclesial communion as means to end: it exists to promote and maintain ecclesial communion."[29] Therefore, an emphasis by the FABC on the Church as a *structured communio* would continue to affirm the importance of the hierarchy in promoting and preserving the unity of the Church, and at the same time, underscore the fact that hierarchy and leadership are enriched by the full participation and inclusion of the whole people of God including lay people.

An ecclesiology that is based on the framework of *structured communio* would seek to explore the implications of this concept as a concrete expression of the nature of the Church as mystery. One of the outcomes of this ecclesiological approach, and the theology of the laity that flows from it, is that the unity of all the faithful is ensured while the ecclesial diversity in unity is fostered and encouraged. It would also affirm that the ordained and religious are defined primarily by their relationships to other members of the Church rather than simply through their possession of special powers or charisms. The theological meaning of a *structured communio*, coupled with the conciliar concept of the Church as the people of God, could serve as a basis and a catalyst for a structural reform at the local level of the Church in Asia to strengthen and expand the role of the laity and empower them to participate more actively in the life and mission of the Church.

The concept of the Church as a *structured communio* is linked intimately to the theme of "ordered" ministries, the third focus that we suggest that the Asian bishops could deepen to enrich their theology of the Church and of the laity. Like the concept of *structured communio*, this ecclesiological matrix preserves the unity of the community, encourages different ministries, and emphasises the

---

27 Walter Kasper, *Theology and Church* (London: SCM Press, 1989) 160.

28 Terence L. Nichols observes that "for authors such as Elisabeth Schüssler Fiorenza, Rosemary Radford Ruether, Leonardo Boff, Sallie McFague, and others, hierarchy means domination *tout court*. The alternative to hierarchy, for these authors, is an egalitarian church." See "Participatory Church," in *Common Calling: The Laity and Governance of the Catholic Church*, edited by Stephen J. Pope (Washington, D.C.: Georgetown University Press, 2004) 112.

29 Francis A. Sullivan, "Authority in an Ecclesiology of Communion," *New Theology Review* 10 (1997) 24.

fact that both forms of ministries, ordained and lay, "are essentially grounded in baptism and all the baptized share a common mission and common identity as the *Christifideles* before they are further specified by state of life and particular ministry."[30] In this framework, one cannot discuss the ministry of the ordained or the lay ministry in isolation from the community and from each other.

Our fourth suggestion involves a deepening of a theology of the laity based on the sacraments of initiation,[31] —especially the sacrament of baptism—"one that situates distinctiveness within the identity and mission that all believers have in common."[32] A baptism-based theology of the laity, which flows from the ecclesiological vision of *Lumen Gentium*, will affirm first of all that baptism is the unifying factor for the Church as the people of God. It also serves as the foundation of the Christian community and offers a basis for a contextual articulation of the identity, role, and lifestyle of lay people. This baptism-centred theology is based upon the conviction that baptism is "the basis or matrix of all the Church's ministries, be

---

30 Susan K. Wood, "Conclusion," in *Ordering the Baptismal Priesthood: Theologies of Lay and Ordained Ministry*, edited by Susan K. Wood (Collegeville, Minn.: Liturgical Press, 2003) 260. For Richard Gaillardetz, "ordered church ministry is a reality broader than the ministry of the ordained (though inclusive of it) and narrower than Christian discipleship." See "The Ecclesiological Foundations of Ministry within an Ordered Communion," in *Ordering the Baptismal Priesthood: Theologies of Lay and Ordained Ministry*, edited by Susan K. Wood (Collegeville, Minn.: Liturgical Press, 2003) 36. In Gaillardetz's view, "in undertaking an ordered ministry, one is ecclesially re-positioned," and this "new ecclesial relationship" is "subject to ecclesial discernment, formation, authorization, and ritualization." Ibid., 36, 48.

31 According to the 1983 Code of Canon Law "the sacraments of baptism, confirmation and the blessed Eucharist so complement one another that all three are required for full christian initiation." See c. 842 §2, *The Code of Canon Law: New Revised English Translation*, prepared by the Canon Law Society of Great Britain and Ireland in association with the Canon Law Society of Australia and New Zealand and the Canadian Can Law Society (London: HarperCollins, 1997) 196. John Paul II further explicates the interrelationship between the three sacraments: "The participation of the lay faithful in the threefold mission of Christ as priest, prophet and king finds its source in the anointing of baptism, its further development in confirmation and its realization and dynamic sustenance in the holy eucharist" (*Christifideles Laici*, no. 14); see also John Paul II, "*Pastores Gregis*," no. 38, *Origins* 33:22 (6 November 2003) 373.

32 Christopher Ruddy, "Ecclesiological Issues Behind the Sexual Abuse Crisis," *Origins* 37:8 (5 July 2007) 124. Ruddy argues that by referring to the lay-centred Church, one is simply replacing one dominant group with another. Ibid. See also Leonard Doohan, *The Lay-Centered Church: Theology and Spirituality* (Minneapolis, Minn.: Winston Press, 1984).

they lay or clerical,"[33] all baptized are called to one and the same holiness, and lay people share equally with the clergy the mission of the Church. This theological focus requires an increased emphasis on the ecclesiological model of co-discipleship, whereby all Christians, clergy, religious, and laity, are first and foremost the baptized, the Christian faithful, and the disciples of Christ. In this common matrix, all members of the Church share responsibility and participate in the same *missio Dei*.

We argue that a more extensive treatment of these proposed theological foci would greatly enrich the FABC's theology of the laity. From this fourfold theological basis we suggest four pastoral initiatives that the bishops of Asia could undertake to make their theology of the laity more relevant and fruitful. These practical suggestions correspond to the "Act" phase or the third moment of their theological methodology.

Four Pastoral Initiatives

First, the bishops of Asia could review the relevance and fitness for purpose of the oft-repeated term "triple dialogue," a leitmotiv that has given their contextual theology a consistent unity, even though the primary intent of the term is pastoral and missionary. In the FABC statements, the term "dialogue" can mean either *dialogus* or *colloquium*, the two conciliar words that have often been translated as "dialogue" but do not necessarily mean the same thing.[34] At Vatican II, *dialogus* is used "whenever the Church is engaged in ecumenical talks or is proclaiming its mission."[35] On the contrary, "when the process is one of interpersonal relationships," or "whenever there are conversations and discussions which do not directly involve the Church hierarchy the word *colloquium* is used."[36] In practice, in the mind of ordinary Asian Christians, the term dialogue tends to conjure up an image of exchanging ideas and viewpoints at an intellectual and theoretical level, or a structured conversation with agreed upon objectives and principles, an exchange

---

33 Gerard Austin, "Baptism as the Matrix of Ministry," *Louvain Studies* 23 (1998) 101.
34 For a comprehensive discussion of the meaning of the term "dialogue" in the documents of the Second Vatican Council, see Ann Michele Nolan, *A Privileged Moment: "Dialogue" in the Language of the Second Vatican Council 1962–1965*, European University Studies, Series 23, Theology, vol. 829 (New York: Peter Lang, 2006). Nolan notes that "the word 'dialogue" is used fifty-four times in one English translation or another across the sixteen documents, with an entire section devoted to the concept in the Pastoral Constitution of the Church in the Modern World." See ibid., 178.
35 Ibid., 221.
36 Ibid., 221.

that is often seen to be beyond the ken of the majority of lay people.[37] This term has also been considered to be "ideologically charged and therefore unhelpful."[38] Therefore, we suggest that the term "triple dialogue" be complemented by, and used interchangeably with, the phrase "triple engagement," a term that in our view better embodies and expresses the orientation of the FABC's theology. It reminds Asian Christians that a true dialogue should not remain at a purely theoretical or spiritual level, but has to be a concrete and sincere engagement and cooperation with others in pursuing the mission of building up the kingdom of justice, peace, and love.[39] This expression is more closely aligned with the contextual and relational character of the FABC's theology because of its emphasis on the concrete, historical and existential engagement between Christians and other Christians.

The Asian bishops could also expand their understanding of the term "triple dialogue" and include a fourth type of dialogue, namely the dialogue and engagement with the national government. In view of the authoritarian nature of several national governments in Asia, a deeper reflection of the FABC on this dialogical dimension would provide local churches in Asia with useful theological and pastoral pointers. This dialogical augmentation could also be of relevance and interest to the Church in China,[40] and the pastoral practice of the Church in Vietnam could serve as a case study.

---

37 Peter C. Phan observes that "in the West, especially in academic circles, the word 'dialogue' usually evokes images of a learned conversation among intellectuals at conferences and symposia." See "Praying to the Buddha: Living Amid Religious Pluralism," *Commonweal* 134:2 (26 January 2007), http://find.galegroup.com/itx/start.do?prodId=AONE (accessed 21 February 2006), Gale Document Number: A159183041.

38 This assertion is attributed to John Allen by Timothy Radcliffe, "Overcoming Discord in the Church," *National Catholic Reporter* (5 May 2006): 6. For John Allen, "In some Catholic circles, pleas for 'dialogue' are believed to mask a relativism in which one theological or ecclesiological stance is considered as good as another, so the aim is simply for everyone to 'get along,' rather than to establish which positions cohere with the faith that comes from the apostles and which don't." Ibid.

39 Peter C. Phan argues that "interreligious dialogue can be practiced by people of faith, irrespective of educational level, social standing, and religious status," and that "such dialogue is not merely a preparatory step toward peacemaking and reconciliation; it constitutes the very process of peacemaking and reconciliation itself, a process that occurs precisely in the acts of living together, working together, and praying together." See "Praying to the Buddha: Living Amid Religious Pluralism," *Commonweal* 134:2 (26 January 2007), http://find.galegroup.com/itx/start.do?prodId=AONE (accessed 21 February 2006), Gale Document Number: A159183041.

40 For an overview of the Church in China over the past fifty years and the new guidelines proposed by Pope Benedict XVI for reconciliation and cooperation in evangelisation

Secondly, it would be of immense benefit to the Asian Church if the FABC could devote much more attention to the theological basis and the pastoral implications of basic ecclesial communities, a privileged form of the local Church and a primary bearer of the mission of the Church. Being also basic human communities, these ecclesial entities represent a new way of being Church in Asia, an ecclesial institution that offers a contextual locus for integrating faith and life, Christianity and citizenry. This typology could be seen as a contemporary image of the early Christian community in the Acts of the Apostles. A more extensive development of this theological construct would provide a basis for lay people to deepen their faith, an opportunity for them to judge the social environment in light of the Gospel, and a catalyst to become more conscious of their missionary role. It would also serve as a springboard for their journey into the world, where they are called to live their common priesthood in the everyday life of the world, and to increase their participation in the life and mission of the Church. In many parts of Asia, this new form of being Church is likely to be the only viable mechanism that offers the laity an environment to nourish their common faith, especially in countries where Christianity is proscribed, and to strengthen their beliefs against the onslaught of new forms of idolatry such as consumerism, relativism, and practical atheism. An increased emphasis on the concept of basic ecclesial communities, where laity and clergy pray and exchange ideas as equal partners, could represent a concrete and modest step in the implementation of a renewal of the structure of the Church, a priority that was foreshadowed by the FABC at the Fourth Plenary Assembly held in 1986. In these basic ecclesial communities, there is "a paradigm shift in the relationship between clergy, religious and lay people. Clericalism falls

---

between underground and official Catholics, see Benedict XVI, "Letter to Chinese Catholics," *Origins* 37:10 (2 August 2007) 145–58. In a special report on religion and public life *The Economist* suggests that "the biggest prize for Christians across Asia is China itself. Some call it 'the Africa of the 21st century', recalling that the number of Christians in that continent rose from below 10m in 1900 to 400m in 2000. Officially, the Chinese government admits to 23m Christians within its borders, but it counts only churches that register with the authorities, and the real figure is probably around three times as high." See "In God's Name: a Special Report on Religion and Public Life," *The Economist* (3 November 2007) 6. The report moves on to predict that China may "end up being both the world's largest Christian country and its largest Muslim one." Ibid., 8–9. Hannah Beech also provides an estimate of about 100 million Christians in China. See "Salvation Armies," *Time* (26 April 2010) 36.

back and lay empowerment advances."[41] This reform of the ecclesial structure, which is underpinned by a focus on the Church as a structured *communio* and an ordered view of ministries, would promote genuine collaboration between clergy and laity in all aspects of ministry, and will no doubt unleash all their talent and energy.

A third avenue that the Asian bishops could take is to follow the lead of Pope John Paul II in *Ecclesia in Asia* and reflect more deeply on the role of the family, youth, and women, as the prime agents of evangelisation, by elevating each of these roles into the main topic of a plenary assembly. First, they could perhaps take as the departure point the ecclesiological model of the family as the *ecclesia domestica* and use it as a basis for developing the identity and role of the family.[42] Second, the Church is duty-bound to provide young people with a solid religious education to equip them to be missionaries and witnesses in the world, which is driven by an inexorable move towards globalisation. In the society of today, many schools and colleges in Asia no longer provide young people with the holistic education they need, displaying instead a reductionist tendency that views education in terms of production, competition, and the market. Finally, being a rich and under-utilised human resource in the Church, women should merit additional attention from the FABC. In fact, despite the changing role of women in society, which owes much to the "genius of women,"[43] they are still under-represented in the life and ministry of the Church. Here the bishops of Asia could draw on the thought of John Paul II who emphasises that "the presence and the role of women in the life and mission of the Church, although not linked to the ministerial priesthood, remain absolutely necessary and irreplaceable."[44] In his view, "today their role is of capital importance both for the renewal and humanization of society and for the rediscovery by believers of the true face of the Church."[45] The dire

---

41 This observation was made in address by Orlando B. Quevedo, Archbishop of Nueva Segovia, Philippines, to the SEDOS Symposium accompanying the Synod for Asia held in 1998, "Seeds of the Kingdom," *The Tablet* (30 May 1998) 696.

42 In 2004, the FABC chose the Asian Family as the topic of the Eighth Plenary Assembly. See FABC VIII, FAPA Vol. 4, 1–61. It is of note that the model of the Church as the family of God was proposed by a Vietnamese bishop at the Second Vatican Council. See Simon Hoa Nguyen Van Hien, Episcopus Dalatensis, ["Intervention at Vatican II], Periodus II, Congregatio Generalis XL," in *Acta Concilii Vaticani II* ([Rome: Typis Polyglotis Vaticanis, 1972]) 42–5.

43 John Paul II, "A Letter to Women," *The Tablet* (15 July 1995) 918.

44 John Paul II, "*Ordinatio sacerdotalis*," *L'Osservatore Romano* (1 June 1994) 1.

45 Ibid.

situation of the family, young people, and women in Asia calls for an articulation of their distinct identity and role in the Church, and for the FABC to provide a fresh direction that pertains to the three main loci of lay life, namely the family, the parish, and the market place.

Finally, the fourth suggestion we submit for consideration is this: that the FABC initiate a more comprehensive and longer term program of formation for the laity to enable them to deepen their spirituality, become better disciples and missionaries of the Word, understand more correctly their rightful place in the Church, and eagerly undertake their own ministry in the mission of the Church understood first and foremost as the *missio Dei*. This baptism-based program of formation will emphasise the common identity and mission of all the faithful, both laity and clergy, who are bound to one another in the one Church.[46] It also affirms that baptism is not just one event but is a part of the process of continual conversion, of being more deeply incorporated in the life of Christ and the Church in Asia, and of living the Gospel in the midst of all earthly activities.

The need for the pastors of the Church in Asia to give a high priority to the formation of lay people and to foster their active and full participation in the Church, has already been spelled out in *Lumen Gentium*, the Dogmatic Constitution that declares that the exalted office of the pastors is "to be shepherds of the faithful and also recognize the latter's contribution and charisms that everyone in his own way will, with one mind, cooperate in the common task."[47] This conciliar statement amplifies what Pope Pius XI had said earlier in an impromptu talk given in 1939 to the young priests of the Canadian College in Rome on the fiftieth anniversary of this college, also his last will and testament as it was his last public audience.[48] Here the Pope encourages the clergy to mobilise lay people to

---

46 Ladislas Orsy notes that one of the "two historical trends that contributed to the loss of sense and practice of participation," in the Church is "the shift in emphasis from the sacrament of baptism to that of orders." See "Participation in the Church as a Seminal Concept," *Origins* 17:46 (28 April 1988) 799. For Orsy, participation is communion. Ibid.

47 *Lumen Gentium*, no. 30.

48 Pope Pius XI's statement is as follows: "I want you to take this message away with you. The church, the mystical body of Christ, has become a monstrosity. The head is very large, but the body is shrunken. You the priests, must rebuild that body of the church, and the only way that you can rebuild it is to mobilize the lay people. You must call upon the lay people to become, along with you, the witnesses of Christ. You must call them especially to bring Christ back to the workplace, to the marketplace." Cited by Alex Carter, *A Canadian Bishop's Memoirs* (North Bay, Ontario: Tomiko Publications, 1994) 50-1; quoted in Ladislas Orsy, "The Church of the Third Millennium," in

be witnesses of Christ in the world. This teaching of *Lumen Gentium* also reflects the thought of John Henry Newman, who, over a century earlier, was concerned "to create of the laity an active force that would be at work both in the Church and in the world at large,"[49] and hence, wanted an educated and faithful laity, "well-catechised and faithful to their baptismal promises."[50] It also echoes a well-worn remark of this most English of holy men that in matters of doctrine as well as in pastoral governance the Church would look foolish without the faith and the participation of the laity.[51] In summary, we believe that the Asian bishops' theology of the laity would be enriched and become more relevant if they follow these possible directions by conducting a new, comprehensive analysis of the current environment, offering a more extensive treatment of the proposed theological topics, and implementing the suggested pastoral initiatives. However, to confidently move into these directions we suggest that a paradigm shift, or a complete change of mindsets, is required to craft a robust theology of the laity, one that encourages a much greater role for the laity in the Asian Church of the future.

Towards a Paradigm Shift in the FABC's Theology of the Laity

Paradigms are ways of construing reality based on certain fundamental assumptions. A shift occurs when one or more of those assumptions are found to be at best questionable. Many analyses of the vocation and mission of the laity proceed from a number of largely unexamined assumptions. Chief among these are the definition of the laity with reference to the clergy, and the insistence that there are two dimensions of the mission of the Church with the proper role of the laity being in the world. If the present tension between the rise of the laity and the role of the clergy is ever to be resolved, these assumptions need rethinking.

The key assumption is the first: that of the laity defined with reference to the clergy and religious. Vatican II did not always provide a positive definition of

---

Common Calling: The Laity and Governance of the Catholic Church, edited by Stephen J. Pope (Washington, D.C.: Georgetown University Press, 2004) 250.

49 Paul Chavass, "Newman and the Laity," in *Newman Today*, edited by Stanley L. Jaki (San Francisco: Ignatius Press, 1989) 50.

50 Ibid., 52.

51 John Coulson, "Introduction," in *John Henry Newman: On Consulting the Faithful in Matters of Doctrine*, edited with an introduction by John Coulson and a foreword by Derek Worlock, Archbishop of Liverpool (London: Collins, 1986) 18-9; see also Derek Worlock, "Foreword," ibid., v. For John Henry Cardinal Newman, "'in all times the laity have been the measure of the Catholic spirit.'" Quoted by Cardinal Cormac Murphy-O'Connor in "Renewing the Parish: 1: Fired by the Spirit," *The Tablet* (31 May 2003) 12.

the term "laity." It was understood to mean "all the faithful except those in Holy Orders or in a religious state approved by the church."[52] The ground for this definition is that there is an ontological difference between the laity and the clergy. This typological definition has been repeated endlessly in the documents of the Church so that the inference from them comes to obscure the fact that a priest is a layperson before being ordained, and does not cease to be a baptized person after receiving ordination. What is needed is to work from inside the mindset of those who hold on to this proposition, and see whether it is possible to induce a shift in that mindset and produce a definition of the laity simply as Christians.[53] To its credit, the FABC, while continuing to maintain an implicit distinction between the clergy and the laity has gone a long way in this direction by adopting a description, not a definition, of the laity as Asian Christians, a concept that underscores the double calling of faith and cultural belonging of lay people, and one that lies at the heart of what it means to be a Christian in Asia.

Only when we come to a positive definition of the laity as Christians can we change the second fixed idea that the mission of the laity has two separate dimensions *ad intra* and *ad extra*.[54] The persistent reference in magisterial documents, despite the emphasis on the unique mission of the Church, has perpetuated the ingrained perception in the mind of the faithful that there are two different realms, the sacred and the secular, and two different kinds of mission, one in the Church and one in the world. These divisions between the Church and the world, and between vocation and mission, were seen in the titles of two major documents of the Church on the laity, namely the 1987 World Synod of Bishops on the "Vocation and Mission of the Lay Faithful in the Church and the World,"[55] and the

---

52 *Lumen Gentium*, no. 31.
53 Yves Congar frequently defines the laity as "Christians *sine addito*." See "The Laity," in *Vatican II: An Interfaith Appraisal* (Notre Dame: University of Notre Dame, 1966) 241, 244; see also "Discussion," ibid., 269.
54 For Avery Dulles, "it would be a mistake…to make a sharp dichotomy between ministry in the church and apostolate in the world, as if it were necessary to choose between them" ("Can Laity Properly Be Called 'Ministers,'" *Origins* 35:44 [20 April 2006] 730).
55 John L. May, Joseph L. Bernardin, Rembert G. Weakland and Stanley J. Ott, "What We Have Heard and What We Will Say," *America* 157:5 (29 August – 5 September 1987) 109. Commenting on the official statements of the 1985 Synod, Joseph Komonchak notes that the "shifts in perspective and emphasis from Council to Synod lead one to fear that the distinction between *Ecclesia ad intra* and *Ecclesia ad extra* has been hardened." See "The Synod of 1985 and the Notion of the Church," *Chicago Studies* 26:3 (1987) 340. Komonchak also cautions against "the common but mistaken separation of the 'nature' and the 'mission' of the Church," and asserts that "the Church does not

FABC's 1986 Fourth Plenary Assembly on the "Vocation and Mission of the Laity in the Church and in the World of Asia." Several aspects of this problem have been articulated over the years including those relating to drawing the demarcation line between the Church and the world, the dichotomy between the sanctuary and the marketplace, and the obstacle to provide an integrated view of Christian life.[56] The division between the vocation and mission of the laity also separates nature and mission, ontology and praxis, and gives a strong impression that the role of lay people does not derive from who and what they are. In recent years, their increased participation in the Church through numerous lay ministries, which is fuelled in part by an acute shortage of priests, gives the lie to this pastoral separation between their mission in the Church and in the world. This observation leads us to advocate the employment of the term "mission" without the division between the *ad intra* and *ad extra* aspects.[57] Such usage would avoid dichotomizing clergy and laity in terms of ministries, in the Church and in the world, respectively.[58] In our view, there is a deep reciprocity between the internal affairs of the

---

first exist 'in its mystery' and then receive a 'mission in history'. Its mystery is precisely a dimension of the historical mission of Christ and therefore cannot be considered 'in itself' and without reference to the concrete tasks its own historical mission requires. And no mission may be undertaken by the Church except as an implication of the mystery from which it takes its rise." Ibid., 338.

56 Elissa Rinere has raised several pertinent questions: "If laity labor primarily 'in the world', what is to be understood about their efforts 'in the Church'?" or "How can a Christian lead a unified and integrated life if the Christian does not live in an integrated environment? "If the Church is separate from the world, does that not imply that the exercise of religion is separate from everyday life?" See "Canon Law and Emerging Understandings of Ministry," in *Ordering the Baptismal Priesthood: Theologies of Lay and Ordained Ministry*, edited by Susan K. Wood (Collegeville, Minn.: Liturgical Press, 2003), 77–8; see also Joseph Komonchak, "Clergy, Laity and the Church's Mission in the World," in *Official Ministry in a New Age, edited by James H. Provost* (Washington, D.C.: Canon Law Society of America, 1981) 168–93.

57 In an address to lay people on the 20th anniversary of *Gaudium et Spes* in Liège, John Paul II discouraged the separation between these two modes of collaboration in the building up of the Church: "'baptisés et insérés dans le monde, tels sont les deux axes de votre condition. Votre terrain d'action est à la fois l'Eglise et le monde." Quoted by Patrick Valdrini, "La mission des laïcs dans le magistère de Jean-Paul II," *Ius Canonicum* 26:51 (1986) 86.

58 For Avery Dulles, "Since the council some have maintained that the clergy have as their proper sphere of operation the inner affairs of the church, whereas lay persons should regard secular matters as their area of competence. The council, however, does not authorize such a sharp division of labor" (*The Reshaping of Catholicism*

Church and the events of the world such that whatever happens in either sphere will have impact in the other. The entire Church is in the world, and all ministries are fundamentally oriented towards the Church's mission to the world in the service of the kingdom of God.[59] This assertion is consistent with the teaching of *Gaudium et Spes* which emphasises that the whole Church, not just the laity, has a secular dimension, and within it, lay people have a particular secular character.[60]

Therefore, we argue that the Church's cause could be enhanced if lay people are defined or described purely and simply as Christians,[61] and the mission of the laity be expressed without the *ad intra* and *ad extra* qualifications. If such a definition and usage could be acceptable to the universal magisterium it would become a foundation for a new ecclesiological framework of cooperation between clergy and laity, one that maintains the unity between them but at the same time allows them to actively engage in specific activities that pertain to their specific vocation and charisms. It could also initiate a pastoral revolution that could reinvent the laity, spur lay activity, and bring about "a springtime as we cannot imagine."[62] Repeating this hopeful expression of Yves Congar, Pope John Paul II declares that "this Christian springtime, many signs of which we can already glimpse, is perceivable in the radical choice of faith, in the genuine holiness of life, in the extraordinary apostolic zeal of many lay faithful, men and women, the young, adults and the elderly."[63] For the pontiff, with the Second Vatican Council "*the*

[San Francisco: Harper & Row, 1988] 27). To support his observation, Dulles cited *Apostolicam Actuositatem*, no. 5, which "exhorts lay persons 'to exercise their apostolate both in the Church and in the world, in both the spiritual and the temporal orders." Ibid.

59 Joseph Komonchak also argues that "there is, after all, no *Ecclesia ad intra* except as an *Ecclesia ad extra*." See "The Synod of 1985 and the Notion of the Church," *Chicago Studies* 26:3 (1987) 340.

60 *Gaudium et Spes*, no. 40; *Lumen Gentium* (no. 38) also teaches that "what the soul is in the body, let Christians be in the world."

61 *Lumen Gentium* (no. 30) prefers to consider clergy, religious and laity as subsets of the more encompassing term Christian faithful: "Having made clear the functions of the hierarchy, the holy Council is pleased to turn its attention to the state of those Christians who are called the laity. Everything that has been said of the People of God is addressed equally to laity, religious and clergy."

62 Yves M.J. Congar, *Lay People in the Church: A Study for a Theology of Laity*, rev. ed., trans. Donald Attwater (London: Geoffrey Chapman, 1965) xviii.

63 John Paul II, "Message of His Holiness John Paul II," in *The Congress of Catholic Laity: Rome 2000*, edited by the Pontificium Consilium pro Laicis (Vatican City: Libreria Editrice Vaticana, 2002) 8.

hour of the laity truly struck, and many lay faithful, men and women, more clearly understood their Christian vocation, which by its very nature is a vocation to the apostolate."[64] This apostolate is indispensable, "if the Gospel is to be the light, salt and leaven of a new humanity,"[65] because as witnesses to Christ, the lay faithful are called "to bring the light of the Gospel to the vital nerve centres of society."[66] Therefore, he encourages lay people to "once again take the documents of the Second Vatican Council in hand to rediscover the great wealth of its doctrinal and pastoral motives."[67] This conciliar treasure, to a large extent, is contained in *Lumen Gentium*, a theological masterpiece that highlights the important function of lay people and its Christological authority by declaring that "until the full manifestation of his glory, he [Jesus] fulfils this prophetic office, not only by the hierarchy who teach in his name and by his power, but also by the laity."[68]

Concluding Remarks

This chapter has offered some modest reflections on the future of the FABC's theology of the laity by making some tentative suggestions as to the possible directions of this theology, after situating it in the global context of society over the past fifty years. These preliminary suggestions include: (i) a new, comprehensive analysis of the current environment, both local and global; (ii) an increased emphasis on four theological themes of *missio Dei*, Church as a structured or ordered communion, lay functions from the perspective of "ordered ministries," and a baptism-based theology of the laity; and (iii) an undertaking of four pastoral initiatives, including a review of the relevance and fitness for purpose of the term "triple dialogue," a more sustained focus and attention to the theological and pastoral meanings of basic ecclesial communities, a deeper reflection on the role of the family, youth, and women as the prime agents of evangelisation, and finally, a longer term and ongoing program of formation for the laity.

While quick generalisations are always misleading, we observe that one of the enduring values of the FABC's theology of the laity is the rediscovery of the

---

64 John Paul II, "Homily of His Holiness John Paul II on the Occasion of the Jubilee of the Apostolate of the Laity," ibid., 12; see also "Message of His Holiness John Paul II," ibid., 15.
65 John Paul II, "Homily of His Holiness John Paul II on the Occasion of the Jubilee of the Apostolate of the Laity," ibid., 13.
66 Ibid., 14.
67 Ibid., 13.
68 *Lumen Gentium*, no. 35.

authentic tradition of the role of the laity, which had for many centuries been constrained in a hierarchical system that views lay people as secondary members of the Church. What this theology offers is a rich and profound interpretation of the mission of the laity as proclamation, witness of life, and dialogical engagement with society, religions, and cultures, and thereby regains its genuine Catholic character. However, in our humble opinion, this theology did not go far enough. In fact, it has not completely extricated itself from the current theological mindset, which is still burdened with a clergy-based definition of the laity and an oft-repeated cliché of mission *ad intra* and *ad extra*. Its main theological motif of triple dialogue also needs to be augmented with the fourth dialogical dimension, one that has been advocated by the Catholic bishops of Vietnam, namely the dialogue with the national government.

As a contextual and relational theology par excellence, the FABC's theology of the laity holds on to a dialogical and dialectic relationship with the world by maintaining a constructive but critical engagement with the local context, and a creative fidelity to the tradition of the Church. While still being a project in progress, and despite its minor ecclesiological deficits discussed above, the FABC's theology of the laity has displayed the features of both a local and a universal theology. It speaks directly to the local audience but its message is also relevant to the whole Church. As the Church in Asia is well into the twenty-first century a central question facing the Asian bishops is what role the laity could and should play in the Church and in the world of Asia. Our suggestion is that the Asian Church will be truest to its identity when all of its members, laity, clergy, and religious, acknowledge their rightful place and distinctive role, actively participate in the Spirit-led mission to build up the body of Christ and the kingdom of God, and boldly proclaim the most decisive event in history, the unique relevance of the triune God in the death and resurrection of Jesus Christ.

Selected Bibliography

1. Primary Sources

1.1 Vatican II

Sacrosanctum Oecumenicum Concilium Vaticanum II. *Constitutiones, Decreta, Declarationes*. Cura et studio Secretariae Generalis Concilii Oecumenicii Vaticani II. Rome: Typis Polyglottis Vaticanis, 1966.

Vatican Council II. "*Ad Gentes Divinitus*. Degree on the Church's Missionary Activity." In *Vatican Council II*: Vol. 1, *The Conciliar and Post Conciliar Documents*, edited by Austin Flannery, 813–56. New rev. edition. Northport, N.Y.: Costello Publishing Co., 1996.

Vatican Council II. "*Apostolicam Actuositatem*. Degree on the Apostolate of the Laity." In *Vatican Council II*: Vol. 1, *The Conciliar and Post Conciliar Documents*, edited by Austin Flannery, 766–98. New rev. edition. Northport, N.Y.: Costello Publishing Co., 1996.

Vatican Council II. "*Dignitatis Hunanae*. Declaration on Religious Liberty." In *Vatican Council II*: Vol. 1, *The Conciliar and Post Conciliar Documents*, edited by Austin Flannery, 799–812. New rev. edition. Northport, N.Y.: Costello Publishing Co., 1996.

Vatican Council II. "*Gaudium et Spes*. Pastoral Constitution on the Church in the Modern World." In *Vatican Council II*: Vol. 1, *The Conciliar and Post Conciliar Documents*, edited by Austin Flannery, 903–1001. New rev. edition. Northport, N.Y.: Costello Publishing Co., 1996.

Vatican Council II. "*Lumen Gentium*. Dogmatic Constitution on the Church." In *Vatican Council II*: Vol. 1, *The Conciliar and Post Conciliar Documents*, edited by Austin Flannery, 350–426. New rev. edition. Northport, N.Y.: Costello Publishing Co., 1996.

Vatican Council II. "*Nostra Aetate*. Declaration on the Relation of the Church to Non-Christian Religions." In *Vatican Council II*: Vol. 1, *The Conciliar and Post Conciliar Documents*, edited by Austin Flannery, 738–49. New rev. edition. Northport, N.Y.: Costello Publishing Co., 1996.

Vatican Council II. "*Sacrosanctum Concilium*. The Constitution on the Sacred Liturgy." In *Vatican Council II*: Vol. 1, *The Conciliar and Post Conciliar Documents*, edited by Austin Flannery, 1–36. New rev. edition. Northport, N.Y.: Costello Publishing Co., 1996.

1.2 John Paul II

Encyclicals

John Paul II. "*Redemptor Hominis.*" Melbourne: A.C.T.S. Publications, 1979.

–. "*Redemptoris Missio.*" *Origins* 20:34 (31 January 1991) 541, 543–68.

Apostolic Exhortations

John Paul II. "'*Christifideles Laici*': Adhortatio Apostolica Post-synodalis ad Episcopos, Sacerdotes et Diaconos atque Religiosos Viros ac Mulieres omnesque christifideles Laicos: de vocatione et missione Laicorum in Ecclesia et in mundo." *Acta Apostolicae Sedis* (1989) 393–521. English text in *Origins* 18:35 (9 February 1989) 561, 563–95.

–. "*Ecclesia in Asia.*" *Origins* 29:23 (18 November 1999) 357, 359–84.

–. *I Will Give You Shepherds: 'Pastores Dabo Vobis': Post-Synodal Apostolic Exhortation of John Paul II to the Bishops, Clergy and Faithful on the Formation of Priests in the Circumstances of the Present Day*. Boston, MA: St. Paul Books and Media, [1992].

–. "*Pastores Gregis.*" *Origins* 33:22 (6 November 2003) 353, 355–92.

Apostolic Letters

John Paul II. "Apostolic Letter to Latin American Religious on the Occasion of the Fifth Centenary of the Evangelization of the New World." *Origins* 20:13 (6 September 1990) 208–16.

–. "*Ordinatio Sacerdotalis.*" *L'Osservatore Romano* (1 June 1994) 1–2.

–. "*Tertio Millennio Adveniente.*" *Origins* 24 (24 November 1994) 401, 403–16.

Books, Addresses, Letters, Messages, Speeches, etc.

John Paul II. "Annual Address to the Roman Curia." *Origins* 17:33 (28 January 1988) 573–6.

–. *The Church: Mystery, Sacrament, Community. A Catechesis on the Creed*. Vol. 4. Boston, Mass.: Books & Media, 1998.

–. *Crossing the Threshold of Hope*. London: Jonathan Cape, 1994.

–. "Do Laity Share in the Priest's Pastoral Ministry?" *Origins* 24:3 (2 June 1994) 40-2.

–. "Finding the True Light." In *The Future of the Asian Churches: The Asian Synod and Ecclesia in Asia*, edited by James H. Kroeger and Peter C. Phan, 58–61. Quezon City, Philippines: Claretian Publications, 2002.

–. "Homily in Oriole Park." *Origins* 25:18 (19 October 1995) 312-4.

–. "Homily of His Holiness John Paul II on the Occasion of the Jubilee of the Apostolate of the Laity." In *The Congress of Catholic Laity*: Rome 2000, edited by the Pontificium Consilium pro Laicis, 11–15. Vatican City: Libreria Editrice Vaticana, 2002.

–. "Message of His Holiness John Paul II." In *The Congress of Catholic Laity*: Rome 2000, edited by the Pontificium Consilium pro Laicis, 3–9. Vatican City: Libreria Editrice Vaticana, 2002.

–. "Propose Suitable Pastoral Lines in the Light of Loreto Discourse." *L'Osservatore Romano* (30 September 1985) 9.

–. "Towards a Common Ethical Code for Humankind: *Address to the Pontifical Academy of Social Sciences 2001*." *Concilium* 4 (2001) 11–4.

1.3 Federation of Asian Bishops' Conferences (FABC)

Collections

Colombo, Domenico, ed. *Documenti della Chiesa in Asia: Federazione delle Conferenze Episcopali Asiatiche 1970–1995*. Bologna: Editrice Missionaria Italiana, 1997.

Eilers, Franz-Josef, ed. *For All the Peoples of Asia: Federation of Asian Bishops' Conferences. Documents from 1992 to 1996*. Vol. 2. Quezon City: Claretian Publications, 1997.

Eilers, Franz-Josef, ed. *For All the Peoples of Asia: Federation of Asian Bishops' Conferences. Documents from 1997 to 2001*. Vol. 3. Quezon City: Claretian Publications, 2002.

–. *For All the Peoples of Asia: Federation of Asian Bishops' Conferences. Documents from 2002 to 2006*. Vol. 4. Quezon City: Claretian Publications, 2007.

Rosales, Gaudencio B. and C.G. Arevalo, eds. *For All the Peoples of Asia: Federation of Asian Bishops' Conferences. Documents from 1970 to 1991*. Vol. 1. Quezon City: Claretian Publications, 1992.

Vimal, Tirimanna, ed. *For All the Peoples of Asia: FABC Documents from 2007 to 2012*. Vol. 5. Manila: Claretian Publications, 2014.

Individual Works

Federation of Asian Bishops' Conferences. *The First Asian Laity Meeting: 4–9 September 1994, Korea*. [Seoul]: Pontifical Council for the Laity, Federation of Asian Bishops' Conferences Office of Laity, Catholic Lay Apostolate Council of Korea, [1994].

–. *Statutes of the Federation of Asian Bishops' Conferences*. Hong Kong: General Secretariat of the FABC, 1995.

–. "Theses on Local Churches." *FABC Papers No. 60*. Hong Kong: FABC, 1991.

1.4 The 1998 Special Assembly of the Synod of Bishops for Asia

Phan, Peter C., comp. and ed. *The Asian Synod: Texts and Commentaries.* Maryknoll, N.Y.: Orbis Books, 2002.

[Synod of Bishops]. "Message to the People of God From the Special Assembly of the Synod of Bishops for Asia." *Origins* 28:2 (28 May 1998) 17, 19–22.

[Synod of Bishops]. "The Synod's Propositions." In *The Asian Synod: Texts and Commentaries*, compiled and edited by Peter C. Phan, 140–65. Maryknoll, N.Y.: Orbis Books, 2002.

1.5 The Vietnamese Episcopal Conference

Pastoral Letters and Communiqués

Hội Đồng Giám Mục Việt Nam [The Vietnamese Episcopal Conference]. *Giáo Hội Công Giáo Việt Nam: Niên Giám 2004 [The Catholic Church of Vietnam: Almanac 2004]*, edited by Văn Phòng Tổng Thư Ký, Hội Đồng Giám Mục Việt Nam [General Secretariat, The Vietnamese Episcopal Conference]. Hà Nội: Nhà Xuất Bản Tôn Giáo, 2004.

–. *Giáo Hội Công Giáo Việt Nam: Niên Giám 2005 [The Catholic Church of Vietnam: Almanac 2005]*, edited by Văn Phòng Tổng Thư Ký, Hội Đồng Giám Mục Việt Nam [General Secretariat, The Vietnamese Episcopal Conference]. Hà Nội: Nhà Xuất Bản Tôn Giáo, 2005.

La Conférence épiscopale du Vietnam. "Lettre commune de la Conférence épiscopale du Vietnam a l'ensemble des prêtres, religieux et laïcs de tout le pays." [Translation by Fr Jean Maïs, Missions Étrangères de Paris]. *Flashes sur le Vietnam* (October 1980).

–. "Lettre commune de la Conférence épiscopale du Vietnam envoyée à la communauté du peuple de Dieu pour l'année 2001." *Églises d'Asie* 338 (1 October 2001) 23–6.

Trần Anh Dũng, ed. *Hàng Giáo Phẩm Công Giáo Việt Nam (1960–1995) [The Hierarchy of the Catholic Church of Viet Nam]*. Paris: Đắc Lộ Tùng Thư, 1996.

–, ed. *Hội Đồng Giám Mục Việt Nam (1980–2000) [The Vietnamese Episcopal Conference]*. Paris: Đắc Lộ Tùng Thư, 2001.

Other Documents

La Conférence épiscopale du Vietnam. "Le culte des ancêtres et des héros: Communiqué de la Conférence épiscopale du Vietnam." *Documentation Catholique* 63 (1966) 467–70.

Hội Đồng Giám Mục Việt Nam [Vietnamese Episcopal Conference]. "Bản trả lời các câu hỏi" ["Responses to the *Lineamenta*'s Questions"]. *Định Hướng* 16 (1998) 81–90.

[Vietnamese Episcopal Conference]. "Toward Genuine Religious Freedom: the Submission by the Bishops of Vietnam to the Seventh Congress of their Country's Communist Party." *Catholic International* 2 (September 1991) 772–4.

Nguyen Minh Nhat [Bishop of Xuân Lộc]. "The Hardships of the Church in Vietnam." *L'Osservatore Romano* 48 (26 November 1990) 2.

–. "Les relations entre l'Eglise et l'Etat: vues par le président de la conférence épiscopale." *Missi* 2 (February 1991) 27.

1.6 Other Primary Sources

Benedict XVI. "*Deus Caritas Est*: Encyclical." *Origins* 35:33 (2 February 2006) 541–57.

–. "Letter to Chinese Catholics." *Origins* 37:10 (2 August 2007) 145–58. Also appeared as "Letter of the Holy Father Pope Benedict XVI to the Bishops, Priests, Consecrated Persons and Lay Faithful of the Catholic Church in the People's Republic of China." http://www.vatican.va/holy_father/benedict_xvi/letters/2007/documents/hf_ben-xvi_let_20070527_china_en.html (accessed 12 July 2007).

Bishops' Conference of England and Wales. *The Sign We Give: Report from the Working Party on Collaborative Ministry*. Chelmsford, Essex: Matthew James Publishing, 1995.

The Code of Canon Law: New Revised English Translation. Prepared by the Canon Law Society of Great Britain and Ireland in association with the Canon Law Society of Australia and New Zealand and the Canadian Can Law Society. London: HarperCollins, 1997.

The Congregation for the Doctrine of the Faith. "Declaration '*Dominus Iesus*': On the Unicity and Salvific Universality of Jesus Christ and the Church." *Origins* 30:14 (14 September 2000) 209, 211–24.

–. "Letter to the Bishops of the Catholic Church on Some Aspects of the Church Understood as Communion." *Origins* 22:7 (25 June 1992) 108–12. Also in *One in Christ* 28:3 (1992) 282–93.

Eight Vatican Offices. "Instruction: On Certain Questions Regarding the Collaboration of the Nonordained Faithful in the Sacred Ministry of Priests." *Origins* 27:24 (27 November 1997) 397, 399–409.

Halton, Thomas. *The Church*. Messages of the Fathers of the Church. Wilmington, Delaware: Michael Glazier, 1985.

Paul VI. "*Homilia.*" *Acta Apostolicae Sedis* 58 (1966) 51–59.

–. "*Ministeria Quaedam, 15 August, 1972.*" In *Vatican Council II:* Vol. 1, *The Conciliar and Post Conciliar Documents*, edited by Austin Flannery, 427–32. New rev. edition. Northport, N.Y.: Costello Publishing Co., 1996.

Pius XII. "*Ad Apostolorum Principis:* Encyclical of Pope XII on Communism and the Church in China, June 29, 1958." In *The Papal Encyclicals 1939–1958*, edited by Claudia Carlen, 365–71. Raleigh, [N.C.]: McGrath Publishing Company, 1981.

–. [Address to the New Cardinals on 20 February 1946] Allocutiones I. *Acta Apostolicae Sedis* 38 (1946) 149.

The Pontifical Council for Interreligious Dialogue and the Congregation for the Evangelisation of Peoples. "Dialogue and Proclamation: Reflections and Orientations on Interreligious Dialogue and the Proclamation of the Gospel of Jesus Christ." *Origins* 21:8 (4 July 1991) 121, 123–135.

Richardson, Cyril C. et al. *Early Christian Fathers*. New York: Macmillan Publishing, 1970.

Taberd, J.L, ed. [Episcopo Isauropolitano, *Vicariio Apostolico Concincine, Cambodie, et Ciampe, Asiatice Societatis Parisiensis, nec non Bengalensis, Socio Honorario*]. *Dictionarium Anamitico-Latinum: Primitus Inceptum ab Illustrissimo et Reverendissimo Episcopo Adranensi, Vicariio Apostolico Concincine*. Serampore [Bengal, India]: Fredericnagori Vulgo Serampore, 1838.

U.S. Bishops. "Called and Gifted: The American Catholic Laity, 1980, Reflections of the U.S. Bishops." *Origins* 10:24 (27 November 1980) 369, 371–3.

–. "Called and Gifted for the Third Millennium." *Origins* 25:24 (30 November 1995) 409–15.

–. "Co-workers in the Vineyard of the Lord." *Origins* 35:25 (1 December 2005) 405–27.

[U.S. Bishops]. *Lay Ecclesial Ministry: The State of the Questions: A Report of the Subcommittee on Lay Ministry*. Washington, D.C.: Committee on the Laity, United States Conference of Catholic Bishops, 1999.

2. Secondary Sources

2.1 On the Documents of the Federation of Asian Bishops' Conferences

Alangaram, Arockiam. "Christ of the Peoples of Asia: Towards an Asian Contextual Christology." Dr. Theol. diss., Leopold-Franzens University of Innsbruck, 1998. Adapted and published as *Christ of the Asian Peoples: Towards an Asian Contextual Christology based on the Documents of the Federation of the Asian*

Bishops' Conferences. Rev. edition. Bangalore: Asian Trading Corporation, 2001.

Anatriello, Sinani. "Spirituality for the Laity in the Toungngu Diocese in the Light of the Documents of the Federation of Asian Bishops' Conferences (FABC)." S.T.D. diss., International Carmelite College (Teresianum), 1999.

Borja, Maria Eliza A. "An Analysis of the FABC Documents on the Asian Family (1979-2013)." Ph.D. diss., Ateneo de Manila University, 2014.

Boromeo, Charles. "Priestly Formation in the Light of the Federation of Asian Bishops'Conferences (FABC): Towards a Model in the Burmese Context." S.T.D. diss., International Carmelite College (Teresianum), 2002.

Bula, Agustinus. "A Study of The Evangelizing Mission of the Church in Contemporary Asia in the Light of the Documents of the Federation of Asian Bishops' Conferences, 1970-1995." Th.D. diss., Pontificia Universitas Urbaniana, 1997.

Chang, Jeffrey G.L. "Ordained Ministries in the Mission and Ministry of the Church in Asia, in Light of the Documents of the Federation of Asian Bishops' Conferences, 1970-2005." S.T.D diss., Fu Jen Catholic University, Taipei, 2007.

Chia, Edmund. "FABC's 'Response' to *Dominus Iesus.*" *East Asian Pastoral Review* 38:3 (2001) 231-37.

-. "Thirty Years of FABC: History, Foundation, Context and Theology." *FABC Papers, No. 106.* Hong Kong: FABC Central Secretariat, 2003.

-. "Towards a Theology of Dialogue: Schillebeeckx's Method as Bridge Between Vatican's *Dominus Iesus* and Asia's FABC Theology." Ph.D. diss., University of Niimegen, 2003.

Cummins, John S. "Asia, Continent at a Crossroads." *America* (14 October 1995) 4-6.

Dinh Duc Dao, Joseph. "Preghiera Rinnovata per una Era Missionaria in Asia." D. Miss., Pontificia Universitas Gregoriana, 1993.

Dupuis, Jacques. "FABC Focus on the Church's Evangelizing Mission in Asia Today." *Vidyajyoti* 56 (1992) 449-68.

Emmanuel, S.J. "Contemporary Catholic Thought on the Vocation and Mission of the Laity in the Church and in the World." *FABC Papers, No. 44.* Hong Kong: FABC Central Secretariat, 1986.

Hai, Peter N. V. "Evaluation of the FABC's Theology of the Laity." *East Asian Pastoral Review,* 47:3 (2010) 234-262.

Hai, Peter N. V. "Features of the FABC's Theology of the Laity." *East Asian Pastoral Review,* 47:1 (2010) 7-37

Hai, Peter N. V. "*Fides Quaerens Dialogum*: Theological Methodologies of the Federation of Asian Bishops' Conferences." Australian E-Journal of Theology

8 (October 2006) 1–26, http://aejt.com.au/__data/assets/pdf_file/0008/378665/
AEJT_8.9_Hai_Fides_Quaerens_Dialogum.pdf (accessed 6 July 2012); translated into Vietnamese by Nguyen Hoang Vinh as "*Fides Quaerens Dialogum*:
Cac Phuong Phap Than Hoc Cua Lien Hiep Cac Hoi Dong Giam Muc A Chau,"
in *Thoi Su Than Hoc* [Contemporary Theological Issues] 55 (January 2012)
110–149.

Hai, Peter N. V. "Laity and Church in the Documents of the Federation of Asian
Bishops' Conferences." *Compass: A Review to Topical Theology* 46: 2 (2012)
13–20.

Hai, Peter N. V. "Lay People in the Asian Church: A Critical Study of the Role
of the Laity in the Contextual Theology of the Federation of Asian Bishops'
Conferences (1970–2001) with Special Reference to John Paul II's Apostolic
Exhortations *Christifideles Laici* (1989) and *Ecclesia in Asia* (1999), and the
Pastoral Letters of the Vietnamese Episcopal Conference." Ph.D. diss., Aus-
tralian Catholic University, 2009.

Hai, Peter N. V. "Lay People in the Asian Church: A Study of John Paul II's Theology of the Laity in *Ecclesia in Asia* with Reference to the Documents of the
Federation of Asian Bishops' Conferences." *Australian E-Journal of Theology*
10 (May 2007) 1–22, http://aejt.com.au/__data/assets/pdf_file/0004/378076/
AEJT_10.4_Hai_Lay_People.pdf (accessed 6 July 2012).

Hai, Peter N. V. "Models of the Asian Church." *Australian E-Journal of Theology* 18:1 (April 2011) 61–73, http://aejt.com.au/2011/volume_18/issue_1/?
article=325557 (accessed 30 April 2011); translated into Vietnamese by
Nguyen Hoang Vinh as "Cac Mo Hinh Giao Hoi A Chau," in *Thoi Su Than
Hoc* [Contemporary Theological Issues] 54 (November 2011) 159–186.

Hai, Peter N. V. "Reflections on the Future of the FABC's Theology of the Laity."
East Asian Pastoral Review 49:2 (April-June 2012) 107–132.

Hai, Peter N.V. "*Sentire cum ecclesia*: Laity and the Call to Holiness in Papal and
Local Theologies." *The Australasian Catholic Record* 89:3 (July 2012) 333–348.

Handoko, Petrus Maria. "Lay Ministries in the Mission and Ministry of the
Church in Asia: A Critical Study of the Documents of the Federation of Asian
Bishops' Conferences 1970–1991." Th.D. diss., Pontificia Universitas Grego-
riana, 1993.

Kadaliyil, Lawrence Abraham. "Toward a Relational Spirit Ecclesiology in Asia:
A Study on the Documents of the Federation of Asian Bishops' Conferences."
Th.D. diss., Graduate Theological Union, Berkeley, 2006.

Mariampillai, D. Bosco M. "The Emerging Asian Theology of Liberation in the
Documents of the Federation of Asian Bishops' Conferences 1974–1986."
Ph.D. diss., University of Ottawa, 1993.

Nam Ki Ok, Marta. "Il ruolo evangelizzatore dei fedeli laici nel contesto socio-religioso in Corea alla luce dei documenti della FABC dal 1980 al 1991." Th.D. diss., Pontificia Universitas Urbaniana, 1996.

Nemet, Ladislav. "Inculturation in the Philippines: A Theological Study of the Question of Inculturation in the Documents of CBCP and selected Filipino Theologians in the Light of Vatican II and the Documents of FABC." Th.D. diss., Pontificia Universitas Gregoriana, 1994.

Nguyen, Thao. "A New Way of Being Church for Mission: Asian Catholic Bishops and Asian Catholic Women in Dialogue: A Study of the Documents of the Federation of Asian Bishops' Conferences (FABC)." Th.D. diss., Graduate Theological Union, Berkeley, Calif., 2013.

Nguyen Van Am. "The Laity in Asia: Mission as Inculturation in the Documents of the Federation of Asian Bishops' Conferences." S.T.D. diss., Jesuit School of Theology at Berkeley, 2001.

Paikada, Matthew. "Characteristics of an Indian Liberation Theology as an Authentic Christian Theology: A Study Based on the Analysis of the Indian Situation and the Documents of the CBCI and the FABC." Dr. Theol., Westphalia Wilhelms University, 1988.

Phan, Peter C. "Human Development and Evangelisation: The First to the Sixth Plenary Assembly of the Federation of Asian Bishops' Conferences." *Studia Missionalia* 47 (1998) 205–27.

Punda Panda, Herman. "Towards Living Together in Harmony: A Study of Interreligious Dialogue as an Effort to Promote Harmony Among Believers of Various Religions, Based on the Federation of Asian Bishops' Conferences (FABC) Documents from 1970–1996." S.T.D. diss., Pontificia Universitas Urbaniana, 2001.

Putranta, Carolus B. "The Idea of the Church in the Documents of the Federation of Asian Bishops' Conferences (FABC) 1970–1982." Th.D. diss., Pontificia Universitas Gregoriana, 1985.

Tan, Jonathan Yun-ka. "'Missio ad gentes' in Asia: A Comparative Study of the Missiology of John Paul II and the Federation of Asian Bishops' Conferences (FABC)." Ph.D. diss., The Catholic University of America, 2002.

–. "Theologizing at the Service of Life: The Contextual Theological Methodology of the Federation of Asian Bishops' Conference [sic] (FABC)." *Gregorianum* 81:3 (2000) 541–75.

Thainese, Alphonse. "Laity in the Participatory Communion in the Local Church of Andhra: An Ecclesiological Inquiry Based on the Documents of the Federation of Asian Bishops' Conferences 1970–2005." Th.D. diss., Dharmaram Vidya Kshetram and Pontifical Athenaeum of Philosophy, Theology and Canon Law, 2006.

Thoppil, James. "Towards an Asian Ecclesiology: Understanding of the Church in the Documents of the Federation of Asian Bishops' Conferences (FABC) 1970–1995 and the Asian Ecclesiological Trends." Th.D. diss., Pontificia Universitas Urbaniana, 1998. Updated and published as *Towards an Asian Ecclesiology: the Understanding of the Church in the Documents of the FABC (1970-2000)*. Shillong, India: Oriens Publications and Asian Trading Corporation, 2005.

Thumma, Lucas. "An Inquiry into the Ethico-Legal Methodology of the Social Teachings of the Federation of Asian Bishops' Conferences from 1970 to 1991." S.T.D diss., Vidyajyoti College of Theology, Delhi, 1996.

Tomko, Josef Cardinal. "A Renewed Church in Asia: A Mission of Love and Service." In *FABC Papers No. 95*, 1-12. Hong Kong: FABC, 2000. Also appeared as "Dialogue, Inculturation and Evangelization in Asia." *Origins* 29 (10 February, 2000) 549–53.

Wilfred, Felix. "The Federation of Asian Bishops' Conferences (FABC)." In *For All the Peoples of Asia: Federation of Asian Bishops' Conferences. Documents from 1970 to 1991*, vol. 1, edited by Gaudencio B. Rosales and C.G. Arévalo, xxiii–xxx. Quezon City: Claretian Publications, 1992.

–. "Images of Jesus Christ in the Asian Pastoral Context: An Interpretation of Documents from the Federation of Asian Bishops' Conferences." *Concilium* 2 (1992) 51–62.

–. "Sunset in the East: The Asian Realities Challenging the Church and Its Laity Today." *FABC Papers No. 45*. Hong Kong: FABC, 1986.

2.2 On *Ecclesia in Asia* and the 1998 Synod for Asia

Amaladoss, Michael. "The Image of Jesus in the *Church in Asia*." *East Asian Pastoral Review* 37:3 (2000) 233–41.

Chia, Edmund. "Interreligious Dialogue in *Ecclesia in Asia*" in *Jeevadhara* 30 (2000) 300–12; also appeared in *East Asian Pastoral Review* 37:3 (2000) 243–55; and as "Of Fork and Spoon or Fingers and Chopsticks: Interreligious Dialogue in *Ecclesia in Asia*." In *The Asian Synod: Texts and Commentaries*, compiled and edited by Peter C. Phan, 273–83. Maryknoll, N.Y.: Orbis Books, 2002.

Fox, Thomas C. "Polite Toward Rome, True to their Mission." *National Catholic Reporter* (28 January 2000) 10–1.

Kavunkal, Jacob. "Church and Mission in Asia in the Light of *Ecclesia in Asia*: A Critical Study." *Jeevadhara* 30 (2000) 290–9.

Neuner, Josef. "*Ecclesia in Asia*: Towards a New Theology of Proclamation." *Third Millennium* 3 (2000) 110–6.

Shan, Paul. "Presentation of the Post-Synodal Apostolic Exhortation Ecclesia in Asia of His Holiness John Paul II on Jesus Christ the Savior and His Mission of Love and Service in Asia: 'That They May have Life and have It Abundantly' (Jn. 10:10).'" *The Japan Mission Review* 53 (1999) 263–76.

Tan Yun-ka, Jonathan. "From *Ecclesia in Asia* to a Mission of Love and Service: A Comparative Analysis of Two Contrasting Approaches to Doing Christian Mission in Asia." *East Asian Pastoral Review* 41:1 (2004) 68–101.

2.3 On the Vietnamese Episcopal Conference and the Catholic Church in Vietnam

Églises d'Asie. "Après vingt années d'attente: Une interview de Mgr Paul Nguyen Van Binh [Archbishop of Saigon]." *Églises d'Asie* 199 (16 May 1995). www. eglasie.mepasie.org (accessed 8 December 2006). Originally published in the daily "Sai Gon Giai Phong" [Saigon liberated], a publication of the Communist Party in Ho Chi Minh City.

–. "Entretien de M. Vo Van Kiet, chef du gouvernement, sur un certain nombre de questions touchant le catholicisme." *Églises d'Asie* 173 (16 March 1994). www. eglasie.mepasie.org (accessed 15 December 2006). Previously appeared in the weekly Công Giáo và Dân Tộc [Catholicism and Nation] (27 February 1994).

–. "Les évêques du Vietnam et la Féderation des conférénces épiscopales d'Asie." *Églises d'Asie* 186 (1 November 1994). http://www.eglasie.mepasie. org (accessed 15 December 2006).

–. "Fidélité et Espérance: Une interview de Mgr Nguyễn Minh Nhật, évêque de Xuân Lộc, président de la Conference épiscopale du Vietnam." *Églises d'Asie* 101 (16 December 1990). http://www.eglasie.mepasie.org (accessed 15 December 2006).

Hai, Peter N. V. "The Contextual Theology of the Vietnamese Episcopal Conference in the 1980 Pastoral Letter." *East Asian Pastoral Review* 48:4 (Oct-Dec 2011) 313–344.

Ha, Van Minh. *Die Laien in der Kirche Vietnams: Eine pastoraltheologische Studie zu ihrer Rolle in Geschichte und Gegenwart.* Frankfurt am Main: Peter Lang, 2001.

Maïs, Jean. "1975–1985: 10 ans de relations entre l'Église et l'état au Vietnam." *Echange France-Asie* (May 1986) 1–26.

–. "Première réunion de la Conférence épiscopale du Vietnam et preparation de la lettre commune." *Flashes sur le Vietnam* (October 1980) 1–3.

Marr, David G. "Church and State in Vietnam." *Indochina Issues* 74 (April 1987) 1–7.

Missi (Magazine d'Information et de Solidarité Internationale). "Chrétiens au Vietnam." [Entire issue devoted to the Catholic Church of Vietnam]. *Missi* 2 (February 1991).

Ostrowski, Brian Eugene. "The Nom Works of Geronimo Maiorica, S.J. (1589–1656) and their Christology." Ph.D. diss., Cornell University, 2006.

Sodano, Angelo Cardinal. "Priests and the 'Catholic Patriotic Association': Excerpt from Cardinal Angelo Sodano's Letter to Bishop Paul-Marie Nguyen Minh Nhat, President of the Vietnamese Episcopal Conference." *Catholic International* 4:2 (February 1993) 7–8.

2.4 Other Books

Amaladoss, Michael. *Making All Things New: Dialogue, Pluralism, and Evangelization in Asia.* Maryknoll, N.Y.: Orbis Books, 1990.

Barnes, Michael. *Theology and the Dialogue of Religions.* Cambridge: Cambridge University Press, 2002.

Baum, Gregory, ed. *The Twentieth Century: A Theological Overview.* Maryknoll, N.Y.: Orbis Books, 1999.

Bernier, Paul. *Ministry in the Church.* Mystic, Conn.: Twenty-Third Publications, 1992.

Bevans, Stephen B. *Models of Contextual Theology.* Maryknoll, N.Y.: Orbis Books, 1992.

Bevans, Stephen B. and Roger P. Schroeder. *Constants in Context: A Theology of Mission for Today.* Maryknoll, N.Y.: Orbis Books, 2004.

Boff, Clodovis. *Theology and Praxis: Epistemological Foundations.* Translated from the Portuguese by Robert R. Barr. Maryknoll, N.Y.: Orbis Books, 1987.

Bouyer, Louis. *The Church of God: Body of Christ and Temple of the Spirit.* Chicago: Franciscan Herald Press, 1982.

Brown, Raymond E. *The Churches the Apostles Left Behind.* London: Geoffrey Chapman, 1984.

Cadière, Léopold. *Croyances et Pratiques Religieuses des Annamites.* [Volume 1]. Preface by Paul Boudet. Hanoi: Imprimerie D'Extrême-Orient, 1944.

–. *Croyances et Pratiques Religieuses des Annamites.* [Volume 2]. Foreword by Louis Malleret. Saigon: Ecole Française D'Extrême-Orient, 1955.

–. *Croyances et Pratiques Religieuses des Annamites.* [Volume 3]. Paris: Ecole Française D'Extrême-Orient, 1957.

Congar, Yves M.J. *Lay People in the Church.* Revised edition with additions by the author. Trans. Donald Attwater. London: Geoffrey Chapman, 1965. [Originally published as *Jalons pour une théologie du laïcat* by Les Editions du Cerf, Paris, 1953. Revised edition, with addenda, published in France in 1964].

–. *Ministères et communion ecclésiale.* Paris: Les Editions du Cerf, 1971.

Cullen, Philomena, Bernard House and Gerard Mannion. *Catholic Social Justice: Theological and Practical Explorations*. London: T&T Clark, 2007.

De Lubac, Henri. *The Motherhood of the Church*. San Francisco: Ignatius Press, 1982.

Doohan, Leonard. *The Lay-Centered Church: Theology and Spirituality*. Minneapolis, Minn.: Winston Press, 1984.

–. *Laity's Mission in the Local Church: Setting a New Direction*. San Francisco: Harper & Row, 1986.

Doyle, Dennis M. *The Church Emerging from Vatican II: A Popular Approach to Contemporary Catholicism*. Mystic, Conn.: Twenty-Third Publications, 1992.

–. *Communion Ecclesiology: Vision and Versions*. Maryknoll, N.Y.: Orbis Books, 2000.

Dulles, Avery. *A Church to Believe in: Dicipleship and the Dynamics of Freedom*. New York: Crossroad, 1982.

–. *Models of the Church*. Dublin: Gill and Macmillan, 1976.

–. *The Reshaping of Catholicism*. San Francisco: Harper & Row, 1988.

–. *The Splendor of Faith: The Theological Visin of Pope John Paul II*. New York: Crossroad, 1999.

Dupuis, Jacques. *Toward a Christian Theology of Religious Pluralism*. Maryknoll, N.Y.: Orbis, 1997.

Faivre, Alexandre. *The Emergence of the Laity in the Early Church*. Translated by David Smith. New York: Paulist Press, 1990.

Fiorenza, Francis Schüssler and John P. Galvin, eds. *Systematic Theology: Roman Catholic Perspectives*. 2 vols. Minneapolis, Minn.: Fortress Press, 1992.

Flynn, Gabriel, ed. *Yves Congar: Theologian of the Church*. Louvain: W.B. Eerdmans, 2005.

Fox, Zeni. *New Ecclesial Ministry: Lay Professionals Serving the Church*. Kansas City: Sheed & Ward, 1997.

Gallagher, Michael Paul. *Clashing Symbols*. London, Longman and Todd, 1997.

Goergen, Donald J. and Ann Garrido, eds. *The Theology of Priesthood*. Collegeville, Minn.: The Liturgical Press, 2000.

Gutiérrez, Gustavo. *A Theology of Liberation: History, Politics and Salvation*. Translated and edited by Sister Caridad Inda and John Eagleson. Rev. edition. Maryknoll, N.Y.: Orbis Books, 1988.

Hall, Douglas John. *Thinking the Faith: Christian Theology in a North American Context*. Minneapolis: Fortress Press, 1991.

Hall, Gerard Vincent. *Raimon Panikkar's Hermeneutics of Religious Pluralism.* Ann Arbor, Mich.: UMI, 1994.

Hamer, Jerome. *The Church is a Communion.* London: Geoffrey Chapman, 1964.

Hastings, Adrian et al., eds. *The Oxford Companion to Christian Thought.* New York: Oxford University Press, 2000.

Hebblethwaite, Peter. *The New Inquisition: Schillebeeckx and Küng.* London: Collins, 1980.

–. *Paul VI: The First Modern Pope.* London: Fount HarperCollins, 1994.

Hennelly, Alfred T., ed. *Liberation Theology: A Documentary History.* Edited with Introductions, Commentary and Translations by Alfred T. Hennelly. Maryknoll, N.Y.: Orbis Books, 1990.

Himes, Michael J., ed. *The Catholic Church in the Twenty-First Century: Finding Hope for its Future in the Wisdom of its Past.* Liguori, Miss.: Liguori, 2004.

Kasper, Walter. *Theology and the Church.* London: SCM Press, 1989.

Kelly, Anthony. *An Expanding Theology: Faith in a World of Connections.* Newtown, NSW: E.J. Dwyer, 1993.

Kinast, Robert L. *Caring for Society: A Theological Interpretation of Lay Ministry.* Chicago: The Thomas More Press, 1985.

Kloppenburg, Bonaventure. *The Ecclesiology of Vatican II.* Translated by Matthew J. O'Connell. Chicago: Franciscan Herald Press, 1974.

Kroeger, James H. and Peter C. Phan. *The Future of the Asian Churches: The Asian Synod and "Ecclesia in Asia."* Quezon City: Claretian Publications, 2002.

Küng, Hans. *The Church.* London: Burns and Oates, 1967.

Küng, Hans and David Tracy, eds. *Paradigm Change in Theology.* Translated by Margaret Köhl. New York: Crossroad, 1991.

Küng, Hans and Walter Kasper. *The Plurality of Ministries.* New York: Herder and Herder, 1972.

Lakeland, Paul. *The Liberation of the Laity: In Search of an Accountable Church.* New York: Continuum, 2002.

Latourelle, René, ed. *Vatican II Assessment and Perspectives: Twenty-Five Years After (1962–1987).* 2 vols. New York: Paulist Press, 1988.

Lauret, Bernard, ed. *Fifty Years of Catholic Theology: Conversations with Yves Congar.* Philadelphia, Pa.: Fortress Press, 1988.

Lawler, Michael G. *A Theology of Ministry.* Kansas City, Mo.: Sheed & Ward, 1990.

Lawler, Michael G. and Thomas J. Shanahan. *Church: A Spirited Communion.* Collegeville, Minn.: The Liturgical Press, 1995.

Leung, Beatrice, ed. *Church & State Relations in 21ˢᵗ Century Asia*. Hong Kong: Centre of Asian Studies, The University of Hong Kong, 1996.

Lonergan, Bernard J.F. *Method in Theology*. New York: Herder and Herder, 1972.

Luzbetak, Louis J. *The Church and Cultures: New Perspectives in Missiological Anthropology*. American Society of Missiology Series, No. 12. Maryknoll, N.Y.: Orbis Books, 1988.

Lyotard, Jean-François. *The Postmodern Condition: A Report on Knowledge*. Translation from the French by Geoff Bennington and Brian Massumi. Foreword by Fredric Jameson. Theory and History of Literature, vol. 10. Manchester: Manchester University Press, 1984.

Marciniak, Ed et al., eds. *Challenge to the Laity*. Huntington, Ind.: Our Sunday Visitor, 1980.

Marr, David G. *Vietnamese Tradition on Trial: 1920–1945*. Berkeley, Calif.: University of California Press, 1981.

McAlister, John T. and Paul Mus. *The Vietnamese and Their Revolution*. New York: Harper & Row, 1970.

McBrien, Richard P. *Ministry: A Theological, Pastoral Handbook*. New York: HarperCollins, 1988.

Miller, John H., ed. *Vatican II: An Interfaith Appraisal*. Notre Dame, Ind.: University of Notre Dame, 1966.

Nolan, Ann Michele. *A Privileged Moment: "Dialogue" in the Language of the Second Vatican Council 1962–1965*. European University Studies, Series 23, Theology, vol. 829. New York: Peter Lang, 2006.

Noll, Ray R., ed. *100 Roman Documents Relating to the Chinese Rites Controversy (1645–1941)*. Translations by Donald D. St. Sure. San Francisco: The Ricci Institute for Chinese-Western Cultural History, 1992.

O'Donnell, Christopher. *"Ecclesia": A Theological Encyclopedia of the Church*. Collegeville, Minn.: The Liturgical Press, 1996.

O'Meara, Thomas Franklin. *Theology of Ministry*. New York: Paulist Press, 1983.

Osborne, Kenan B. *Ministry: Lay Ministry in the Roman Catholic Church: Its History and Theology*. New York: Paulist Press, 1993.

Panikkar, Raimon. *The Unknown Christ of Hinduism: Towards an Ecumenical Christophany*. Revised and enlarged edition. London: Darton, Longman & Todd, 1981.

Phan, Peter C. *Being Religious Interreligiously: Asian Perspectives on Interfaith Dialogue*. Maryknoll, N.Y.: Orbis Books, 2004.

–. *Christianity with an Asian Face: Asian American Theology in the Making*. Maryknoll, N.Y.: Orbis Books, 2003.

–. *In Our Own Tongues: Perspectives from Asia on Mission and Inculturation.* Maryknoll, N.Y.: Orbis Books, 2003.

–. *Mission and Catechesis: Alexandre de Rhodes and Inculturation in Seventeenth-Century Vietnam.* Maryknoll, N.Y.: Orbis Books, 1998.

–, ed. *The Gift of the Church: A Textbook on Ecclesiology in Honor of Patrick Granfield.* Collegeville, Minn.: The Liturgical Press, 2000.

Pieris, Aloysius. *An Asian Theology of Liberation.* Edinburgh: T&T Clark, 1988.

–. *Love Meets Wisdom: A Christian Experience of Buddhism.* Maryknoll, N.Y.: Orbis Books, 1988.

Pope, Stephen J., ed. *Common Calling: The Laity and Governance of the Catholic Church.* Washington, D.C.: Georgetown University Press, 2004.

Quatra, Miguel Marcelo. *At the Side of the Multitudes: The Kingdom of God and the Mission of the Church in the FABC documents (1970–1995).* Quezon City: Claretian Publications, 2000. [Translated and edited from "Regno di Dio e Missione della Chiesa nel Contesto Asiatico: Uno Studio sui Documenti della FABC (1970–1995)." D. Miss., Pontificia Universitas Gregoriana, 1998].

Rahner, Karl. *Theological Investigations.* Vol. 20, *Concern for the Church.* Translated by Edward Quinn. London: Darton, Longman & Todd, 1981.

Ratzinger, Joseph. *Church, Ecumenism and Politics: New Essays in Ecclesiology.* Middlegreen, Slough, England: St Paul Publications, 1988.

Rausch, Thomas P. *Catholicism in the Third Millennium*, 2nd Edition. Collegeville, Minn.: The Liturgical Press, 2003.

Richard, Lucien, Daniel T. Harrington, and John W. O'Malley, eds. *Vatican II: The Unfinished Agenda: A Look to the Future.* New York: Paulist Press, 1987.

Rowland, Christopher, ed. *The Cambridge Companion to Liberation Theology.* Cambridge: Cambridge University Press, 1999.

Sanks, T. Howland. *Salt, Leaven, and Light.* New York: Crossroad, 1992.

Schillebeeckx, Edward. *The Church with a Human Face: A New and Expanded Theology of Ministry.* London: SCM Press, 1985.

–. *Ministry: Leadership in the Community of Jesus Christ.* New York: Crossroad, 1981.

Schreiter, Robert J. *Constructing Local Theologies.* Maryknoll, N.Y.: Orbis Books, 1985.

–. *The New Catholicity: Theology Between the Global and the Local.* The Boston Theological Institute Series, vol. 3. Maryknoll, N.Y.: Orbis Books, 1997.

Schreiter, Robert J., ed. *Mission in the Third Millennium.* Maryknoll, N.Y.: Orbis Books, 2001.

274

Tavard, George H. *The Church, Community of Salvation: An Ecumenical Ecclesiology.* Collegeville, Minn.: The Liturgical Press, 1992.

Taylor, Philip, ed. *Modernity and Re-enchantment: Religion in Post-revolutionary Vietnam.* Vietnam Update Series. Singapore: Institute of Southeast Asian Studies, 2007.

Thomas, Pascal. *Ces chrétiens que l'on appelle laïcs.* Paris: Les Éditions Ouvrières, 1988.

Tillard, J.-M.R. *Church of Churches: The Ecclesiology of Communion.* Translated by R.C. De Peaux. Collegeville, Minn.: The Liturgical Press, 1992.

Vorgrimler, Herbert, ed. *Commentary on the Documents of Vatican II.* Vol. 1. New York: Herder and Herder, 1967.

Walters, Malcolm. *Globalization,* 2nd edition. London: Routledge, 2001.

Weigel, George. *Witness to Hope: The Biography of Pope John Paul II.* New York: HarperCollins, 1999.

Wicks, Jared. *Doing Theology.* New York: Paulist Press, 2009.

Wijsen, Frans, Peter Henriot and Rodrigo Mejía, eds. *The Pastoral Circle Revisited: A Critical Quest for Truth and Transformation.* Maryknoll, N.Y.: Orbis Books, 2005.

World Council of Churches. *Baptism, Eucharist and Ministry.* Faith and Order Paper No. 111. Geneva: World Council of Churches, 1982.

Wood, Susan K., ed. *Ordering the Baptismal Priesthood: Theologies of Lay and Ordained Ministry.* Collegeville, Minn.: Liturgical Press, 2003.

2.5 Other Articles

Alesandro, John. "The Code of Canon Law: Past, Present and Future." *Origins* 37:23 (15 November 2007) 357–70.

Amaladoss, Michael. "Contextual Theology and Integration." *East Asian Pastoral Review* 40:3 (2003) 266–71.

Anglican-Roman Catholic International Commission. "The Church as Communion: Agreed Statement by the Second Anglican-Roman Catholic International Commission." *Origins* 20:44 (11 April 1991) 719–27. Also in *One in Christ* 27:1 (1991) 77–97.

Atkinson, Joseph C. "Family as Domestic Church: Developmental Trajectory, Legitimacy, and Problems of Appropriation." *Theological Studies* 66 (2005) 592–604.

Austin, Gerard. "Baptism as the Matrix of Ministry." *Louvain Studies* 23 (1998) 101–13.

Baum, Gregory. "The Impact of Marxist Ideas on Christian Theology." In *The Twentieth Century: A Theological Overview*, edited by Gregory Baum, 173–85. Maryknoll, N.Y.: Orbis Books, 1999.

Beech, Hannah. "Salvation Armies." *Time* (26 April 2010) 32–6.

Bernadin, Joseph L "Ministry: In Service of One Another." *Origins* 15:9 (1 Agust 1985) 132–8.

Bowden, John. "How Vatican II Changed the Church: 6: Priest Behind the Scenes." *The Tablet* (16 November 2002) 10–1.

Chantraine, G. "Le laïc à l'intérieur des missions divines." *Nouvelle Revue Théologique* 109 (1987) 362–81.

Chavass, Paul. "Newman and the Laity." In *Newman Today*, edited by Stanley L. Jaki, 49–78. San Francisco: Ignatius Press, 1989.

Cincinnati Archdiocesan Pastoral Council. "An Expanded View of Ministry." *Origins* 16:31 (15 January 1987) 553, 555–68.

Coffey, David. "The Common and the Ordained Priesthood." *Theological Studies* 58 (1997) 209–36.

Collet, Giancarlo. "Theology of Mission or of Missions ? The Treatment of a Controversial Term." *Concilium* 1 (1999) 85–92.

Collins, John N. "A Ministry for Tomorrow's Church." *Journal of Ecumenical Studies* 32:2 (1995) 159–78.

–. "Fitting Lay Ministries into a Theology of Ministry: Responding to an American Consensus." *Worship* 79:3 (May 2005) 209–22.

Collins, Raymond F. "Did Jesus Found The Church? Which Church?" *Louvain Studies* 21:4 (1996) 356–64.

Comblin, José. "The Signs of the Times." *Concilium* 4 (2005) 73–85.

Congar, Yves. "The Conciliar Structure or Regime of the Church." *Concilium* 167 (September 1983) 3–9.

–. "Laïc et Laïcat." In *Dictionnaire de Spiritualité*, vol. 9, 79–108. Paris: Beauchesne, 1976.

–. "The Laity." In *Vatican II: An Interfaith Appraisal*, edited by John H. Miller, 239–49. New York: Association Press, 1966.

–. "My Path-Findings in the Theology of Laity and Ministries." *The Jurist* 32 (1972) 169–88.

–. "Pneumatology Today." *American Ecclesiastical Review* 167 (1973) 435–49.

–. "Prêtre, Roi, Prophète." *Seminarium* 23 (1983) 71–82.

–. "Quelques problèmes touchant les ministères." *Nouvelle Revue Theologique* 8 (October 1971) 785–800.

–. "'Real' Liturgy, 'Real' Preaching." *Worship* 82:4 (July 2008) 310–22.

–. "Sur la trilogie: Prophète-Roi-Prêtre." *Revue des Sciences Philosophiques et Théologiques* 67 (1983) 97–115.

Cool, Michel. "Le testament du Panzerkardinal." *L'Express* (20 March 1997) 68, 70.

Coriden, James A. "Ministry." *Chicago Studies* (Fall 1976) 305–15.

Crispin, Philip. "Church's Best-Kept Secret." *The Tablet* (11 June 2005) 8–9.

De La Potterie, I. "L'onction du Christ." *Nouvelle Revue Théologique* 80 (1958) 225–52.

–. "L'origine et le sens primitif du mot 'laïc." *Nouvelle Revue Théologique* 80 (1958) 840–53.

Donnell, John C."Vietnam 1979: Year of Calamity." *Asian Survey* 20:1 (January 1980) 19–32.

Doohan, Leonard. "Contemporary Theologies of the Laity: An Overview Since Vatican II." *Communio* 7 (1980) 225–42.

–. "Lay People and The Church." *The Way* (July 1992) 168–77.

–. "Theology of the Laity." In *The Modern Catholic Encyclopedia*, edited by Michael Glazier and Monika K. Hellwig, 493–5. Newtown, Australia: E.J. Dwyer, 1994.

–. "Theology of the Laity." In *The New Dictionary of Sacramental Worship*, edited by Peter E. Fink, 636–44. Collegeville, Minn.: The Liturgical Press, 1990.

Dulles, Avery. "Can Laity Properly Be Called 'Ministers." *Origins* 35:44 (20 April 2006) 725–31.

–. "Can the 'Word' Laity Be Defined?" *Origins* 18:29 (29 December 1988) 470–9.

–. "John Paul II and the Advent of the New Millenium." *America* (9 December 1995) 9–15.

–. "John Paul II and the New Evangelization." *America* (1 February 1992) 52–9, 69–72.

–. "*Sensus Fidelium.*" *America* (1 November 1986) 240–2, 263.

Dupuis, Jacques. "The Church's Evangelizing Mission in the Context of Religious Pluralism." *The Pastoral Review* 1:1 (2005) 20–31.

Emmanuel, S.J. "Asian Mission for the Next Millennium." *The Way* (April 1999) 103–117.

Fisher, Peter. "*Koinonia* and Conflict." *Theology* 104:822 (November-December 2001) 420–8.

Ford, John. "Ministries in the Church." In *The Gift of the Church: A Textbook on Ecclesiology in Honour of Patrick Granfield*, edited by Peter C. Phan, 293–314. Collegeville, Minn.: The Liturgical Press, 2000.

Freire, Paulo. "Conscientizing as a Way of Liberating (1970)." In *Liberation Theology: A Documentary History*, edited with Introductions, Commentary and Translations by Alfred T. Hennelly, 5–13. Maryknoll, N.Y.: Orbis Books, 1990.

Gaillardetz, Richard R. "The Ecclesiological Foundations of Ministry within an Ordered Communion." In *Ordering the Baptismal Priesthood: Theologies of Lay and Ordained Ministry*, edited by Susan K. Wood, 26–51. Collegeville, Minn.: Liturgical Press, 2003.

–. "The Theology Underlying Lay Ecclesial Ministry." *Origins* 36:9 (20 July 2006) 138–43.

Gilchrist, J. "Laity in the Middle Ages." In *New Catholic Encyclopedia*, vol. 8, 331–335. Washington D.C.: The Catholic University of America, 1967.

Gispert-Sauch, George. "John Paul II: Christology, Dialogue, Mission." *Jeevadhara* 35:209 (September 2005) 371–80.

–. "The New Protestant 'Pope'." *Vidyajyoti* 67:10 (October 2003) 853–4.

Gómez, Felipe. "The Missionary Activity Twenty Years After Vatican II." *East Asian Pastoral Review* 23:1 (1986) 26–57.

–. "Signs of the Times." *East Asian Pastoral Review* 26:3–4 (1989) 365–86.

Goosen, Gideon. "A New Relationship Between the Ministerial and Baptismal Priesthoods." *Compass* (Winter 1997) 17–24.

Green, Thomas J. "The Church and the Law." In *The Gift of the Church: A Textbook on Ecclesiology in Honour of Patrick Granfield*, edited by Peter C. Phan, 373–94. Collegeville, Minn.: The Liturgical Press, 2000.

Groody, Daniel G. Groody, Daniel G. "Crossing the Divide: Foundations of a Theology of Migration and Refugees." *Theological Studies* 70 (2009) 638–67.

Groppe, Elizabeth T. "The Practice of Theology as Passion for Truth: Testimony from the Journals of Yves Congar, O.P." *Horizons* 31:2 (Fall 2004) 382–402.

Gutiérrez, Gustavo. "The Task of Theology and Ecclesial Experience." *Concilium* 176 (1984) 61–4.

Hagstrom, Aurelie. "Theology of Laity." In *New Catholic Encyclopedia*, 2nd edition, vol. 8, 290–93. Washington, D.C.: Gale in Association with the Catholic University of America, 2003.

Hahnenberg, Edward. "Ordained and Lay Ministry: Restarting the Conversation." *Origins* 35:6 (23 June 2005) 94–9.

–. "The Vocation to Lay Ecclesial Ministry." *Origins* 37:12 (30 August 2007) 177–82.

–. "When the Church Calls." *America* 195:10 (9 October 2006) 10–4. http://find.galegroup.com/itx/start.do?prodId=AONE (accessed 11 October 2007); Gale Document Number: A152742193.

Hai, Peter N. V. "The Laity in Historical Context." *East Asian Pastoral Review*, 46:4 (2009) 334–356.

Haleblian, Krikor. "The Problem of Contextualization." *Missiology: An International Review* 11:1 (January 1983) 95–111.

Harrington, Daniel J. "The Collaborative Nature of the Pauline Mission." *The Bible Today* 42:4 (July 2004) 200–6.

–. "Paul and His Co-Workers." *Priests and People* (August-September 2003) 320–5.

Hennelly, Alfred T. "Theological Method: The Southern Exposure." *Theological Studies* 38:4 (December 1977) 709–35.

Himes, Kenneth R. "Globalization with a Human Face: Catholic Social Teaching and Globalization." *Theological Studies* 69 (2008) 269–89.

Holland, Joe. "Roots of the Pastoral Circle in Personal Experiences and Catholic Social Tradition." In *The Pastoral Circle Revisited: A Critical Quest for Truth and Transformation*, edited by Frans Wijsen, Peter Henriot, and Rodrigo Mejía, 1–12. Maryknoll, N.Y.: Orbis Books, 2005.

Huntington, Samuel P. "The Clash of Civilizations?" *Foreign Affairs* 72:3
(Summer 1993) 22–49.

International Consultation Between the Catholic Church and the World Evangelical Alliance. "Church, Evangelization and the Bonds of 'Koinonia'." *Origins* 33:19 (16 October 2003) 310–20.

International Theological Commission. "Christianity and the World Religions." *Origins* 27:10 (14 August 1997) 149, 151–66.

Kaiser, Robert Blair. "How Vatican II Changed the Church: 5: Priest Behind the Scenes." *The Tablet* (9 November 2002) 8–9.

Kasper, Walter. "The Mission of Laity." *Theology Digest* 35:2 (Summer 1988) 133–8.

–. "On the Church: A Friendly Reply to Cardinal Ratzinger." *America* (23–30 April 2001) 8–14. Also in *The Furrow* 52:6 (June 2001) 321–32, and *The Tablet* (23 June 2001) 927–30.

–. "The Theological Anthropology of *Gaudium et Spes*." *Communio* 23 (Spring 1996) 129–40.

Kelly, Anthony J. "Whither 'Australian Theology?': A Response to Geoffrey Lilburne." *Pacifica* 12 (June 1999) 192–208.

Kilian, Sabbas J. "The Meaning and Nature of the Local Church." *Catholic Theological Society of America Proceedings* 35 (1980) 244–55.

Klostermann, Ferdinand. "The Laity." In *Commentary on the Documents of Vatican II*, edited by Herbert Vorgrimler, vol. 1, 231–52. New York: Herder and Herder, 1968.

Komonchak, Joseph A. "Church and Ministry." *The Jurist* 43:2 (1983) 273–88.

–. "Clergy, Laity, and the Church's Mission in the World." *The Jurist* 41:2 (1981) 422–47.

–. "How Vatican II Changed the Church: 8: What Road to Joy?" *The Tablet* (30 November 2002) 11–2.

–. "Ministry and the Local Church." *Catholic Theological Society of America Proceedings* 36 (1981) 56–82.

–. "The Synod of 1985 and the Notion of the Church." *Chicago Studies* 26:3 (1987) 330–45.

–. "Vatican II as an Event." *Theology Digest* 46:4 (Winter 1999) 337–52.

König, Franz Cardinal. "How Vatican II Changed the Church: 11: 'It Must Be the Holy Spirit." *The Tablet* (21–28 December 2002) 4–6.

Kroeger, James. "'Signs of the Times': A Thirty-year Panorama." *East Asian Pastoral Review* 26:2 (1987) 191–6.

Küng, Hans. "Global Business and the Global Ethic." *Concilium* 4 (2001) 87–105.

–. "Islam: Radical Changes in History – Challenges of the Present." *Concilium* 5 (2005) 93–102.

Legrand, Lucien. "Vocation à la mission dans le nouveau testament." *Spiritus* 113 (1988) 339–52.

Le Tourneau, D. "Le sacerdoce commun et son incidence sur les obligations et les droits des fidèles en general et des laïcs en particulier." *Revue de droit canonique* 39 (1989) 155–94.

Ligier, Louis. "'Lay Ministries' and their Foundations in the Documents of Vatican II." In *Vatican II Assessment and Perspectives: Twenty-Five Years After (1962–1987)*, vol. 1, edited by René Latourelle, 160–76. New York: Paulist Press, 1988.

Linnan, John E. "Ministry Since Vatican II." *New Theology Review* 3 (1990) 33–45.

Magnani, Giovanni. "Does the So-Called Theology of the Laity Possess a Theological Status?" In *Vatican II Assessment and Perspectives: Twenty-Five Years After (1962–1987)*, vol. 1, edited by René Latourelle, 568–633. New York: Paulist Press, 1988.

Marshall, John. "How Vatican II Changed the Church: 7: My Voyage of Discovery." *The Tablet* (23 November 2002) 8–9.

Martinez, German. "An Ecclesiology of Peace." *Theology Digest* 38:3 (Fall 1991) 235–9.

McCord, H. Richard. "Lay Ministry: Living its Questions." *Origins* 19:46 (19 April 1990) 757, 759–65.

Melloni, Alberto. "How Vatican II Changed the Church: 4: A Speech That Lit the Flame." *The Tablet* (2 November 2002) 7–8.

Menard, Camil. "L'ecclésiologie des théologiens de la liberation: Contexte général and analyse de quelques questions ecclésiologiques discutées par Leonardo Boff." *Eglise et Théologie* 19 (1988) 349–72.

Meyer-Wilmes, Hedwig. "The Diversity of Ministries in a Postmodern Church." *Concilium* 3 (1999) 69–88.

Miller, J. Michael. "Three Megatrends Influencing Catholic Higher Education Globally." *Origins* 36:36 (22 February 2007) 565–73.

Miller, Vincent J. "Where is the Church? Globalization and Catholicity." *Theological Studies* 69 (2008) 412–32.

Missi. "Une Eglise sous haute surveillance: Les difficiles rapports entre l'Etat communiste et les catholiques." *Missi* 2 (February 1991) 16–9.

Murphy-O'Connor, Cormac. "Renewing the Parish: 1: Fired by the Spirit." *The Tablet* (31 May 2003) 11–2.

Neuner, Peter. "Aspekte einer Theologie des Laien." *Una Sancta* 43 (1988) 316–24.

–. "Was ist ein Laie?" *Stimmen der Zeit* 210 (1992) 507–18.

Nguyễn Thế Anh, "From Indra to Maitreya: Buddhist Influence in Vietnamese Political Thought." *Journal of Southeast Asian Studies* 33:2 (June 2002) 225–41.

Nichols, Terence L. "Participatory Church." In *Common Calling: The Laity and Governance of the Catholic Church*, edited by Stephen J. Pope, 111–26. Washington, D.C.: Georgetown University Press, 2004.

Nicolás, Adolfo. "Christianity in Crisis: Asia. Which Asia? Which Christianity? Which Crisis?" *Concilium* 3 (2005) 64–70.

Niermann, Ernst. "Laity." In *Encyclopedia of Theology: The Concise Sacramentum Mundi*, edited by Karl Rahner, 814–5. London: Burns and Oates, 1975.

Nilson, Jon. "The Laity." In *The Gift of the Church: A Textbook on Ecclesiology in Honour of Patrick Granfield*, edited by Peter C. Phan, 395–413. Collegeville, Minn.: The Liturgical Press, 2000.

O'Mahony, Anthony. "Into the Age of Uncertainty." *The Tablet* (19 July 2008) 4–5.

O'Malley, John W. "Vatican II: Did Anything Happen?" *Theological Studies* 67 (2006) 3–33.

O'Malley, William. "The Church of the Faithful." *America* (19 June 1993) 6–10.

O'Meara, Thomas F. "Beyond 'Hierarchology.'" In *The Legacy of the Tübingen School: The Relevance of Nineteenth-Century Theology for the Twenty-First Century*, edited by D.J. Dietrich and M.J. Himes, 173–91. New York: Crossroad, 1997.

Ormerod, Neil. "A Dialectic Engagement with the Social Sciences in an Ecclesial Context." *Theological Studies* 66 (2005) 815–40.

–. "Mission and Ministry in the Wake of Vatican II." *Australian EJournal of Theology* 1 (August 2003) 1–11.

Orsy, Ladislas. "Participation in the Church as a Seminal Concept." *Origins* 17:46 (28 April 1988) 796–800.

Osborne, Kenan B. "Envisioning a Theology of Ordained and Lay Ministry: Lay/ Ordained Ministry-Current Issues of Ambiguity." In *Ordering the Baptismal Priesthood: Theologies of Lay and Ordained Ministry*, edited by Susan K. Wood, 195–227. Collegeville, Minn.: Liturgical Press, 2003.

–. "The Meaning of Lay, Laity and Lay Ministry in the Christian Theology of Church." *Antonianum* 63 (1988) 227–58. Also condensed as "The Meaning of Lay, Laity and Lay Ministry." *Theology Digest* 36:2 (Summer 1989) 113–9.

–. "A Profile of the Baptized Catholic Christian at the Beginning of the Third Millennium." *The Catholic World* (January-February 1996) 35–8.

Parrella, Frederick J. "The Laity in the Church." *Catholic Theological Society of America Proceedings* 35 (1980) 264–86.

Phan, Peter C. "Asian Christian Spirituality: Context and Contour." *Spiritus* 6 (2006) 221–7.

–. "The Christ of Asia: An Essay on Jesus as the Eldest Son and Ancestor." *Studia Missionalia* 45 (1996) 25–55.

–. "Christian Social Spirituality: A Global Perspective." In *Catholic Social Justice: Theological and Practical Explorations*, edited by Philomena Cullen, Bernard House and Gerard Mannion, 18–40. London: T&T Clark, 2007.

–. "Cultures, Religions, and Power: Proclaiming Christ in the United States Today." *Theological Studies* 65 (2004) 714–40.

–. "Ignacio Ellacuría, S.J. in Dialogue with Asian Theologians: What Can They Learn from Each Other?" *Horizons* 32: 1(Spring 2005) 53–71.

–. "Method in Liberation Theologies." *Theological Studies* 61 (2000) 40–63.

–. "Possibility of a Lay Spirituality: a Re-examination of Some Theological Presuppositions." *Communio* 10:4 (1983) 378–395.

–. "Praying to the Buddha: Living Amid Religious Pluralism." *Commonweal* 134:2 (26 January 2007). http://find.galegroup.com/itx/start.do?prodId=AONE (accessed 21 February 2006); Gale Document Number: A159183041.

–. "Theology on the Other Side of the Borders: Responding to the Signs of the Times." *CTSA Proceedings* 57 (2002) 87–120.

–. "Vietnamese Catholics in the United States: Christian Identity Between the Old and the New." *U.S. Catholic Historian* 18:1 (2000) 19–35.

Phan Đình Cho. "The Laity in the Early Church: Building Blocks for a Theology of the Laity." *Triết Đạo:Journal of Vietnamese Philosophy and Religion* 4:2 (2002) 36–53.

Pieris, Aloysius. "The Roman Catholic Perception of Other Churches and Other Religions after the Vatican's *Dominus Iesus.*" *East Asian Pastoral Review* 38:3 (2001) 207–30.

–. "Vatican II: Glimpses into Six Centuries of Its Prehistory." *East Asian Pastoral Review* 44:4 (2007) 302–15.

Pike, Douglas. "Vietnam in 1980: The Gathering Storm." *Asian Survey* 21:1 (January 1981) 84–92.

Potvin, Thomas R. "Le baptême comme enracinement dans la participation à la triple fonction du Christ." In *Le laïcat: Les limites d'un système. Actes du Congrès Canadien de Théologie*, 141–190. Montréal: Fides, 1986.

Power, David N. "Priesthood Revisited: Mission and Ministries in the Royal Priesthood." In *Ordering the Baptismal Priesthood: Theologies of Lay and Ordained Ministry*, edited by Susan K. Wood, 87–120. Collegeville, Minn.: Liturgical Press, 2003.

Provost, James H. "Ministry: Reflections on Some Canonical Issues." *The Heythrop Journal* 29 (1988) 285–99.

Radcliffe, Timothy. "Overcoming Discord in the Church." *National Catholic Reporter* (5 May 2006) 5–8.

Rahner, Karl. "Die bleibende Bedeutung des Zweiten Vatikanischen Konzils." *Stimmen der Zeit* 197 (1979) 795–806.

–. Towards a Fundamental Theological Interpretation of Vatican II. *Theological Studies* 40:4 (December 1979) 716–27.

Ramsey, Jacob. "Miracles and Myths: Vietnam Seen through Its Catholic History." In *Modernity and Re-enchantment: Religion in Post-revolutionary Vietnam*, edited by Philip Taylor, 371–98. Vietnam Update Series. Singapore: Institute of Southeast Asian Studies, 2007.

Ratzinger, Joseph. "The Local Church and Universal Church." *Origins* 15:22 (14 November 1985) 370–6.

Rayan, Samuel. "Third World Theology: Where Do We Go From Here ?" *Concilium* 199 (August 1988) 127–40.

Rikhof, Hervi. "The Competence of Priests, Prophets and Kings: Ecclesiological Reflections about the Power and Authority of Christian Believers." *Concilium* 197 (1988) 53–62.

–. "The Ecclesiologies of *Lumen Gentium*, the *Lex Ecclesiae Fundamentalis* and the Draft Code." *Concilium* 4 (1995) 54–63.

Rinere, Elissa. "Canon Law and Emerging Understandings of Ministry." In *Ordering the Baptismal Priesthood: Theologies of Lay and Ordained Ministry*, edited by Susan K. Wood, 68–84. Collegeville, Minn.: Liturgical Press, 2003.

Ruddy, Christopher. "Ecclesiological Issues Behind the Sexual Abuse Crisis." *Origins* 37:8 (5 July 2007) 119–26.

Rush, Ormond. "The Offices of Christ, *Lumen Gentium* and the People's Sense of the Faith." *Pacifica* 16:2 (2003) 137–52.

Sanks, T. Howland. "Globalization and the Church's Social Mission." *Theological Studies* 60 (1999) 625–51.

–. "Reading the Signs of the Times: Purpose and Method." In *Reading the Signs of the Times: Resources for Social and Cultural Analysis*, edited by T. Howland Sanks and John A. Coleman, 3–11. New York: Paulist Press, 1993.

Schineller, Peter. "Inculturation as the Pilgrimage to Catholicity." *Concilium* 204 (August 1989) 98–106.

Schreiter, Robert J. "Faith and Cultures: Challenges to a World Church." *Theological Studies* 50:3 (September 1989) 744–60.

–. "Mission in the Third Millennium." In *Mission in the Third Millennium*, edited by Robert J. Schreiter, 149–61. Maryknoll, N.Y.: Orbis Books, 2001.

–. "The Theological Meaning of a Truly Catholic Church." *New Theology Review* 7 (November 1994) 5–14.

Senior, Donald. "The Biblical Heritage and the Meaning of Vocation: Address to Third Continental Congress on Vocations." *Origins* 31:46 (2 May 2002) 760–6.

Sesboüé, Bernard. "Y a-t-il une différence séparatrice entre les ecclésiologies catholique et protestante?" *Nouvelle Revue Théologique* 109 (1987) 3–30.

Staudt, Brian. "The Lay-Cleric Distinction: Tragedy or Comedy?" *Church* 12:3 (Fall 1996) 47–50.

Sullivan, Francis A. "Authority in an Ecclesiology of Communion." *New Theology Review* 10 (1997) 18–30.

–. "The Evangelizing Mission of the Church." In *The Gift of the Church: A Textbook on Ecclesiology in Honour of Patrick Granfield*, edited by Peter C. Phan, 231–48. Collegeville, Minn.: The Liturgical Press, 2000.

Taber, Charles R. "Contextualization." *Religious Studies Review* 13:1 (January 1987) 33–6.

Tan Yun-ka, Jonathan. "From 'Missio *ad* Gentes' to 'Missio *inter* Gentes'. I.: Shaping a New Paradigm for Doing Christian Mission in Asia." *Vidyajyoti* 68:9 (September 2004) 670–86; "From 'Missio *ad* Gentes' to 'Missio *inter* Gentes'.

II.: Shaping a New Paradigm for Doing Christian Mission in Asia. *Vidyajyoti* 69:1 (January 2005) 27–41.

The Economist. "In God's Name: a Special Report on Religion and Public Life." *The Economist* (3 November 2007) 1–20.

The Tablet. "Towards Justice and Dignity." *The Tablet* (30 September 2006) 2.

Torfs, Rik. "*Auctoritas – potestas – jurisdictio – facultas – officium – munus*: a conceptual analysis." *Concilium* 197 (April 1988) 63–73.

Trần Văn Toàn. "La doctrine des 'trois pères': Un effort d'inculturation du christianisme au Vietnam." *Mission* 9:1 (2002) 89–104.

U.S. Bishops' National Advisory Council. "The Thrust of Lay Ministry." *Origins* 9:39 (13 March 1980) 621, 623–6.

Valdrini, Patrick. "La mission des laïcs dans le magistère de Jean-Paul II." *Ius Canonicum* 26:51 (1986) 81–92.

Vu Kim Chinh. "Cooperation as Mutual Liberation – Background of Emerging Relationship Between the State and the Catholic Church in Vietnam." In *Church & State Relations in 21ˢᵗ Century Asia*, edited by Beatrice Leung, 175–202. Hong Kong: Centre of Asian Studies, The University of Hong Kong, 1996.

Waaijman, Kees. "Lay Spirituality." *Studies in Spirituality* 10 (2000) 5–20.

Walsh, Michael. "How Vatican II Changed the Church: 10: U-turn on Human Rights." *The Tablet* (14 December 2002) 7–9.

Wiesel, Elie. "Pope John Paul II: Pointing the Way to Reconciliation." *Time* (26 April 2004) 67.

Wilfred, Felix. "Inculturation as a Hermeneutical Question: Reflections in the Asian Context." *Vidyajyoti* 52 (1988) 422–36.

Wilkins, John. "How Vatican II Changed the Church: 1: Earthquake in Rome." *The Tablet* (12 October 2002) 10–1.

–. "How Vatican II Changed the Church: 2: Unfinished Business." *The Tablet* (19 October 2002) 10–2.

Williams, A.N. "Congar's Theology of the Laity." In *Yves Congar: Theologian of the Church*, edited by Gabriel Flynn, 135–59. Louvain: W.B. Eerdmans, 2005.

Wood, Susan K. "Priestly Identity within Parish Identity." In *Ordering the Baptismal Priesthood: Theologies of Lay and Ordained Ministry*, edited by Susan K. Wood, 175–94. Collegeville, Minn.: Liturgical Press, 2003.

Woodrow, Alain. "How Vatican II Changed the Church: 3: Diary of an Insider." *The Tablet* (26 October 2002) 11–3.

Wulf, Friedrich. "Über die Herkunft und ursprünglichen Sinn des Wortes 'Laie'." *Geist und Leben* 32 (1959) 61–3.

Zauner, Wilhelm. "Laien und Priester – eine Kirche." *Theologische Praktische Quartalschrift* 135:3 (1987) 205–212. Condensed as "Laity and Priests: One Church." *Theology Digest* 36:2 (Summer 1989) 127–31.

Zotti, Mary Irene. "Cardijn: A Priest Who Believed in the Priesthood of the Laity." *The Living Light* 23:4 (June 1987) 307–15.

Index

A

Ad Gentes 6, 26, 28, 109, 113, 138, 145, 148, 157–158, 210, 215, 244

Apostolate of the Laity 1–2, 112, 257

Apostolicam Actuositatem 1–2, 25–28, 109, 112–113, 164, 174, 256

Asian Bishops' Meeting 4–5, 53, 55, 76, 81, 161

Asian Colloquium on Ministries in the Church 58, 80, 89, 98, 127–130, 144, 155

Asian context 46, 52, 56–57, 65, 72, 82, 84, 87–89, 98, 122–123, 134–135, 144, 150, 153, 158, 163, 168, 177, 182, 184, 191, 229, 233

Asian cultures 63, 65, 70, 72, 158, 185, 188

Asian family 11, 53, 92, 101

Asian Integral Pastoral Approach 13, 63–65, 77, 83, 104

Asian Synod 14, 53, 168–170, 173, 176, 180, 183, 185–186, 191, 197, 212, 222

B

basic ecclesial communities 13, 32, 34, 65, 77, 98, 100, 104, 107, 110, 122, 128, 139, 146, 149–151, 153, 156, 158, 162–164, 237, 250, 257

Benedict XVI 219, 230, 232, 249

Bishops' Institute for Lay Apostolate 5, 101, 103

C

call to holiness 31, 84, 201, 222, 224, 226, 236–237

Catholic social teaching 235, 240

Challenges of Asia 4, 59, 90, 97

charisms 89, 103, 112, 119, 124, 127–128, 135, 144, 167, 174, 246, 252, 256

Christifideles Laici 16, 38, 164–167, 174, 177, 179–180, 192, 225–227, 230, 233, 236–237, 242, 247

Christological 1, 85, 115, 124, 156, 163, 166, 172, 179, 193, 199, 204, 223, 232, 237, 257

Church and State Relations 217

common priesthood 1, 13, 27, 84, 87, 106, 112, 114–116, 124, 128, 130–131, 160, 222–223, 250

communion in mission 162

communion process 65, 77

Communism 205, 207, 229

community of faith 14, 44, 55, 105, 107, 122, 124–125, 130, 137, 139, 141, 145, 150, 153, 156–157, 159, 161–163, 178–179, 193, 237–238

Confucianism 212, 213–214

contextualisation 46, 48, 76, 98, 106–107, 161, 236

D

dialogue and solidarity 118, 139, 150, 153, 158, 162–163, 237

Dignitatis Humanae 218

disciple-community 153, 162–163, 237

discipleship 14, 39, 81, 84, 87–88, 94–95, 98, 105–107, 116, 120, 131, 150, 158–159, 161–162, 175, 224, 233, 236, 247–248

E

Ecclesia in Asia 6, 9, 14–15, 17, 160, 164, 166, 167–194, 197, 221–222, 226, 229–230, 233, 237–238, 242, 251

Ecclesiam Suam 199, 205, 208

ecclesiological foundations 235, 237

ecclesiological frameworks 28, 147, 222, 227

ecclesiological models 140, 142, 159, 237

Evangelii Nuntiandi 16, 58, 148, 215–216

evangelisation 7–8, 37, 56, 58, 63, 70, 79, 85, 92, 110, 118–119, 122, 139, 153, 159–160, 164, 166–167, 171, 173, 175–176, 178–179, 181, 183–184, 186–187, 189, 191, 193, 213, 215, 219, 236–237, 249, 251, 257

F

FABC. See Federation of Asian Bishops' Conferences 5–6, 66, 107, 132, 161, 183–184, 197, 228, 245, 251

faith seeking dialogue 67

Federation of Asian Bishops' Conferences 4–5, 10–11, 13–14, 79–80, 83, 96, 98, 111, 117, 137, 155, 157, 160–161, 166, 170, 191, 221–222, 226, 230, 233, 242–243

formation of the laity 62, 122

G

Gaudium et Spes 1–2, 6, 18, 26, 28, 30, 33, 70, 109–110, 113, 164, 192, 200, 203–204, 208–209, 215, 217–218, 227, 231, 255, 256

gift of faith 171–172, 174–175

gift/task 169, 171–175, 177, 179, 187

H

holiness of life 177, 194, 197, 231, 256

I

identity of the laity 80, 113, 125, 222

inculturation 8, 10, 13–15, 46, 56, 67, 71, 85, 86, 88, 95, 118, 125, 168–169, 171, 173, 176, 179, 193, 210, 212–214, 222, 229, 234, 237, 239–240

interreligious dialogue 13–14, 54, 62, 65, 68, 71–72, 86, 88, 95, 105, 125, 146, 173, 177, 180, 181–183, 186, 189, 193–194, 234, 249

J

John Paul II 6, 9–10, 15, 17–19, 28, 38, 40, 55, 58, 88, 142, 148, 152, 160, 164–169, 171–184, 186, 188–194, 197, 199–200, 203, 205, 221–230, 232–235, 237–238, 242, 247, 251, 255–257

John XXIII 6, 165, 199

Joseph Ratzinger 1, 40, 55, 151–153

K

kingdom of God 7, 10, 26, 35, 37, 84, 87, 89, 94, 99, 105, 107, 118, 120–122, 131, 140, 144, 149, 153, 157, 159–160, 182, 190, 224–225, 227, 235–237, 244, 256, 258

kingly 3, 25, 27

L

lay ministries 12, 32, 42, 88, 90, 107, 112, 118–119, 132, 155, 255

lay spirituality 13, 23, 94–95, 120–121, 123

Leonard Doohan 21, 23–24, 31–32, 42, 44, 127, 129–130, 235, 247

liberation theology 34, 60–61, 68–69
local church 11, 43–44, 71, 137–138,
    149, 151, 153, 188, 206
Lumen Gentium 1–3, 6, 25–29, 33,
    107, 109, 112, 115–116, 123–125,
    132, 164, 172, 174, 177, 183, 215,
    223–224, 226–227, 236, 245, 247,
    252, 254, 256–257

M
meaning of ministry 21
ministries of the laity 91, 94
missio Dei 145, 157, 243, 248, 252,
    257
mission as service 158
Mission as Solidarity 209
Mission as Witness of Life 215
mission of inculturation 13, 15
mission of the laity 1, 12–13, 15, 81,
    83, 88, 109, 123, 165, 167, 172,
    193, 225, 229, 236, 253–254, 256,
    258
mission process 63
mission to the world 162, 215, 231,
    256

N
new way of being church 64–65,
    138, 143, 147, 151, 153

O
option for the poor 8, 56, 69, 89, 93,
    125, 128, 229, 234–235
ordered ministries 133, 243, 257

P
pastoral cycle 60–61
Paul VI 5, 58, 76, 81, 98, 148, 155,
    161, 190, 197, 199, 200, 204–205,
    208, 210, 215, 228, 231–232, 238
people of God 1–2, 21, 25, 27–28,
    30, 36, 39, 80, 82, 85, 87, 91, 94,

103, 106, 111, 113, 114, 116, 118,
    126, 128, 132, 143, 160, 166, 170,
    173, 196, 199, 201, 203, 209, 216,
    225, 226–227, 244, 246–247
Pius XI 205, 208, 252
Pius XII 30, 164, 205–206, 208
pneumatological 94, 124, 142–145,
    153, 156, 223, 237
priesthood of life 13, 79, 84, 87,
    96–97, 106, 110, 112–115, 117–
    118, 121, 124, 128, 135, 160, 236
priestly 3, 11, 25, 27, 82, 87, 95, 97,
    106–107, 121, 128, 134, 160, 162
Proclamation and Dialogue 181
proclamation through dialogue 187
prophetic 3, 25, 27, 59, 61, 77, 82,
    87, 97, 106–107, 113, 116, 125,
    128, 134, 144, 149, 160, 162, 215,
    217, 220, 257
pusillus grex, 7

R
Redemptor Hominis 6, 172, 199, 203,
    205, 229
reign of God 86, 88, 101, 149, 225

S
Second Vatican Council 1, 24, 28,
    30, 33, 42–43, 45–46, 88, 103,
    109, 111–112, 131, 155, 193–194,
    196–197, 205, 210, 215, 217, 231,
    240, 245, 248, 251, 256
see, judge, act 59, 97, 123, 125, 236
sentire cum ecclesia 229
service of life 146
signs of the times 6, 54, 61–62, 70,
    77, 83, 85, 123, 125, 144–145,
    157–158, 163, 195, 218, 242
small Christian communities 44, 65,
    98, 100, 107, 110, 125, 144
social teachings of the Church,
    98–99, 104, 107

Stephen Bevans 46, 48, 67
structured *communio* 245–246, 251

T
theological methodologies 13, 17,
19, 42, 49, 57, 63, 66, 76, 96–97,
111, 235–236
theological pluralism 52, 67, 71, 77
Theology as Service to Life 65
Triple dialogue 69

V
Vatican II 1–4, 6, 9–10, 16–19,
21, 24, 25, 27–31, 33, 36, 38,
42–45, 47, 58, 70, 76, 95, 109–112,
115–116, 119, 122, 125–126,
130–132, 134, 137–138, 141–143,
148, 150–151, 155–156, 159–160,
163–165, 172, 178, 180–181, 186,
189–190, 192, 194, 199, 203–204,
208, 210, 215–217, 222, 227, 229,
231–232, 234–235, 237, 245, 248,
251, 253–254
VEC. See Vietnamese Episcopal
Conference 226, 238
Vietnamese Episcopal
Conference 9, 16–17, 195–196,
199, 207, 228, 230, 233, 235, 242
vocation of the laity 216, 227

W
witness of life 14, 166, 176, 180,
191, 193–194, 201, 203, 215–216,
219, 222, 226, 229, 233, 235, 238,
258

Y
Yves Congar 1, 3, 8, 12, 22, 30–31,
114–115, 120, 125–128, 138, 147,
235, 254, 256